D0438303

THE TRUSTED LEADER

THE TRUSTED LEADER
BUILDING THE RELATIONSHIPS
THAT MAKE GOVERNMENT WORK

Terry Newell
Leadership for a Responsible Society

Grant Reeher
Syracuse University

Peter Ronayne
Federal Executive Institute

CQ PRESS

A Division of Congressional Quarterly Inc.
Washington, D.C.

CQ Press
1255 22nd Street, NW, Suite 400
Washington, DC 20037

Phone: 202-729-1900; toll-free, 1-866-4CQ-PRESS (1-866-427-7737)

Web: www.cqpress.com

Copyright © 2008 by CQ Press, a division of Congressional Quarterly Inc.

All rights reserved. No part of this publication may be reproduced or transmitted in any form or by any means, electronic or mechanical, including photocopy, recording, or any information storage and retrieval system, without permission in writing from the publisher.

Cover design: Lorraine Donneke

∞ The paper used in this publication exceeds the requirements of the American National Standard for Information Sciences—Permanence of Paper for Printed Library Materials, ANSI Z39.48-1992.

Printed and bound in the United States of America

11   10   09   08   07   1   2   3   4   5

Library of Congress cataloging-in-publication data

The trusted leader: building the relationships that make government work / [edited by] Terry Newell, Grant Reeher, Peter Ronayne.
    p. cm.
  Includes bibliographical references and index.
  ISBN 978-0-87289-427-3 (alk. paper)
  1. Administrative agencies—United States—Management. 2. Executive departments—United States—Management. 3. Organizational effectiveness—United States. 4. Political leadership—United States. 5. Interpersonal relations. I. Newell, Terry. II. Reeher, Grant. III. Ronayne, Peter. IV. Title.
JK421.T88 2008
352.3—dc22

                                                                2007029050

Contents

Section I. Relationships: The missing link in government reform

Terry Newell, Grant Reeher, and Peter Ronayne

The success of government depends on competence and trust. American government has grown dramatically in the past seventy-five years, and evidence indicates that it has accomplished much. Yet many Americans distrust government, and that distrust threatens its future success and the social capital that underlies democratic institutions. Efforts to build trust, especially in the career, institutional leadership of government, are essential. Most strategies to improve government, however, have focused on macro-level changes, such as strategic planning, organizational structure, systems, oversight, and measurement. These changes work only if attention is paid to micro-level changes: building personal relationships.

Terry Newell

Building trust requires being a values-based leader. When leaders violate followers' core values, they forfeit their trust. But public service leaders face conflicting value demands. How do they navigate among constitutional, citizen, organizational, professional, and personal values that often conflict? They need at least five skills to do so: act with integrity, listen, tolerate dissent, involve others, and make moral decisions. Using those skills in their personal leadership, in their organizations, and on the public stage is essential for values-based leadership.

Section III. Building relationships across organizational boundaries understand their agencies, build partnerships, and focus on what appointees do best—craft strategy and manage externally. Career officials must seek to understand the appointee's view of the world, extend a helping hand, keep their organizations in good working order, and be tolerant of potential initial appointee missteps.

munications technology offers a unique opportunity to involve citizens, but using it well requires that leaders adopt an e-governance *rather than an* e-government *approach to their Internet-based outreach efforts. In e-governance, citizens are actively included in the governing dialogue and encouraged to work together among themselves, with the agency serving as facilitator. Approaches to engaging citizens in this way can be drawn from electoral politics, commerce, and the experiences of selected U.S. and international government agencies.*

People trust government if they have a good experience with it. Yet most government agencies lack the concepts and tools to think carefully about and engineer positive citizen experiences. Such experiences depend on addressing the emotional, not just the cognitive, needs of citizens. Exceptional citizen experiences with government require attention to three types of sensory clues. Leaders must orchestrate functional clues: Do their programs, processes, forms, and systems work as intended? The emotional payoff comes when they get mechanic clues (the physical or virtual setting in which service is provided) and humanic clues (the people who serve citizens and how they act) right.

The United States enjoys a dominant and potent combination of military, economic, cultural, and political power, but that power is relatively ineffective if the world does not trust the nation and its leaders. Building trust requires government officials who have a sense of American history and how it has shaped the American worldview. Government leaders also need to appreciate how other nations view the United States and the constellation of forces shaping global interactions and issues. In addition, leaders must possess the skills and knowledge to be effective internationally. The evidence suggests, however, that too many government leaders lack this critical understanding and these skills.

Government was not designed to be easy. Its leaders face intense pressure, conflicting demands, and a seemingly intractable set of hoops through which to jump. After all, the Framers decided that preserving freedom was more important than efficiency. So what can civil service leaders do? Turning in a solid professional performance is not enough. Leaders must build trust. To do so, they must engage citizens in their own government, however messy that may get. They must also help the public understand how government works and how to affect the governing process. Will doing this earn the civil servant the public's admiration? No. But making a difference where it really matters makes the civil servant's job worthwhile.

Contributors

Lou Carbone (B.A., political science) is the founder, president, and chief experience officer of Experience Engineering, a Minneapolis-based experience management firm. He has spent more than two decades in the development of experience value management theory and practice in a broad range of industries, including travel, health care, retail, technology, financial services, manufacturing, and education. He is the author of *Clued In: How to Keep Customers Coming Back Again and Again.*

Alfred L. Cooke (Ph.D., counseling) is the director of the Federal Executive Institute's Center for Organizational Performance. He has been an organization development and human resources specialist for twenty years and focuses on leadership development, organizational consulting, strategic planning, human resources development, learning organizations, corporate university development, training, and program development. He was previously dean of graduate studies and later dean of education at Marygrove College in Detroit, Michigan, where he developed new master's degree programs in educational leadership and social justice. Prior to that, he was assistant director of human resources and chief learning officer at Detroit Edison Company. He has also held the position of director of the American University/National Training Laboratory (AU/NTL) master's degree program in organization development and has taught at the university and secondary levels. He recently edited a reference book on human relations training and group facilitation, *Reading Book for Human Relations Training,* for the NTL Institute.

Grace Cummings (B.A., international relations) is the founder of Working with Congress, a company that designs and conducts seminars to help people understand and effectively participate in the legislative process. Since 1995 she has pursued her passion for teaching as an adjunct faculty member at the Federal Executive Institute. She has also served as executive director of the Faith & Politics Institute, chief of staff to Reps. James O. McCrery of Louisiana and John H. Kingston of Georgia, and a consultant and staffer on a variety of political campaigns and public relations efforts.

Dan Fenn Jr. (A.M., government and international relations) is adjunct lecturer in executive programs at the Kennedy School of Government and former director of the John F. Kennedy Library in Boston, which is part of the National Archives and Records Administration. He was most recently special assistant to the chancellor, University of Massachusetts, Boston. His earlier government experience includes service as a staff assistant to President John F. Kennedy, commissioner and vice chairman of the U.S. Tariff Commission, and special assistant to Sen. Benjamin A. Smith of Massachusetts. He served two terms as a selectman in his hometown of Lexington, Massachusetts, and is the author or editor of numerous books and articles.

Beverly R. Fletcher (Ed.D., organization development) is a member of the senior faculty at the Federal Executive Institute. Her work focuses on organization development, transformation concepts and applications, and justice issues. Fletcher is the author of several books, one of which—*Organization Transformation Theorists and Practitioners: Profiles and Themes*—deals with how organizations are facing dynamic forces in the social environment that require them to either transform or cease to exist. Before coming to the institute, Fletcher served as an independent consultant to national and international organizations in leadership, strategic planning, conflict management, team development, executive coaching, and large-scale change. Her graduate-level teaching includes the human relations program at the University of Oklahoma, the management program at the University of Maryland University College, and the business administration and public administration programs at American University in Washington, D.C.

Gail Funke (Ph.D., economics) is a member of the senior faculty at the Federal Executive Institute. Among her accomplishments are research and publications on public policy, policy analysis, and economics, as well as extensive experience in strategic planning, coaching, and team facilitation for federal, state, and local governments. She recently completed a project on the policy implications of welfare reform in a major Virginia city. Her duties at the institute include program coordination, classroom teaching, and large-group presentations.

Russ Linden (Ph.D., organizational leadership) is a management educator and author who specializes in organizational change and performance issues in the public and nonprofit sectors. He has his own consulting firm and is an adjunct faculty member at the Federal Executive Institute and the University of Virginia, where he teaches leadership classes to government executives. His research and teaching interests include collaborating across organizational boundaries, creating customer-focused organizations, and managing relationships in the workplace. His most recent book is *Working Across Boundaries.*

Robert Maranto (Ph.D., political science) teaches political science at Villanova University. He has served in government; taught at numerous colleges and universities; and with others has written or edited eight books, including *Beyond a Government of Strangers: How Career Executives and Political Appointees Can Turn Conflict to Cooperation, The Second Term of George W. Bush,* and *A Guide to Charter Schools.* He serves under April Gresham Maranto, Tony Maranto (b. 1999), and Maya Maranto (b. 2004).

George Mitchell (M.A., economics; M.A., political science) is a doctoral candidate in political science at the Maxwell School of Citizenship and Public Affairs at Syracuse University. His current research involves contemporary international relations theory and computer modeling. Before joining Syracuse, he was a research analyst in the private sector on Middle East policy issues.

Bill Murray (Ph.D., public administration) is an adjunct professor at Virginia Polytechnic Institute and State University. He has worked in state government in the legislative and executive branches.

Terry Newell (Ed.D., educational administration) is currently director of his own firm, Leadership for a Responsible Society, and an adjunct faculty member at the Federal Executive Institute. He previously served as dean of faculty at the institute and in that capacity was responsible for its four-week, interagency Leadership for a Democratic Society program for senior federal government officials. In his twenty years at the U.S. Department of Education, he worked on educational innovation in elementary and secondary schools and higher education; he also served as director of training. His most recent work has focused on ethics and values-based leadership. Newell's publications have addressed values and ethics in leadership, organizational change, the future and its implications for leadership, and diversity and its effects on organizations and leaders.

John W. Pickering (Ph.D., American government) is president of the Commonwealth Center for High-Performance Organizations, a management consulting firm in Charlottesville, Virginia, working with executive teams in the public, nonprofit, and private sectors to improve organizational performance and manage large-scale organizational change. He served as deputy director and a senior faculty member of the Federal Executive Institute; was an executive with the U.S. Department of Housing and Urban Development; and taught political science and public administration at Lamar University, Florida State University, and Memphis State University. He is also an adjunct faculty member at the Federal Executive Institute and the University of Virginia's Weldon Cooper Center for Public Service.

Ron Redmon (M.A., public administration) has had a highly successful private practice as a leadership coach and consultant for the past fifteen years, following his own distinguished career as a federal executive. His clients have included cabinet secretaries in the federal government and corporate chief executives. He serves on the adjunct faculty of the Federal Executive Institute, where he has taught coaching to approximately 1,000 government leaders. In addition, he has designed and delivered some of the institute's most impactful and well-regarded customized leadership development programs. Previously, he served for six years as the senior leadership coach for the Excellence in Government Fellows program of the Council for Excellence in Government in Washington, D.C. His training and development as a coach have been with most of the premier contributors to the field, supplemented by continuous learning in the fields of dialogue, general semantics, human dynamics, and systems theory.

Grant Reeher (Ph.D., political science) is associate professor and director of graduate studies in the Political Science Department at Syracuse University's Maxwell School of Citizenship and Public Affairs. He is also on the adjunct faculty at the Federal Executive Institute. He is the author, coauthor, or coeditor of numerous books, including *First Person Political: Legislative Life and the Meaning of Public Service* and *Click on Democracy: The Internet's Power to Change Political Apathy into Political Action.* He has also published many editorial essays on various political topics, including pieces in the *New York Times, Chicago Tribune, Newsday, Philadelphia Inquirer,* and *Ottawa Citizen.* He writes a regular political column for the *Syracuse Post-Standard.*

Peter Ronayne (Ph.D., international affairs) is dean of faculty at the Federal Executive Institute, where he also directs the Leadership for a Democratic Society program and cofounded FEI's Center for Global Leadership. He is the author of *Never Again? The United States and the Prevention and Punishment of Genocide since the Holocaust* and coauthor of the most recent update of *Biography of an Ideal,* a history of the U.S. civil service for the U.S. Office of Personnel Management. He is currently writing a biography of Secretary of State Madeleine Albright and is at work on a project that chronicles the history of Generation X. A former Presidential Management Intern, Ronayne also teaches as an adjunct professor in the Department of Politics and in the School of Continuing and Professional Education at the University of Virginia.

Preface

We know from our personal lives that relationships are central to our well-being. This fact is no less true in government. Viewed from the outside, government is a complex set of structures, regulations, and programs. On the inside, it takes good relationships fostered by the people working there for government to function well. And even though good relationships alone cannot restore the trust in government that has been lost in recent years, they are essential to its revival. Strengthening those relationships is the subject of this book.

Because this volume is about relationships, we seek to have a productive one with you, the reader, and we employ several devices toward this end. First, the chapters are designed to stand on their own, so you may read them in any order you wish. Second, the chapters conclude with sections providing useful tips for leadership success and resources for further learning. Third, because the best relationships are reciprocal, we invite you to contact us—using our e-mail addresses below—with your own stories about the importance of building relationships in government, the tips and techniques you have learned from your own practice, and ideas about what additional questions we should address in this book in the future. Every book on this topic is a single snapshot of best thinking and practice. With your help (and some luck in sales) we can make future editions even better through our relationship with you.

Max De Pree, former CEO of Herman Miller, a popular office furniture company also noted for its dedication to ecodesign and building a high-commitment work culture, once said, "The first responsibility of a leader is to define reality. The last is to say thank you. In between the two, the leader must become a servant and a debtor." To the extent we have defined reality in this book, we owe thanks and are indebted to many who made it possible. This book would not exist without the contributions of the chapter authors, and so we thank them first. Second, we thank the thousands of public leaders, at all levels of government, who not only have taught our authors the lessons contained in these pages but also serve as successful daily reminders of how, at its best, government works for the American people. These dedicated civil servants have earned our trust, our respect, and our great admiration.

We thank the faculty and staff of the U.S. Office of Personnel Management's Federal Executive Institute (FEI), whose behavior toward each other and the career government leaders they educate has, for forty years, built trust and relationships and supplied the inspiration for this book. In particular we thank Tom Towberman, former director of FEI, for encouraging us to share our knowledge and experience and for his sustaining enthusiasm.

Charisse Kiino at CQ Press has been a splendid editor, supportive and directive in turn and in combination, as the situation demanded. The quality of the book was greatly enhanced by the excellent editorial work of Dwain Smith, Carolyn Goldinger, and Lorna Notsch, as well as by the marketing assistance of Chris O'Brien. Catherine Farley's expert proofreading and Enid Zafran's comprehensive indexing further strengthened the quality of this work. We also thank Tim Martinez, Cyndee Schweigert, and Chris Stevens for helping to proofread the manuscript. We thank Jeff Stonecash at the Maxwell School of Citizenship and Public Affairs for inserting our questions into the Maxwell Poll on Civic Engagement and Inequality. And we thank Greg Maslak at Syracuse University for suggesting the approach to the book's cover design.

Finally, each of us thanks the other two for their dedication and their bonhomie, and each of us also has a special thank you to offer:

To Carol, my teacher and role model on how to build relationships and trust—and who has shown me the power of both to foster success in life and work;

To David Reeher, modeler of quiet and trusted leadership;

To Vincent and Claire Ronayne, who lived and taught a lifetime's worth of trust and service.

| Terry Newell | Grant Reeher | Peter Ronayne |
| ResponsibleLeadr@aol.com | gdreeher@maxwell.syr.edu | Peter.Ronayne@opm.gov |

*I*ntroduction

The context for
leading democracy

TERRY NEWELL, LEADERSHIP FOR A RESPONSIBLE SOCIETY;
GRANT REEHER, DEPARTMENT OF POLITICAL SCIENCE, MAXWELL SCHOOL
OF CITIZENSHIP AND PUBLIC AFFAIRS, SYRACUSE UNIVERSITY;
AND **PETER RONAYNE,** DEAN OF FACULTY, FEDERAL EXECUTIVE INSTITUTE*

*People could not trust what they read. Uncertainty follows
distrust, fear follows uncertainty, and, under conditions such as
these, terror follows fear.*

— John M. Barry, *The Great Influenza*

BETWEEN 1918 AND 1919, nearly a third of all Americans suffered under
the "Spanish Flu," a strain of the subtype H1N1 virus. More than 500,000
people died. The pandemic overwhelmed the nation's nascent public health
system. Consumed by the Great War, the federal government barely acknowledged the crisis or devoted any resources to address it, short of trying
to limit its spread in overcrowded military camps. People could not trust
what little the government said or did, and widespread public fear resulted.

Almost a century later, the United States faces the prospect of an even
worse flu pandemic. But much has changed. The federal government has
constructed a national public health infrastructure; its Centers for Disease
Control and Prevention has been studying and tracking flu viruses for
decades; and government agencies have forged ongoing links with the World
Health Organization. The federal government has created a national pandemic flu plan that is integrated with international efforts and supplemented
by state and sometimes local designs. Information on what steps to take and
how to respond is widely available.

---

*The views expressed here are the author's and do not necessarily reflect those of the
Federal Executive Institute or the U.S. Office of Personnel Management.

1

In many ways, we are much better prepared this time, but success in confronting a pandemic virus is by no means certain. Whether citizens respond positively and calmly depends as much on the trust they have in public leaders and institutions as on the technical preparations made by federal, state, and local governments. That trust in turn depends on healthy working relationships within and across government agencies and among a wide range of private and not-for-profit institutions. Without effective relationships, the response to the flu will show signs of disorganization and failure, and trust will suffer, leading to panic or even terror.

The government response to Hurricane Katrina—by most accounts as disastrous as the storm itself—makes the current concern real. But it does not make future failure inevitable.

The growth and performance of government

Public health and hurricane preparedness represent just two of the areas in which government grew dramatically during the twentieth century. Since 1947 the number of cabinet level federal agencies has doubled, and the per capita federal expenditure has more than tripled (from just under $2,000 to more than $7,000, in current dollars).[1] By some estimates, state and local government has grown even more rapidly. Per capita expenditure quadrupled during the same period (from under $1,000 to more than $4,000, in current dollars).[2] The number of people employed by state and local government also grew, from 3.3 million to 19.2 million between 1946 and 2005, far outpacing the rate of growth in population as a whole and dwarfing the 2.6 million employees in today's federal government.

The eight cabinet agencies created at the federal level since the end of World War II testify to the fact that citizens expect more from government. In areas as diverse as space exploration, disease control and prevention, social services, environmental protection, transportation, and homeland security, citizens' expectations of the federal government far exceed those in earlier times and would no doubt shock the architects of our constitutional structure. This growth has occurred under Democrats and Republicans alike. The reason? The issues that public leaders now face are more numerous, more complex, more international in scope, and they require more systemic solutions.

In the midst of rising demand and public investment, how has government performed? Any tendered response is open to debate, but a careful study led by Derek Bok of Harvard University, using seventy-two indicators in various policy fields (such as economic prosperity, quality of life, oppor-

Figure I.1 Trust in the federal government

Percentage

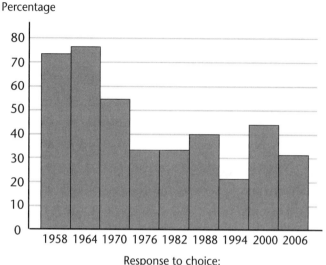

Response to choice:
"Most of the time/just about always does the right thing"

Source: American National Election Studies and the Council for Excellence in Government.

tunities, personal security, and values) suggests that government made considerable progress from the 1960s to the 1990s. The improvement was not uniform, but the outcome was far better than the prevailing image of government implies.[3] A Harris poll completed in early 2007 shows a similar pattern, at least among the thirteen agencies studied. More than 70 percent of Americans polled said that six of the agencies did an "excellent" or "pretty good" job, and only four of the agencies scored under 60 percent. The highest scoring agency (84 percent) was the Centers for Disease Control, and the lowest (40 percent) was the Social Security Administration.[4]

Trust in politics and the political leaders of government

While the quality of government performance may be mixed, public perceptions about government's trustworthiness are not—and they are not good. As Figure I.1 shows, the percentage of Americans who "trust the government in Washington to do what is right" most of the time or just about always declined from a high of 76 percent in 1964 to a low of 21 percent in 1994, before rebounding somewhat to 31 percent in 2006.

Between 1958 and 2004, the proportion of Americans reporting that government wastes "a lot" of their tax money increased from 43 percent to 61 percent. The proportion reporting they do not have a "say in what government does" increased from 28 percent in 1958 to 43 percent in 2004. The proportion reporting that "government is run for the benefit of all" declined from 64 percent in 1964 to 40 percent in 2004.[5]

Lack of trust is especially pronounced for elected leaders. When asked in 2006, "Would you generally trust each of the following types of people to tell the truth, or not?" just 48 percent trusted the president, and a mere 35 percent trusted unidentified members of Congress.[6]

The supposed causes of declining trust in government are a source of both consternation and disagreement.[7] Some link the downward trend in trust to dissatisfaction with the president and Congress.[8] Others suggest that the root of the problem is dissatisfaction with politicians, political parties, and government policies more generally.[9] Still others say that skepticism about government was sown in Americans from the start and that the fertile ground of our innate suspicion has been watered not only by contemporary social values questioning all authority but also by the conviction that the political process lacks fairness and integrity.[10] On the other hand, Americans' unrealistically high expectations for government also likely play a role. The growing tendency of the media to paint a negative picture of government no doubt contributes.[11] In addition, denunciation of government by politicians, more pervasive negative political advertising (witness the 2006 midterm elections), and sharper partisanship add to the problem.[12] And the list of probable suspects goes on.

Trust in the institutions and career leaders of government

Much of the distrust in national polls may be linked to short-term elected leaders, their actions, and our views about them. Career civil servants, however, are the enduring public face of government and comprise its inner institutional structure. Career civil servants carry a special responsibility for fostering trust. On them depends not only the delivery of more than $2.9 trillion in federal programs and services, but also the ability of citizens to trust the specific instruments of government even if they do not trust political leaders and political institutions. Distrust of elected leaders may deplete the political capital with which they can govern, but distrust of career leaders can erode the broader social capital on which rests the long-term confidence in American democracy.

Perceptions of the trustworthiness of civil servants appear to be mixed. In a 2006 Harris poll, only 62 percent of Americans reported that they would trust civil servants to tell the truth—higher than the figures for political leaders, but down from the 70 percent reporting trust in 1998.[13] A Hart poll for the Council for Excellence in Government in 2006 found that only 44 percent of Americans reported having "quite a lot" or "a great deal of confidence" in civil servants (17 percent reported "very little confidence").[14] On the other hand, some studies have found that although Americans dislike and distrust government as a whole, they respond more positively when asked about their specific interactions with government officials in a particular program or agency—in the same fashion that citizens dislike Congress as an institution, but like their own representative.[15] Data from the American Customer Satisfaction Index, for example, suggest that government agencies are on the whole viewed by their "customers" as performing about as well as firms in the private sector, though admittedly some agency services are rated much lower.[16]

Recent findings from Syracuse University's Maxwell Poll on Civic Engagement and Inequality—in which we were able to insert two questions directly related to the public's views about the federal bureaucracy—strike similar chords.[17] Like other national surveys, general questions about government yielded grim results. On the eve of the 2006 midterm elections, only 35 percent of the respondents agreed with the statement that "you can generally trust public officials to try to do the right thing." And 52 percent agreed that "people like me don't have much say about what government does." But when asked more specifically about federal employees, 56 percent agreed with the statement that "the people working for the federal government are competent," and 65 percent said that in their own interactions with federal government workers, they had "been treated with respect." In fact, only 12 percent actively disagreed with this statement; the others either had no clear opinion or had not, to their knowledge, interacted with federal employees.

Regardless of the exact degree of trust in the civil service and career civil service leaders, that trust is under stress. As value conflicts in society intensify, they are brought into the administration of government programs. Career leaders in government receive broadly worded and sometimes contradictory legislative mandates as lawmakers pass on or gloss over unresolved issues. Civil servants confront polarized citizens and groups as they seek to implement the unclear will of Congress and the administration. Perceived—and in some cases real—failure of government agencies to accomplish highly public missions or to address persistent problems is almost inevitable. Ultimately, trust in career government leaders and institutions suffers.

The danger to democracy

A government ill executed, whatever it may be in theory, must be, in practice, a bad government.

Alexander Hamilton, *Federalist Paper,* No. 69

If citizens perceive that government is "ill executed," even if some of the reasons are unavoidable, democratic governance is called into question. If the bird flu pandemic arrives, a public that does not trust government will ignore its pleas for quarantine and the targeted distribution of flu vaccines to health care workers and those most at risk. This result could quickly lead to panic and the failure of government in a self-fulfilling prophecy.

Lack of trust in the civil service operates at many levels. It creates skepticism among constituency groups and members of Congress, threatening the level of financial resources and political capital civil servants enjoy. Distrust can also decrease the voluntary compliance with laws and regulations, on which so many government programs depend. All this leads to greater congressional oversight and micromanagement of agency operations. As Figure I.2 on page 7 illustrates, these consequences, in addition to the lower morale sure to infect government employees beset by mostly negative messages, can form a spiral of worsening distrust and performance.

As we have argued, distrust is not just a problem within the public. It also takes a toll among agencies, many of which must collaborate with each other to achieve public purposes. Consider the need for the Defense and State Departments to work together to fix or prevent the failure of states abroad because such failed states pose a growing risk to the United States. If career leaders in these agencies and their subcomponent organizations cannot build effective relationships based on mutual trust and relationships that enable coordinated planning, training, and execution, their joint mission will prove unworkable.

Lack of trust among career civil servants also has an impact *inside* agencies. Distrust across functional boundaries within agencies, for example, restricts the free flow of information and personnel essential to solving complex problems requiring collaboration across organizational structures. The resulting poor performance and negative publicity make recruitment and retention of talented civil servants more difficult, even while many government employees are approaching retirement age and need to be replaced.

Figure I.2 When trust declines

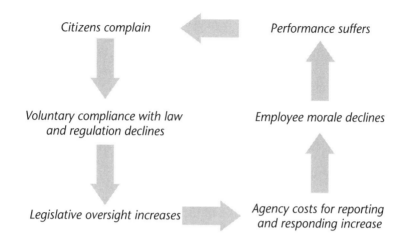

Citizens complain ← Performance suffers

↓ ↑

Voluntary compliance with law
and regulation declines

Employee morale declines

↓ ↑

Legislative oversight increases → Agency costs for reporting
and responding increase

These effects also come at a time when trust in government by government employees themselves is under threat. Although government employees generally like their jobs, the trust they report in their immediate leadership chain of command receives lower marks, as Table I.1 shows. When employees lack trust in their superiors, organizations lose the creativity and commitment essential to high performance.

Table I.1 Trust within the federal government

Question	Response
"I have a high level of respect for my organization's senior leaders."	Strongly agree: 15.1% Agree: 35.0%
"My organization's leaders maintain high standards of honesty and integrity."	Strongly agree: 15.6% Agree: 35.2%
"How satisfied are you with the policies and practices of your senior leaders?"	Very satisfied: 9.1% Satisfied: 32.6%
"Promotions in my work unit are based on merit."	Strongly agree: 9.2% Agree: 30.6%

Source: Federal Human Capital Survey, U.S. Office of Personnel Management, 2006.

The central role of career leadership in building institutional trust

As a candidate for president, Jimmy Carter noted that economy and efficiency are necessary but insufficient to build effective government. Honesty, integrity, compassion, love, and justice are important too—for these qualities build the relationships and trust that make economy and efficiency possible.

Because of their short tenure and public exposure, political leaders find it difficult to build trust. But career civil servants can have more success. And while generating political trust is largely outside the control of career civil servants, building institutional trust is not.

> *Nowhere in the Constitution of the United States, or the Declaration of Independence, or the Bill of Rights, or the Emancipation Proclamation, or the Old Testament, or the New Testament, do you find the words "economy" or "efficiency." Not that these words are unimportant. But you discover other words like honesty, integrity, fairness, liberty, justice, patriotism, compassion, love—and many others which describe what human beings ought to be. These are the same words which describe what a government of human beings ought to be.*
>
> —Jimmy Carter, *Why Not the Best?* 1976

By fostering institutional trust, career civil service leaders can enhance both performance and the perceptions of their agencies. As Steven Van de Walle and Geert Bouckaert suggest in Figure I.3, public perceptions of agencies have an indirect but significant effect on public perceptions of government as a whole.[18] Although what happens inside and across agencies is not solely responsible for what the public thinks of government, it does make a difference.

For career civil servants, the core question is this: How can we strengthen relationships and instill trust inside and outside our organizations so as to foster agency success and positive public perceptions?

This book focuses on the central role played by career civil service leaders in building trust in themselves and their organizations. Our thesis is that trust matters and that it can be developed. Our focus is on the development of trust through building effective relationships among career civil service leaders, their employees, people in other organizations in the executive branch, the legislature, and the citizenry. We devote considerable attention to the federal government, but the arguments and insights apply with equal

Figure I.3 Multiple influences on trust in government

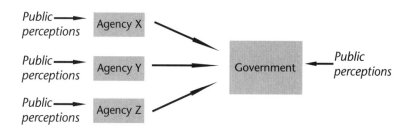

Source: Steven Van de Walle and Geert Bouckaert, (2003) "Public Service Performance and Trust in Government," *International Journal of Public Administration,* 26, 8/9 (2003): 891–913.

force at the state and local level. Relationships and the trust they engender or thwart were as important when Alexander Hamilton speculated about bureaucracy as they were 200 years later when Jimmy Carter reminded us that caring about those you serve is an essential measure of success, and they will be equally important in this century.

This argument rests on looking inside the "black box" of each of the agencies in Figure I.3. Figure I.4 on the following page suggests that agency performance and therefore public perceptions rest on both macro-level and micro-level factors.

Most efforts to improve government have focused on macro-level changes. Efforts as diverse as the Government Performance and Results Act (GPRA) (strategy and measures); the creation of chief financial officers, chief information officers, and chief human capital officers (systems); performance management and pay banding (measures and systems); outsourcing (systems); the Office of Management and Budget's Program Assessment and Rating Tool (PART) (measures); and frequent reorganizations (structure) all have a common goal: to alter the performance of agencies so as to meet public purposes and foster positive public perceptions.

The argument we make is that comparable emphasis on the micro-level change efforts to build shared values, effective relationships, and therefore enhancing trust has been lacking. At best, the designers of macro-level changes have taken for granted the presence of shared values, sound relationships, and trust—they are assumed to exist. At worst, they have been ignored or viewed as the "soft stuff" that requires neither attention nor action.

Figure I.4 Macro- and micro-level change levers in organizations

Agency X

Trust and relationships: The critical connection

Building shared values, effective relationships, and trust are the "hard stuff" and can neither be assumed nor ignored in fostering high performance in government.

For the purposes of this book, we define trust as a foundational confidence among citizens, including government workers themselves, that government agencies and the people who work in them will act in a reasonably consistent way to promote their shared values and interests and respond to their long-term needs and wants. Like trust in other realms, trust in government is ultimately anchored in perceptions of integrity, inclusion, reciprocity, fairness, competence, and reliability—and it both depends upon and fosters excellent working relationships.

In *The Trusted Leader*, we have chosen to focus on the leadership of career civil servants because we believe they have powerful leverage over the culture within their organizations. Using that power effectively may not guarantee institutions that earn the trust of the American people, but using that power ineffectively surely guarantees that such trust is lost.

Our definition of trust leads to several closely connected observations that are essential to the argument of this book.

Box I.1   Trust within the federal government

Trust is a foundational confidence among citizens, including government workers themselves, that both government agencies and the people who work in them will act in a reasonably consistent way to promote their shared values and interests and respond to their long-term needs and wants. Like trust in other realms, trust in government is ultimately anchored in perceptions of integrity, inclusion, reciprocity, fairness, competence, and reliability—and it both depends upon and fosters excellent working relationships.

First, as Figure I.4 suggests, trust is foundational. It underlies and affects all work done within and across agencies. Without it, little of value can be accomplished.

Second, trust proceeds from the inside out. Interpersonal trust is essential to building team and organizational trust, which is essential to building trust with other agencies and among members of the public.

Third, lack of trust at any point in this chain has negative effects downstream. Lack of trust among intelligence agencies in sharing data, for example, can have a deadly effect on a military operation, even if trust and performance among military personnel is exceptional.

Fourth, trust is anchored in a relationship. We cannot speak of trust unless we speak at some level of trusting someone. Therefore, to build trust, we must build relationships.

We do not mean to belittle the importance of macro-level mechanisms for enhancing individual and organizational performance, nor do we mean to diminish the importance of performance itself in building trust. Rather, we argue that effective relationships and trust, anchored in shared values, make other government improvement efforts possible. Poor relationships and distrust between Congress and the agencies, for example, lead the latter to offer GPRA targets that are so easy that they are sure to be met or to disguise data when real results are not as promised. Poor relationships and distrust undermine efforts at personnel reform, as unions and management seek ways to protect themselves from the damage each assumes the other intends to inflict. Similarly, the power of information technology to enhance government productivity and citizen involvement in government exists only in theory until those who are to use such technology trust each other enough to communicate with honest information—or to communicate at all.

Trust, relationships, and social capital

The importance of effective relationships seems intuitive, but talk of relationships often produces criticism that this "soft stuff" is neither useful nor learnable. The research record does not support such criticism.

The terminology used to talk about trusting relationships in the research literature often focuses on the term *social capital*.[19] High-quality relationships in which trust and positive regard are maximized represent positive social capital. Social capital, it turns out, is critical to organizational success. In a wide-ranging survey of the research and theory of social capital formation in organizations, Janine Nahapiet and Sumantra Ghoshal concluded: "Social capital facilitates the development of intellectual capital by affecting the conditions necessary for exchange and combination to occur. . . . One of the important barriers to the transfer of best practice within organizations is the existence of arduous relations between the source and recipient. Where relationships are high in trust, people are more willing to engage in social exchange in general, and cooperative interaction in particular." [20]

In another survey of the research, Gareth Jones and Jennifer George concluded that "shared values and expressions of positive affect typically result in individuals wanting to cooperate and to do whatever they can for the common good; hence, they will define their roles broadly to include whatever acts they are capable of performing that contribute to common goals and raise performance and competitive advantage." [21] And, speaking even more directly to the link between social capital and organizational success, Mark Bolino, William Turnley, and James Bloodgood argue that "Individuals in a group are more comfortable with uncertainty and less resistant to change when they like one another . . . workgroups in which members like one another may be more flexible, better able to adapt to a changing environment, and higher performing." [22]

Evidence from research on emotional intelligence demonstrates that building effective relationships that enhance trust and thereby create social capital requires a set of skills that can be learned. Daniel Goleman and the Consortium for Research on Emotional Intelligence place these skills (Box I.2) into four clusters.[23]

These clusters and their associated skills have distinct and important interconnections. Self-awareness is necessary for self-management, and social awareness skills are critical for managing relationships. Futher, if you cannot manage yourself, it is unlikely you will be good at managing relationships.

Goleman's work also demonstrates that emotionally intelligent leaders—in our terms, leaders who can build relationships and trust—are more

Box I.2   Emotional intelligence skills

Self-awareness	Emotional self-awareness	
	Accurate self-assessment	
	Self-confidence	
Self-management	Emotional self-control	Achievement
	Transparency	Initiative
	Adaptability	Optimism
Social awareness	Empathy	
	Organizational awareness	
	Service orientation	
Relationship management	Development of others	Influence
	Inspirational leadership	Conflict management
	Change catalyst	Teamwork and collaboration

Source: Adapted from *Emotional Competence Inventory (ECI) Technical Manual,* June 2006, 3–4; *www.eiconsortium.org/research/ECI_2.0_Technical_Manual_v2.pdf.*

successful at creating organizational climates that foster the flexibility essential to innovation, commitment to a common purpose, a sense of responsibility, clarity around mission and values, high standards of performance, and the linking of performance to rewards.[24]

The plan for the book

Trust is a social good to be protected just as much as the air we breathe or the water we drink. When it is damaged, the community as a whole suffers; and, when it is destroyed, societies falter and collapse. . . . Trust and integrity are precious resources, easily squandered, hard to regain.

—Sissela Bok, *Lying: Moral Choice in Public and Private Life,* 1978

Governing is a social act, and effective governance therefore requires social competence. Career leaders in government who can build relationships that produce trust have met a necessary, if not sufficient, condition for leading democracy. Philosopher Sissela Bok is correct to argue that trust once lost is hard to regain. This book is aimed at showing government leaders how to build effective relationships that foster the "social good" she so rightly prizes.

This is not a book of theory, although theory underlies every chapter. It is instead a book of practice. We emphasize lessons learned on the front lines of leading government organizations and the perspectives, skills, and tools that the most effective leaders have mastered.

To set the overall context for the book, chapter 1 focuses on values-based leadership. Government leaders take an oath of office that rests on a set of constitutional values they pledge to support and defend. Yet these are not the only values they must address. The mix of personal, employee, organizational, professional, and societal values that confront them in their daily decisions requires patience and wisdom to navigate. Terry Newell defines the sea of values across which government leaders sail, the perspectives and skills required to do so, and the importance of being a values-based leader in establishing sound relationships and trust.

Building on the groundwork of chapter 1, section II looks at how government leaders must act to build effective relationships and trust *within* their organizations. In chapter 2, Beverly Fletcher and Alfred Cooke argue that understanding yourself and leading yourself must be the precursor to building relationships with and leading others. Leaders who neglect this personal work are trying to launch a ship without ballast or rudder. If you don't know and trust who you are, why would anyone else? If you can't change yourself, how can you hope to change anything or anyone else?

Chapter 3 demonstrates how authentic leaders, those who have done their personal homework, can serve as masterful coaches to develop the self-awareness and self-leadership needed in those who work for them. Ron Redmon describes the mindset of an effective coach, the behaviors and skills coaches must master, and the principles that guide them. Together, chapters 2 and 3 enable the government leader to forge the central structure on which all else depends—the productive interpersonal relationship.

In chapter 4, Gail Funke helps leaders build the first of the more complex structures essential to leading democracy: effective teams. In too many organizations, the whole is less than the sum of its parts. Good individuals do not automatically make for good teams, and this chapter explores why teams are essential and how leaders foster them. Funke argues that the leader must not only attend to the skills and practices necessary for the team and its members—the microenvironment of teams—but also that the leader must act to support a team-based organization—the macroenvironment for teams. How can leaders establish the rewards, systems, structures, and leadership essential for the success of the teams they rely upon?

Section II concludes with a focus on the broader organization. John Pickering picks up where the focus on teams leaves off. Pickering asks: How do you bring about large-scale organizational change that produces high-performing government organizations? He argues that the prevailing industrial model, based on a leadership philosophy of command-and-control, must be replaced by a model based on a consultative-participative leadership philosophy. The work of leadership in high-performing organizations, Pickering tells us, involves addressing seven central questions and using five change levers. Everyone must participate in this work. It requires building and drawing upon relationships that cut across functions and hierarchical levels.

High-performing organizations, under the guiding hand of leaders who have built strong relationships and trust within, do not always sail alone. Other organizations with other agendas must be considered. The chapters in section III are based on the belief that career civil servants must lead in a broader context than the team or organization—they must lead *outside* the organization as well as inside it. Government leaders must find ways to collaborate with those in other organizations. Readers will not be surprised to find that building relationships and trust are essential here as well.

In chapter 6, Russ Linden focuses on three general paths that lead to collaboration across organizational boundaries and five basic elements necessary for collaboration to succeed. Without finding or forging a shared purpose, a sense of urgency, having the appropriate people at the table, developing a credible process for working together, and having one or more champions, cross-organizational collaboration remains a hope, not a reality. With these basics in mind, he then addresses strategies that leaders can use to move collaboration from a promise to a program—as well as what to do when some of the basics are missing. Given the growing need for cross-organizational collaboration to meet complex public problems, the ability to collaborate is a critical leadership skill.

In chapter 7, Robert Maranto addresses one of the most delicate types of collaboration that effective leadership entails—how to work across the career-political divide. Why do some career employees have such negative views of their political leaders, and why do some political appointees distrust career leaders? Maranto explores the myths each holds of the other and what they can—indeed, must—do to forge the honest communication and sincere trust essential for their work together. The wall of distrust between career and political public servants is, in Maranto's view, neither inevitable nor unbreachable. Chapter 7.1 carries this argument down to the state government level. The mechanics of career-political relationships differ in important ways at the state level, but the underlying need to forge trust and build effective relationships is the same.

Through the wisdom of the Founders, we have three branches of government, and little happens when they fail to work together for the common good. As James Madison would remind us, we have a system in which ambition is engineered to counteract ambition—legislative-executive suspicion is to a considerable degree built into our nation's political DNA, and it is necessary and helpful, but only up to a point. When suspicion turns to rancor, democracy suffers. Grace Cummings, in chapter 8, focuses on how career leaders in government can build productive relationships with Congress. Executive branch leaders serve two masters, she argues, their own bosses and 535 others on Capitol Hill. They are in a constitutional vise they cannot escape. But knowing how to work with the Hill, what members and staffers expect, and how career leaders in government can be honest and effective—and therefore faithful to their own constitutional role—is the territory she crosses. Chapter 8.1 demonstrates how the need to work effectively with the legislative branch plays out at the state level.

The Preamble to the Constitution reminds us that career leaders in government are here for a reason, six of them to be exact: to "form a more perfect Union, establish Justice, insure domestic Tranquility, provide for the common defence, promote the general Welfare, and secure the Blessings of Liberty to ourselves and our Posterity." Sound relationships and strong bonds of trust within the branches and organizations of government are necessary to achieve the Preamble's promise, but they are not sufficient. As Lincoln reminded us at Gettysburg, government must be "by the people" as well as "for the people," which means trusting the people and also asking for trust from them. *Washington Post* columnist Jim Hoagland expressed this point well when he observed that "demanding trust from the public without extending it invites great skepticism. Correcting this is one of modern history's great challenges." [25]

In chapter 9, Grant Reeher and George Mitchell suggest that one of the best ways to trust the people—and improve government as a result—is to engage the public in governance. Electronic communications technology offers a unique opportunity to involve citizens. They recommend that federal executives adopt an e-*governance* rather than just an e-*government* approach to their Internet-based outreach efforts, one in which citizens are actively included in the governing dialogue and encouraged to work together among themselves, with the agency serving as facilitator.

Lou Carbone argues in chapter 10 that we build trust among citizens when they have a good experience with government. Because they cannot *not* have an experience when they interact with government agencies and employees, the only choice for leaders is the quality of that experience. Drawing on research from psychology, sociology, and marketing, Carbone maintains that the citizen's experience can be engineered so that it meets not just the rational but also the emotional needs that an individual expects in any service encounter. Those who file their taxes electronically, for example, have a far better experience with the Internal Revenue Service than do those who file paper returns. Both get their taxes done, but e-filers come away with a better feeling about the process. Not surprisingly, the IRS is encouraging more people to file electronically. Carbone shows us how to arrange service clues, the sensory inputs that are always present in an experience, to produce a better experience, and more positive feelings, in every citizen interaction.

Chapter 11, the last in section III, reminds us that almost every issue and program in government also has an international dimension or can be affected by global events. Peter Ronayne therefore argues that building relationships and trust across national borders is also important. The skills required to do so can be learned, and acquiring these skills is essential to success in everything from promoting U.S. businesses abroad to fostering global health, addressing global warming, and fighting terrorism.

The book concludes with Dan Fenn's passionate and poignant reminder that the Founders did not set out to make the civil service leader's job easy. Unlike the private sector, the public sector was consciously designed to frustrate anyone who attempts to craft leadership. While Madison understood that we have "engineered an inefficient government to keep men free," citizens often view such inefficiencies as examples of poor government performance. Career leaders in government, Fenn suggests, bear a special responsibility to help the public understand why government works as it does. They need to foster public participation, be transparent and frank, and keep trying to serve the public good even when they meet the resistance. Finally, career leaders in government have a special responsibility to enliven their daily work with honor, grace, and admiration not only for the public but also for themselves. Americans owe their public servants a debt of thanks, he concludes. We must try to earn it, even though we may rarely receive it.

Notes

1. Garrett and Rhine (2006), 14–15.
2. Ibid., 17.
3. Bok (1997). See also Light (2002).
4. Harris Poll No. 10, February 6, 2007. See: *www.harrisinteractive.com/harris_poll/index.asp?PID=726.*
5. American National Election Studies at *www.electionstudies.org.*
6. Harris Poll, July 7–10, 2006, as reported at *www.pollingreport.com/values.htm.*
7. See, for example, Barnes and Gill (2000). The authors sought to replicate the Derek Bok study in New Zealand, with strikingly similar results.
8. Luks (2001).
9. Van de Walle et al. (2002).
10. Nye, Zelikow, and King (1997).
11. Paterson (2000).
12. Nye, Zelikow, and King (1997).
13. Harris Poll, July 7–10, 2006.
14. Hart (2006).
15. Goodsell (2003).
16. Operated by the University of Michigan, the American Customer Satisfaction Index rates participating organizations/programs using a sophisticated telephone survey and methodology. At the end of 2006, the average score for all federal agencies on a scale of 0-100 was 72.3, compared to 74.9 for the private sector. Within government, scores varied from as low as 51 for individual paper filers at the IRS to 87 for buyers of numismatic and commerative coins at the U.S. Mint. See *www.theacsi.org/government.htm.*
17. The Maxwell Poll is a nationally representative poll of adults. Details can be found at *www.maxwell.syr.edu/campbell/Poll/Index.htm.*
18. Van De Walle and Bouckaert (2003).
19. See Fukuyama (1995) for an extended treatment of trust and social capital in the performance of societies.
20. Nahapiet and Ghoshal (1998). Although this study focuses on building social capital in organizations, Fukuyama (1995) provides evidence that social capital formation in societies depends similarly on trusting relationships.
21. Jones and George (1998).
22. Bolino, Turnley, and Bloodgood (2002).
23. Goleman (2000a) presents the research case, and the emotional competence inventory (ECI) is the primary research tool that measures the four skill clusters. For information on the ECI, visit the Web site of the Consortium for Research on Emotional Intelligence at *www.eiconsortium.org.*
24. Goleman (2000b).
25. Hoagland (2006).

1 Values-based leadership for a democratic society

TERRY NEWELL, LEADERSHIP FOR A RESPONSIBLE SOCIETY

*For we must consider that we shall be as a city upon on a hill.
The eyes of all people are upon us.*

—Gov. John Winthrop, aboard the *Arbella,* 1630

AS THE *ARBELLA* APPROACHED BOSTON HARBOR, one of the first government executives in their new land reminded his followers that a life based on high moral values would not only ensure their survival and success but also was essential because of the public nature of their undertaking. Winthrop's exhortation was anchored in religious experience, but secular officials throughout American history have used his words to remind us that our nation—and our government—is still a "city upon a hill." [1] As leaders of government, we are expected to live and lead by high moral values. Values-based leadership builds relationships and trust. This statement is more than a nice sentiment. In a democracy, values-based leadership is essential.[2]

Ursula Henderson led by high moral values. As director of a veterans service center in the Department of Veterans Affairs, she faced the daunting challenge of managing veterans' claims with speed and compassion in an office where employees processed one file after another in a seemingly endless stream of boring bureaucratic work. Rather than remind them of their job descriptions and performance standards, she chose to remind them of Lincoln's Second Inaugural Address, that their job was "to care for he who has borne the battle, for his widow and his orphan," the same words carved in granite on their headquarters in Washington, D.C. She chose to draw on her own passion for helping veterans and tell them a story from a movie about a severely disabled World War I veteran (*When Johnny Came Marching Home*). In the movie, the vet is bandaged from head to toe and can communicate only by blinking his eyes in Morse code. She wanted her staff to see that, in her words, "each file has a face." In short, she chose to lead by reminding them of the core values at the heart of their own lives and enshrined in the history of their agency. She lifted them to an ennobling public purpose. She demonstrated values-based leadership.[3]

Why does values-based leadership matter in government?

Ursula Henderson is not alone. Values-based leadership in government—the practice of leading individuals and organizations from a set of shared core moral values embodied in the leader's behavior and the organization's processes, products, and services—is widespread. But it is neither easy nor inevitable. Bureaucracy, the way we structure and run government agencies, does not automatically produce values-based leadership. The reliance upon hierarchy—objective, rule-based, and loyal action—is not inherently moral. Faithful bureaucrats throughout history have done immoral acts. The Tuskegee Syphilis Study, conducted by the U.S. Public Health Service from 1932 to 1972, demonstrated that what Hannah Arendt called the "banality of evil" was not limited to Nazis.[4] But if not easy or inevitable, values-based leadership in government is still necessary. It builds trust, fosters effective relationships, and helps the bureaucracy to promote democracy.

Values-based leadership matters because core moral values underlie our commitment to each other as members of this nation. The Declaration of Independence enshrines "Life, Liberty and the pursuit of Happiness" as natural rights that precede government and whose protection is the only legitimate basis on which some may govern others. The "consent of the governed" rests on honoring voters' core moral values, and when those values are dishonored, consent is withdrawn.

The Constitution promises that our Union will only be "more perfect" if it will establish "Justice . . . and secure the blessings of Liberty." It proclaims a set of moral ends. It also prescribes a set of moral means by which we govern, including the need to respect majority rule, minority rights, and due process.

Values-based leadership matters because it instills trust in the citizens of the United States. As Robert Greenleaf argues in *Servant Leadership,* trust comes when people have confidence in the leader's values and competence.[5] Skill in the mechanics of governing is necessary but not sufficient to earn the public trust. Leaders need the power that comes from principle, not just the technique that comes from talent. Without trust, the constitutional compact does not work.

Values-based leadership matters because we want our nation to be that "city upon a hill." To the extent government executives lead by and demonstrate core moral values, they help build what Joseph Nye, former dean of Harvard's John F. Kennedy School of Government, calls "soft power."[6] American values and culture can build support for U.S. foreign policy and U.S. goals in the world if our values gain the admiration of people in other nations. In this sense, the "soft power" of values and culture complements the "hard power" that technology, military might, and economic prowess seek to provide. As other civilizations have learned, hard power may be necessary, but it is never sufficient for long-term leadership on the world stage. Other countries have to admire what a nation lives by as well as what it lives with. When values-based leadership falters, as it did so strikingly at Iraq's Abu Ghraib prison, for example, soft power suffers. We cease to live up to our aim to be that "city upon a hill."

Although Nye was primarily concerned with the international influence wielded by soft power, the importance of values-based leadership matters domestically as well. Nearly three-fourths of Americans feel that government would inspire substantially greater confidence if it focused on "respecting the moral values of the public," according to surveys by the research firms of Peter Hart and Robert Teeter.[7]

Values-based leadership matters because significant academic research shows that it is the most effective leadership approach over the long run. James McGregor Burns, in his classic, *Leadership,* contrasted three ways to lead.[8] Coercive or raw power works only until it is overthrown from within or from the outside. Transactional leadership, in which people follow because they are promised practical returns, such as a certain standard of living, can last a while longer. Eventually, however, the governed decide that the promises at the heart of the transaction are no longer met or no longer attractive. Only transformational leadership, where people are drawn together by core values they share, can be sustained over the long term. People want to see their values take root. Transformational—values-based—leadership works because it appeals to followers' most deeply felt values and in so doing empowers them to become leaders in their own right to sustain these values over time.

Values-based leadership matters because we are in a knowledge economy, especially in government. In a knowledge economy, success comes to those with the best ideas. Survival as a nation depends on thinking not only better but faster than those who would do us harm. How do we get the best thinking from not just our employees but citizens in general? It has to be freely given. We cannot compel knowledge contributions. People are more likely to share their creative thinking when they see it is in service to what they value. Values-based leadership releases this energy of innovation.

Finally, values-based leadership matters because it sustains organizations even as the people in them move on. In *Built to Last,* Jim Collins and Jerry Porras show that organizations lasting for generations have very few things in common. They differ in their size, structure, systems, skills, and strategies. But one thing they share is that they are all driven by a set of unchanging core values. Their leaders embed these values in the organization's culture.[9] Collins and Porras draw their examples from the private sector, such as Johnson & Johnson, whose core value around the safety of its products led it to pull every capsule of Tylenol from store shelves when a deranged man spiked a few with cyanide. Their point applies equally well to public organizations. The Marine Corps (see Box 1.1) is values-based and rightly viewed as a leader in this regard even by private sector firms who visit its headquarters in Quantico, Virginia, to learn its values-based leadership approach.

Why do career leaders in government need to be values-based leaders?

Values-based leadership matters in our democracy, but does it necessarily follow that bureaucrats themselves must practice it? Isn't the job of career leaders in government just to administer the laws? Can't we leave value-based decisions and leading by values to elected officials who, after all, are the only ones the people directly entrust with leading?

As the Introduction demonstrated, democracy is not that simple. About 2,000 political leaders are responsible for the overall direction of the executive branch, but it is the daily actions of more than 6,500 career senior executives, 50,000 managers and supervisors, and 2.6 million executive branch employees that translate that direction into action. At the state and local government level, nearly 20 million civil servants dwarf the size of the political leadership. Programs, policies, and behavior that are either faithful or not to our shared core values as a nation are the result. Unless career civil servants are also values-based leaders, the chain of constitutional leadership has a fatal, weak link.

George Washington sensed this intuitively in his first administration when he said that "In every nomination to office I have endeavored . . . to make fitness of character my primary objective." Abigail Adams stated it even

Box 1.1   Core values of the U.S. Marines

HONOR: The bedrock of our character. The quality that guides Marines to exemplify the ultimate in ethical and moral behavior; never to lie, cheat, or steal; to abide by an uncompromising code of integrity; to respect human dignity; to have respect and concern for each other. The quality of maturity, dedication, trust, and dependability that commits Marines to act responsibly; to be accountable for actions; to fulfill obligations; and to hold others accountable for their actions.

COURAGE: The heart of our Core Values, courage is the mental, moral, and physical strength ingrained in Marines to carry them through the challenges of combat and the mastery of fear; to do what is right; to adhere to a higher standard of personal conduct; to lead by example, and to make tough decisions under stress and pressure. It is the inner strength that enables a Marine to take that extra step.

COMMITMENT: The spirit of determination and dedication within members of a force of arms that leads to professionalism and mastery of the art of war. It leads to the highest order of discipline for unit and self; it is the ingredient that enables 24-hour a day dedication to Corps and Country; pride; concern for others; and an unrelenting determination to achieve a standard of excellence in every endeavor. Commitment is the value that establishes the Marine as the warrior and citizen others strive to emulate.

Reaffirm these Core Values and ensure they guide your performance, behavior, and conduct every minute of every day.

Source: Marine Corps Values: A User's Guide For Discussion Leaders, 2–7; can be found at *www.tecom.usmc.mil/utm/6-11B.pdf.*

more clearly when writing to her son, John Quincy Adams, himself destined for a life of public service: "Great Learning and superior abilities, should you ever possess them, will be of little value and small Estimation unless Virtue, Honor, Truth and Integrity are added to them."

Washington and Adams may have been principally concerned with elected or appointed leaders, but their words apply just as forcefully to civil service leaders. Federal employees, for example, take a solemn oath of office to "bear true faith and allegiance" to the Constitution and to "well and faithfully" discharge their duties. The definition of faithful is to be "steadfast in affection ... firm in adherence to promises ... and true to the facts or a standard"—moral values in service of a moral obligation.[10]

Box 1.2   Core values of the U.S. Constitution

Moral Ends

"We the People of the United States, in Order to form a more perfect Union, establish Justice, insure domestic Tranquility, provide for the common defence, promote the general Welfare, and secure the Blessings of Liberty to ourselves and our Posterity, do ordain and establish this Constitution for the United States of America."

Values-based means

Representative, elective government
Subordination of military to civil authority
Free exercise of religion, press, speech, assembly, and petition
Security against unreasonable search/seizure
Trial by jury
Divided powers/checks and balances
Majority rule/minority rights
Due process of law

The U.S. Congress recognized the importance of leading by core moral values for all civil servants when, in the Code of Ethics for Government Service enacted in 1958, it stated as the first item: "Put loyalty to the highest moral principles above loyalty to persons, party, or Government department."

What values guide values-based leaders?

On the surface, values-based leadership seems simple and direct. Who would argue that leaders should not have strong moral values they exemplify in their daily work? Below the surface, however, people get nervous. Don't we want our civil servants to keep their values to themselves? What values are we talking about, and aren't moral values the purview of religious faith rather than secular government? In a democracy, people inevitably have value conflicts. Do we want unelected government executives choosing among competing values?

These questions have lasted as long as our Republic, and they have no easy answers. But that does not mean they are unanswerable. Although we may never agree as a nation on a full set of moral values we all share, that does not mean we don't share many. Nor does it mean that we relieve our leaders of the requirement to identify and lead by moral values. Consider the

Figure 1.1 Core values worldwide

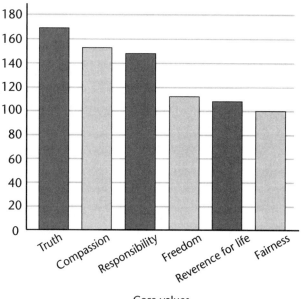

Core values

Source: Adapted from Rushworth Kidder, *Moral Courage* (New York: William Morrow, 2005).

alternative. If we do not want our public servants to adopt and lead by a set of core moral values, we risk relieving them of the need to think about and be accountable for morally acceptable action. So the question is not *whether* but by *which* moral values we want them to lead.

There are at least four ways to answer this question. Our Constitution offers the first and most important response. It encompasses a set of moral ends, established largely by the Preamble. It also encompasses a set of values-based means that we are held to "support and defend" (see Box 1.2). Values-based leaders must ask themselves if their actions adhere to these values.

A second guide is a set of core personal values. The popular notion that "everything is relative" is in fact not the case. Research by the Institute for Global Ethics finds that a small number of moral values are shared across the world. The institute's research includes surveys, contextual analysis, interviews and workshops, all of which ask the same basic question: What values count the most for you in living your daily life?

Figure 1.1 on page 25 presents the results of a study conducted of 272 attendees at the State of the World Forum in 1996, a group that represented forty countries and fifty different faith groups. The data represent the frequency count when people selected their top five values from a list of fifteen. The same core values turn up at the top of the list in every other study the institute has conducted. These values speak to the importance of respecting the worth of each human being. Whether adherence to these values is anchored in one's religious faith or not, who would want a world—or a public official—for whom these values did not guide action?

Although the most often mentioned values may not represent the full set of core personal values that should guide public servants, they demonstrate that the question of what those values are is not "up for grabs." They are a small, not an infinite number.[11]

A third guide is a set of professional values that emerges from two centuries of public service excellence—and failure. This group incorporates constitutional and personal core values and moves them into the realm of administrative behavior. They are captured best in codes of ethics crafted by those entrusted with furthering the profession of public administration and the behavior of public administrators. The ethical code of the American

---

Box 1.3   American Society for Public Administration code of ethics

1. **Serve the public interest:** Serve the public beyond serving oneself.

2. **Respect the Constitution and the law:** Respect, support, and study government constitutions and laws that define responsibilities of public agencies, employees, and all citizens.

3. **Demonstrate personal integrity:** Demonstrate the highest standards in all activities to inspire public confidence and trust in public service.

4. **Promote ethical organizations:** Strengthen organizational capabilities to apply ethics, efficiency, and effectiveness in serving the public.

5. **Strive for professional excellence:** Strengthen individual capabilities and encourage the professional development of others.

Source: American Society for Public Administration, www.aspanet.org. Each of these five broad areas contains four to eight behavioral statements that define expected actions of public administrators.

Society for Public Administration presents an excellent example of a powerful statement of professional values that must guide government executive action.

Yet another set of values that has some claim on career leaders are those inherent in and often formally established by their technical professions. These values should be consistent with constitutional and public administration values—and must be given secondary place if they are not. The values of the professions (for example, law, engineering, psychology, medicine) offer another set of standards that career civil servants in particular professions can use to guide their actions.

Even beyond constitutional, personal, public service, and professional values lay the additional value realms of organization, family, community, and religion. The question for career leaders in government quickly becomes not "are there values that must guide my actions?" but "how do I choose among the value claims upon me?" Answering that question demands mastery of a set of skills essential to values-based leadership.

What skills do values-based leaders in government need?

If government executives want to be values-based leaders, they need a set of skills with which to approach their work. Values without skills are like engines without fuel—they are all potential energy. Skills move values into action. Any of the wide range of competencies in leadership skill lists might be called upon in a given instance by a values-based civil servant, but some will *always* be called upon. We suggest at least the following five:

1. Acting with integrity.
2. Listening.
3. Tolerating dissent.
4. Involving others.
5. Moral decision making.

Acting with integrity

Values-based leaders must be honest. In its simplest expression, this means they must not lie. Although one might "have to lie" at some point in a career to protect those in imminent physical danger—for example, an intelligence agent whose truthfulness would put his own or others' lives in jeopardy—these instances are more rare than we might believe or wish to think.[12]

Deception . . . strikes at the very heart and essence of democratic government. It allows those in power to override or nullify the right vested in the people to cast an informed vote. . . . Deceiving the people for the sake of the people is a self-contradictory notion in a democracy, unless it can be shown that there has been genuine consent to deceit.

— Sissela Bok, *Lying: Moral Choice in Public and Private Life*, 1978

"Telling the truth" seems like a straightforward principle. Asked if a report has been prepared to meet a congressional mandate, the path to truthfulness is an honest "yes" or "no." Leaders in government are faced with many situations, however, in which they may convince themselves that there are alternatives that are not exactly lies. For example, is withholding negative data about the performance of the organization a lie, if the request did not specify this type of information? What about suppressing a dissenting view on the meaning of intelligence data? Does a report that includes only statistics that buttress the organization's position represent a lie?

As Box 1.4 suggests, the territory between "the truth, the whole truth and nothing but the truth" and "an outright, known falsehood" contains a number of choices, which test moral principles. Failing to think carefully about these choices can ease the leader's way onto the slippery slope that makes future errors in truthfulness both easier to make and harder to see.

At a deeper level, integrity means "firm adherence to a code of . . . moral values."[13] One's behavior must be integral—in other words, consistent with professed moral values. In this sense, telling the truth is necessary but not sufficient for acting with integrity, which can also be defined as "the quality or state of being complete or undivided." To be a leader within this definition of integrity, moral words must match moral deeds. When a government executive has this kind of integrity, no one need worry if the lofty rhetoric he or she hears is somehow divorced from the actions seen. It is this kind of leadership that builds trust.

Listening

No one can be a values-based leader without the ability to listen. This means wanting to hear what others say and understanding the values behind their deeply held beliefs as much as it means having a set of skills that enable listening (for example, active attention, paraphrasing what we hear, and probing

Box 1.4   The path between truth and falsehood

The truth, the whole truth, and nothing but the truth

Evading the subject
Partial truth
Withholding information
Distorting data
Manipulating statistics
Being vague
Presenting only one side of the argument
Suppressing dissenting views
Leaking selected information
Using a false analogy
Saying nothing
Spinning the story

An outright, known falsehood

Note: The list of actions above, between the whole truth and an outright falsehood, is not meant to suggest any rank order.

for understanding). It means having empathy for another even when we do not agree. To have empathy, the leader must work at getting inside another's thoughts and feelings—a task that is as important to attempt as it is impossible to fully achieve. Listening also means spending time on the other person or group's agenda as well as on our own, and it means understanding ourselves well enough to know when our own values, motives, and assumptions may be blocking the message others are trying to send.

Tolerating dissent

This "skill" rarely shows up on a list of leadership competencies, but government executives who cannot tolerate dissent cannot "well and faithfully" "support and defend" the Constitution. The Framers believed that dissent was not only inevitable but necessary in a republican form of government. As Jefferson noted, "error of opinion may be tolerated where reason is left free to combat it." [14] But reason must be allowed to speak. Values-based leaders accept this requirement not only in the public arena but also inside their own organizations. Research is clear that government leaders who cannot tolerate dissent in their own ranks make bad, even disastrous decisions. For example, the NASA *Challenger* and *Columbia* accident investigations both concluded that the inability to promote and hear dissenting views contributed directly to these tragedies. As the Columbia Accident Investigation Board noted in its report: "The organizational structure and hierarchy blocked effective communication of technical problems. Signals were overlooked, people were silenced, and useful information and dissenting views on technical issues did not surface at higher levels. What was communicated to parts of the organization was that O-ring erosion and foam debris were not problems." [15] In both cases, the highest moral value of the preservation of life was somehow subordinated to lesser values.

A related characteristic of values-based leaders is their ability to tolerate ambiguity. A leader must hold off from closure—at least long enough to hear and consider dissenting views. The leader must accept that he or she has neither all the data nor all the answers and that uncertainty accompanies tough decisions. Leaders who *have* to decide before they need to decide often rue the decisions they make.

Involving others

Values-based leaders in government seek to include people in the decisions that affect their lives. Our Madisonian system demands multiple voices to protect liberty and relies on the belief that hearing different views contributes to better decision making. Social science research also shows that people commit to those values and actions they have a hand in shaping.[16] People resist change when they are frozen out of it. They are more likely to embrace it when they see it as their change—something that acknowledges and incorporates their values. Even though values-based leaders know that the final decision on both values and actions will rarely accept every input they receive, they aim to have people feel they have had a chance to be heard.

Moral decision making

Values-based leaders are more likely than other leaders to make sound, moral decisions. Being honest, listening, tolerating dissent, and including others are necessary but not sufficient skills to help leaders do the right thing. When faced with many alternatives and counterpressures, civil service leaders need the ability to think through the problems they face. This skill is not only a matter of using decision tools but also a matter of using moral imagination. If they don't know the questions to ask, and if they don't ask enough questions, their decisions will be shortsighted at best and destructive of core values at worst. To be human is to be limited by one's own "mental models," the way one makes sense of the world. Values-based leaders find ways to transcend the limits of their own thinking—to imagine the values conflicts they face from multiple perspectives and to see multiple moral choices about moving ahead.[17]

The questions in Box 1.5 can help leaders take a systematic look at making decisions with an eye to the value-based points of view at stake.[18]

Box 1.5   Exercising moral imagination: Questions to ask

Get the facts

1. What is the values dilemma as you see it? What values seem at issue as you define the problem?

2. Who are the stakeholders and how do they see the issue? What values matter for them?

3. What is at stake for you? What are your motives?

4. What are the relevant facts?

5. What values are in conflict now that you have a deeper understanding of the problem?

6. What assumptions are you and others making that might need to be tested?

Identify options

7. Who has responsibility to resolve this dilemma?

8. What results would define success for you? For other stakeholders?

9. What are all of the possible options?

10. What are the positive and negative consequences of the most promising options?

Make and implement a decision

11. What option best satisfies your core values while acknowledging and faithfully considering the values that matter to others?

12. How will you implement the chosen option and mitigate negative impacts?

What is the stage on which values-based government leaders act?

Values and skills come together in action. "All the world's a stage," Shakespeare reminded us. Government leaders know full well that they are always on stage. Their on-stage actions deliver or deny the promise of democracy. Their actions demonstrate or deny their understanding of the values that matter to those they serve. The three stages for values-based leadership action are: the public, the organizational, and the personal. These stages almost always overlap in practice.

The public stage

Anyone whose agency or action has received negative press on the front page of a major newspaper knows that leadership contrary to core moral values is the easiest way to invite public scorn. Those who break the law, violate regulations, or engage in ethically abhorrent behavior usually get the sanction they deserve. The simplest rule for values-based leaders: don't do wrong.

Unfortunately, avoiding wrong is not necessarily doing right. Values-based leaders in government must also:

Keep the public purpose in mind. Everything government does has a public purpose. That purpose enshrines core values in an organization's legislation, mission, and vision. Values-based leaders can always explain how their actions are faithful to that core purpose—and their employees can explain it, too. People say that Sen. Herman Talmadge, while visiting Cape Canaveral in the early 1960s, asked a janitor what his job was. The janitor's reply—"My job is help us get a man to the moon"—led Talmadge to become a fervent supporter of NASA, which until that time had struggled to get sufficient funding. Talmadge reasoned correctly that if a janitor knew that his job was contributing to a grand public purpose, so did everyone else (see Box 1.6). The story may be apocryphal, but it demonstrates that NASA's core purpose served as an ennobling statement for its workforce as well as the rest of America. NASA has had tough times to be sure, but core values and a core purpose see one through—something government leaders can draw upon when their agencies are confronted with adversity.[19]

Encourage the expression of differing interests. As discussed above, values-based leaders encourage—or at least support—the expression of different points of view and the values that underlie them in the belief that better

---

Box 1.6   The NASA vision for the future

To improve life here,
To extend life to there,
To find life beyond...

As only NASA can

---

policies and programs will emerge from a conversation in the light than from one hidden in shadow. Their belief is anchored in considerable research on decision making, much of which argues for the value of disagreement.[20] On the public stage, values-based leaders are adept at using a range of methods to encourage healthy dialogue, including, for example, town-hall meetings, focus groups, surveys, Web sites, and personal conversations with main stakeholders. They also incorporate the spirit as well as the letter of the Administrative Procedures Act (APA) in their work. Originally passed to ensure that the expansion of government ushered in by the New Deal did not mean a distancing of government from public accountability, the APA has been expanded and refined. It provides multiple ways to encourage and listen to differing views. Requiring agencies to keep the public informed about their organization, procedures, and rules; providing for public participation in the rulemaking process; and establishing uniform standards for the conduct of formal rulemaking—all features of the APA—are important mechanisms that leaders who seek to build trust among the public they serve will use to open their decision making to a range of views.

Educate the public about the governing process. Encouraging differing views is most productive when there is a broad public understanding of how government works. Without an appreciation that we are a society that depends on collaboration and compromise, differing views can easily become shrill demands. Many Americans lack sufficient civic knowledge, and the result is that they act more like customers than citizens. As customers, they see paying taxes as the only obligation they bear. They don't have to participate in learning and thinking about public issues. They don't have to accept any responsibility for participating in public discourse and crafting solutions. They don't have to like paying for anything that may benefit others. In short, they don't have to have much civic-mindedness. They have only to vote and complain. They see their relationship to the nation as a contract not a covenant.

Figure 1.2 Dwight Waldo's ethical obligations of a public servant

Source: Adapted from Rosemary O'Leary, *The Ethics of Dissent* (Washington, D.C.: CQ Press, 2006), 17.

This way of thinking can easily lead to distrust when the "deliverables" of the contract are, in their view, not forthcoming. By reaching out to citizens, explaining the process of governing, and helping them play a useful role, career civil service leaders can do much not only to build good policy and good programs but also to enhance trust. Reaching out may be difficult and leave the civil service leader open to criticism (as our concluding chapter in this book demonstrates), but it is both the price we pay and the promise we make as those who govern.

Make tough decisions that involve value trade-offs. Public executives deal with issues that lack easy, widely acceptable answers. These tough decisions almost always involve trade-offs among competing values. Where do we safely store nuclear waste? How do we balance the need to fight terrorism with protecting personal privacy? How can we provide for the aging baby boomer population without unfairly burdening the younger generation? As Dwight Waldo (see Figure 1.2) noted years ago, values-based leaders know that they have obligations to many individuals and groups whose values pull

Figure 1.3 Moral horizons: Expanding the scope and timeframe of the leader's concerns

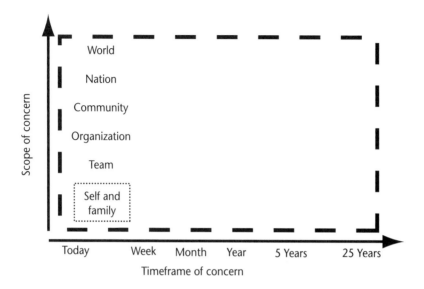

in different directions.[21] As a result, they recognize that they will often make decisions that please no one fully. They make them anyway, secure in the knowledge that they have allowed differing values to be expressed and considered. And they can articulate how they have addressed concerns about differing values in the decision-making process.

Consider the implications of potential actions on affected communities and the future. Most decisions involve what to do *now* in the context of a specific situation and group of stakeholders. But the impact of these decisions can have profound ripple effects on wider audiences and future points in time. Shifting resources to increase police protection in a troubled area may be the most sensible and politically expedient thing to do when faced with crime reports in the news, but the values-based leader will also ask additional questions before making this decision: How will this shift affect other parts of the community and their needs? Will increasing what we spend on police protection mean we have to decrease the budget in other areas and, if so, what effect will this have in the years ahead on preventive programs such as education, job training, and youth centers?

As Figure 1.3 shows, a government leader can set a wide or narrow limit on the scope of whose values to consider when facing the moral implications of prospective actions (the vertical axis). The leader can also consider the impact of potential decisions over a short time or longer span of time (the horizontal axis). At worst, a public leader cannot see beyond the immediate impact of a potential action on himself and his immediate needs (the dotted box in Figure 1.3). But a values-based leader will set the horizon farther out in time and space. Although few decisions must consider the worldwide impact many years into the future (the dashed box), it is also true that few decisions are only a matter for one individual or one organization and their short-term interests.[22]

Stay in their constitutional role. Career government executives, who report to elected or appointed officials, are tasked with carrying out the policies and programs these officials direct—except where actions would be illegal, unethical, and/or unconstitutional. At times they must subordinate their personal values and professional beliefs, a very stressful role to play. A government executive may not agree with the policy to ban drug sale imports from Canada, fund a particular program, or ignore a pressing need out of political expediency, but that does not make those actions illegal or unethical. Nor do such actions give the leader the justification to refuse direction from above or to leak information to the media. The values-based leader should express her views to her boss (see the section below on loyal dissent), but also remember that it is political not career leadership that has been elected and is answerable to the voters.[23]

The organization

Government executives are also on stage within their organizations. Creating a sense of trust and being effective outside in the public arena are rarely possible for a leader and her or his organization unless values based leadership also exists inside. Values-based leaders in government can take specific actions such as the following:

Foster a sense of public service. Just as Ursula Henderson did for her employees in the veterans service center, values-based government leaders demonstrate a passion for public service and instill it in their employees. They remind their workers of the core public purpose that created their organization. They also remind their employees of the core values behind that public purpose, values that come ultimately from the Constitution and the Declaration of Independence. Ben Scaggs at the Environmental Protection Agency in Research Triangle Park, North Carolina, may not have told the public about Elliott, a nine-year-old asthmatic who could not play baseball when the air was unhealthy. But he told his employees about him, because making the air cleaner for Elliott—and thousands like him—is what brought Ben to work each day. Even though his office and his staff were in support roles to those concerned with the Clean Air Act, he wanted his staff to know the importance of what they were supporting. And so, in the best traditions of values-based leaders, he exhorted his employees to find their own Elliott so that each of their days at work would be driven by the desire to serve.

Promote core values. Executives must articulate and reward behavior consistent with core values. For many employees, the biggest disconnect is between published values statements that hang on agency walls and their perception of how their leaders act. If the leader values integrity, he should publicly recognize the employee who has discovered a mistake and called attention to it. Even better, he should admit mistakes to employees. The leader who acknowledges in a staff meeting, for example, that a decision he made did not work out creates an environment that allows employees to admit their mistakes and moves from the bureaucratic tendency to place blame to the moral tendency to forgive. If a leader values creativity, she should recognize the experiment that failed—and even embarrassed the agency in the process. If collaboration is a value, the leader should not give all the recognition and awards to solo performers.

> Ali Bahrami, a leader in the Transport Airplane Directorate of the Federal Aviation Administration made organizational values come alive every day. Several years ago, on a Friday at 3 pm, he received a call of a "positive finding" on the vertical tail structure of an Airbus 300. Translated, that means the airworthiness of all similar planes was called into question. As Ali said, describing what happened next: "Some of us worked through the weekend to define a plan in order to assure the safety of the fleet. By Monday morning, we had a plan. On Wednesday, at about midnight, we prepared an airworthiness directive which required certain actions. The same folks were at work the next day at 5:00 am so that they could respond to potential inquiries." No one can doubt the values of service, safety, and commitment that permeate Ali Bahrami's organization, values he promoted in his own action and so clearly instilled in his employees.[24]

Promoting core values also implies identifying the small number that are both essential and on which there can be agreement. Organizations are most effective and efficient when their members agree on (and can easily recall) the core values that guide them.[25]

> *I remember one of our first off-sites (at TSA). I asked around the table as to whether or not we had core values at TSA. They said, "Oh, sure." I said, "Well, how many do you have?" They said, "Oh, I think there might be like 10 or 11." I said, "Is anybody here able to recite those for me?" Of course, they could not, because they hadn' t internalized them. We were at that point about three weeks old as an organization.*
>
> —James Loy, former administrator,
> Transportation Security Administration

Ensure that employees do not confuse organizational means with constitutional ends. The reason for organizational policies, systems, and procedures is to achieve a public purpose. Many employees, forgetting the purpose, act as if the rules are the end not the means. They confuse organizational values with the constitutional values that must have primacy in their work. They deny a request for assistance because the forms have not been filled out perfectly rather than helping the applicant correct the problem. Admittedly, government agencies often have to struggle to appropriately balance organizational with constitutional values, but government executives lead that balancing act. It is not easy. Do employees bend the rules to respond to the needs of a citizen, or do they "treat everyone the same?" Values-based leaders in government do all they can to put public service above process. They encourage employees to challenge the rules and focus on the right.

Create an ethical culture and foster ethical conversations. People will confront ethical issues even (perhaps especially) in the best-led organizations. Should we adopt a policy that some in the public angrily protest? What do we do when asked to verify information publicly that we privately doubt is accurate? What should we say when asked to support a policy with which we personally disagree?

Values-based leaders expect such questions to come up. They engage employees in thinking them through. They use ethical issues as the basis of conversations in staff meetings, aimed at helping employees and the organization do the right thing. They create an ethical culture by ensuring that core values drive the organization. This task is one of leadership architecture in

Figure 1.4 Elements of an ethical culture

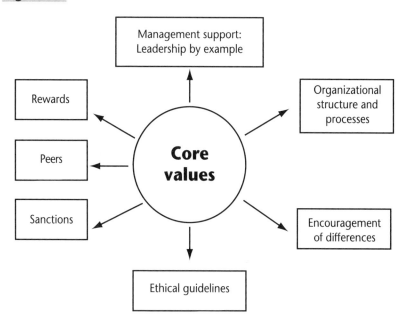

which they must ensure that all of the elements of such a culture exist, operate effectively, and support each other (see Figure 1.4).

Part of fostering this ethical culture is to remind employees of their constitutional oath of office. The Federal Executive Institute, for example, readministers the oath to all graduating government executives. The U.S. Air Force does so in a public ceremony to every officer receiving a promotion. In this action, its senior officers show, by the example of their behavior, that fidelity to the Constitution is essential to leadership.

The self

Career civil servants cannot be values-based leaders on the public stage or within the organization if they have not mastered the skills or lack the temperament to behave that way themselves. Leading from a values base means living from one. Government executives must do at least three things in their "always on stage" behavior, using the skills discussed above.

Model values-based leadership behavior. We are all faced with moral temptations—those decisions where we know that one choice is wrong—morally and often legally as well. These choices are easy for values-based leaders. They are covered by laws and formal ethical codes aimed at avoiding problems such as conflicts of interest and inadequate financial disclosure. Quite simply, faced with these choices, values-based leaders do the right thing. The tougher choices government leaders face are those between two or more courses of action all of which may be morally and legally right, and all of which may have some negative outcomes. Rushworth Kidder of the Institute for Global Ethics calls such situations ethical dilemmas.[26] They have no easy answers because a values-based case can be made for more than one choice. Does a leader give an employee a good recommendation for another job because he wants to move on and needs the promotion to support his family, even though he has not been a stellar performer? Or does the leader tell the whole truth when called for a reference? Values-based leaders have developed a way to think about such issues and make reasoned and reasonable decisions. Or to put it in the words of political scientist Louis Gawthrop, they can differentiate between what they *can* do and what they *should* do.[27] They do not confuse what is permissible with what is the best and most ethical course of action. They engage in self-reflection and model the way they want their followers to behave. They also often explain and engage their employees in discussion about value conflicts in their work. In this way, they also model the importance of dialogue in bringing diverse points of view to grappling with value dilemmas.

Engage in loyal dissent. Values-based leaders do more than encourage dissent from those who report to them—they practice dissent as well. They know how to take a stand when they disagree on a tough issue where core values might be violated—their own, organizational, and/or constitutional. As John Johns, former dean at the National Defense University and former faculty member at the Federal Executive Institute, reminds us, we have many ways to act in between the extremes of silence and whistle-blowing (see Box 1.7). Values-based government executives know how to practice loyal dissent. They may still ultimately have to blow the whistle, but that action, which often removes them from further significant influence in their organizations, is the last resort, not the first.

Act with moral courage. Acting ethically and engaging in loyal dissent where needed often require courage. Not everyone welcomes or applauds moral action. Physical bravery, the kind seen in battle, is what we usually think of when talking about courageous action, but most of the situations career leaders in government face will not call for that. Moral courage is what transforms ethical thinking into ethical action, and a government executive

Box 1.7   Guidelines for loyal dissent in government*

1. Choose your issues carefully. Dissent tries the patience of superiors. Use your credits for dissent judiciously.

2. Do your homework and think it over. Do not shoot from the hip every time you disagree.

3. Clearly take ownership for your dissent.

4. Don't personalize the challenge; focus on the issue. Remember that reasonable people can honestly differ, sometimes with strong convictions, on issues.

5. Be objective and balanced in your analysis of the issue. Each of us is a product of our own unique experiences and we view the world based on those experiences. Try to put yourself in the shoes of the opposition, remembering that higher officials tend to view issues in a broader context.

6. Don't paint your superiors into a corner by challenging their judgment in public (or at a staff meeting unless the superior asks for a discussion of the issue), especially if they have taken a public stance.

7. Do not expect radical change in opposing views.

8. Know your boss. What are his/her central values and does the issue at hand relate to those central values? If so, change will be difficult.

9. Provide alternatives to the position you are challenging, i.e., don't be merely negative.

10. Choose your time to challenge. In general, try to get your oar in the water before a position has been announced.

11. Recognize when you have pushed the limit. Bosses differ in their tolerance of dissent, even when it is loyal.

12. Always remember that you may be wrong; you may even be ideologically biased.

13. Accept defeat graciously, i.e., don't pout. On the other hand, if you cannot live with the decision, from a moral standpoint, you have the option of going to higher authority, or ultimately resigning. (You may also feel justified in contacting Congress, interest groups, or the media. This **may** be loyal dissent in some instances, but it is often called "whistle-blowing" and is judged by different criteria than loyal dissent.)

---

*This version is slightly abbreviated. For the full version, by John Johns, see *Constitutional Literacy Reader* (Charlottesville, Va.: Federal Executive Institute).

Figure 1.5 Moral courage

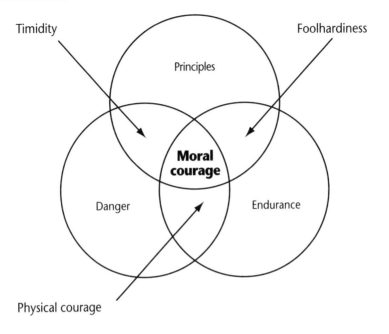

Timidity

Foolhardiness

Principles

Moral courage

Danger

Endurance

Physical courage

Source: Rushworth Kidder, *Moral Courage* (New York: William Morrow, 2005), 185.

cannot be a values-based leader without it. Kidder argues persuasively that moral courage comes at the intersection of three circles of thinking, as illustrated in Figure 1.5.[28] The first is the sphere of principles. A leader cannot take moral action unless it is in service to moral values. The second is the sphere of danger. If the leader is going to exercise moral courage, he must consider the hardships: ostracism from social groups, personal loss of a job and benefits, and/or the anguish and ambiguity that come with not knowing what taking a stand will mean for the leader's organizational and personal life. The third is the sphere of endurance. Exercising moral courage often means a long, hard struggle against great odds with uncertain success. Note that Kidder argues that moral courage requires all three. Jumping into action on principle may be just foolhardy if the leader has not carefully evaluated the danger (hardships) being faced. Considering principles and danger but not engaging in enduring action is just timidity. Acting despite danger without thought as to the moral principles involved is physical courage and may be laudable in some situations, but it is not the same as moral courage.[29]

Conclusion

Values-based leadership in government is both essential and possible. It can be studied, understood, and learned. It can be instilled in others and enshrined in organizational practices. It builds trust, fosters productive relationships within and outside agencies and is essential to democratic governance. Values-based leaders—and organizations—are made, not born. They result when government executives see themselves in service to citizens. And service to citizens is what being a civil servant means, after all. It requires, among all else we have discussed, a large portion of humility.

It may seem odd to end this prescription for the behavior of values-based leaders in government with a paean to humility. Aren't leaders supposed to be charismatic, resolute, visible, and sure-footed? Was Washington humble? Lincoln? The short answer is yes, and they were charismatic, resolute, visible, and sure-footed, too. Humility is not a shrinking away from the world. It is an acceptance of one's ultimately small place in the grand scheme of things, of one's debt to so many others (whom we call followers and citizens), of one's human limits. It also indicates a stance of openness to what others have to contribute and to the values that matter to them.

This very finding has emerged in recent research on leadership. In *Good to Great*, Jim Collins asked what, if anything, was commonly shared among leaders who took well-performing organizations and turned them into great ones.[30] He found only two personal qualities. One was an intense will to succeed, and the other was great humility. Their humility created an atmosphere of trust and built powerful relationships that served them and their organizations well. Their humility helped them become values-based leaders.

George Washington spent forty years in public service. He led troops in the French and Indian War. He took command of the Continental army and led it through eight years of hardship to ultimate victory. He served as president of the Constitutional Convention in 1787, and he served two terms as the first president of the United States created by that convention. At the end of his public service, Washington, who might well have been president for life if he wished, chose instead to relinquish power. In his Farewell Address in 1796, he spoke of his hopes for the country, his lessons for preserving the still fragile democracy, and his personal gratitude for the honor of serving. Among his final words to a grateful nation was the recognition that a president too was human after all: "In the discharge of this trust," Washington said, "I will only say that I have, with good intentions, contributed towards the Organization and Administration of the government, the best exertions of which a very fallible judgment was capable."

This is values-based leadership at its very best.

Tips for leadership success

- Identify the core values that drive you in your life and work. These are the source of your power and passion, both of which are essential for leadership.
- Lead by attending to your core values. Recognize when your actions would violate these values and summon the moral courage to behave in a way that represents the best ethical traditions of government service.
- Be faithful to your oath of office and accept that you have taken an obligation that means subordinating your personal agenda to serving the public good.
- Approach your civil service leadership role with a sense of humility. Accept that there is much you do not know and perspectives you have not considered and find ways to learn and be open to alternative views.
- Build your skills in and exercise your ability to have integrity, listen, tolerate dissent, include others in decision making, and use moral imagination to consider a broad range of perspectives and options to act in a values-driven way.
- Build an organizational culture that supports keeping the public purpose in mind, expressing dissent, considering value trade-offs that accompany contested issues, and examining the long range implications of potential actions on all those affected by them.

Resources for further learning

For a broad overview of values-based leadership and moral reflection in public life, consider reading:

Terry Cooper, *The Responsible Administrator: An Approach to Ethics for the Administrative Role*, 4th ed. (1998). Cooper first presents a model for thinking about and addressing ethical questions and then tackles ethics at a practical level for the individual and the organization.

Janet Denhardt and Robert Denhardt, *The New Public Service: Serving, not Steering* (2003). The authors suggest that the new public service sees the role of the civil servant as fostering democracy through active engagement of citizens in the creation and implementation of policy. The new public service requires the public administrator to think about what it means to create the good society and civic virtue.

Louis Gawthrop, *Public Service and Democracy: Ethical Imperatives for the 21st Century* (1998). Gawthrop argues that democracy can be preserved only when public officials imbue their thinking and action with three core moral values—faith, hope, and love. Effective pubic service, he maintains, requires a moral center not just following the law.

John Rohr, *Public Service, Ethics, and Constitutional Practice* (1998). Bureaucrats are not isolated from the policy process just because they are unelected. Rohr maintains that career civil servants can avoid abusing their power if they anchor their thinking in regime values—the constitutional values that shape society and should guide their thinking.

For focusing on specific issues and skills civil service leaders must address, consider reading:

Joseph Badaracco Jr., *Leading Quietly* (2002). Although the heroic, larger-than-life leader is sometimes needed in society, Badaracco argues that most situations are best addressed through the quiet leader, a person who does the right thing effectively but without fanfare. He identifies the eight tactics and three traits that characterize their actions.

Sissela Bok, *Lying: Moral Choice in Public and Private Life* (1978). Bok addresses under what conditions, if any, lying may be justified and the implications of lies on public trust.

Rushworth Kidder, *Moral Courage* (2005). The ability to think through ethical dilemmas is necessary but not sufficient to being an ethical person. The second ingredient needed is moral courage. It consists of deciding on the core principles and values that matter, understanding the dangers (to reputation, livelihood, and so forth) that may attend acting morally, and having the endurance to act and persist despite obstacles.

Patricia Werhane, *Moral Imagination and Management Decision Making* (1999). Why do good managers make unethical decisions? Werhane suggests that they may become locked into a particular conception of their role, a particular narrative of how the world works, a particular mental model that makes it almost impossible for them to see things from any other vantage point. Moral imagination, the ability to see a situation from different perspectives and to create and consider alternatives for appropriate action, is essential to managerial decision making which is both effective and moral.

Web sites useful for exploring values-based leadership include:

Center for Ethics and the Professions, Harvard University, *www.ethics.harvard.edu*. The center encourages teaching and research about ethical issues in business, education, government, law, medicine, and public policy.

Ethics Resource Center, Washington, D.C., *www.ethics.org*. The center focuses on ethics research and education related to creating ethical individuals and organizations in the public and private sectors.

Government Accountability Project, Washington, D.C., *www.whistleblower.org/about/index.cfm*. This organization focuses on enhancing occupational free speech for government and private sector workers. It has a large focus on supporting whistle-blower protections.

Institute for Global Ethics, Camden, Maine, *www.globalethics.org*. Started by Rush Kidder, the institute promotes ethical behavior in individuals, institutions, and nations through research, public discourse, training, and practical action.

Josephson Institute of Ethics, Marina del Rey, California, *http://josephson institute.org*. The Josephson Institute conducts programs and workshops for leaders including legislators and mayors, high-ranking public executives, congressional staff, editors and reporters, senior corporate and nonprofit executives, judges and lawyers, and military and civilian police officers.

Office of Government Ethics, Washington, D.C., *www.usoge.gov*. This is the site of the federal government agency charged with overall management of ethics legislation and regulations enacted for political appointees and career civil servants who work for the federal government.

Notes

1. Winthrop (1630). More recent and high-level uses of the image of America as a "city upon a hill" include John F. Kennedy's speech in Boston on January 20, 1961, the day before his inauguration as president, and President Reagan's Farewell Address to the nation on January 11, 1989.

2. The notion of a "city upon a hill" is used here to reflect a view and an expectation that those who govern must demonstrate and build moral values in their roles as leaders and designers of organizations. Some who quote Winthrop use his passage to suggest that somehow America is special among nations, even selected by God to be a shining light to the world.

That argument for American exceptionalism is antithetical to values-based leadership as it is used in this chapter because it assumes that Americans are better than the other peoples of the world. Such thinking runs directly contrary to the posture of humility toward and deep respect for others at the heart of values-based leadership.

3. Ursula Henderson attended the Federal Executive Institute of the U.S. Office of Personnel Management in Class 247. This information is taken, with her permission, from the "leadership challenge" she prepared. The leadership challenge is an activity in which all program executives engage. It is their statement of how they wish to lead their organization into the future. Other examples taken from FEI executives in this chapter are also used with their permission.

4. Arendt (1963) offers a chilling study of what she refers to as the "banality of evil" as she traces the life and bureaucratic career of Adolph Eichmann, the civil servant perhaps most responsible for implementing Hitler's "Final Solution." In the Tuskegee Syphilis Study, physicians failed to provide penicillin to some African American patients even after its curative effects on the disease were known, just so researchers could study the progression of the disease in untreated patients. President Clinton formally apologized for this moral breach on May 16, 1997.

5. Greenleaf (1977).

6. Nye (2004). See chapter 11 for a fuller treatment of the importance of values in international leadership.

7. Based on a nationwide survey of 1,003 American adults February 20–24, 1997, conducted by the firms of Peter Hart and Robert Teeter for the Council for Excellence in Government.

8. Burns (1978).

9. Collins and Porras (1994).

10. *Merriam-Webster's Collegiate Dictionary,* 11th ed. (Springfield, Mass.: Miriam-Webster, 2003), 450.

11. Using evidence from ninety-seven samples in forty-four countries, Shalom Schwartz (1994) demonstrates that the same values, clustered in very similar ways, show up in the cultures of a wide range of nations. Although certain value clusters may carry different weights in different cultures, there does appear to be a universal structure and content to the value set overall.

12. Bok (1978) is a seminal work in this area. Bok offers a set of considerations for those in public and private life to use in determining if a lie is justified. The quote here is taken from the chapter, "Lies for the Public Good."

13. Merriam-Webster, 450.

14. Jefferson (1801).

15. See Columbia Accident Investigation Board Final Report, chap. 8, 201, August 26, 2003.

16. The field of organizational development, pioneered in the 1960s and 1970s, draws heavily on research showing that participation breeds commitment as well as better solutions. For two more modern treatments of the same issue, see Heifetz (1994) and Kouzes and Posner (2002). Heifetz demonstrates that the significant problems facing public sector leaders lack technical ("one right answer") solutions and that only the involvement of others can lead to the adaptive solutions needed. Kouzes and Posner draw upon research showing the power of engagement to build a shared vision and a common commitment to act.

17. See Werhane (1999) for a cogent and thought-provoking discussion of the importance and elements of moral imagination.

18. Many writers have crafted ethical decision-making models and questions. An excellent book that lays out a number of approaches is Lewis (1991).

19. NASA's core purpose statement cited here was in place during the *Columbia* shuttle disaster. It has since been revised given NASA's new focus on manned lunar and Mars landings.

20. For example, see Janis (1989), Sunstein (2003), and Surowiecki (2004).

21. Waldo (1988).

22. For a brief article on the concept of moral perimeters, see Kidder (2005b).

23. An excellent work on this topic is O'Leary (2005). Situations may arise in which a career civil service leader's personal or professional values are so much in the public interest that acting overtly or covertly against political leadership may be justified on ethical grounds. Such "guerrilla" action should be taken only after very careful deliberation, however, because civil disobedience is a practice that can seriously undermine democratic governance.

24. Quote is taken from the written description of Ali Bahrami's Leadership Challenge at the Federal Executive Institute. The document is undated.

25. See, for example, Jehn (2001). Quoted in Sunstein (2003), Jehn says: "For a team to be effective, members should have high information diversity and low value diversity. For a team to be efficient, members should have low value diversity. For a team to have high morale (higher satisfaction, intent to remain, and commitment) or to perceive itself as effective, it should be composed of participants with low value diversity."

26. Kidder (1995).

27. Gawthrop (1998).

28. Kidder (2005a).

29. Much of the physical courage shown in battle or by law enforcement officers or firefighters also includes moral courage. The two are not mutually exclusive. When a soldier risks her life to save her comrades, she has usually thought carefully about the values of accomplishing a critical mission and self-sacrifice for others before that moment arrives. This not only endows her physical courage with moral courage, it is often that moral courage that has made the physical courage possible.

30. Collins (2001).

2 Self-awareness and leadership success

BEVERLY R. FLETCHER, SENIOR FACULTY, FEDERAL EXECUTIVE INSTITUTE*
AND ALFRED L. COOKE, DIRECTOR, CENTER FOR ORGANIZATIONAL
PERFORMANCE, FEDERAL EXECUTIVE INSTITUTE*

What lies behind us and what lies before us are tiny matters compared to what lies within us.

—Ralph Waldo Emerson

You make your life your own by understanding it.

—Warren Bennis

TIM APPLIED FOR A POSITION within his agency that would have been a promotion for him. He successfully competed in a multiphased interview process and was told that he had been selected, but several months passed, and the selection was still not formalized. Tim was feeling some doubt at this point. He was disappointed to learn indirectly that his current boss had communicated with the would-be new supervisor and asked that Tim not be given the new job because he was needed for his current program. None of this was communicated directly to Tim, even though he had informed both bosses that he would be pleased to work with them on transition plans.[1]

Tim faced a career-defining moment. How he responded would be guided by how well he understood himself. And his response would have a profound effect on his chances for the promotion, his career, and his relationships with both of these supervisors. Although Tim was not in control of whether he got the position, he was in control of how he responded to the news.

The hard work of understanding oneself is not a destination where one arrives with complete and perfect self-awareness. Instead it is a lifelong journey in which one strives to become more self-aware at each milestone. The premise for this chapter was laid out in chapter 1: becoming a values-based

---

*The views expressed here are the author's and do not necessarily reflect those of the Federal Executive Institute or the U.S. Office of Personnel Management.

leader is not just a matter of picking values from a list; rather, it involves a lifetime of building self-awareness, engaging in authentic behavior, and being able to change.

Research suggests that if a leader is to be successful, self-awareness is ongoing internal work that is essential.[2] A basic assumption is that the process of becoming self-aware is never complete; instead, it is a way of life. The focus therefore must be on developing leaders who are in a continual mode of self-learning.

Warren Bennis, a highly regarded pioneer in the field of organizational change and leadership, indicates that a leader cannot learn from someone else how to become fully self-aware. He notes important lessons to be learned in the self-discovery process:

> You are your own best teacher. . . . Accept responsibility. . . . Blame no one. . . . You can learn anything you want to learn. . . . True understanding comes from reflecting on your experience.[3]

Robert Tannenbaum, UCLA professor emeritus of the Anderson School of Management and one of the originators of the field of organization development, comes to a similar conclusion when he writes that leadership effectiveness relies on having an integrated knowledge of one's leadership behaviors, but, more important, effectiveness depends on developing an *internalized knowledge of self.*[4]

A model of leadership success

Figure 2.1 displays two major components of successful leadership: self-awareness and other awareness. Leadership success depends on gaining self-awareness through self-examination and change while also gaining willing followers through other awareness and adeptly influencing people to follow.

This chapter primarily focuses on the top portion of Figure 2.1—the self-awareness limb. Self-awareness involves self-reflection, values exploration, engaging in authentic behavior, and being able and willing to change. Although we explore the top half of the figure in more depth, it is important to keep in mind that the bottom half implies that trust develops only by understanding oneself and simultaneously understanding others.

The matrix of the relationship between self and others is activated when answering the question, "Who are we?" The process of defining who we are together and successfully establishing that relationship is the basis for building trust. Values-based leadership therefore is the practical outcome of suc-

Figure 2.1 Components of leadership success

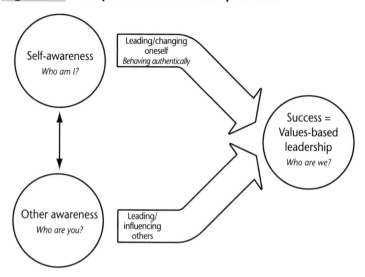

cessfully understanding and managing oneself while developing trusting and mutually influencing relationships.

In our model, leadership success is measured in terms of the achievement of values-based leadership. Another way to look at this is to think of success as the achievement of a state in which the individual makes appropriate self- and other affirming choices. Self-efficacy is a proactive process in which the individual is able to make self-affirming choices based on fundamental self-knowledge and esteem.[5] A simple formula describes this process:

Self-awareness = Self-knowledge + Self-affirmation ➡ *Self-efficacy*

Mary is a senior executive faced with a critical meeting in which the new agency director is going to discuss a change in the organization. Mary is concerned about one of the proposals that she believes fundamentally alters the agency's mission. Furthermore, this aspect of the agency's mission is the primary reason why Mary became a public servant fifteen years ago, and it continually provides her with the motivation to do her challenging job. Most of the other senior managers in the agency favor the proposed new direction. Prior to the meeting, Mary wonders whether she should go along with the change or voice her concerns. At some point, she asks herself, "Who am I?" She comes to the difficult conclusion that she must voice her concerns in an authentic way based on her core values and self-awareness. Mary engaged in a process of reflecting on and becoming more aware of herself that ultimately led to self-efficacy; as a result, she performed an important service to her organization.

Similarly, when you need to influence others and make decisions affecting others, the following formula has implications for successful leadership: *Other awareness = Other knowledge + Other affirmation* ➡ *Other efficacy*

Although the focus of this chapter is on the first of these two formulas (self-awareness) the second formula has far-reaching implications for leaders. To be effective in her dialogue with the organization, Mary must be able to suspend her judgments about the motivations of the other managers. She must understand their underlying assumptions and interests and affirm them as individuals in order to collaboratively develop creative ways that address both their interests and hers and build trust. The implications for other efficacy[6] should be kept in mind as it comes into play in Chapters 3 and 4 on coaching and team building.

Self-awareness: "Who am I?"

Knowing others is wisdom, knowing yourself is enlightenment.

—Lao-Tzu

Knowledge of the self is the mother of all knowledge.

—Kahlil Gibran, *The Philosophy of Logic*

Self-knowledge is cognitive information we have about various fundamental aspects of our character. It is the information we gather through observing and reflecting on our past experiences and behaviors. It comes as a result of self exploration such as, "I am proficient at ____." "I am not good at ____." "I have a preference for____." "Given a choice between ____ and ____, I tend to choose ____." "I am recognized for my ability to ____." "I most often see myself as ____." The list goes on.

The Myers-Briggs Type Indicator (MBTI) personality preferences; interest preferences in the Strong Vocational Interest Blank; personal sketches from a multitude of leadership profile instruments, and knowledge gained from multirater feedback—from those who supervise, report to, and are organizational peers—are all formalized means of gaining self-knowledge. Less formal, and perhaps equally as valuable, is observing one's own choices, behaviors, personal preferences, and habits, which are often overlooked indicators of self.

On Monday Julie, an instructor at a residential education center, is scheduled to meet with her boss, Stan, to go over the faculty schedule for the upcoming year. Last year, program coordination work, which involves being the "up-front" visible presence for a large class, was divided equally among five instructors. Although Julie completes her coordination tasks competently, she does not enjoy this part of her job. As an introvert, she experiences a high level of stress and finds that coordination tasks significantly drain her energy and reduce her effectiveness in other areas. Because the organization is short two instructors, it is now more important than ever for everyone to do their fair share of coordinating to make it all work. Julie wonders, however, if a simple division of labor is truly the best way to use the various talents that are available. Susan and Greg, two of her colleagues, are gregarious extroverts who thoroughly enjoy the "onstage" processes of coordinating large programs and do so with ease and grace. Both have expressed a preference for coordinating programs over most of the other instructor duties. Julie, however, is a whiz with program design and truly enjoys the more intimate setting of the small classroom and feels most effective there. She decides to bring up her concerns at Monday's meeting.

Knowing one's preferences is important self-knowledge that allows one to make effective choices about when to assume responsibility and when to seek to delegate to others.

Self-affirmation is the affective component of self-awareness. It represents what we like or esteem about who we are. Self-affirmation is highlighted by how we answer questions such as: "I value _____ about myself." "I like that I am _____." "It is important that others respect my _____." "I like myself because _____." "I try to let others know that _____ is important to me." Such responses get at the nature of what one appreciates about oneself. They reflect the affective and emotional responses that we need as human beings to validate who we are. For Julie, it was important to focus her attention on the strengths that she brought to the team rather than on what she may have perceived to be her shortcomings as an introvert. By focusing on what she likes and values about herself, Julie was effective in talking with Stan, who agreed to her suggestion that those who have the greatest strength in doing coordination work be assigned more of it.

Self-efficacy is conscious and affirming choice-making.[7] The formulaic rule suggests that if you have a clear understanding of yourself and affirm the goodness and value that is in you, you will be able to make effective self-affirming choices. Efficacy also suggests that if you have knowledge of others and affirm their value, you will make "other affirming" choices as well. Efficacy is values-based. One's values are at the core of choice-making whether one makes choices about self or others.

Harvard professor Howard Gardner sums up the need for doing the hard work of developing self-awareness:

> I want my children to understand the world, but not because the world is fascinating and the human mind is curious. I want them to understand it so that they will be positioned to make it a better place. Knowledge is not the same as morality, but we need to understand if we are to avoid past mistakes and move in productive directions. An important part of that understanding is knowing who we are and what we can do.[8]

Tools for building self-awareness

> *Look well into thyself; there is a source of strength which will always spring up if thou wilt always look there.*
>
> — Marcus Aurelius

Over time we tend to develop patterns and ways of doing things that blind us to new possibilities and prevent us from seeking new knowledge that might change the way we see the world and therefore the choices we make. Gardner might well have spoken directly to us as leaders. What he suggests is that the goal of leadership is to make the best choices grounded in the knowledge of oneself and affirming who we are.[9] Among the many accepted ways to enhance self-awareness are:

- Knowing what is important—values exploration
- Doing your autobiography
- Keeping a journal
- Examining your behavior through the "ladder of inference"
- Inviting feedback
- Receiving mentoring and executive coaching

Knowing what is important—values exploration

Values are emotionally charged and powerful mechanisms for ordering our existence. Our values play themselves out every day and in every area of our lives. They identify what is important to us in every aspect of ourselves. Many of us act out of values that we have never consciously considered. Successful leadership requires that we understand our values and what motivates us to make the choices we do. When we have not consciously looked at our values, we can find ourselves in trouble without knowing that it is the result of conflicting values. Similarly, when we have not defined our values, we do not have a firm basis for identifying and comparing our options and making effective decisions.

Values exploration can be as simple as asking "What do I value?" and discovering the sources of your responses to this question. Do your answers come from a spiritual or religious practice? Are they based in a cognitive and rational orientation? Are they from rules of behavior and guidelines learned in your childhood? Understanding where values came from may be an important step in defining what they are, which ones are "core," and which are merely idealized or espoused. A simple values exploration exercise such as the one in Box 2.1 is a useful way to start exploring your values and also identifying possible conflicting values. An individual is asked to select his personal "top ten" values from a longer list of possibilities. The act of choosing

---

Box 2.1   Values exploration exercise

What are your top ten personal values and your top ten organizational values? Do they complement each other or come into conflict? What problems, if any, do conflicts (for example, valuing truth but also loyalty) create for you as a leader? Feel free to add others.

Personal values
(these matter most to me)
(*examples*)
- truth
- trust
- openness
- love
- family
- justice
- mercy
- freedom
- community
- economic security
- learning
- achievement
- harmony

Organizational values
(these matter most to my organization)
(*examples*)
- accountability
- responsibility
- creativity
- quality
- productivity
- teamwork
- integrity
- loyalty
- timeliness
- customer focus
- diversity
- effectiveness
- efficiency

from a longer list helps him clarify what values are most central and which may operate more at the periphery of his life. In addition, he can add other values to the list.

Tim, with whom we began this chapter, realized that his organizational desire to be loyal and a team player conflicted with some of his core personal values, especially his belief in justice (he had applied for and been selected for the job) and desire for achievement (he truly wanted the promotion). He struggled to find a way to honor both sets of values and decided to raise his concern with his current boss in a direct but nonconfrontational way. Although it was a difficult conversation, in the end they resolved the problem: he would report to his new job in another month, during which time he would train his successor. Being self-aware helped Tim deal with his sense of betrayal—and far more successfully than if he had just demanded satisfaction from his boss.

Doing your autobiography

A full or partial autobiography or memoir is a useful tool for exploring one's values, how they developed, and what effect they have had. Even the straightforward process of examining significant events in one's life and trying to discern what impact they had can be a powerful way to better understand one's values.

The basic premise of any autobiographical technique is that one goes back as far as one can remember and identifies significant events at the different stages of growth and development. Once identified, the questions of who was involved and why the event was important can lead to understanding how values developed and what in fact those values may be. It is useful to approach the exercise by finding a quiet place to do this work without interruption. Quieting one's own judgmental voice and accepting what is revealed as useful information for self-discovery (not as criticism of one's life) is important.

The example in Figure 2.2 is a Lifeline Exercise done by a federal executive. In completing this exercise, Jim discovered a number of connections he had not previously seen that helped him to understand his reactions to major decisions made in his agency. By listing the critical events in his life that stimulated significant emotional responses, Jim was able to go beyond his immediate reactions to recent similar events and make several important decisions for both his agency and himself.

Figure 2.2 A lifeline exercise

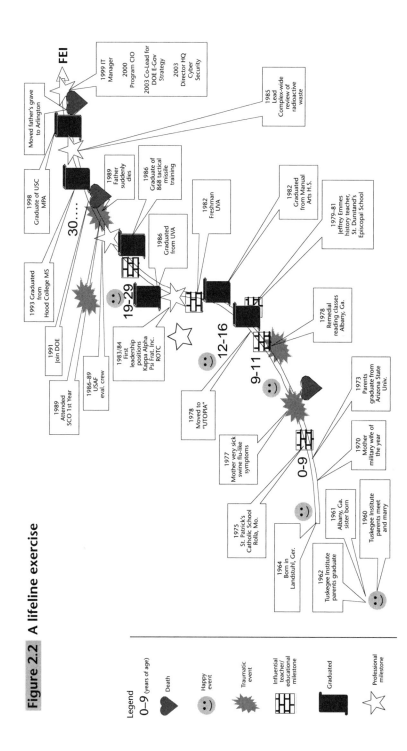

FEI

1999 IT Manager

2000 Program CIO

2003 Co-Lead for DOE E-Gov Strategy

2003 Director HQ Cyber Security

Moved father's grave to Arlington

1985 Lead Complex-wide review of radioactive waste

1998 Graduate of USC MPA

1989 Father suddenly dies

1986 Graduate of 868 tactical missile training

30....

1982 Freshman UVA

1986 Graduated from UVA

1982 Graduated from Manual Arts H.S.

1993 Graduated from Hood College MS

1979–81 Jeffrey Emmes history teacher, St. Dunstand's Episcopal School

19–29

1978 Remedial reading classes Albany, Ga.

1991 Join DOE

1983/84 First leadership positions Kappa Alpha Psi Frat. Inc. ROTC

12–16

1989 Attended SCO 1st Year

1986–89 USAF eval. crew

1978 Moved to "UTOPIA"

9–11

1973 Parents graduate from Arizona State Univ.

1977 Mother very sick flu-like symptoms

1970 Mother military wife of the year

1975 St. Patrick's Catholic School Rolla, Mo.

0–9

1961 Albany, Ga. sister born

1960 Tuskegee Institute parents meet and marry

1964 Born in Landstuhl, Ger.

1962 Tuskegee Institute parents graduate

Legend

0–9 (years of age)

Death

Happy event

Traumatic event

Influential teacher/ educational milestone

Graduated

Professional milestone

Jim realized that the military values so prevalent in his background, recently reinforced when he moved his father's grave to Arlington National Cemetery, had made him overly dependent on a leadership style that assumed—and expected—strict adherence to a chain of command. This value cut against the more collegial culture in his agency, especially with the newer and younger employees he supervised. He struggled to find a way to honor his core values while acknowledging that they need not be firmly applied in all cases in his relationships with direct reports.

Keeping a journal

The journal is an ongoing repository of experiences, thoughts, actions, and beliefs. It is a way of capturing internal thought processes and emotional responses so that they can be more systematically explored for meanings, underlying assumptions, and patterns. Keeping a journal can be formal in that one can set guidelines for what one will capture; or it can be random, exploratory, unstructured, and impromptu. Deciding how to go about keeping a journal and analyzing the results are often difficult tasks for novice journal writers. Perhaps the best way to get started is to find a quiet time and place each day and just start writing about experiences without judgment or attention to sentence structure, spelling, and grammar. The act of simply writing down information is often a sufficient stimulus for making greater sense of an experience. The writings will eventually provide enough data to look more systematically for trends, meanings, conclusions, inferences, and residual learning.

Margaret James Neill is a well-known teacher of how to keep a journal. She points to several good reasons for this approach, such as experimenting with new behavior; developing an internal feedback system that clarifies and reminds you of "what, how, and where" categories of information; freely expressing and exploring your feelings; learning more about your personal patterns and history and your current status; and enhancing your capacity to be aware of the inner dynamics of your life.[10]

Leadership development consultant Lawrence Porter proposes guidelines for keeping a journal to enhance self-awareness. He writes:

> Keeping a journal is one way of organizing and reviewing one's experiences. One way to do this uses a three-step process. First, describe the experience, i.e. "what happened"? Second, write your

Box 2.2   An excerpt from Paul's journal

(date)

What happened?

Today I met with Margaret to go over her performance appraisal. My appraisal of her work was in my opinion extremely positive. It was my intention to use most of the time allotted to talk with her about my expectations of her and the staff in implementing my vision for the future of our group. However, she reacted to the appraisal with anger and accused me of belittling her. Her exact words were "I have never had a poor performance appraisal in my life. How dare you propose to assess my work and give me a negative appraisal when you have been here for only five months!"

My reactions

I was taken aback by her strong emotional reaction and my first impulse was to refute her accusations using strong language. I felt that her response was inappropriately aggressive and I was extremely disappointed as I had expected better from her. I found it very challenging to withhold voicing my automatic response to her outburst.

I am proud that instead of an automatic rebuttal, I observed my own anger at the exchange and formulated two responses: "Tell me more about how this appraisal impacts you." And "How would you like to word the appraisal so that it more accurately reflects your perceptions of your performance?"

By holding off on my emotional response and engaging her in a conversation, I was able to get her perspective and begin to develop an understanding of where she was coming from. I left the session with her agreeing to reword the appraisal. We will get together tomorrow to discuss it.

What I learned

This incident has brought home to me the need to be sensitive not only to the cultural expectations I have, but those of others in this new situation. I will have to be careful to clarify my intentions and expectations in ways that are different from my previous position. I need to be more sensitive to the paradigm differences that exist here and weigh my responses based on a careful self-review.

reactions to the experience, what you thought, felt, wanted, and did. Finally, write what you learned from what happened.[11]

Paul is a new federal executive from the private sector, who is now a supervisor of a small subgroup in his new agency. Box 2.2 on page 59 is an excerpt from his journal.

However you use it, the journal lends itself to self-exploration and awareness. Leaders who allow themselves to reflect upon their experiences find fertile ground in which they can grow and change.

Because life is complex and experiences rarely repeat themselves exactly, do not just think in terms of what you would do in the exact same situation. Think about what can be taken from the experience and applied to other related and even unrelated situations. The journal is a good place to engage in this type of broad thinking. Go back to previous journal entries and look for generalizations, patterns, tendencies, and underlying principles. When we think more broadly we make our reflection time significantly more beneficial.

As a general rule it is appropriate for leaders to think systemically about their own behavior just as they do about the organizations in which they operate. Systems thinking requires attention to relationships that sometimes have effects that are not obvious.

Examining your behavior through the "ladder of inference"

Cynthia was confused by the reactions she was getting from Tom, one of the executive assistants who works for her. Every interaction they had was fraught with what Cynthia believed was aggressive and dismissive language from Tom. He had also begun to ignore her in ways that she felt were rude. After several "slights" from Tom, Cynthia decided to give him the same "cold shoulder." She made a decision to interact with him on a very limited basis and only when necessary to complete vital work.

Tom took Cynthia's response to him as confirmation of his initial negative response to her. Cynthia then saw Tom's "escalated rude behavior" as evidence that she should continue to avoid Tom as much as possible. Over time the situation with Cynthia and Tom deteriorated because they both failed to recognize the assumptions they were making about each other's behavior.

Before you can effectively challenge your assumptions, you must first become aware of when you are making them. The ladder of inference is a concept that helps to explain how humans very naturally go about making assumptions.[12] An inference is a conclusion derived from beliefs regarding what are thought to be facts. According to the ladder of inference (see Figure 2.3), we tend to assume that our beliefs and actions are objectively based on

Figure 2.3 The ladder of inference

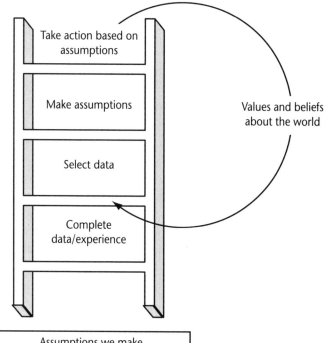

- Take action based on assumptions
- Make assumptions
- Select data
- Complete data/experience

Values and beliefs about the world

Assumptions we make

- What I value is most important/worthy
- What I believe is true
- The "truth" is obvious
- My beliefs are based on real data
- The data I select are "the real data"

Source: Adapted from the work of Chris Argyris. See Peter M. Senge, *The Fifth Discipline* (New York: Doubleday, 1990).

observable data in the "real world," and we are surprised when others do not see the "truth" as clearly as we do.

Chris Argyris, professor emeritus at Harvard Business School, says that data by which we make sense out of the world of events and experiences are all around us in infinite quantities. To keep from becoming overwhelmed by these vast amounts of information, we have developed the important ability to select limited amounts of data and make inferences from them based upon assumptions that come from our values, beliefs, and previous experiences.

Our actions in turn are based on the assumptions that we make, which then leads us to narrowly select data in future experiences that are similar. We do this to the extent of ultimately not even seeing the other data—especially those that contradict our assumptions. The irony is that without this ability to "narrowly select data," it would take an inordinate amount of time to understand our world of experiences. Consequently, making decisions would be time-consuming, costly, and even dangerous to us in many ways.

Therefore, our ability to make inferences is a good thing; it is useful in that it helps us to quickly understand what is happening and to make timely decisions. Paradoxically, this ability also poses an obvious danger—one that can lead us into taking faulty actions. If we are not aware that we are making an inference based on incomplete data, we will believe that the assumptions we make are indeed "the facts," that what we believe about the situation is most important and most worthy of attention, that what we know is absolutely "the truth," that the truth is obvious; and that our actions are based on "real data" because, naturally, the data we select are *the* real data.

By using the understanding gained from the ladder of inference, we can improve our self-understanding, communication with others, and leadership by exercising:

- Self-reflection: Becoming more aware of our own assumptions and beliefs and the data they are based on; and
- Self-disclosure (authentic self-presentation): Making our assumptions and beliefs and the data they are based on more visible to others through a process of dialogue.

According to Terry Newell:

> If we acknowledge that our actions may be based on selecting only certain data, meanings we assign to data (based on cultural and personal experiences and biases), assumptions we make, and/or our beliefs about the world, then we must also acknowledge that other people, with other ways of looking at the same hard data, may have different points of view worth considering. We can then offer our meanings, assumptions, and beliefs as hypotheses, subject to examination and change.[13]

The ladder of inference helped Cynthia and Tom. During a confrontation session initiated by Cynthia, they were able to clarify their inaccurate inferences and challenge their assumptions about each other. They each became more aware of the words they were using and how those words could be misinterpreted. They came to see that they were each making assumptions based on paying attention to only some of their actions and statements—in other words, selecting data to confirm their suspicions of each other—and entirely missing the supportive actions and messages each was trying to send. After their talk, Cynthia and Tom were able to reconcile their working relationship before it deteriorated beyond repair.

Inviting feedback

In our quest for self-knowledge, we may tend to think more highly of ourselves than we ought or, conversely, we may in our own minds exaggerate our weaknesses and look down upon ourselves. We need a realistic view of our strengths and weaknesses if we are to know our true selves. How we see ourselves may be clouded by messages we received early in life or by faulty or outdated assumptions that we have nurtured over the years. (See Figure 2.4.)

Paradoxically, we need other people to help us see ourselves more clearly, even though others have played a part in our skewed view of ourselves. We

Figure 2.4 Feedback is self-awareness in relationship with others

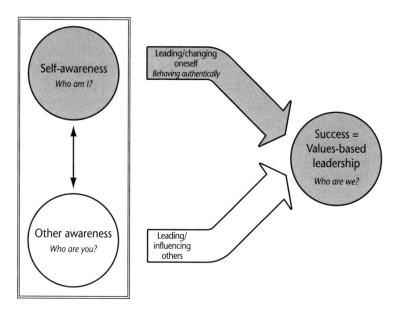

may not be prepared to face ourselves as viewed through others' eyes, but it is unlikely that anyone can totally avoid feedback: It comes at us in every moment that we live and take action. To deny feedback is to make a decision to isolate oneself from others and from life. Feedback is the way we learn about ourselves, others, the world around us, and the consequences of our behaviors. That interaction between ourselves and others is depicted in our original model, Figure 2.1, but with a different title: Feedback is self-awareness in relationship with others.

To get a better understanding of who you really are, you must be prepared to receive feedback about yourself from others. Joseph Luft and Harry Ingham, two well-known psychologists, created the Johari Window, a concept that helps us better understand the intersections between what others know about us and what we know about ourselves. This two-by-two matrix (see Figure 2.5 on following page) provides a visual metaphor for seeing into oneself.[14]

There are things we and others know about us and things that we and others do not know about us. When we know something about ourselves that corresponds with what others know about us, those things are in the upper left quadrant (Window 1)—the open, free, public, or known area.

Those things about ourselves known only to ourselves and hidden from others are in the hidden or private area (Window 3). Some people also refer to this area as the *mask,* the *façade,* or the *idealized self.* This area is accessible only by you and is in the area where you can work on self-disclosure or authentic self-presentation. Whenever you act authentically in congruence with who you truly are, you reduce the size of the hidden area, which becomes part of Window 1—the open area. It is this area that Cynthia and Tom opened up by sharing more about themselves as they made use of the ladder of inference.

One of the most difficult parts of this model for some people to accept is the fact that we all have blind spots, and, unfortunately, others have a clearer view of them than we do ourselves. The blind area (Window 2) contains those things that other people know about you that you cannot see about yourself. This is where feedback is particularly useful. If the feedback you receive is about one of your blind spots, it is a most amazing gift—one that takes courage for the other person to give and may not always be appreciated by the recipient. It is a gift from someone else to you of a part of yourself. Cynthia and Tom also fruitfully explored this area when they finally sat down and, through conversation, realized that they were each blind to the

Figure 2.5 The Johari Window

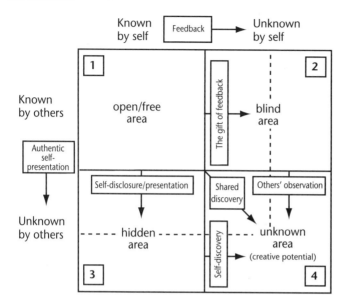

Source: Adapted from Alan Chapman, *The Johari Window,* 2003 online presentation at *http//unpan1.un.org/intradoc/groups/public/documents/UNSSC/UNPAN022136.pdf.* Based on Joseph Luft and Harry Ingham, *The Johari Window: A Graphic Model for Interpersonal Relations* (Los Angeles: University of California, Western Training Lab, 1955).

assumptions they were making about the other—such assumptions often go unchecked.

According to noted sports psychologist and consultant Linda Bunker, blind spots (Window 2) and masks (Window 3) can also be "derailers" for a leader.[15]

> For example, if some mannerism, habit, or eccentricity I have is irritating to others but I don't see it in myself, it may stand in the way of effective communication. Or if I continue to "hide" or shield important personal information from others (perhaps thinking it is demonstrating my courage or strength) it may inadvertently send a message to colleagues that it is not OK to share their personal concerns or challenges.

Perhaps the most profoundly inspiring area of the model is in the lower right quadrant—the unknown or to be discovered area (Window 4). These are the things that neither you nor others know about you. It is the area of greatest creative potential and deep self-discovery—we truly do not know the limits of our potential. The important question to ask about this area is "How do I tap my unknown potential?" The answer to that question may seem simple—through utilizing a combination of authentic self-presentation (which opens up the known area and reduces the hidden area) and feedback (which also opens up the known area and reduces the blind area). These two things—authentic self-presentation and receiving feedback—can change your life in positive ways.

If you tell others that you want feedback, you must really mean it and allocate time for it. If not, you will do more harm than good to the level of trust in the relationship. People may be understandably reluctant to give you feedback because doing so is risky for the giver. When someone declares his inner thoughts about you, he is in fact self-disclosing and making himself vulnerable to you, and must then contend with your reactions. If the giver is unsure of your intentions, open invitations will be nonproductive. People will watch your body language and pay attention to your responses to test if you really mean it. If negative comments raise your personal defenses, people will soon conclude that you only want positive comments and will censor their remarks accordingly.

To avoid these problems, start small by asking only individuals you trust and who know you well. Ask for feedback about specific behaviors. For example, "When I did/said ____, how did you interpret my intentions? what did you feel? what did you think? what were your reactions?" Receive their comments nondefensively without rebuttal: "yes, but ____" is interpreted as being nonreceptive to the feedback. Also remember to thank them and acknowledge their gift. As you gain more skill at asking for and receiving feedback nondefensively, continue asking others for the feedback you need.

A useful way to get feedback and test your assumptions at the same time is to clearly state the conclusions you arrived at about an experience and then ask selected individuals what conclusions they drew from that same experience. Compare notes with others as a way of engaging in a dialogue about the different perceptions. Avoid debating about who is right or wrong; one can learn much from simply attempting to understand different perceptions.

Another valuable tool for receiving feedback is a 360 degree (or multirater) assessment instrument. Such tools were developed because of the complex nature of asking for and receiving honest feedback from a number of different groups of people (peers, direct reports, and bosses) and should not be used as a replacement for interpersonal face-to-face feedback needed from individuals. When used appropriately and skillfully, 360 degree feedback can open doors to powerful follow-up conversations. In the context of this discussion, 360 degree assessments are used as a development tool, not as a tool for appraising performance. Moreover, if the purpose for using a 360 degree assessment is something other than developing one's interpersonal and leadership skills, it does not fall into the category of feedback discussed in this chapter. The value of 360 degree feedback is directly linked to the integrity of the process, and the integrity of the process is measured in terms of its purpose, administration, and the usefulness of its analyses. Characteristics of an effective 360 degree assessment tool are:

- The focus: to enhance self-awareness
- The goal: interpersonal and leadership development
- The method: instruments completed anonymously by direct reports and peers (the one exception to anonymity is the direct supervisor)
- The outcome: analyses provided in recognized, tested, and quantifiable categories (for example, the federal executive core qualifications/competencies)[16]

Feedback can provide learning opportunities for us if we can use the observations and reactions of others to become more aware of ourselves and the consequences of our behaviors. Feedback can help us become more aware of what we do, how we do it, and how it affects others—which can help us modify behaviors and become more effective in our interactions and communication. Asking for and receiving feedback requires courage, skill, understanding, and respect for self and others.

Receiving mentoring and executive coaching

> *To thine own self be true; and it must follow as the night the day, thou can'st not then be false to any man.*
>
> —Shakespeare, *Hamlet*

As career government executives with busy schedules and multiple pressures, it is not surprising that we have difficulty finding time to think about who we are, our strengths and weaknesses, our drives and personalities, our habits and values. In turn, a low level of self-awareness makes it almost impossible to be consistent ("true") in our words and actions. Congruence between who you are, your words, and your actions demonstrates the deeper meaning of the word *integrity*. How can you demonstrate integrity if the self is unknown? According to writer and artist Jennifer Hautman, without self-awareness, we continue to get "caught up" in our own internal dramas and unknown beliefs and values, allowing unclear thought processes to determine our feelings and actions.

> If you think about it, not understanding why you do what you do and feel what you feel is like going through your life with a stranger's mind. How do you make wise decisions and choices if you don't understand why you want what you want? It's a difficult and chaotic way to live never knowing what this stranger is going to do next.[17]

Mentoring and coaching are two effective "tools" in the quest for consistency, authenticity, integrity, and trust.

WHAT IS MENTORING? A successful leader must be able to make good choices and produce effective action. Using a mentor is a process that aids decision making and effective action. A mentor is a veteran of the organization who focuses on transferring organizational knowledge to his or her protégé. The knowledge transfer is most often about critical processes, contacts, and interpersonal relationships that are unwritten and without which one cannot effectively perform in the organization.[18] A mentor helps the executive to expand his or her contacts and networks; focuses the executive's attention on critical assignments and activities; provides words of wisdom from his or her own experience; and gives support and encouragement. A mentor enhances self-awareness through giving feedback, encouraging self-reflection, and asking good questions that challenge the executive to examine his or her assumptions. A mentor, by sharpening the protégé's awareness of the organizational context, can also help the developing leader understand data and go down the ladder of inference before making a serious organizational mistake. Mentors are invaluable, and it is difficult to succeed in any complex organization without one.

WHAT IS EXECUTIVE COACHING? Executive coaching is a partnership between an individual executive and a trained coach to enhance the executive's current and future effectiveness in his or her organization. An executive coach works with an individual executive to identify the executive's developmental goals and pursue a plan for achieving those goals. Coaches draw from a broad knowledge base and an extensive repertoire of assessment and learning tools. Coaching assists the executive to increase self-awareness, understand the implications and consequences of his/her behaviors, and develop new skills and competencies designed to achieve the executive's particular goals. Executive coaching is voluntary, confidential, and tailored to the expectations and schedules of the individual executive.[19] Successful coaching involves the development of a trusting relationship and requires a good fit between the executive and the coach. Unlike mentoring, the executive coach need not have an understanding of the organization to be effective.

George has experienced difficulty communicating with Frank, his peer, and one of two directors in the agency. Frank did not attend meetings that George regularly scheduled, but George made an effort to show up at Frank's meetings. Frank seldom sought George's input when he needed to collaborate, and he avoided eye contact with George whenever the two were in meetings together. Frank seemed to consistently find ways to oppose suggestions from George. When asked to respond to George's requests, Frank usually gave short, curt answers. George was concerned about the ill effects his poor relationship with Frank had on the organization and he decided to get help by seeking the services of an executive coach. The coach helped George see his own behavior and how it might be affecting the relationship. George agreed to do the following:

- Write a letter to Frank identifying his concerns in nondefensive and nonaccusing language.
- In the letter request a meeting in "neutral territory" and suggest the possibility of a third party to facilitate the meeting if Frank so desired.
- In the meeting lay out the issues (again using nondefensive and nonaccusing language); talk about their underlying common interests and the importance of improving their relationship for the good of the organization.
- Role play with the coach to practice choosing words to use and those to avoid in attempting to reach a mutually satisfactory outcome with Frank.

George wrote the letter. Frank agreed to meet but did not want a third party involved. Although George and Frank will probably never be best friends, others in the organization have seen a notable improvement in their working relationship and a marked improvement in the collaboration between their groups.

The importance of changing—finding the time

> *There was that law of life, so cruel and so just, that one must grow or else pay more for remaining the same.*
>
> —Norman Mailer

> *People often say that this or that person has not yet found him or herself. But the self is not something that one finds, it is something one creates.*
>
> —Thomas Szasz

One of the main reasons leaders give for not doing the work that enhances self-awareness and change is "I'm too busy—I don't have enough time." Making the time necessary to do this work is essential. Leaders find the time in various ways and places. You do not need hours at a stretch; even a few minutes a few times a day can make a powerful difference. You have time regardless of how busy your schedule is—you just have to carve it out.

- Reflect in the shower.
- Reflect on the commute to and from work.
- Reflect in the moments before you go to bed.
- Reflect with your family or significant other, either one-on-one or in a small group conversation, over meals.
- Convert some of your television or other recreational time into reflection time.
- When you set up your schedule each day, week, month, or quarter, schedule in reflection time.

Finding the time will help you discover who you are. When you know who you are, you may have a need or desire to change, and changing demands an emotional transition, a lot of effort, and a considerable amount of courage. Being self-aware will help you move closer to living your values and enable you to make more suitable choices that enrich your life and the lives of others in the organization. Being self-aware will help build your self-confidence as you become more true to yourself and authentic in every action. The ultimate benefits are improving your organizational relationships and gaining trust.

Tips for leadership success

In summary, the following practices may be helpful as public sector leaders seek to increase their level of self-awareness:

- Increase your knowledge of what you value through values exploration.
- Write your memoirs or your autobiography.
- Write in your journal daily.
- Examine your behavior through the ladder of inference.
- Invite feedback from others.
- Find an organizational mentor.
- Get an executive coach.

Resources for further learning

Additional resources on self-awareness and related topics include the following:

Books:

Alfred Cooke et al., *Reading Book on Human Relations Training,* 8th ed. (1999). A resource for anyone who wants to understand the dynamics of human interaction, this comprehensive collection of essays is for human resource professionals, leaders, managers, consultants, trainers, and students. The collection is divided into major skill-building areas, all necessary for improving professional effectiveness: communications, diversity, conflict, reentry (after the training experience), history and background of laboratory education, self-awareness, support systems, experiential learning, and group dynamics.

Howard Gardner, *Frames of Mind: The Theory of Multiple Intelligences* (1983). Gardner started a national debate with the theory of multiple intelligences, which holds that a unitary measure of intelligence does not take into account a variety of intelligences possessed by humans including mathematics, logic, music, language, and psychological perception. This seminal work outlined his theory, which started with seven intelligences and has grown to eight.

Spencer Johnson, *Who Moved My Cheese?* (1999). Johnson, a physician, created this "story" to help him deal with a difficult change in his life. It showed him how to take his changing situation seriously but not take himself so seriously.

Matthew McKay and Patrick Fanning, *Self-Esteem: A Proven Program of Cognitive Techniques for Assessing, Improving and Maintaining Your Self-Esteem*, 3rd ed. (2002). This work offers cognitive techniques for overcoming destructive emotions and provides a guide for challenging the inner critic. The authors suggest practical ways to realize what is happening, stop self-judgment, gain perspective, and heal past wounds. The result is an opportunity to change core beliefs about one's identity and potential. New to the third edition is an exploration of the importance of goal setting in maintaining self-esteem.

Brian Roet, *The Confidence to Be Yourself* (2001), takes you step by step through a confidence-building process. Roet introduces the idea of a "spectrum" of confidence, one end being total confidence, and the other, insecurity and fear. His confidence-building technique encourages the reader to identify a realistic position on the spectrum and work toward full confidence. Roet includes case histories, exercises, and confidence boosters.

Martin Seligman, *Learned Optimism: How to Change Your Mind and Your Life* (1998). Seligman uses research he conducted on optimism as a basis for providing suggestions for individuals to move from pessimism to a more positive way of seeing the world. Optimism psychology is in the field of cognitive science. Seligman's thesis is that the attitude of optimism has significant benefits for the individual and it can be practiced and learned.

Media Seminars:

Jack Canfield, *Self-Esteem and Peak Performance* (1989), is an audio cassette seminar from CareerTrack Publications.

Hattie Hill-Stoks et al., *Women, Power and Self-Esteem: Take Charge of Your Own Well-being* (1990), comes from Career Track Publications.

Notes

1. This story and others in the chapter are based on real people and events, but the names have been changed.

2. Weisinger (1998), 4, discusses how self-awareness is the basic building block of emotional intelligence. Sosik and Megerian (1999), 367, examines the impact on performance; Delmhorst (2006), 1, and Halverson et al. (2002), 3, look at 360 degree leadership evaluation; Lash (2002), 1, looks at top leaders and self-awareness; Goleman et al. (2002), 30, discusses self-awareness as foundational for effective leadership.

3. Bennis (1989), 55–56.

4. Tannenbaum (1999), 221.

5. Cooke (1995), 1.

6. Ibid.

7. Ibid.

8. Gardner (1999), 180.

9. Gardner (1999).

10. Neill (1999), 209.

11. Porter (1999), 217.

12. Chris Argyris developed the "ladder of inference" in the 1960s. He is perhaps best known for his seminal work on learning organizations. A discussion of the ladder of inference can be found in Senge (1994).

13. Newell (2004).

14. Luft and Ingham (1969).

15. Bunker (2001).

16. For Office of Personnel Management's (OPM) Executive Core Qualifications (ECQs), see 28 Senior Executive Service (SES) competencies on OPM's Web site: *www.leadership. opm.gov/AboutUs/Qualification/index.aspx.*

17. Hautman's Web site is *www.selfgrowth.com.*

18. Porter (2000).

19. Federal Executive Institute and Federal Consulting Group (2002), 1.

3 Coaching: A leadership imperative for the twenty-first century

RON REDMON, PRESIDENT, THE REDMON GROUP

IMAGINE HAVING ENOUGH TIME IN YOUR WORKDAY to try the leadership concepts, strategies, and tools offered in this book. For that to happen, one thing would have to change for many of us. We would need to find a way to stop, or at least slow down, the revolving door of people constantly coming to us with questions, particularly questions they are probably capable of answering for themselves, if they have the right support.

The answer for leaders is not to lock their employees out, but to learn how to coach them. Coaching will cut down on many of the interruptions and allow the leader to put more thought and energy into leading. More important, employees who are coached attain higher levels of performance, take more ownership of their work, and become more self-directed. In short, they experience greater fulfillment. And so do their leaders.

When taken seriously, coaching requires practice and rigor, constant examination of one's attitudes and beliefs, and willingness to learn as much as the people one coaches. Coaching opens doors to a new and deeper understanding of oneself, other people, and the world in general. At its most artful, coaching transcends skills and techniques. It is a way to lead people by engaging their minds, their hearts, their aspirations, and their highest selves. Indeed, the central proposition of this chapter is that the skills, behaviors, and mindset of coaching are no longer options for leaders; instead, they have become prerequisites for leadership success because of the nature and pace of change in the world and the necessity for genuinely new thinking.

This chapter will give you a sense of what is involved in coaching, context for its use in the workplace, and perspective on its role in twenty-first century leadership. It is not possible to explain in detail how to coach in these few pages, so think of this chapter as sticking your toe in a pond. If it feels good, wade in a little—get a book from the resource list at the end and read more. If that is tantalizing, go for a dip in the pond—get some formal training. Several excellent programs are also listed in the resource section.

What is coaching?

In 1980 the Department of Defense launched an advertising campaign to attract young men and women into the new all-volunteer army. The campaign slogan, "Be All You Can Be," quickly made its way into the popular lexicon. It is a succinct way to express what coaching is about. If you have had a relationship with someone who challenged you to be all you can be, who helped you find your own answers to whatever you were dealing with or working on (versus telling you what to do or what you should do), who left you feeling more able and sure of yourself, and who wanted to see you succeed even when you might have lost confidence in yourself, you were being coached.

For most people, the word *coaching* is customarily associated with sports. Of the many things an athletic coach does, assessing performance and developing talent are most similar to coaching in an organization. Both involve establishing performance and developmental targets; praising and encouraging; providing feedback on results, strategies, skills, and attitudes; and serving as a partner to their charges so they can hold themselves accountable for achieving agreed upon goals.

These two realms of coaching have had even more in common since the mid-1970s when Tim Gallwey's best-selling book, *The Inner Game of Tennis*, came out. It was Gallwey's contention that the opponent within one's head is at least as formidable as the one on the other side of the net, and perhaps even more. The book spawned a revolution in the coaching of tennis, followed by *Inner Skiing* and *The Inner Game of Golf*, with the same outcome in those sports. All were predicated on the premise that if a coach can help a person remove or reduce the internal obstacles to better performance, the person's natural abilities, experience, and intuition will take over and unlock his or her untapped potential. At its core, Gallwey's approach was not to teach people, but to help them learn.

In the workplace, the grist for this learning consists of the issues and problems that occur in the course of employees' day-to-day activities. A vital role for an effective leader is to spot the learning opportunities embedded in these events, dilemmas, successes, and failures and help employees extract insights and lessons that can improve their performance in the future. Coaching is the vehicle for this learning. It is an exercise in critical thinking without being critical of the thinker.

The story of Bob and Lisa: A different kind of "two-minute drill"

According to most studies, people's number one fear is public speaking. Number two is death. Death is number two. Does that sound right? This means to the average person, if you go to a funeral, you're better off in the casket than doing the eulogy.

— Jerry Seinfeld

Lisa was honored to be selected as the new deputy division director. It meant being part of an entirely different operation and working for Bob, widely regarded as a masterful leader. Her only concern was that the job included periodic presentations to the bureau's senior management. Bob understood Lisa's concern. Earlier in his career he needed to participate in Toastmasters, a club where members learn public speaking skills, for several months before he was able to speak confidently in public and inspire his audience to action. He wanted Lisa to succeed, and quickly. Her speaking responsibilities were important to the job, and she had to get up to speed. She was a superstar among the technical ranks of their agency and clearly had potential for a bright future in management.

When they were identifying Lisa's performance objectives for the coming year, Bob said, "I recall from your interview for this position that the public speaking duties were of concern to you. What's your thinking about that now?" He listened carefully as she described how in her technical work she had done a lot of writing, but had never been expected to speak in front of audiences larger than a division staff meeting.

"Frankly," she said, "I'm scared to death."

"I can identify," Bob remarked. "A little apprehension keeps us on our toes, but we certainly don't want your nerves to get in the way, so that's definitely something to work on. Let me ask you, what is it about public speaking that scares you?" Bob inquired in an empathetic tone.

"I'm scared I'll lose my place, embarrass myself, and the organization," Lisa replied. "I pride myself on being fully prepared, knowing my material inside and out. I've been told I'm actually quite articulate and that people enjoy hearing what I have to say. And I can't recall a time when I was stumped to come up with an answer to a question. It's nerves, I guess. Once I get nervous, it's hard for me to collect my thoughts and stay on message."

"Have you ever been this nervous about anything before?" he continued.

"It's been a while for sure," Lisa said, with a furrowed brow that told Bob she was pondering his question. "I guess it was back in eighth grade, being in the school play. Stage fright really got me."

"What did you do about it?" [Bob's patient and focused demeanor as he asked his question told Lisa this conversation was important to him and he was sincerely interested in her situation.]

"The thing that helped most was getting comfortable with the surroundings—the stage, the lights, staring out into that huge auditorium. Looking back on it, I can remember staying after school to practice walking out on the stage and taking it all in, over and over. I had my lines down cold. It was something about the space, the environment that unnerved me."

"Is there anything about that experience that could help with what you're dealing with here? Any ideas about what you might do?"

"Now that you ask, I suppose it could be the same thing happening again," Lisa speculated, her worried look brightening slightly.

"Go on," Bob said.

After a moment's thought, Lisa asked, "Do you think it would be possible to go with you to some meetings in the bureau director's conference room? I think it would help if I can be in there and start to get to know the senior officials a bit. And maybe I could chair a couple of my committee meetings in there to get used to the surroundings."

"I'm sure all that can be arranged. We'll begin next week. And let me know what else you come up with and anything more I can do to support you. In addition, I propose that you and I present together at the upcoming senior staff retreat. That will give you a target to shoot for that's coming up soon. What do you think?"

"Sure. That would be great, Bob. Thank you."

"I'm confident you'll get past your nervousness in short order, Lisa. By the way, if you want another resource, a chapter of Toastmasters meets in our building. I found that helpful when I was learning and would be glad to tell you about it sometime, if you like."

This two-minute exchange between Bob and Lisa is an example of a simple coaching conversation. Brief and straightforward as it is (and much of coaching can be), it contains a number of important elements common to all effective coaching. Notice what Bob did.

First, he used the occasion of performance planning with Lisa to focus on her developmental needs, making clear that he values continuous learning as part of her job.

Second, he listened attentively, seeking to understand what was going on with Lisa without assuming that he knew. His part in the dialogue was essentially to invite her to explore what she might do to help herself. Note that Bob's challenge with public speaking was not the same as Lisa's—an important detail that can be easily overlooked by a leader who does not listen attentively, but instead is consumed by her or his own thoughts and eagerness to dispense advice. Getting ready to speak is not listening!

Third, he picked up on Lisa's emotional state when she said, "Frankly, I'm scared to death." Masterful leaders know to respect employees' feelings. They are part of a person's reality and can influence the choices he or she makes every bit as much as reasoning. (This skill is part of emotional intelligence addressed in the Introduction.) Bob signaled that he understood how Lisa was feeling when he said, "I can identify" and added, "A little apprehension keeps us on our toes." Notice that he used *we* language rather than *you* language, which helped build rapport with Lisa before moving the conversation forward (". . . we certainly don't want your nerves to get in the way, so that's definitely something to work on"). Another important dynamic at work here is that an expression of feelings indicates there is trust in a relationship. Lisa felt comfortable enough with Bob to say how she really felt, which told him she would be open to his inquiries.

Fourth, Bob resisted the temptation to offer Lisa advice, which kept the ball in her court. Her nervousness about speaking is her developmental challenge, not his. It might be true that participating in Toastmasters could help Lisa, and it would have been easy for Bob to just tell her so and be done. But giving advice to people when one's intent is to foster development comes with an Achilles heel. Advice relieves people of having to figure out a solution to their problem themselves (and, how often do employees *not* follow advice from their boss?). In that way, giving advice unnecessarily creates or reinforces dependency in a relationship. The result of giving advice (versus coaching) is that the person learns to rely on the thinking of others, rather than thinking for himself. Part of coaching's power comes from a truism of human behavior: people are more motivated to pursue a strategy of their own making.

Certainly, situations arise when advice or direction is called for, such as when there is only one correct or proven best way to do something or time is critical. Those occasions, however, are more rare than leaders who operate in "tell" mode are willing to admit. Time is critical when urgency is mandated, not when it is just not a convenient time. Leaders of Bob's caliber know they have to make time to develop employees, not wait for it to show up.

Bob used an approach that is very effective when the goal is to help someone change behavior. He tapped into Lisa's past experiences by asking, "Have you ever been this nervous about anything before?" Answering the question helped her see that she could help herself rather than look to someone else for a solution. What she will carry away from their conversation is a lesson that goes well beyond an immediate step to resolve her nervousness. It is easy to forget just how much one has experienced in life but not always easy to see how applicable these experiences can be to a current situation. A skillful question can help. Bob's question was an example of Tim Gallwey's premise in action.

A more complex issue or situation naturally would call for coaching of a more complex nature, taking an entirely different path. It might involve exploring Lisa's assumptions about the matter at hand, what it would look like if things turned out the way she wanted (in other words, a preferred future), what the obstacles are for getting there, what she would do if there were no constraints on her choices, or any number of other coaching techniques and devices. The point of coaching, however, is always the same: thinking differently generates new possibilities for action, and new possibilities for action open the door to better results. The value added by coaching as a means to better results lies in the increased self-confidence, self-direction, self-accountability, and self-correction that arise when one is in a process of discovery navigated by oneself.

Bob got Lisa to suggest something specific she could do to get into action, offered his support, and proposed a commitment that she agreed to, which was to present together. The commitment, even though informal, was critical to Bob's effective coaching because it established a near-term benchmark by which both of them could observe Lisa's progress.

Most important, Bob entered this conversation with the intention of helping Lisa build her capacity for effective action. Although the issue at hand might not seem all that significant on the surface, it provided Bob with an occasion to establish an important boundary and a useful baseline in their new relationship. The boundary is that he is able to share Lisa's concerns and be supportive, and at the same time he expects her to think for herself and be self-directed. Establishing a boundary is central to coaching. It makes clear where the responsibility lies for resolving the situation or issue without leaving the employee feeling abandoned. The baseline was to establish listening and inquiry as a norm for their interactions. Lisa will have far more complex issues to grapple with as she moves into her role as Bob's deputy. She now knows she can count on his interested ear, his probing questions, his support, and even his suggestions. She also knows he will not step in to rescue her when he believes she is capable of helping herself. That's coaching.

Of the many things that can be seen in this simple example, two stand out. First, Bob is highly purposeful in what he says. He clearly is aware of what he is trying to achieve and chooses his words and his tone with intent. This degree of rigor is true of all good coaching. Although coaching might appear to be a casual conversation, it is anything but. Second, we get several glimpses into the mindset that Bob brought to this conversation with Lisa. From those glimpses we can surmise pretty well what Bob believes and values and how he views the world generally. A leader's mindset is critical to effective coaching and is a major factor in its success, as much or more than the skills themselves. It is akin to an untrained eye watching a professional tennis match and concluding that the game is all about shot-making and stamina. An experienced observer, by contrast, knows that beneath what is apparent on the court lies a whole other world of deep concentration, self-control, and strategy worthy of a world-class chess match. So it is in coaching.

A mindset for coaching in the twenty-first century

A rock pile ceases to be a rock pile the moment a single person contemplates it, bearing within the image of a cathedral.

—Antoine de Saint-Exupéry

The quote from Saint-Exupéry is a philosopher's way of describing a unique and powerful quality of the human mind—its ability to begin manifesting the potential that is all around us simply by noticing that it is there. It is a poetic expression of where coaching begins.

A mindset is a mental attitude, a way of looking at something. It reflects our beliefs and values and is informed by the norms of the culture and era in which we live. It reflects the theories we have adopted about how the world works and is shaped by the lessons we have learned. It is a window through which we see the world. In coaching, the primary pane in this window has to do with how we regard people. At the core of every successful coach's mind are three beliefs:

1. Most people are good at heart and try to do the best they can with what they have.

2. Most people have an inherent desire to learn and steadily improve themselves.

3. Most people are motivated by contributing what they do well to something larger than themselves and that makes a difference in the world.

Certainly, it cannot be said that these beliefs hold for every person, but they are reasonable assumptions upon which to build relationships with people, rather than starting from a place of doubt or skepticism. It is choosing Douglas McGregor's Theory Y over his Theory X.[1] According to McGregor—MIT management professor, psychologist, and business theorist—organizations often work from assumptions that most people prefer to be directed, are not interested in taking on more responsibility, and want safety above all else. Such assumptions, he said, lead to a belief, and a set of corresponding actions, that employees are motivated primarily by money and the threat of punishment. He labeled these assumptions and beliefs Theory X. By contrast, McGregor postulated that people have the potential to be self-directed and highly creative if properly motivated; that they are not naturally lazy and unreliable. These beliefs he called Theory Y.

Perhaps McGregor's most enduring contribution to our understanding of organizational dynamics and human motivation were the lenses through which we can observe and understand the impact of a leader's assumptions about people on the behaviors of employees. In addition to these beliefs about people, other panes in this figurative window include respect for diversity, humility, empathy, optimism, curiosity, and comfort with paradox and ambiguity.

Respect for diversity in this context extends far beyond appreciation for or tolerance of our differences in the familiar terms of race, creed, age, gender, religion, ethnicity, or national origin. It goes to the most fundamental aspects of who we are as human beings: how we think, how we learn, how we communicate, how we interrelate. It involves a wide array of variables, from personality type and the "multiple intelligences" identified by Harvard professor Howard Gardner to learning styles and the nature of one's emotional intelligence, to name just a few.[2] This is not to suggest that a leader must become a psychologist. What it does suggest is that a leader of people will not succeed without a basic understanding of the core theories of human behavior and motivation, as well as an awareness of the many ways in which each of us is unique. It means noticing those differences and seeing them, not as things to be managed, but as wellsprings of new thinking that can improve a product or service or how we work together.

This story from a vice president of the World Bank makes the point. She had just announced at an all-hands meeting the forthcoming flattening of her sizable organization to put employees closer to their customers. An employee approached her after the meeting to express her deep consternation at this news. The employee, a native of India, had been raised in that country's system of castes, within which people are born, marry, and die, and which people accept as the way to keep society from disintegrating into chaos. As a result, she could not contemplate, much less appreciate, how the organization could function without hierarchy. She was truly shaken at the thought. It was an eye-opener for the leader—a highly capable, well educated, thoughtful woman—and a lesson that she says she recalls regularly to remind herself how different we can be in very fundamental ways, especially in terms of what resides in our heads.

Humility is not always associated with leadership, but is certainly a main ingredient of wisdom. Consider John Wooden, a Hall of Fame college basketball coach. He was frequently quoted as saying, "It's what you learn after you know it all that really counts." [3] Leaders who leave space in their thinking for new ideas, new perspectives, and perhaps entirely different assumptions to arise, regardless of their years of experience, demonstrate true humility. That space in one's thinking is what people are noticing when they say someone is "open." It attracts us because we experience it as an invitation; we are drawn into it. It is comfortable to be with people like that; it is easy to trust them. Humility is an elixir for relationships that truly great leaders and coaches demonstrate. When Max DePree, the iconic former chairman of the board of Herman Miller, left Switzerland after working there for some time, his Swiss co-workers presented him with a fireman's hat inscribed, "I don't know for sure." As he recounts the story, "They apparently thought it unusual to have an American manager who admitted that he didn't know everything. I still try to remember how much there is that I don't know." [4] A leader at the pinnacle of corporate America who can admit to not always having the answer should be an example for leaders at every level everywhere.

> *Make your ego porous. Will is of little importance, complaining is nothing, fame is nothing. Openness, patience, receptivity are everything.*
>
> —Rainer Maria Rilke

Out of humility arises empathy, the capacity to imagine oneself in another's place and understand the other's feelings, motives, needs, and actions.

This is not necessarily to agree with or condone them, but to better understand the individual behind them. In *Sacred Hoops*, championship basketball coach Phil Jackson shares what empathy looks like at the highest level in his world.

> Pro basketball is a macho sport. Many coaches, worried about showing any sign of weakness, tend to shut down emotionally and ostracize players who aren't meeting their expectations. This can have a disturbing ripple effect on the players that undermines team unity. In my work as a coach, I've discovered that approaching problems of this kind from a compassionate perspective, trying to empathize with the player and look at the situation from his point of view, can have a transformative effect on the team. Not only does it reduce the player's anxiety and make him feel as if someone understands what he's going through, it also inspires the other players to respond in kind and be more conscious of each other's needs.[5]

There, in the words of a coach/leader whose name is synonymous with success in the take-no-prisoners world of professional sports, is an important lesson: empathy reduces apprehension, builds trust, and inspires others to greater awareness of their teammates as human beings. Without genuine respect for people, humility, and empathy, coaching will be perceived as manipulation—a crass attempt to use legitimate principles, methods, techniques, and skills to deceive or convert another to one's point of view. In the end, such attempts are only destructive.

In the mindset of every great leader and great coach the proverbial glass is half full. They are optimistic about the future, hopeful in the face of adversity, and confident in their abilities and those of their team members. They see and appreciate what is, rather than lament what is not. From this simple tenet an entire philosophy about organizations, called Appreciative Inquiry (AI), was born. Its father, David Cooperrider, professor at the Weatherhead School of Management at Case Western Reserve University, describes AI as "involving the systematic discovery of what gives 'life' to a living system when it is most alive, most effective, and most constructively capable." [6] It is about what inspires, what energizes, what encourages and sustains. It is about possibilities for the future, not blame for the past. Planting the seeds of one's coaching, indeed one's leadership, in the soil of AI is to adopt a new paradigm that breaks with a long, and at times painful, tradition of thinking of organizations and the people in them as a set of problems to be fixed.

Curiosity is the "juice" behind coaching. This curiosity is not nosiness, but a genuine, respectful desire to understand how others think. Understanding how others think permits us to view the world through their eyes, to appreciate what they see as possible or impossible, and to comprehend how they arrived at their conclusions. By understanding others' thinking, one is in a position to posit an alternative perspective, to observe something that is missing, or offer a distinction that might lead to them thinking differently. Curiosity (without judging) opens this door by gently piercing the veil of the conditioned mind, which is the province of knowledge and therefore, by definition, is limited to what is already known.

What is not known is the domain of imagination. Imagination is stimulated by curiosity, one's own or another's. No less an intellect than Albert Einstein said that imagination is more important than knowledge. As he elaborated in a now-famous observation, "The significant problems we face today cannot be solved by the same level of thinking that created them." In other words, we must think anew, we must think differently, if mankind is to progress. Thinking differently, or "outside the box," as we are regularly implored, is easier to say than to do. The classic nine-dot exercise is simple proof. The goal is to connect all the dots in a three by three matrix with a single line without lifting the pencil from the paper. Trying it for the first time, most people are stumped. It demonstrates the grip that conventional thinking has on most of us. Curiosity then is crucial for leaders to understand their colleagues' thinking, as well as their own, so that issues and problems can be addressed in new ways. As Einstein suggested, this is not problem solving by using what we know; rather, it is about challenging our assumptions, examining our biases, removing our filters, and imagining a future not extrapolated from the present or the past.

> *A shoe manufacturing company sends two marketing reps to a region in Africa to assess the potential for new business. One sends back an e-mail, "Situation hopeless. No one wears shoes." The other writes back enthusiastically, "Fantastic business opportunity. No one has shoes."*

Finally, today's leader must be comfortable with paradox and ambiguity, two constants in our complex and continuously changing world. Paradoxes—seeming contradictions—are all around us, for example, the ever-present call to do more with less. Paradoxes compel us to step out of our familiar mental models to consider "both/and," not just "either/or" thinking. Paradoxes beget possibilities. At Toyota, this principle is being put to use at the corporate level. In an interview with the *Detroit Free Press,* published December 27, 2006,

Matthew May, author of *The Elegant Solution: Toyota's Formula for Mastering Innovation,* made this comment: "In order to drive innovative thinking, Toyota purposefully sets strategic goals in direct conflict with one another and demands simultaneous achievement. Why? Because these competing goals cannot be met without everyone thinking differently. The artful setting of opposing stretch goals mandates innovation."

Ambiguity is a lack of clarity, a state of uncertainty, the shades of gray that color relationships and much of what leaders deal with in organizations. To be uncomfortable with ambiguity is to need more structure, control, or assurance than the world usually provides. Structure, control, and assurances certainly have their place in organizations, but in the extreme they can extinguish the energy in a human endeavor, reducing it to rote process, and constrain an organization's ability to respond with adaptability and flexibility.

These hallmarks of the mindset of a coach, in whatever context or vocation, afford us a way to see the people, events, and circumstances around us in the light of flux, potential, and possibility. Just as important, they generate and continuously recycle trust in our relationships. Who does not trust someone who accepts and respects us just the way we are? Or is humble, has empathy for our wants and needs, curiosity about our views, and demonstrates hope and strength in the face of the world's challenges? This kind of mindset is critical to one's authenticity, one's credibility in coaching, and to the quality of leadership called for today.

A culture that supports coaching

To optimize the power of coaching throughout an organization a leader must create a climate in which it is valued, welcomed, and expected. A coaching-rich culture can lead to transformational change for individuals and the whole enterprise. The preconditions for such a culture are trust, alignment, a priority of learning, and the institutionalization of commitments.

Trust

My colleagues make it abundantly clear in other chapters that effective leadership in democratic institutions is grounded in and relies upon a trusting relationship between the leader and his or her followers. The components of that relationship are one's trustworthiness and behaviors that signal a willingness to trust others. Trustworthiness was addressed eloquently by Terry

Newell in Chapter 1, citing a quote from Abigail Adams, the wife of one president and the mother of another. It bears repeating here: "Great Learning and superior abilities, should you ever possess them, will be of little value and small estimation unless virtue, honor, truth and integrity are added to them." In short, character trumps knowledge or talent. We must earn the right to be trusted by others by demonstrating our worthiness of their highest regard.

In a leader's relationship with an employee, behaviors that signal willingness to trust include:

- Creating "space" in which the employee can do his or her job free of unnecessary interference;
- Steadily assigning more responsible duties and providing the means to accomplish them; and
- Making it clear that one believes in the employee to achieve what is expected.

For some leaders these behaviors might require letting go of a comfortable way of interacting with others in order to take a risk on someone else. Risk begets trust. These behaviors reflect a commitment to employees that goes beyond the mechanics of adequate supervision.

> How many of your direct reports would agree with the statement,
> "My leader wholeheartedly wants to see me succeed"?
> If not all of them would, what would be different if they did?
> Would you say that is true of your boss?
> How does that make you feel?

When leaders make the success of employees paramount, healthy, effective organizations are grown. This is not altruism, but strategic, bottom-line leadership. Larry Bossidy, former CEO of AlliedSignal, said it well when he observed, "In the end, we bet on people, not strategies." [7] Coaching is the most effective way for leaders to secure that bet.

Alignment

When Jack Welch was CEO of General Electric, he often visited its corporate university at Crotonville, New York, to tell program participants his expectations of them as members of the GE management team. One of their primary tasks, he said, was to continuously define and clarify for their employees what he called "the field of action." He would draw a rectangle on a whiteboard and label the four sides *mission, vision, values,* and *results.* The point was that unless employees are on the same "field"—that they understand these four essentials of the organization in roughly the same way—they are not aligned and are therefore prone to misunderstandings, suboptimization of their efforts, and even failure.[8] It is a simple and useful construct for leaders in general and especially beneficial for creating a culture in which coaching can take root and thrive. It ensures a foundation of shared understanding and precludes the development of alternative assumptions about purpose, direction, and expectations.

Learning as a priority

Learning is the fertile soil in which coaching takes root. In his book, *Competing for the Future,* internationally renowned consultant and London School of Business professor Gary Hamel asked, "Are we learning as fast as the world is changing?" This is one of the most profound questions a twenty-first century leader can contemplate. Consider the implications for an organization if the answer to that question is no.

In 1995 Dr. Janet Woodcock, director of the Center for Drug Evaluation and Research (CDER) at the Food and Drug Administration, understood those implications better than she might have liked. Her organization was under intense scrutiny by a Congress grown impatient with CDER's inability to adapt to changes in the pharmaceutical industry vis-à-vis FDA's regulatory responsibilities. Legislators were pushing to constrain the center's authority and slash its funding. Woodcock told her management team that the only thing worse than being shut down entirely would be for Congress to make them "irrelevant." She rallied her team to rethink their long-held assumptions about CDER's role and how it worked, create a culture of learning, and embrace innovation. In essence, she coached her organization to a new understanding of itself, to a different way to be. What she and they accomplished over the next two years literally became a case study in public sector leadership and the value of learning as a strategic priority to drive change.[9]

The lesson here for coaching is that for any individual, team, or organization to adopt new behaviors (meaning to change), it must first make learning a priority. Otherwise, new behaviors will result from extrinsic motivators

Box 3.1   An organizational culture
for the twenty-first century

The U.S. Coast Guard has a mission that spans more than 120,000 miles of coastline and inland waterways. It operates with fewer people than the New York City Police Department and an annual budget that is less than the cost of a new aircraft carrier.

How does it do so much so well with so little? The answer, according to Admiral James M. Loy, former Coast Guard commandant, is ". . .simple and cultural. The foundation is commitment to leadership development. All personnel, from the youngest recruit to the senior-most admiral, are immersed in the culture of leadership and expected to practice it on a daily basis."

This culture is based on a leadership model developed at the Coast Guard Academy and has as its foundation character and values, including integrity, respect, commitment, honor, and trust. Standing upon this foundation are fourteen core competencies, some traditional, such as vision and goals, expertise, teamwork, decisiveness, and some of more recent vintage, such as connectivity, empowerment, and coaching/mentoring.

What is the upshot of this culture? In Admiral Loy's words, "All this preparation eventually meets the serendipitous filter of opportunity. People must be coached to keep their eyes and ears open to new possibilities, cracks in the competition's armor, and new niches in the marketplace. This approach is affirmed by the success and efficiency of the Coast Guard. It is the values-based leadership culture that explains how the organization can be agile enough to shift its focus during a major natural disaster. It clarifies how the Coast Guard was able to save 33,000 lives while other response organizations were waiting for someone to lead."*

---

*Donald T. Phillips and James M. Loy, *Character in Action: The U.S. Coast Guard on Leadership* (Annapolis, Md.: Naval Institute Press, 2003). The lives saved refer to the Coast Guard's work during and after Hurricane Katrina.

such as a willingness to please the boss, a desire to get along, or a "this too shall pass" mentality. Extrinsic motivators evaporate once the stimulus is gone and often leave behind a residue of ill will and cynicism. With learning as a shared priority, the groundwork is laid for coaching to make sense and be appreciated by employees.

Once learning has been established as a priority, organization members need to make a practice of exchanging constructive feedback with one another on a regular basis, preferably in real time. Feedback is central to what can be the most important learning in any organization—what we learn about ourselves, the human players in the narrative. Coaching is the catalyst that converts that feedback into action, which leads to improvement. Without the mechanism of purposeful language (coaching), feedback is little more than information and data about one's behavior that can lie fallow for want of tilling and nurturing.

Creating such an organizational culture can be difficult for leaders who focus predominantly on the immediate or the near term. Such is the pressure where priorities are continually in flux, where players regularly change, or the prevailing value is "What have you done for me lately?" Difficult or counterintuitive as it might seem, creating a learning culture is precisely the work that leaders must undertake to ensure the future success of their organization. It requires taking a longer view, making the explicit commitment to developing people, respectfully challenging one another's thinking, being persistent about seeing new possibilities, and freely offering and receiving feedback. The best tool of all is the leader's own example. We know it is possible to create such a culture because the U.S. Coast Guard is doing it (see Box 3.1).

Commitments

A commitment is a pledge or a promise to do what one says one will do. Without a commitment to action, coaching can easily dissipate into little more than an interesting conversation with no practical effect. It is a commitment to action that generates momentum through steady gains and ultimately brings success. As in the case of Bob and Lisa, a commitment can take the form of an informal, almost tacit, agreement or something more formal or structured. What is crucial is that the significance of commitments is understood and embraced by employees, and the practice of honoring them becomes institutionalized in the organization's culture. Without commitments, energy and time are squandered, morale suffers for lack of direction and accomplishment, and mediocrity prevails.

What makes coaching a leadership imperative for the twenty-first century?

The Chinese have an aphorism: "May you live in interesting times." Indeed we do, most especially the leaders coming into their own at the start of a new century. Their leadership challenges include the exponential explosion of knowledge; rapid globalization along with increasing awareness of the impact of our actions on others far away; higher degrees of interdependence that necessitate collaboration across time, space, and organizational and national boundaries; the technology-enabled availability of data and information at every level and in every corner of the organization; the technology-enabled fluidity of work schedules and sites; and the constant arrival of new technology itself; a more educated workforce than at any time in history, composed of a blend of salaried employees, contractors, grantees, and partners of all kinds in an unprecedented mix of cultures and generations; the talent wars and the exodus of expertise and wisdom of the baby boom generation—all in a vortex of swirling priorities and a mind-numbing demand for speed and more speed. If these factors were not challenging enough, in large bureaucracies like government, this new reality is occurring within antiquated structures, with antiquated processes, and often with antiquated notions about what leadership needs to be.

In 1989 Peter Vaill, among the most influential organizational change theorists of our time, coined the term "permanent whitewater" to characterize the conditions he saw emerging as we moved into the information age.[10] Little more than a decade later, we have already moved beyond the information age into what is being called the intangible economy. This kind of economy is driven not by access to raw materials, transportation, and physical markets, but by the flow of data, images, and symbols. In this economy, brick and mortar are no longer assets of choice; rather, they have been replaced by brand, intellectual property rights, human capital, and knowledge transfer.[11] The twenty-first century—in which every aspect of life is immersed in the technologies of PCs, PDAs, CDs, DVDs, HDTV, IM, iPods, XBOX, WiFi, Wikis, and Wii—is a whole new world compared to the era of black and white television in which today's senior leaders came of age. This degree of change in the stunningly brief period of just half a century constitutes a fundamental transformation in history. As you read this, others are occurring in many fields and most institutions.[12] For example, no one knows what will be revealed through the Human Genome Project, only that a transformation in biology is under way. Our basic understanding of life is literally under a microscope. What we do know, however, is that transformations require and result in new thinking. That was Einstein's point. We also know that thinking does not transform itself. It requires a catalyst, a mechanism. Coaching is one such mechanism that is readily available to leaders all the time, everyday.

In these periods of seismic shifts in history, human behaviors lag well behind all other changes. To be effective today, leaders must adopt new paradigms for their role in the enterprise. The command and control style of leadership that emerged in the industrial era (and remains even now in some dark organizational corners) is at best futile and at worst damaging in light of the challenges facing twenty-first century leaders. To succeed in a world that does not stand still, organizations can no longer consider it a luxury to have self-directed and self-correcting employees at every level. It is an imperative for their very survival. To develop such employees, leaders must tap the passion, aspirations, knowledge, experience, talent, and potential of everyone around them. They must lead by example. They must lead by calling forth. They must lead as coaches.

Conclusion

Coaching is a set of skills for a leader's toolkit: deep listening, inquiry that broadens and deepens thinking, mindful presence, encouragement, goal setting, and the willingness to hold employees accountable for their own commitments (for starters). Coaching also can be a way for leader and employee to frame their relationship, to move beyond the boss-subordinate paradigm based in power to a truly adult-adult alliance grounded in shared purpose, values, aspirations, and goals. At yet another level, coaching can be the means to more fulfillment, both for the person doing it and the person receiving it. In business terms, coaching provides a path to greater employee productivity, and by extension, organizational effectiveness.

At an even higher order of impact, coaching can be a catalyst for transformational thinking, a new way of approaching problems that goes to the underlying premises and assumptions by which individuals, organizations, and society operate.

No matter how one thinks about it, coaching is an act of connecting— connecting leader and employee, connecting an issue or situation to a larger context where its significance is clearer, connecting cognition and emotion, head and heart, what exists to what could be.

Coaching is an uncommonly positive, powerful, and strategic tool for a leader in relationship to employees and the organization as a whole. It is positive because it affirms the employees, seeks the best in them, and calls upon them to clarify and operate from their values and aspirations to be their best selves. It is powerful because it relies on the employees' thinking, intuition, wisdom, and experience, enabling them to see new possibilities and make informed choices, where perhaps all they knew before was "this is the way it has always been done." It is strategic because it looks forward, calls for systems thinking, and is about learning and change.

Coaching can stop the revolving door of people coming to us with questions, particularly those that they are capable of answering for themselves with the right support. It can provide us an entry into being a new kind of leader, enjoying the paradox of greater impact with less control.

Bill O'Brien, the highly respected CEO emeritus of Hanover Insurance, had this to say on the subject of twenty-first century organizations and leadership: "Our traditional organizations are designed to provide for the first three levels of Abraham Maslow's hierarchy of human needs—food, shelter, and belonging. Since these are now widely available to members of modern society, these organizations do not provide anything particularly unique to command the loyalty and commitment of people. The ferment in management today will continue until organizations begin to address the higher order needs: self-respect and self-actualization." [13] No doubt Einstein would have added "new thinking."

That is the imperative leaders must address in the twenty-first century if their organizations are to remain relevant. Ultimately, coaching is a tool, a process that brings the full potential of a leader's team to bear on the enormous challenges of organizations and of our time. What would be different if your employees were coached?

Tips for leadership success

When their work is done, of the great leaders people will say, "We did it ourselves."

—Lao Tzu

The following principles are offered as considerations for those interested in integrating coaching into their leadership practice.

- Coaching is grounded in the leader's beliefs and expectations about other people and a trusting relationship with employees.
- The primary purpose of coaching is to develop the capacities of the other person. The focus of the conversation is the task or situation at

hand, and therefore coaching can occur at any time.

- The larger context of the coaching is a common understanding of the organization's mission, vision, values, and desired results that is shared by both the leader and the employee.
- The leader who coaches sees herself more as a resource for people than as a manager of processes or things.
- Coaching is about possibilities, as opposed to established ways of doing things; it is therefore a vehicle for learning and organizational change.
- As with leadership, the most powerful coaching is by example. Leaders who coach must be models of whatever they expect from those they coach as well as open to coaching themselves.[14]

Resources for further learning

For a broader foundation on coaching as a leadership competency, consider reading:

Marshall Goldsmith, Beverly Kaye, and Ken Shelton, eds., *Learning Journeys* (2000). This compendium of life stories and lessons from a veritable who's who of leadership practitioners and thinkers demonstrates the importance of learning how to learn as a foundation for success.

William Isaacs, *Dialogue and the Art of Thinking Together* (1999). Isaacs is the master of an essential element of twenty-first century leadership: being able to talk together in honest and generative ways. A must read.

Michael Marquardt, *Leading with Questions* (2005). Marquardt asserts that leaders model the way by asking questions that elicit thinking in others and by demonstrating their willingness to learn and change. He examines every side of this approach to leadership and the implications it has for organizations and the people in them.

Susan Scott, *Fierce Conversations* (2004). Two of Scott's lessons pertain to all of us: (1) the conversation is not about the relationship; the conversation *is* the relationship, and (2) never mistake talking for the conversation. Real stories, easy to read, and immediately applicable.

Rosamund Zander and Benjamin Zander, *The Art of Possibility* (2000). Many talk about transformed thinking; the Zanders deliver. With lessons from their experiences in art, business, music, and psychology, they help us understand how to turn our thinking on its head and see the world from radically new perspectives.

For more specifics about how to coach, coaching styles, and coaching language, consider:

Thomas G. Crane, *The Heart of Coaching* (2001). Best choice for busy executives interested in learning enough to get started. Includes helpful graphics to make coaching as straightforward as possible and immediately applicable in small doses.

Robert Hargrove, *Masterful Coaching* (1995). A seminal work in the field that is at once practical, philosophical, educational, informative, and entertaining. Simple to read, very advanced in concepts and techniques.

James M. Hunt and Joseph R. Weintraub, *The Coaching Manager: Developing Top Talent in Business* (2002). A clearly written, practical compendium of basic and advanced coaching skills and techniques along with useful scenarios and case studies from the authors' research and experiences and research in a coaching program for MBA students at Babson College.

Below is a selection of coach training programs the author knows personally and is comfortable recommending. All are certified by the International Coach Federation (ICF), the discipline's governing body, as meeting its rigorous standards. Note: some include forms of coaching, such as life coaching, or aspects of coaching, such as starting a practice, not needed by leaders in organizations.

Coaches Training Institute, San Rafael, Calif., *www.thecoaches.com.*

Georgetown University, Washington, D.C., *www.cpd.georgetown.edu/leadership-coaching.html.*

The Hudson Institute, Santa Barbara, Calif., *www.hudsoninstitute.com.*

Newfield Network, USA, LLC, Boulder, Colo., *www.newfieldnetwork.com.*

New Ventures West, San Francisco, Calif., *www.newventureswest.com.*

Notes

1. McGregor (1960).
2. Gardner (1983).
3. Wooden (1997).
4. DePree (1992).
5. Jackson (1995).
6. Cooperrider (2005).
7. Bossidy and Charan (2002).

8. GE videotape of one of Welch's appearances at Crotonville, loaned to the consulting team of the Federal Quality Institute, Washington, D.C., in 1993.

9. The author served as the principal organizational development consultant to Dr. Woodcock and her senior leadership team during this period. Woodcock's efforts are chronicled in "Growing Leaders for Public Service," by Ray Blunt, from *The Business of Government*, November 2003, published by the IBM Center for the Business of Government.

10. Vaill (1989).

11. Goldfinger (1994) is credited with having first coined the phrase, by which he meant, "The source of economic value and wealth is no longer the production of material goods, but the creation and manipulation of dematerialized content." In 2000 the European Commission published "The Intangible Economy—Report of the European High Level Expert Group on the Intangible Economy," which added this observation (p. 5), "The 21st century business landscape is often characterised as 'old economy' plus internet. As a metaphor this has the appeal of simplicity, but is misleading. Today, the pursuit of competitive advantage requires a radical shift of mindset away from our old-world business models and practices. The clarity of 20th century markets was based on a system of fixed boundaries, with one-to-one trading relationships, linear value-chains and balance sheet accounting concepts. The economy today operates without fixed boundaries, and this has far-reaching implications for companies, financial markets, public institutions and regulators."

12. See "The 2007 SHIFT Report—Evidence of a World Transforming," by the highly regarded Institute for Noetic Sciences, Petalumna, Calif., *www.noetic.org*.

13. Senge et al. (1994), 24.

14. From the training course, "Coaching Skills for Executives," created and taught by the author at the Federal Executive Institute, Charlottesville, Va.

4 Leading for team success

GAIL FUNKE, SENIOR FACULTY, FEDERAL EXECUTIVE INSTITUTE*

Teams strengthen the performance capability of individuals, hierarchies, and management processes.
— Jon R. Katzenbach and Douglas K. Smith,
The Wisdom of Teams

ON SEPTEMBER 11, 2001, the United States suffered a grave attack on its soil. No one will ever forget where they were and what they were doing when the planes hit. The damage in physical and human terms was devastating and has taken literally years to sort out.

As the country struggled to resume its national life, many questions arose: How could this happen? Could it have been prevented? Were there early warning signals? Did anyone at the federal level have information in advance that could have helped?

As it turned out, there was information in the government environment that might have helped. We will never know for certain that the attacks could have been prevented. What we do know, however, is that not enough information was shared between the major intelligence agencies. The extant knowledge in each agency could have contributed to a more informative whole, which clearly would have raised the consciousness level about the possibility, the type, and the imminence of the attacks. Part of the problem was that people did not trust their counterparts in other agencies. Ordinary citizens on a doomed plane seemed more able to mitigate the potential damage of the terrorists.[1] Many in the country, the government, and indeed, the world, were disturbed to know that, for example, the FBI and the CIA were not working together in a team-like manner or routinely sharing critical information, even though U.S. security, internal and external, was entrusted to their care.[2] Their mission statements might differ in letter, but certainly not in spirit.

---

*The views expressed here are the author's and do not necessarily reflect those of the Federal Executive Institute or the U.S. Office of Personnel Management.

The case for teams

Fortunately, the consequences of lack of teamwork are usually not this egregious. If, however, we accept the words of Jon Katzenbach, noted specialist and author on teams, and others, teams represent the simplest, most straightforward process change an organization can make to improve its productivity, reduce duplication, and raise performance.[3] In government, where stagnant budgets and declining discretionary funds are the order of the day (and the future), teams can improve output without requiring more resources, and the consequences can be quite substantial.

So if groups and teams accomplish far more than the same number of individuals working independently, if their use can mitigate the effects of flattened public sector budgets, and teamwork and "groupwork" indeed constitute the template of the twenty-first century workforce, what are the individual and organizational implications for future leaders? Often tempered by independence and autonomy, today's leaders must undergo a sea change if they are to be proactively prepared for the challenges awaiting them. The hallmarks of today's executive environment are complexity and interdependence. A leader simply cannot accomplish her agenda without engaging people in true collaborative association: the leader's work requires that others be substantively engaged in the "production process." Furthermore, public sector leaders confronted with static or shrinking budgets can actually create leverage with a team-based environment and accomplish far more than in an individuated, "stovepiped" arrangement, in which organizational entities rarely if ever interact and see more advantage to maintaining their turf than in collaboration and cooperation.

Countless situations and structures throughout government would benefit from greater or more efficient use of teams and teamwork: the response to Hurricane Katrina at all levels of government, the standup of the conglomerate Department of Homeland Security that followed 9/11, strategies for managing BRAC (base realignment and closure) mandates, agency reorganizations—the list is seemingly without end. Yet we encounter a patchwork of application: some agencies—NASA, for example—make extensive use of teams, but others do not, are coming late to this opportunity, or see teams as of limited use. Why?

The answer lies in our leaders and in our organizational history.

For most of my career in government, I believed that I needed to do it all—in other words, to set out the plan and direct the work; but as I moved up to leadership positions, I couldn't do that—there simply weren' t enough hours in the day. Then I came to FEI and discovered that real leaders are not solely re-sponsible for doing the work; they are responsible for getting the work done.

—Participant in the Leadership for a Democratic
Society Program, Federal Executive Institute

I honestly thought I was doing my organization a favor by lay-ing out the work and assigning tasks; then, at an off-site, the staff revealed that they felt left out and de-motivated when I did that. And up to that eye-opening point, I felt martyred for shouldering all that responsibility!

—Participant in the Custom Teambuilding
Program, Federal Executive Institute

The Federal Executive Institute (FEI), a residential executive education facility established in 1968 for senior career federal government leaders, con-tinues to hear statements like these from seasoned as well as new executives in leadership positions. When FEI began, it was routine for faculty to meet participants who functioned as "lone rangers" in accomplishing their work functions. The institute uses a model represented as "Leadership at the 'T' "—a construct that depicts and contrasts the skills necessary early in one's career with the skills necessary for leadership positions assumed later in one's career (see Figure 4.1).

As one rises up the leadership ladder (represented by the T's vertical bar), the balance shifts from reliance on personal skills, such as technical ex-pertise, to interpersonal skills, working with others, and building teams and coalitions. At the top of the pyramid (the T's horizontal bar), the strategic leadership level, one's success depends most heavily on the ability to work in a team framework across organizational boundaries. Therefore, the very things that contribute to success early on are the same things that need to be "unlearned" or emphasized less as one's career progresses.[4]

How can leaders understand the value of teams and teamwork and them-selves become skilled implementers and users of this approach? How can

Figure 4.1 Leadership at the "T"

Strategic leadership
- Strategic thinking
- Political savvy
- Vision
- External awareness
- Influencing/negotiating

Team leadership
- Team building
- Interpersonal skills

Technical leadership
- Professional and technical skills

today's (and tomorrow's) leaders effectively initiate team-based approaches in both their immediate environments and the virtual world of geographically dispersed teams? And what are the organizational sine qua nons for becoming an effective user and implementer of teams? This chapter explores the meaning of teamwork, the factors necessary for its effective implementation, and how one major learning institution, FEI, fosters the understanding and use of teams and the necessity of creating a compatible organization environment for a different production process and use of teams.

The chapter discusses the several levels of learning and understanding that are necessary for the team approach to be used effectively in the public sector. It rests on the central tenet of this book: the building of trust and the establishment of relationships. Without these foundational steps, the leader cannot hope to use teams effectively. We then turn to institutionalizing teams in the greater organizational structure, to specific activities for building and maintaining teams, and to special applications, such as virtual teams.

Leader, first know thyself and build trust

The journey of 10,000 miles begins with a single step.

—Aphorism

Trust is the foundation of real teamwork. [T]here is nothing soft about it. It is [the most] critical part of building a team.

—Patrick Lencioni, *The Five Dysfunctions of a Team*

If trust is central to effective teams, the leader needs to understand the meaning and importance of trust and to be able to practice it in her daily work life. Yet many leaders "go it alone," trusting no one and relying solely on themselves. Or, they fail to understand the process for building trust, both for themselves and for the people with whom they work. Trust in this context is not merely assuming someone will not steal from the office or will show up on time even when you are not there (although that is certainly part of it). Rather, the trust we emphasize here is the willingness to be vulnerable, to abandon a position of "always right," to be willing to admit when you are wrong or need help. For the executive used to "going it alone," this adjustment can be a major, life-changing one. In the public sector, going it alone has been a long-standing characteristic, handed down through generations of public servants.[5] Leaders must know themselves well enough to understand if they are engaging in this tendency as well as know how to generate the trust essential to breaking from this outdated paradigm.

The work at FEI has always begun with this knowledge in mind; the program is focused on not only building trust but also on allowing executives to see the advantage that increased trust can have in public organizations. From the beginning, personal disclosure is used as a tool in creating the trust necessary for participant learning teams (called Leadership Development Teams) to function. Chapter 2, "Self-awareness and leadership success," more fully discusses the techniques of self-awareness that are used in this safe environment. These activities, although not as in-depth as they may be used in the FEI experience, can serve as templates when the executives seek to implement teams in their back-home situations. The willingness to self-disclose, be open, and be vulnerable is critical to team cohesion and performance. And it all starts with the leader.

The usual result of the FEI experience is that participants start to understand that openness and disclosure need not spell professional purgatory for the executive who practices them. They learn the steps for creating the safe environment where trust can flourish. And they see first hand the results and achievements of groups that create and maintain a high level of trust.

The second development of this FEI process is that participants very quickly forge relationships that are strong, enduring, productive, and grounded in trust. Strong trusting relationships are not about agreeing all the time, but about having firm foundations that allow people to air their concerns and disagreements openly and then resolve them together. Individuals who can do this are strengthened by the process.

For teams to function and flourish over the long haul, trust and sound relationships are crucial, and they start at the top—with the leader or executive. Who can say how 9/11 might have unfolded had the leaders of the various intelligence agencies trusted one another and put this trust into practice—if they had experienced a history of successful working relationships, of sharing information more freely? If they had experienced ups and downs, but felt more certain in their belief in the value of trust, relationships, and cooperation to themselves and the nation?

Another important outcome of this process is that government executives understand that trust and relationships precede rather than follow task and content. Clarity on work tasks does not in any way cause trust and sound relationships to occur. In fact, often groups who put the cart before the horse in this fashion find that later they cannot resolve even the simplest disagreements because they neither learned nor practiced trust and never developed effective relationships that transcend the work at hand.[6]

This process often causes considerable discomfort for public executives, who, although they accept and understand the necessity for teamwork and groupwork and the foundation of trust and relationships, are concerned about their personal abilities in championing such an approach at their own agencies. Among their concerns typically are their personality preferences and their approach to influence.

At FEI, self-awareness (see chapter 2) is considered a key to leadership success. One success measure is the ability to participate in and lead team development. Leaders who understand their own preferences will be more effective and build stronger teams. Personality preferences are addressed through the use of the Myers-Briggs Type Indicator (MBTI), although other valid and reliable instruments that address preferences are also useful.[7] The MBTI identifies innate preferences that are manifested through behavior along four main dimensions: (1) one's source of energy (internal/Introvert or external/Extravert); (2) information gathering (detail/Sensor or big picture/ Intuitive); (3) decision making (impersonal/Thinker or personal/ Feeler); and (4) approach to work and life (decisive and systematic/Judger or open and spontaneous/Perceiver). The capital letters combine to form sixteen types, and each type brings gifts and skepticism to the team process.

Knowing one's MBTI and that of the group allows teams to self-diagnose opportunities as well as pitfalls, which are discussed later in the chapter. For the leader, this kind of information can be invaluable in implementing and supporting teamwork in the agency. Type is a tool for insight, not for avoidance. Leaders need to be aware of several things when utilizing the MBTI with teams:

- A team with a preponderance of the same four-letter types may suffer from "groupthink" and lack challenges to its decision-making process and actual decisions. In this situation, the leader needs to see that provocative questions are asked and alternatives considered.
- A team with a preponderance of one or more of the individual letters needs to be sure that all members are heard and the most common preference does not exert undue influence. For example, extraverts might dominate the conversation, and the ideas of introverts are not heard; or sensors are preoccupied with detail, while intuitives refuse to get specific; or judgers want to use voting to save time when consensus would be a better option; or perceivers resist coming to closure when it is long overdue.
- Using the MBTI to plan teamwork can be extremely useful to the success of the team. The instrument gives team members a neutral language when addressing conflicts and concerns.[8]
- Each member of the team has a great deal to contribute. The leader can help this happen.[9]

The complex environment and effective utilization of teams

No one in my unit thinks we need a team because we all know what the work is. But with flat budgets, I don't think we can get even the same work done without a cooperative approach. We simply can't afford to let our mission fail.

—EPA branch chief, upon engaging FEI
to lead a team formation effort

The task was likely to be long and strenuous, and an ordered mind and a clear programme were essential if we were to come through without loss of life.

—Ernest Shackleton, *South*[10]

One need only look to evolving work patterns and dependencies to appreciate the need for teamwork and groupwork. A quarter century ago, more work was accomplished by individuals working alone than is the case today. We are simply more dependent on other groups and people to accomplish our agendas. This dependency creates the need for people to understand how to (truly) work together. Working together is not "we are in the same location, and I do my work, you do yours"; rather, it is more of "my work is your work" and vice versa.

A successful team or group approach appears tantalizingly easy, yet nothing could be less true. Teams are more than collections of individuals who formerly worked independently and now work together. Their effective utilization requires a broad systems approach not only to the work itself but also to the organization within which the work is conceived and executed. The capable leader will analyze the work environment for correct employment of the team or group approach. In general, the default should be when teams are not needed, rather than when they are. Because of the synergy of teams, all creative, strategic undertakings benefit most from this approach. Teams can take many forms: large, small, long-term, short-term, and each has its own purpose. So, once having committed to the team approach, the leader then forms the team(s) to best suit the needs of the project or organization.

This section provides the background and principles around team formation that the leader must know to be her most effective in utilizing this powerful production process. Some considerations are in order as we proceed. First, team-based environments require special attention to human relations and morale. People are being asked to assume new and different responsibilities that can feel like additional work, perhaps without a financial incentive. The research tells us that money is not a productivity motivator, but recognition and appreciation are. The skillful leader will pay attention to HR concerns and be attentive to teams without micromanaging them. Second, as with many new initiatives, they are often "expensive now" but "cheap later." It is no different with teams: when learning the protocol, including the sometimes difficult task of working collaboratively, progress may seem slow. The attentive leader recognizes this phenomenon and knows that once the team reaches "steady state," this duality will dissipate. Third, the question often arises of how long it takes for the team to gel. The answer is: it depends. If the work is long-term, complex, or the relationships strained, months may elapse, depending on the methodology used to form the team. Later in this chapter, I discuss appropriate methodologies for getting teams off to a rapid and effective start.

The goals need to be clear, as do the life span of the team and its organizational fit (see the macro environment section below). Many teams will have limited task and time frames, and these limits need to be clear at the beginning. It is important to have ways to integrate the work of the team into the overall organizational structure. Too often teams "float alone," and their work is never truly acknowledged or assimilated into the overall organization.

Five questions to ask when using a team approach

Leaders considering the use of teams in government settings need to consider several questions before designing and launching a team-based effort.

1. ARE THE WORK TASKS INTERDEPENDENT; CAN THEY BE, OR SHOULD THEY BE? Trying to answer this question can be confusing at first because the work initially is being performed separately. In addition, potential team members who are skeptical of teams or unwilling to work with others may create all kinds of reasons why the work at hand does not depend on others for their success.[11] The EPA branch chief's employees believed they had no reason to interact, much less have mutual dependencies; they said their individual jobs were totally different, even though all were in the same branch. A long-standing culture of independence reinforced this belief. The MBTI preferences for sensing and intuition often apply here. Sensors may believe that the work is best left in its current, tried-and-true organization. Intuitives may imagine possibilities in new formations. Each may be right, which is why it is important to ask the question and answer it truthfully—which may require some thought and discussion. If it was apparent that the work tasks were interdependent, perhaps the team approach would have been tried a long time ago.

2. IS THE WORK SHORT-TERM OR LONG-TERM? Katzenbach points out that many high-functioning teams engage productively and at high-energy levels for a limited time because of the nature of the work and the excitement of the potential outcome.[12] In these short-term cases, the project itself may generate sufficient energy to motivate a group to form a team and conduct the work. The leader's task is to keep the group focused on the goal. Relationships and trust are not inessential, but they take a secondary role to the goals of the team. When the project is finished, the group disbands. If the project is likely to take a long time, however, the leader must give care to building relationships and trust, or the team will be unable to sustain itself as conflict and controversy arise—and they will. The lack of this foundation will endanger the team's work.

3. WILL THE PARTIES EVER WORK TOGETHER AGAIN? Trust and sound relationships are essential if the individuals on the team are likely to encounter one another in other groupwork situations, which are becoming more common. Interagency task forces may have two or more members from a cooperating organization, or a matrix approach may be implemented in a division. People could encounter each other in a variety of situations, and if the experience was negative or unproductive—in other words, no trust, poor relationships—in the first place, the second round will be worse. At a more global level, any agency seeking to use teams would do well to develop trust in the beginning and make sure everyone is on the same page with regard to group trust and group conduct.

4. WHAT IS THE NATURE OF THE RELATIONSHIP BETWEEN THE VARIOUS INDIVIDUALS? Warm, personal, and trusting relationships tend to endure. People in such relationships may disagree, but they know what to do to resolve their differences. Poor prior relationships will only endanger the work of the team(s) if not addressed at the beginning. If the situation is openly hostile, individual coaching and other activities may be warranted in addition to team development activities for the group. Individuals who perceive their relationships with others as "either/or" may need to be treated more directly,[13] transferred, or given other duties if not resolved.[14]

5. WHY SHOULD WE FORM A TEAM? This question is essential. In government, the overriding issues are flat budgets and the need for agency effectiveness. But an additional argument can be that we can actually do more! Eight branch chiefs that teamed up at a large federal agency found

Table 4.1 Six-box model

Organizational element	Definition
Purpose	Goals and vision of the team; how its work relates to the overall organization
Relationships	How we manage and coordinate the work of the team with the rest of the teams and the overall organization
Helpful mechanisms	Resources and organizational support systems
Rewards	How appropriate behavior is recognized and rewarded
Structure	How the work of the organization functions: time, tasks, physical space, work schedules
Leadership	Keeping the "boxes" in balance
Environment (a "seventh" box)	Everything else, including the way the organization relates to its external customers— in essence, this is not a "box" but a surrounding element

Source: Weisbord (1978). "Environment" may be considered as the box that contains all the other boxes and wider external forces. Weisbord does not list it as a "box," reserving that term for what takes place *inside* the organization.

that not only was their workload more bearable, but also their influence with higher management increased and some outputs actually went up—deadlines met sooner, better reports, and so forth. At a more individual level, the leader had better be ready to answer the "why" question before proceeding too far. Bear in mind, however, that additional benefits often emerge as the team does its work and the synergy takes over.

The macro environment

> *I never realized that I'd need to make so many other organizational adjustments to use the team approach. But once I did, things went even better. For example, the "Teamwork" award has been really popular and motivating.*
>
> —FEMA branch chief

Teams do not operate in an organizational vacuum. In fact, trying to do so is one reason teams fail. Only when the organization is in complete alignment with the work process will the work products be of the quality desirable and necessary for the future. Once the decision to employ teams is made, the diligent leader will give careful attention to the total organization and the processes within the organization that either support the team approach or are not harmonious with it and must be changed. For example, many federal agencies are geared toward supporting processes and systems that reinforce and reward individual effort. This culture encourages teamwork opponents to "ride out" the leader who dares to change the status quo. A leader can, however, ensure that the team approach becomes firmly ensconced in her organization. Following Weisbord, [15] she will find several leadership principles to which she can turn (see Table 4.1 on previous page). Called the six-box model, it is immensely useful as a framework for analyzing change.

1. Purpose. The leader (the word *leader* in this section refers to the overall leader of the organization or work unit; the team leader is discussed under micro issues) always clearly articulates the purpose of the team, its overall goals, the relationship of its work to the overall organization, and the congruence of goals if multiple teams are being used. Even the team name is important: Eschew names such as "Red Team" and "Team A" whenever possible, as they have a way of trivializing the team when the name could be a source of pride or dignity. Reminders from the leader about team goals are in order as well. The leader is aware of the team's progress and when it may require redirection. In addition, the leader keeps the overall agency work unit informed of the rationale for teams, how they will be deployed, and the goals they support. This information is written and posted in ways consistent with the agency's culture, for example, on a communal bulletin board.

2. Relationships. The leader orchestrates the management and coordination of the team(s). She ensures that teams do not work at cross-purposes, that they communicate with each other, that organizational processes support the teams, and that the teams appropriately interface with people and technology as necessary to carry out their work. She also gives attention to relationships within the team, whether the members are a group of peers or come from several organizational levels. With respect to the work at hand, teams are essentially groups of equals, which may require orientation for members used to a hierarchical environment. Supervisors and team leaders may require additional training from an expert in collaboration and conflict management. One easy strategy is to create cross-team groups that meet with

the leader regularly to inform her about how the teams are working and on what. As the teams become more sophisticated, the leader may not need to attend every meeting.

3. Helpful mechanisms/support systems. Overall organizational alignment dictates that the leader pays attention to the many subsystems within the unit that could either support or derail the team. The team may need a budget to promote its work, to rent rooms, hire facilitators and specialists, and create and copy reports. Performance evaluations (see rewards section) will need to be aligned with the responsibilities of group as well as individual accomplishment. Policies and procedures, such as permission for off-site activities, may need to be changed. The serious leader realizes that teams may not initially know what resources they need or that they will be provided. Sometimes the prevailing office space locations will need adjustment to accommodate the team, if the team members are not already in the same place.

4. Rewards. Are there incentives for all that needs doing? This element is critical because reward systems tell us about our performance and what is expected. Many organizations utilize teams extensively, but maintain individual performance as the standard for end-of-year evaluations. This practice effectively removes any incentive for the individual to cooperate in a team environment.[16] Are interim rewards or recognition provided for the work of the team? Is the team treated with respect and its work valued? People laboring in the relative anonymity of a cooperative environment still benefit from the reinforcement that may more regularly accompany individual effort. Is the team accorded safety in the work environment? In other words, is the leader making sure that people can feel free to speak up and do their best work; is status associated with the work of the team; do individuals have the same chances for advancement, increased responsibility, and other rewards? This element is not easy to address, although the adage "what gets measured gets done" would apply here. The individual performance evaluations "exceeds fully successful" or "outstanding" need special attention in a team environment so that recognition of individual accomplishments does not overshadow appreciation of group (team) work. This is the opportunity for the leader to identify special behaviors: "The work of the team is implemented and functions as a model for other teams."

5. Structure. How do the various structures of the organization support the work of the team? The leader decides what type of team is needed and al-

locates the workload of the team and its charge/goals (task structure), assures that the team has dedicated time and space to do its work, and manages potential areas of conflict that the team's work may engender, but most important, the leader assures that the work and needs of the team(s) are integrated into the overall organization, that the work of the team "fits" with the other work of the unit. It is in this domain that the leader ensures that the originating work unit of the team member understands the responsibility of this individual and facilitates arrangements for the unit's work to be done in the absence of the individual. The surest way to a dysfunctional team is to neglect the necessary work restructuring that must occur if the day-to-day work *and* the team work are to get done. Not addressing this problem is a common error, but one easily avoided with some thought and collaboration with employees. A city administration almost doomed the team approach by making two major mistakes: expecting team members to stay late to finish work that went undone while they attended team meetings and expecting other workers in the team member's department to attend to that person's work as well as their own. Strategic thinking and planning beforehand avoid these common errors.

6. Leadership. This box references the leader, who keeps all the boxes in balance. Any initiative benefits from the holistic view of this model, and the savvy leader is constantly reminding herself to pay attention to everything that is going on. In the end, it is the leader who manages all these boxes and enables the team to do its best work, unfettered by inappropriate disruption or internal snafus. We realize that practitioners will replace our general comments with specific actions; our purpose here is to provide an inclusive, guiding framework.

7. Environment. The environment box is the "everything else" box. In some ways it is not really a box because it surrounds the total organization. It manages the external environment for the team, including customers, suppliers, competitors, and regulators. For example, under a team approach, the formerly one-on-one meetings with customers may be replaced with the whole or part of the team participating in such interactions. External actors must then be made aware that decision making is now a diffused activity and that the people they deal with may change depending on which team member is acting as representative. Outsiders must be told that the team has full support, and the leader minimizes internal team management disruptions through boundary management, either intra- or interorganizationally.

Some words about culture and gender

> *I decided to use a team approach at my new office in Texas. We had used teams very successfully in Florida, and I was excited about the prospect. Imagine my surprise when I encountered resistance, even hostility! It was a tough road, and I learned a lot. We're doing OK now.*
>
> —NASA senior manager

Leaders, federal or otherwise, need to be aware of the culture of the organization before championing or adopting a vast team approach if one is not in place. The senior manager from NASA had experienced success with her teams, and it was her preferred method of operating. This enthusiasm was not initially shared at her new location. Simply barging in with the assumption that others will see it the way you do will not always gain goodwill. The careful executive assesses the organization's culture before taking the leap. For federal executives who change jobs on an average of every two years, this is sage advice. Adopting a team approach in your new organization should be addressed using principles of organizational change.[17]

As for gender, the early work by noted researcher and writer Carol Gilligan has been adopted by several writers who claim that there are real gender differences that will play out in egalitarian workplaces. Gilligan posited the "web" concept for the first time, introducing the managerial metaphor that has formed the basis of much recent writing about women's unique style. Basically, she suggests that life for women is circular and connected, rather than linear and autonomous, and the implications for organizational life are clear: men will wish to be alone at the top, valuing independence and fearing closeness; women will wish to be in the middle, valuing affiliation and fearing isolation.[18] Other writers claim that women's natural style gravitates toward a team, a connected approach. Pat Heim, author and consultant in the area of management and gender differences, characterizes this pull as women's desire to keep the organization "flat" rather than hierarchical.[19] These authors and others concede that one may also find women managers in hierarchical environments and men managers in team environments. The form should follow the function, and the main pitfall here is to default to our natural or preferred style, when the choice needs to be attuned to the situation. Our NASA manager happened to be a woman entering a predominantly male office, but she came from a mixed-gender office.

The micro environment

My role in the project was only to manage the relationships of the work team. Someone else managed the technical work. I made it clear from the outset that I would require as much autonomy for my role as the other manager did for his. I got it, and we came in early and under budget.

—A winner of the 2006 Federal Executive
of the Year Award and FEI participant

In addition to macro or organization-wide issues, the leader must attend to the internal dynamics of team functioning. The more attention the leader pays to the fine details of the team, the less he will need to worry about its work. In the work setting, this begins with the posture the leader takes with respect to teams. For example, initiating the use of teams involves familiarizing individuals in the organization with the unique responsibilities and opportunities of working in a collective environment. Certain "unlearning" may be in order, such as thinking that collaborative work is inappropriate and results in loss of professional identity. The leader may need to reassure individuals about this with visible evidence such as revised performance evaluations and changes in policy directives. Training and team monitoring may be needed until the team has reached "steady-state," particularly around roles and decision making. It is impossible to overestimate the value of this up-front work. A team with the firm foundation of trust coupled with strong relationships will outperform its less-prepared counterparts. This extra

Table 4 .2 Basic team definitions

Team element	Components
Membership	The kinds of people, groups, and viewpoints that should be represented on a team
Roles	The sets of constructive or destructive behaviors that help or hinder the team in its work
Teamwork	The team stages of sharing; levels of cooperative behavior
Team process	Activities necessary to start and then support the team over time

effort is worth it later. FEI participants spend the first full week of their four-week program building trust and forming relationships. Many of these groups are still active after years away from the institute.

The following features of teams can be found in other work on teams, although perhaps not all in one place and certainly not with applications to the public sector. The unique hire-fire restrictions, as well as the changes in leadership that often accompany changes at the political level in the executive and legislative branches, plus the complex external environment of the government executive, make attention to the details of teams even more crucial. The elements are summarized in Table 4.2 on page 111.

1. Membership. Team membership should be representative of the skills necessary but also provide a venue for general organizational contribution. Top-heavy teams may contribute less to the overall product than teams that are representative of all organizational levels, depending on the team's charge. On the Manhattan Project, Robert Oppenheimer would not have wanted a team representative of all organizational levels, and his approach might work well in agencies with a strong scientific focus, such as NSF, NIST, or NIH, or if the focus is senior management.[20] In many work units where the work is not strictly scientific, or the need is for work unit implementation of a policy, cross-representational teams function well and provide substantial side benefits. First, the team representatives are goodwill ambassadors to their work units, relieving management of the difficult task of "translation" when seeking to inform about the team's work. Second, the very act of representation serves to quell the voices of the office "disagreers"—indeed, seek to people your team with a cross-section of naysayers as well as supporters. Third, you as leader are automatically provided with a communication mechanism about what is going on back in the units. Representation takes many forms; better to have your potential adversaries or opponents under the tent rather than outside engaging in target practice.[21] In some cases, it may be useful to include contractors on certain teams and in certain activities. One agency took this approach because contractors were intimately involved in the agency's work and sat at desks in the same work space. To exclude these individuals would have meant losing valuable input and sacrificing some of the cooperative camaraderie that had grown up. If you are concerned about contractors being privy to certain internal functions, such as budgets, establish some ground rules. In this case, the contractors were aware of the contractor-sensitive issues and did not attend sessions that addressed them.[22]

2. Roles. Teams function differently from traditional, hierarchical organizations. As such, many members will be unfamiliar with what is essentially a "flat" structure. The team leader is not "the boss." [23] This is a situation in which the leader (you) needs to clarify this role with the team leader and the team itself. The role of team leader is a unique one and does not/should not involve actual authority over members of the team. The team leader coordinates, facilitates, convenes, serves as liaison with management, conveys information, and otherwise helps the team do its work. Employees unwilling to accept this should be left in less-obvious and less-harmful positions.

Because all teams have many functions that need fulfilling, the team roles may change over time and according to the situation. Again, as we move from a hierarchical, manager-centered formulation, the leader needs to be familiar with and to familiarize his teams with the various roles that each can/might play. There are several taxonomies, and two are discussed here as reasonably inclusive of the possible and necessary roles.

Creative, supportive, and administrative roles. All of these roles are essential to effective team functioning. During a team meeting, one person might play all of these roles, and all are essential for beneficial results. Creative behaviors include idea generation, suggestions that lead to addressing problems from different perspectives ("What would we do if we knew we couldn't fail?" "What if we had an unlimited budget?") and reframing ("Perhaps our problem isn't lack of resources, but poor deployment of resources."). Supportive behaviors are just that: cheering on an idea, thinking of ways to apply the idea, or generally boosting the team. Administrative behaviors help keep the team on track and include the people who serve as timekeepers, interface with other affected groups, keep the records, and handle communication. The team leader is responsible for making sure the behaviors occur, either naturally or through a format, and creating a "good" place for those agency "rebels" who are always questioning.

Task, relationship, and self-oriented behaviors. In this construct, only the first two are positive behaviors; the third refers to self-centered behaviors that undermine the team. Task behaviors include keeping the team on track, paying attention to the task, keeping time, and monitoring progress. Relationship behaviors are directed at keeping the team functioning on an emotional level, making sure everyone is included, that all ideas are heard, and that the well-being of the team members, not just its task accomplishment, are attended to. The Executive of the Year award winner essentially had this task as her full-time job for several months. It is the one to which the leader should pay the most attention because government employees are almost always task-oriented, not relationship-oriented.

Self-oriented behaviors are destructive, more directed at enhancing the person rather than furthering the work of the team, and they are lethal if not addressed early. Sometimes such individuals can be brought into the fold and sometimes they cannot. After a period of reasonable effort, perhaps involving individual work with the team member, the leader must make the hard decision: removal from the team or even the organization.[24]

3. Teamwork. The team is working toward higher and higher levels of collaboration, shown here in order from the first stage of sharing information to the most advanced stage of sharing power and decision making.

• Share information.
• Share ideas, jointly problem solve.
• Share resources.
• Share power, decision-making authority.

Initially, team members share information, an important first step. Many organizations have little internal knowledge about what others are doing and as a result perform at less than optimum levels. The extent of the knowledge in a room with ten team members is tenfold the individual, which, albeit a tautology, still bears repeating. This stage of the team (see orientation below) contributes to establishing trust and expanding the knowledge domain. Much has been written on team interpersonal processes, and it all begins with a "who am I, who are you?" kind of dialogue. At this stage, teams begin to engage in conversations and activities that give them a chance to "try their wings" in more complex situations. At FEI, we begin with sharing activities (for example, individual "Web pages," personal story-telling, and simulations) and then move to more challenging team projects.

Once trust and information sharing have been established, the next stage begins the real work of the team as it engages in creative activities and addresses the charge for which it was formed. At this stage the team synergy is formed, and approaches and solutions transcend individual input. The trust-building stage is the necessary precursor, however, as the environment must be safe for the creative energy to emerge. It is important to note that the stages of team development are often iterative. A more challenging activity may lead some members to revisit trust as the opportunities for conflict increase. The team is then reminded of its purpose, its ground rules, or norms, and, ideally, addresses the conflict or difficulty in an open fashion.

Sharing resources is a considerably higher level of team attainment as it indicates that the team has started to view itself as an entity, rather than a collective. The final stage, the apex, comes when power and decision making are shared. Every team member sees himself or herself as part of a whole, a whole that is larger than its parts. This level of trust is not insignificant. It means that each member of the team trusts the other members to act in his or her behalf and vice versa.[25] It also means that the team can function at full effectiveness when not every member is present. Given the complex and demanding nature of government work, this point is crucial. It is common for leaders to be called away at a moment's notice to deal with one of the many external stakeholders in its environment. Work cannot cease when this happens.

4. Team Process. There are several major team processes that, if followed, will increase trust, create positive relationships, and improve the success rate of the team.

Orientation. All teams need a formal orientation. It may be brief or extensive, but it needs to happen. Without it, the work of the team may be slowed and the full value of the group never realized. Orientation is usually the first meeting, at which the leader (of the organization or work unit) gives the charge, reaffirms the organizational goals that the team's work supports, outlines time and resource parameters, establishes meeting times, articulates arrangements for work coverage, and so forth. A NASA participant at FEI shared that she had taken the MBTI numerous times because her agency believes that any new team needs a formal orientation, including the preference profile of each member.

Then the team begins its self-management and trust-building, usually commencing with the establishment of team *norms,* the ground rules by which the team agrees to "live." They are generated by the team and can/should include: confidentiality, how time to speak will be shared, respect, active listening, and others the members decide to adopt. The norms provide a scorecard that the team can use to evaluate its behavior; when a norm is violated, the team usually will engage in some corrective behavior and a reaffirmation of the norm. It may be necessary to add to the list of norms over time.

A targeted trust-building activity also helps speed the team toward its work. Some groups use a communication instrument such as the MBTI, but many activities are available. They should match the expected duration of the team; in other words, a long-term team needs to spend more time on such matters than a team with a one-month deadline. The important thing is that such activities begin to build a separate *team identity,* which greatly improves team functioning and results. In a government bureaucracy, team identity can be invaluable. The branch chiefs who decided to work together as their own team greatly increased their work pride, energy, and output.

The orientation is a critical matter, and leaders should not omit this phase, but rather adjust the "front-loading" to the charge, importance, and duration of the team's work. Situations in which prior interactions have been strained require more intervention than groups that interact frequently. A professional facilitator often speeds the start of the team, and his services may be required throughout the process. It is a delicate process to facilitate a group and be part of the group as well, so using an "outsider" frees up all team members to interact fully. And, depending on the decision model of the group and the frequency or infrequency of its formal interaction, professionals may again save the group time. Any leader who has tried to facilitate his or her high-stakes meeting probably knows this all too well. Many government agencies have in-house facilitators who can be engaged through the HR department. If the group meets only once a month or so, each meeting will require some reorientation and reminding about norms, decision-making processes, and other agreements. In addition, if the subject matter is likely to be contentious, and/or the commitment of all team members is critical for implementation, outside professionals or serious attention to the foregoing are essential.[26] The National Coalition for Jail Reform, during its active years in the 1980s, engaged a professional from the American Arbitration Association to begin each semiannual meeting with a session on the consensus rule that the group agreed to as part of its norms. The work of the coalition was at once delicate, conflict-prone, and critical. This one protocol step allowed it to accomplish major reforms.[27]

One outcome of this phase (a norm, actually) should be the agreement that the team's work goes forward regardless of how many are in attendance. This norm not only encourages attendance, but also eliminates a common problem that many teams face—essentially "re-doing" their work every time they convene. This problem is a major cause of team disaffection and dysfunction and has the effect of allowing one person or a small number of people to "hamstring" the team. When the work moves forward, people stay engaged and the team stays productive.[28] But this norm cannot substitute for commitment to the team. The leaders must organize agency processes to accommodate the team schedule.

Ongoing assessment. Regular team assessments of team health, progress and protocol on task, and creative and administrative behaviors are necessary. Another approach could use the frame of task, relationship, and self-oriented behaviors and assess how they contribute to or degrade the life and work of the team. The norms developed in the first stage provide a useful barometer of the team's functioning. Occasionally, some type of conflict management or resolution will be necessary (see midcourse corrections below), or the team may simply need to validate its direction and work thus far. Given the structure of the federal workplace, it may be wise to build regular assessments into the team's schedule.

Midcourse corrections. Any number of problems may beset a team as it progresses: It may need new members; a member may leave, necessitating a skill check and recruitment; the charge may be altered; the working environment may change; the boss may be transferred; the time may quicken (or lengthen); or the decision-making process may break down. In the case of new members, or one less member, the operative concept is "new team." Whenever the composition of the team changes, the effect is essentially creation of a new team because the relationships and skill mix are different. A new, albeit brief, orientation for the team is in order. The norms may be affirmed rather than reconstructed, but the essential concept is that the team once again views itself as the unique entity that it is.

Certain midcourse strategies, such as "force field analysis" or conflict management training, may be useful tools for the team. In force field analysis, the team analyzes its present state of operations and then identifies driving and restraining forces that are keeping it in the present state, rather than in a more desirable future state—the completion of the team project.[29] Next, the group identifies the actions it can take to mitigate the restraining forces (a more productive strategy than increasing drivers that may already be at their maximum). For example, absences of critical team members may be slowing the work; the team may be meeting too infrequently and spending excessive time on catching up; some team members may lack the authority to speak for their work unit; there may be petty disagreements; the team may need additional training in how to use a consensus model; and so forth. At FEI, we argue that the midcourse correction is one of the most valuable tools a leader can use. After-action reviews have their place, but it is far more appropriate to stop the train from proceeding to the wrong station.

Decision making. In general, if long-term commitment to the decision is required for effective implementation and acceptance throughout the organization, the consensus rule works best. Majority votes are best used for short-term situations with no stakeholder impact. Unanimity is difficult to achieve under the best circumstances, though always worth a straw vote to check positions. The team can develop its own decision rules but needs to recognize that the intriguing speed of a majority vote in a contentious situation only creates winners and losers, the latter often feeling no compunction to support a decision they oppose.[30] So, consensus is time-consuming in the beginning and very speedy at the end. Consensus differs from unanimity in that the final decision may vary from the original proposition, but is one that the entire team can live with—an important consideration. The group polls its members, who identify the offending portions, and concessions, language adjustments, and additions are made until each person agrees not to dispute the decision. One of the most helpful parts of the consensus process is that the team is reminded of (and affirms) what its goals and outcomes are. This "eye on the prize" helps keep the group on track and softens the way to consensus.[31]

Team member contributions. Sometimes, team members do not all pull their own weight. A lack of effort may create resentment on the team and raise the possibility of inferior products because the team composition usually reflects the skill mix necessary for optimum results. This problem needs to be addressed even before the team starts its work, in the norm-setting stage. Assumptions need to be clarified, including queries such as "Will everyone here be able to fully participate? What will we do as a team if this is not the case?" The norms help create the space for the team to have a productive discussion if someone is not contributing. The ways to address this situation are too numerous for these pages, but include direct statements ("Mary, it appears that you're not going to be able to put in the time on this team. Would you like to recommend a replacement?") or a slightly more indirect approach ("As we write our final report, it appears that we are each going to need about fifteen hours to do this. Is there anyone for whom this is a problem? Would you like to still be listed as a 'contributing' member?"). A professional facilitator can help in this situation. Again, the possibility of nonparticipation reinforces the need for regular meetings and a reorientation time for each, however short. Otherwise, problems fester under the surface and can undermine a team's productivity just when it needs it most. Finally, the government leader needs to make her own preferences and positions clear.

Team communication. Each team needs its own communication strategy. However structured, the team needs to speak with one voice, which may require writing scripts for team members who report back to their groups or units, or the appointment of a single team spokesperson. It may require that all team members are present at certain larger meetings to reinforce the solidarity. Any question put to an individual member that the team has not addressed should not be answered but instead brought to the larger group. Regular and frequent communications are necessary, because when a group of people meets privately there is always great curiosity about what has transpired.[32]

Virtual teams

I never thought we could work together. Before this session I considered ____ our adversary, a force to be opposed, ignored, or neutralized—certainly not a partner with the same goals that I have. The trust we have established will help all of us do our jobs better. Now I look forward to the future.

—Virtual Team/Community of Practice participant at an FEI virtual team session

Home is where the site is.

—Jessica Lipnack and Jeffrey Stamps, *Virtual Teams*

Our rapidly evolving technological world requires that we address the virtual aspects of teams as well. Alternative worksites, long distance work, telecommuting, and regional or branch offices are now mainstream arrangements. New technology allows us to simulate a meeting environment that approaches an in-person model. Many forces drive the move to virtual teams or geographically dispersed teams. These forces include: the value of collaborative work, the importance of knowledge management, the necessity to include geographically dispersed members, and competitive forces active in getting the work done. In addition, the nature of government work and difficult budgets dictate cost-effective and time-sensitive ways to work together. One agency was able to maintain its services in the face of budget cuts by adopting a (more) virtual approach to what had been extensive travel schedules and costs. The time and money saved by this rethinking (and it was a major rethinking for an organization that relied, even thrived, on travel) more than compensated for the budget cuts. Many opposed this "new" approach, but clear heads prevailed, and now the virtual approach is central to its operations. Attention to basic principles, structure, and operating protocols will much improve opportunities for success and longevity in a virtual environment. The following provides a broad overview of how a team leader might utilize a virtual approach. Bear in mind that the steps, process, and organizational requirements are still necessary, albeit modified for the virtual environment.

The different kinds of virtual work include geographically dispersed management, individual projects (requiring group input), group projects, and community of practice teams. The latter is a group tied by common and critical interests, for example, the defense intelligence community, where acting individually could produce dangerously suboptimal results. The advantage of virtual work for government is that it allows agencies to reap the considerable benefits of more teamwork with individuals and groups who do not work near each other. In other words, through virtual team protocol, the government manager can implement teams throughout his organization and even across organizational boundaries.

1. Virtual team components. The components include virtual leadership (the leader is physically distant from the group); virtual operations/operating agreements (the team determines how it will function, for example, by teleconferences, videoconferences, or periodic in-person meetings, and how attendance/participation is structured); the team charter (the team norms, goals, outcomes—what the virtual group actually commits to—which is a fairly time-consuming activity); and the virtual team process (similar to the activities discussed above except that the members are dispersed).

2. Initiating the virtual team. Although the work of the team will be geographically dispersed, an initial face-to-face meeting is much to be desired. Trust- and relationship-building activities are best conducted in person. If the work of the team is highly sensitive, such as when FEI conducted virtual team building with representatives from different agencies in the defense intelligence community after 9/11, there really is no other way. At the initial meeting, team members get to know each other, affirm or reaffirm their individual, then collective visions and mission, and engage in the various activities that start to build trust. Confidentiality is particularly critical, as the team has only this opportunity to address it directly.

Because the face-to-face time of the team is so limited, this initial session becomes more crucial and the topics more diverse, as the team must also address potential derailers of the team, meeting schedules and protocol, and other issues that would be handled by nonvirtual teams in ongoing meetings.

It is at this initial session that the team charter or working agreement is developed. It is a statement of the group, its members, its internal name, and the things to which it has agreed, beginning with its purpose and its goals. Deciding the team norms and other operating principles and procedures are the next steps. The expected use of technology often results in training sessions using forms of groupware in which the members practice communicating electronically. Protocols for teleconferences can be developed. It is also during this period that participants can voice their hopes and fears about the team and its virtual nature. When members are face-to-face, the time is best used to set in place methods for the team's work.

3. Operational practices of the virtual team. In addition to the practices outlined above, the team also needs protocols for defining success, troubleshooting, conflict management, integrating new or additional members (including definitions of membership), recognition and rewards, and communications. Sustaining the work of the virtual team is more problematic than for on-site teams because the initiation and actual convening of a meeting can be cumbersome. In addition, the integration of the products of the team must be discussed so that all have ownership, make contributions, and receive appropriate credit. A virtual team can have spokespersons, as long as the team agrees on the products put forward.

If the virtual team spends sufficient up-front time on these issues, its work is much more likely to go forward than if these steps receive scant attention.

4. Technology. The technology available for maintaining virtual teams is excellent and continues to improve. At a general minimum, the teleconference works to keep all in touch, but chat rooms, private Web sites, virtual team buildings (with different "rooms" for different activities), and video teleconferences (VTCs) significantly enhance the work of the team.

Summary

The public sector executive has much to gain and nothing to lose by effectively implementing and utilizing a team approach. As the comments and examples here illustrate, this approach can be used in many settings. Some undertakings will be large and far-reaching, others more short-term and simply oriented. Basically, however, most work can be performed more effectively in a group setting. By careful attention to the guidelines and processes outlined here, the leader can assure that group/team activities are used appropriately and have the optimum possibilities for success. It is important for federal managers to pay close attention to the environment and approach team implementations strategically. Proper orientation activities; modifying organizational processes to more fully reinforce, support, and accommodate teams; midcourse correction, and adjustment of team process to fit the tasks and relationships at hand are all the duties of the leader. Properly attended to, the public leader will be effective in utilizing this style to the benefit of his or her organization and the American people. Diminishing budgets and increased public scrutiny demand that we do nothing less.

Tips for leadership success

- Be aware of the culture when implementing a team approach.
- If teams are new to the organization, utilize principles of change management.
- Analyze your rationale for teams; for example, is there task interdependence?
- Know whether the teams are short-term or long-term and adjust accordingly.
- Allow sufficient time for front-end activities of building trust and relationships.
- Be prepared to regroup as the team finds its way.
- Deal directly and immediately with those who would undermine the team process.
- Remember the answers are always in the team. It is one reason why leaders use them.
- Revise and adjust the organizational processes to support and reinforce teamwork.
- Be available to provide the team time and other resources.
- Allow time for midcourse corrections.
- Enjoy the increased output and effectiveness of your team approach!

Resources for further learning

Nancy J. Barger and Linda K. Kirby, *The Challenge of Change in Organizations* (1995). An explanation of reactions to change from the perspective of the

Myers-Briggs Type Indicator. Yields insight into how different types might respond to new initiatives, such as teams.

Leslie Bendaly, *Games Teams Play* (1996). Contains more than fifty games and exercises to help teams develop productive ways of working together.

William Bridges, *Managing Transitions: Making the Most of Change,* 2nd ed. (2004). Quite simply the best book on transition available. Essential in understanding human reaction to new initiatives.

Carol Gilligan, *In a Different Voice* (1982). The original volume on gender differences in group approaches and conduct.

Sally Hegelsen, *The Female Advantage: Women's Ways of Leadership* (1990). Studies of evidence and application of Gilligan's findings in the workplace.

Elizabeth Hirsh, Katherine W. Hirsh, and Sandra Krebs Hirsh, *Introduction to Type and Teams,* 2nd ed. (2003). Team building using the Myers-Briggs Type Indicator.

Jon R. Katzenbach and Douglas K. Smith, *The Wisdom of Teams* (2003). All around good advice and insight.

Patrick Lencioni, *The Five Dysfunctions of a Team: A Leadership Fable* (2002). Easy to follow with excellent framework and advice.

——— *Overcoming the Five Dysfunctions of a Team* (2005). Builds on the original work.

Jessica Lipnack and Jeffrey Stamps, *Virtual Teams: Reaching Across Space, Time, and Organizations with Technology* (1997). This is one of the fine books on virtual teams, with good overall explanations and assistance.

A. H. Maslow, "A Theory of Human Motivation," *Psychological Review* 50 (1943): 370–396. The original work on creating safe workplaces and the hierarchy of human needs.

Ernest Shackleton, *South* (1998). Reprint of Shackleton's 1914–1916 diary of his 600-day struggle to keep his men alive in the Antarctic and the teamwork required to do so.

Marvin R. Weisbord, *Organizational Diagnosis: A Workbook of Theory and Practice* (1978). Excellent (and still the best) reference on organizational functions. Essential to know when instituting organizational change.

John H. Zenger, Ed Musselwhite, Kathleen Hurson, and Craig Perrin, *Leading Teams: Mastering the New Role* (1994). Another helpful reference.

Notes

1. Ironically, the passengers on Flight 93 came together and functioned as a very high performing team for those brief and fatal moments.

2. This is not to ignore the very real institutional barriers that prevail in government and often make cooperation a difficult, if not impossible, process.

3. Katzenbach and Smith (2003).

4. Larry Smith, a former adjunct professor at FEI, with Harvard and Capitol Hill experience, created this useful construct. Teresa Spearman, former FEI Executive in Residence, frequently used the term *unlearnings* to identify what we need to stop doing to be successful.

5. One of the blessings (and curses) of the public sector and its bureaucracy is its ability to sustain itself independently of the individual, so that the nation's work is not subject to the vagaries of new hires and subsequent frequent or dramatic organizational and policy changes. The downside is that many practices become institutionalized and are hard to alter without considerable individual and group work.

6. Team development is not a journey for the timid. It is very tempting to start with the so-called "real work" rather than the relationships because the latter are often difficult to facilitate and the person may be met with resistance. This road is fraught with danger. Once on task, it is hard to get back to trust and relationships. Many retreats and off-sites stop at this point, with no foundation or tools for future unpredictable obstacles.

7. The MBTI, one of the most widely used preference instruments in the world, has myriad applications, including insights for leadership. Based on the theoretical work of Swiss psychologist Carl Jung and his U.S. followers, Kathryn Briggs and her daughter Isabel Briggs-Myers, it uses a detailed self-report instrument to identify innate preferences about perception, energy, and lifestyle. It is extremely useful not only for self-awareness but also for understanding others. Its value in team formation, communication, and maintenance is unparalleled.

8. The Myers-Briggs Type Indicator is excellent for teams. It is nonintrusive, yet addresses the strengths and blind spots of the group, provides an excellent structure for problem-solving (type dynamics) and in general gives the team a common language for talking about itself and to each other. It is not highly "personal" and avoids the suggestion of intimacy about teams that is off-putting for some.

9. See Hirsh et al., 2003, for a thorough and insightful approach to understanding and applying type to teams.

10. Possibly the greatest work on leadership and the team approach ever written. *South* was Shackleton's diary for the fateful attempted Antarctic crossing of 1914–1916.

11. An organizational culture that has emphasized competition as a way of enhancing productivity will be especially taxed to embrace a cooperative approach.

12. Katzenbach and Smith (2003).

13. This was the case for two individuals at the Department of Transportation. Each defied and undercut the other, and they refused to work cooperatively. Eventually, all that remained for the supervisor was a coercive approach, which he used. Each individual's performance evaluation was partially dependent on how their partnership functioned. This strategy achieved the short-term results the supervisor wanted: they grudgingly cooperated. Eventually, one of the individuals left the agency.

14. Lencioni (2002) observes that sometimes it is necessary to invite people to leave the team, or—as in the case of the senior leadership team of the company in the book—the organization. It is always a difficult decision because in the short term the group is affected adversely. Most leaders who employ this last-resort strategy are pleasantly surprised by the team's acceptance. They saw it coming too.

15. Weisbord (1978).

16. One government agency, seeking to use teams more effectively in a contentious and competitive office environment, was advised to incorporate team cooperation and behavior into the annual employee performance reviews. The manager demurred, claiming that the evaluations would then "not be useful in other jobs." The group is still contentious and uncooperative.

17. The work of Bridges (1984) is always relevant here. Moving from an individual to a team approach can invoke the same sense of loss and identity and require the same kind of adjustment process that accompanies other organizational changes. Move forward but tread carefully.

18. Gilligan (1982).

19. Heim (1994).

20. Oppenheimer's leadership of the Los Alamos team is legendary for his genius in managing the egos and motives of a disparate group of gifted scientists. His story is probably most instructive for managing elite teams.

21. A city administration made effective use of the "big tent" strategy by including (at the facilitator's insistence) opponents as well as supporters of a controversial initiative they sought to implement. Almost by dint of their inclusion, the opponents (after some initial de rigueur posturing) became staunch supporters and were of immense assistance in garnering administrationwide support.

22. This is where an early affirmation of public service values can help career employee and contractor alike in understanding the purpose of the team and its work.

23. A federal agency using a team approach mistakenly appointed an individual as team leader who refused to accept that in this role he was not the boss. The team required many hours of intervention because this particular person was unable and/or unwilling to relinquish control. The better choice for this intractable individual would have been removal. As it turned out, the team never achieved its potential, and its resentment of the leader never abated. His retirement brought many sighs of relief.

24. A Federal Highway Administration team member consistently degraded the team and its members. The team functioned well when he was absent. At two off-sites (the second being necessary only because of his lack of cooperation and an unfortunate way to spend taxpayer dollars), the rest of the team finally gave up on converting him into a committed team member and developed strategies to isolate him. It was a suboptimal approach, perhaps, but one that let the other, high-performing team members maintain their energy and organizational commitment. He finally left and was never missed.

25. Some elected (and other) groups with low trust never move out of the "committee of the whole" into subcommittees because no one trusts a subunit to act on their behalf. It is a cumbersome yet common phenomenon.

26. Each team member brings a set of KSAs (knowledge, skills, and abilities) to the effort. In addition, they bring presuppositions, attitudes, and concerns about the work of the team. Ignoring these in the process stage creates deeper problems in the decision-making and implementation phase.

27. For example, the membership ranged from the American Civil Liberties Union to the Sheriff's Association and the National Association of Police Chiefs—not groups that normally interact, much less see eye-to-eye. Yet they agreed on many positions in their work with the coalition and achieved necessary reforms in the nation's jails.

28. A federal training facility that was using cross-functional teams for the first time encountered this problem repeatedly. At each meeting the (essentially) new membership would revisit decisions and change them, resulting in virtually no progress. A subsequent team, seeking to not make the mistakes of the past, adopted the "go forward" position as one of their ground rules, and the team performed at a very high level.

29. From the work of Curt Lewin, force field analysis is a powerful tool in many settings.

30. This model in effect allows team members to go back to their units and undermine the group decision unless the team agreed to support every decision. Usually, with voting, the true attitude of the minority comes out in unproductive ways, such as "this is what *they* decided."

31. It is helpful at every meeting to reaffirm the team goals, verbally, using a timeline or whatever device helps keep members centered. Team members have other responsibilities, and this reminder helps people focus on the work at hand.

32. Ben Bissell, a noted change management authority, used to comment that in the absence of information, people simply make up their own—with the concomitant clean-up problems for the team because denying a negative is practically impossible.

5 Building high-performance organizations

JOHN W. PICKERING, PRESIDENT, COMMONWEALTH CENTER
FOR HIGH-PERFORMANCE ORGANIZATIONS

*Knowing is not enough, we must apply. Willing is not enough,
we must do.*

—Goethe

THIS BOOK IS ANCHORED IN THE FACT that trust is the product of relationships—relationships between individuals, between top management and the entry-level workforce, and between citizens and government. Consider, however, the following two situations. You are the top manager of a large Navy industrial facility that must improve performance dramatically or be closed. To accomplish this, you have to downsize the civilian workforce by half or more and set aside years of tradition to change production processes. And you must do so while dealing with multiple unions. Or you have just become city manager in a medium-sized eastern city. The city council is supportive but is pushing for the city to be more responsive to rapidly evolving public needs for services and the public's demand for more participation in decisions. At the same time, however, you have inherited a set of senior managers focused exclusively downward into their own units; the mindset of the organization is largely "stovepiped"; it's "our unit first and the heck with everyone else." These are real scenarios faced by managers in organizations we have worked with over the past thirty years. How do you build and maintain trust in situations like these? Managers will often say, "I have a technical background! No one prepared me to deal with this kind of challenge!"

Such reactions supply the departure point for this chapter, which distills lessons found in the literature and applied practice base from the fields of organizational development, change management, and process improvement

Copyright © 2007 Commonwealth Centers for High Performance Organizations; text
and figures used with permission.

to produce a handy roadmap leading to higher performance. Our approach—which we call the high-performance organizations (HPO) diagnostic/change model—assumes that (1) after years of observation, federal, state, and local government and nonprofit organization managers and employees are experts on their own organizations; but (2) they may not have been exposed to an extensive organizational theory background and so need a framework to effect change; and (3) they want to be part of a positive change process, continually driving their organizations toward becoming higher performing organizations.

The HPO diagnostic/change model

The high-performance organization diagnostic/change model was developed in the early 1990s and has been evolving ever since, as we work with organizations. The academic theory and applied lessons from well-run organizations that underpin the model are not new. They are loosely based on the causal model of Rensis Likert, a pioneer in organizational behavior; author and researcher Marvin Weisbord's six-box model; McKinsey Company's Seven S model; and others in the management literature.[1] The model has been refined and expanded over the years, based on our work with scores of federal, state, and local government organizations, nonprofit agencies, and a few private sector entities. The HPO model (see Figure 5.1) is a classic systems model—input, throughput, output, feedback. Inside the model, it moves from the three *conceptual* change levers of leadership, vision, and values, through the three *applied* levers of strategy, structure, and systems, to impact organizational performance. There is also a feedback loop to our organization's environment, which is critical to secure the support of those outside the organization for our continued efforts to improve performance.

To make the model more "diagnostic" in nature, we later added seven key diagnostic questions (KDQs) to integrate with the model's six change levers:

1. What is high performance for us?
2. How would we know if we were high performing?
3. According to whom are we high performing?
4. Why do we need to be high performing?
5. Is what we are doing the right "what"?
6. How good are we at delivering our products and services?

Figure 5.1 The high-performance organization diagnostic/change model

Key: CL = change lever KDQ = diagnostic question

7. How are we going to treat each other, our partners, our customers, and our stakeholders?

The interaction between the KDQs and the change levers produces a thought process and roadmap for improvement. One final point: the black box surrounding the model represents the organization, but when we ask managers or employees to name their organization, they are confused. Do we mean their immediate unit, their branch, division, or their larger organization? The answer, naturally, is yes. They need to apply the model and the KDQs to themselves personally, to their immediate unit, to the intermediate units above them, and to the organization as a whole. Then they need to ensure alignment or "nesting" of the answers to the KDQs at each level of the organization, one into the other.

The seven key diagnostic questions

One way to understand the model is through the seven key diagnostic questions that can help an organization evaluate its foundational assumptions and causal reasoning. These KDQs can lead an organization to define more completely the work required in each of the change levers. This chapter examines each of the KDQs in considerable detail as well as several change levers.

KDQ 1: What is high performance for us?

Members at all levels of an organization must agree on the answer to KDQ 1—for the organization as a whole, for their individual units, and for themselves. Without agreement, individual members of the organization, acting alone and in isolation, have little chance to accidentally arrive at a common understanding of what high performance is or how to achieve it. If individuals, units, and the organization as a whole are not aligned on what high performance is, then no matter how talented or committed the individual members are, the organization will be unlikely to achieve the outcomes and impacts it seeks. Yet, from the way many organizations operate, this appears to be exactly what they believe will happen. They seem to be saying: "Hire good people, let them figure out on their own what high performance is for them, and then start off in that direction." Instead, organizations that want to begin moving toward higher performance must establish a collaborative process for articulating and sharing a common organizational vision of what high performance is, for creating nested visions indicating how each unit fits into the whole, and for aligning individual members in the organization with these nested visions.

It is, moreover, not enough for an organization to define high performance as just "wanting to be the best"—especially if it is the organization, acting alone without customer participation, that gets to define what best means. Consider the all too common mistake made in the apocryphal story about the dog food factory that wanted to make the best dog food in the world and hired the world's foremost experts to produce excellent (in their view) dog food. There was only one problem: dogs would not eat the food. In this respect, our use of the term *high performance* appears to be similar to what leadership researcher and writer Jim Collins means by the term *great* in his book *Good to Great*.[2] It is possible to be merely good, maybe even the best among a mediocre lot of competitors, but it takes substantially more to be great or, in our language, high performance.

KDQ 2: How would we know if we were high performing?

Organizations seeking high performance must, as a part of understanding what high performance is, address a second question: And how would we know if we were high performing? This question implies a system of measurements that will let us know if we are moving in our intended direction. I want to emphasize, however, that this is the *second* question, not the first. We have seen some organizations trying to implement a performance measurement process without first agreeing on what high performance is.

We often run an in-class exercise to illustrate that most people have a pretty good intuitive notion of what high performance looks like, in other words, a generic definition of high performance. We point out that they have experienced organizations all their lives and that each of these encounters—whether a good experience or a bad one—adds to their notion of what high performance in organizations means. To help them uncover these sometimes unconscious attitudes and beliefs, we select a type of organization, for example, a laundry/dry cleaners, and ask participants what they think high performance means in this example.

Immediately, participants begin yelling out things like: "I want my clothes back; I want them clean; on hangers with light starch; no broken buttons or crushed lapels. . . ." Others say: "I want them to treat me in a friendly and respectful way; I want the laundry close to where I work or live; I don't want to take vacation time to go to the laundry—they need to be open when I'm not at work; they need to handle problems well; I don't want to have to go to the manager to get satisfaction; the first person I deal with should be able to handle the issue." Eventually, someone says: "And I want it at a competitive price; I don't want to have to pay the price of the shirt to get it back!"

At this point, we ask: "So who were you in this exercise?" They answer: "The customer." So then we ask: "What if you are a residential neighbor of the laundry? Would your ideas of what high performance means change?" The answer: "Absolutely: I want it quiet, and 'green,' and good at handling traffic, and clean, and well-designed. . . ." Finally, we ask: "What if you were a long-term investor in the laundry; would your definition of high performance change again?" Again, the answer is: "Sure. Now I want profit!" When we explore what produces profit, we find that the laundry needs to be good at generating revenue and minimizing costs. Few of our participants would agree that generating profit is the primary objective of the public/nonprofit sectors; rather, most would say that accomplishing the mission is the primary objective. On the other hand, if we look at the causal sequence involved in achieving these objectives, we see that things are not so different as they seem in these two different worlds: the business world would say they need to focus on serving customers to generate revenues and on minimizing costs to generate a profit, and the public/nonprofit sectors would say they need to generate revenues and minimize costs to accomplish the mission. As a result, we can use many private sector approaches, thought processes, and tools in the public sector; we just have to recognize that the ultimate objectives are different in the two worlds.

Out of the laundry exercise, the class generates a generic definition of high performance, which includes the following factors:

Factor 1: Quality of products and services (meeting the wants, needs, and expectations of the customers)

Factor 2: Outstanding customer value (satisfaction, responsiveness, service, timeliness, convenience, courtesy, competence of staff, problem resolution)

Factor 3: Sound financial performance (generating revenue, minimizing costs, good business model, efficient systems)

These generic factors are common in almost every organization we work with and can produce a lively discussion of whether a unit/department/organization can define and measure these factors as they relate to the specifics of their situation. The three factors are not mutually exclusive—that is, when we are talking about one of them, it almost always overlaps one or both of the other two factors. Let's explore each of these in more detail.

Factor 1. Quality of products and services requires a focus on the customer's wants/needs/expectations and on the organization's support systems/work processes—two very different perspectives that result in two different dimensions of quality. The first dimension is a focus on the customer and requires that we produce products and provide services that meet the customer's wants, needs, and expectations. Moreover, it demands that enough interaction take place between the supplier and the customer to ensure that a clearly defined agreement exists about what will be delivered. We call this dimension design and features quality. Visualize it as a vertical scale with the bottom labeled "modest design and features quality" and the top labeled "complex design and features quality." Using a car analogy, think Corolla-level features—outstanding fit-and-finish, repairability, and reliability, but modest design and features, compared to Lexus-level features—all the same features as Corolla, but offering more complex design and features. This does not mean the Corolla is a poor choice. It simply has fewer features and therefore costs less. What is appropriate—Lexus, Camry (the mid-point on the scale), or Corolla—is a decision for purchasers based on their needs, preferences, and budget (see the vertical scale in Figure 5.2).

If we deliver too low on the design and features quality dimension, we will have dissatisfied customers, who are likely to complain that we are delivering poor quality. On the other hand, if we deliver too high and try to

Figure 5.2 The definition of quality

charge the customer for the additional features, we will again have dissatisfied customers, who could say we are forcing them to accept excess features
they do not want to pay for and accuse us of trying to bait and switch, running up the bill, or gold-plating. If we exceed their wants/needs/expecta-
tions and do it for free (that is, at no additional cost to the customer), we
may have delighted customers, but we also run the risk of inflating our customers' expectations beyond our ability to deliver in the future. And we may
be providing more complexity than our customer wants, needs, and/or expects, leading them to describe our products or services as cumbersome, not
intuitive, or too hard to use.

We may want to make the business decision to add features we know a
customer wants and not charge them as a way of cementing a relationship or
seizing market share, but we need to clearly understand the implications of
doing so. It is critical to reach agreement on the level of design and features
quality the business is going to deliver (or, if multiple levels are required for
varying customer needs, then the agreement is around when to deliver each
level). To leave it up to each individual is to invite the delivery of a full spectrum of products and services varying from poor design and features quality
through gold-plating, most not pleasing the customer and potentially wast-
ing resources. One way to do more with less is to stop gold-plating and apply
the saved resources to increased production. We will revisit this dimension of
quality when we discuss KDQ 5: Are we delivering the right "what"?

The second dimension of quality is execution quality. It reminds us of the
work of W. Edwards Deming, Joseph M. Juran, and others in the world of

"quality" programs (for example, Quality Circles, Total Quality Management, and today's LEAN/Six Sigma in manufacturing).[3] This dimension requires us to have excellent execution quality, defined as the ability of the organization to perform flawlessly a best-practice process. We must also be as near flawless as possible in our planning, design, engineering, and production processes and in our people training and development, procurement, contracting, facilities, and other support systems.

We can visualize execution quality as a horizontal scale, running from left to right, with the left end of the scale labeled "poor execution quality" and the right end as "excellent execution quality" (Figure 5.2). The two questions to ask ourselves about our organization on this scale are: Do we have the right process (best-practice processes for delivering the design and features required) and are the processes being done right? (is there excessive rework, scrap, warranty?). If our processes are not best-practice, we would have a high cost of compliance; in other words, doing an inefficient process perfectly is still inefficient. If, however, we have a best-practice process but execute it poorly, we would incur the high cost of *non*compliance because doing a best-practice process poorly is also inefficient. If we were delivering excellent execution quality, we would be running the appropriate best-practice processes in a near flawless way. Another way to do more with less is to move to the excellent (right) side of this dimension. We will revisit this discussion of "How good are we?" briefly under KDQ 6.

Factor 2. Customer value in the HPO model has to do with the relationship side of our interaction with customers, citizens, and others. Recall in the laundry example that seminar participants said, "I want them to treat me well; I want the laundry located close to where I live or work; I don't want to take vacation time to go there." What if the laundry owner was to give us back perfect clothes and then insult us as we walked out the door? The quality was perfect, but the relationship was not, and it is the relationship part that constitutes customer value. Customers will use terms such as *dependable, reliable, convenient, responsive, satisfying, fast,* and *pleasant* to describe their desires on this factor. The problem here is that one size does not fit all; instead, each customer selects from this market basket of items those she desires, and the supplier needs to figure out what items they are and deliver them.

Before we can do this analysis, we need to identify our current and future customers, understanding that they come in lots of different flavors (especially in the government world) and that they often have conflicting wants, needs, and expectations. We address how to do this analysis when we get to KDQ 3: According to whom?

Factor 3. Financial performance relates to our ability to generate revenue, minimize our costs, evaluate profitability, generate accurate contract estimates and winning bids, and justify our investments. Doing this analysis in the public sector can be difficult. Historically, government organizations have focused primarily on design and features quality and not on execution quality, customer value, or financial performance. Indeed, in many cases, the government's financial management systems (budgeting, procurement, contracting, and so forth) have not been designed to provide units with the information they need to make sound financial decisions. Think of the messages these systems send to us: "Here's your allowance to run your program—we really don't care what you need; this is all you get. It's based on what you got last year plus or minus a little, depending on economic conditions and administration priorities. Don't overspend your allowance (but the numbers are always late to you, so you won't really know how you're doing). Don't underspend your allowance, or you'll lose it and get less next time. And don't steal a nickel of it." But, by implication, you could waste a billion of it! Rarely do we see a demand that a unit demonstrates that it is best-practice, that it has a sound business model, that its causal model has been tested, and that it can show that it produces the mission's desired outcomes. To be fair, at the federal level the Government Performance Results Act (GPRA), OMB's Program Assessment Rating Tool (PART), and the President's Management Agenda are efforts to improve the system, but much more needs to be done—especially at the unit level of organizations.

In the HPO model, high performance is defined as the simultaneous delivery of all three of these elements—quality products and services, outstanding customer value, and sound financial performance. We call the simultaneous delivery and continuous improvement of these factors "Pick 3," and because we want these three factors to be delivered over time, the expectation is really Pick 3+, where the plus is consistent and sustainable performance over time. It is a rare organization that performs at the Pick 3+ level.

Over the years, we have worked with many organizations that have performance metrics, but often they are not capable of answering the most fundamental questions: What are we trying to achieve (our desired outcomes and impacts) and how would we know if we were? Organizations tend to measure what is measurable, which can translate, especially in the public sector, into a focus on activities and tasks, intended to demonstrate compliance with legislation or regulations—to show to Congress, the city council, or the public that work is being performed (a focus on activity). We would argue that high performance in the public/nonprofit sectors translates into mission accomplishment at a level defined by the organization's vision (a focus on outcome).

KDQ 3: According to whom are we high performing?

The third KDQ requires us to do a thorough analysis of the environment outside the black box from Figure 5.1. The box represents us: our unit/ department/organization. The environment includes customers and other stakeholders who can affect us as an organization. In the public and nonprofit sectors, the concept of customer appears to be more complex than in the private sector. Customers certainly include those who use the products and services we produce (our beneficiary chain customers), but they also include our food chain customers (those who provide us with funding and/or policy direction), our partners (people and entities inside and outside our unit/organization with whom we must work to produce value for our beneficiaries), and our competitors (those with whom we can or do compete). In addition, customers include stakeholders who do not belong in the preceding categories, but who can influence us in sometimes positive, but more often, potentially negative ways. They include the press, regulatory agencies, investigative entities such as inspectors general, and the Government Accountability Office. The power of this analysis, referred to as strategic customer value analysis (SCVA), is that we are now able to see where overlaps and conflicts exist between what one beneficiary customer or funding source wants/needs/expects and the desires of others. Figure 5.3 places these actors into a graphic display, showing the interactions between *us* and the various flavors of *them*.

In addition to understanding where we are today relative to customer expectations, KDQ 3 often leads us to develop a more collaborative relationship with our customers, for it is not only important that we understand their wants, needs, and expectations today, but that we understand what their requirements are likely to be in the future. If we are to remain high performing, we will need to build strategies that increase our value to our customers over time and that will deliver the outcomes required by our vision and mission.

Figure 5.3 Strategic customer value analysis (SCVA)

KDQ 3. According to whom are we high performing?

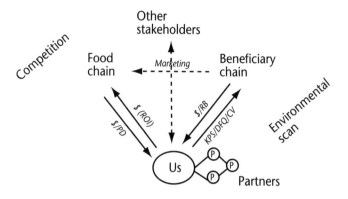

Key: $ = Money; PD = Policy direction; ROI = Return on investment; RB = Repeat business;
KPS = Key products and services; DFQ = Design and features quality; CV = Customer value;
P = Partners

KDQ 4: Why do we need to be high performing?

The fourth KDQ gets at a critical factor in successful change efforts: the issue of organizational energy to sustain our improvement efforts over time. What if we cannot answer this question to the satisfaction of our workforce? Employees will not support the change effort for the time required for our performance to improve. If the literature on large-scale organization change is correct in saying that sustained effort is required for five to seven to ten or more years to achieve lasting organizational change, then we will need to tap a variety of energy sources. University of Michigan professor Noel Tichy, former GE organization development adviser, argues that all of us need to develop a "teachable point of view"—a succinct, personal, and compelling set of arguments capable of being delivered with passion to ourselves, our coworkers, our subordinates, and others reminding us of the importance of improving our performance.[4]

When we ask participants why their organizations need to be high performing, nine times out of ten the first answer will be some version of "threat to our survival"; in other words, we'll lose to our competitors; our citizens will be dissatisfied and elect a micromanaging council; we'll be outsourced. So when we ask, "A threat to your survival is an energy source?" the response is a resounding "of course!" But what kind of energy source is it? It is negative energy. And if an organization is under threat to survival for a long period of time, those employees who can leave do so to escape the stress, while others hunker down and seem to say "kill me, already." This drop in morale leads to lower, rather than higher, performance over time. We have described threat to survival as a "short-term, nonrenewable energy source." So what else is available as an energy source?

The second reason for needing to be high performance is self-pride: "I need to be part of something high performing just because I need it for me." When asked if this one is a renewable energy source, the answer is yes. But when asked if self-pride can be injured by the organization, the answer is again yes. The good news, based on our experience, is that even when self-pride has been injured, most people will come back to us when allowed to experience self-pride again.

These two sources can be used in almost any kind of organization, but pressing our participants, I often ask: "So you're telling me there's no difference between the mission of your organization and that of a tobacco company?" Now, many private sector firms have moral purposes equivalent to public/nonprofit sector organizations: Johnson & Johnson is a good example. But the one energy source that the public/nonprofit sectors generally have in abundance is higher moral purpose. It matters whether we are high performing or not because the missions we have are critical to society. When I ask why I had to work so hard to discover this energy source, many participants will respond that they don't talk about it out loud, but it's what keeps them doing what they're doing. When I ask participants if their organizations use this energy source effectively, some say yes and can explain how, but most generally say no, we could do better.

KDQ 5: Is what we are doing the right "what"?

The fifth KDQ begins to integrate the thinking and analysis done to this point into a more concrete set of specifications. We saw this question earlier when we were discussing design and features quality (see the vertical scale in Figure 5.2). To be able to answer this question effectively we must engage the following more specific questions:

- What are/should be our key products and services (KPS) to meet the wants/needs/expectations of our customers—now and in the future?

- Are we providing our products and services to the right customers? If we have the right products and services, but the wrong customers, maybe we should fire some customers and get some new ones? On the other hand, if we have the right customers and wrong KPS, then we need to change the products and services. Are we *effective* in serving our customers?
- Do we produce excellent customer value, according to the beneficiary chain, food chain, partners, and other stakeholders?
- What is or should be our organization's unique niche? (To answer this one it is helpful to ask: Who would miss us if we were gone?)
- What should we take responsibility for accomplishing in the near term (next three to five years) and the longer term (ten to thirty years)? What is/should be our major impact or outcome goal?
- How do these efforts contribute to achieving our larger vision—our definition of high performance?

The product of this particular effort is clarification and revision of our core purpose and reason for being—essentially we must confirm, revise, or construct our mission and unique niche. An example comes from the U.S. Environmental Protection Agency's Office of the Inspector General. Historically, the purpose of the IG had been to ensure that the agency complied with law and regulation and that efforts were undertaken to prevent fraud, waste, and abuse. While important, the inspector general and her staff realized that these activities were insufficient. Greater emphasis was needed on the intention of Congress in establishing these laws. Results (outcomes/impacts) mattered. Effectiveness mattered, and to that extent the IG's office refocused its efforts on making a contribution to the improvement of the environment and human health. Compliance to law and regulation was necessary, but mindless compliance that produced no outcome/impact benefits was also wasteful. To address this new emphasis area, the IG established the Office of Program Evaluation to determine whether EPA's programs would result in the impacts and outcomes intended, even if all the statutory and regulatory directives were executed perfectly.

KDQ 6: How good are we at delivering our products and services?

We looked at the sixth KDQ when we were discussing execution quality (see the horizontal scale in Figure 5.2). Are we as *efficient* as we can be in delivering our main products and services? Do we have the right business strategy (business model) and organizational structure? Are our systems and processes best-practice and executed flawlessly? Note that the last three items mentioned here (strategy, structure, and systems) are the three applied change levers in the HPO model (see Figure 5.1).

Let's begin by looking at our overall business strategy/business model. If we were a small business making a pitch to the bank to secure a loan, we would need to lay out a convincing argument that we really know our business, that our business model is robust—that it will work no matter what economic or other conditions we encounter—and that we have considered whether we should do all the work ourselves versus outsourcing or partnering. Do you recall People Express Airlines, the first of the low-cost airlines? It had great values, was a fun place to work, and *Harvard Business Review* couldn't write enough case studies about it. But here was their business strategy, their niche: low cost vacation travel. Not a robust enough strategy, as it turns out. Let me add one main word and a connector word to that strategy statement: low cost *business* and vacation travel. So, now what airline are we talking about? Southwest. How are they doing? They modified the strategy of People Express into a robust business strategy and then delivered flawlessly. In the business strategy/business model area, we might want to ask ourselves the following more specific diagnostic questions:

- If our strategy/business model is the very same one that got us here, is it capable of getting us to the next level as well? Will it allow us to effectively and efficiently accomplish our vision, mission, and strategic goals?
- What is our competitive advantage based on?
- Do we know our key business functions? Do we need to close out some business lines to better align with our future direction and to generate resources to fund new initiatives?
- Do we have a sound approach to strategic outsourcing decisions? How do we handle "surge" demand and/or surplus production capacity?
- Can we explain our key business assumptions and our causal model for getting results?

The next factor for examination is organizational structure. We need to evaluate our current structure and change it if we believe a different organizing principle would allow us to fulfill our vision and strategy. Most organizations we work with have inherited a stovepiped structure from their industrial model past, so examining structure might be threatening to the established order. Specific diagnostic questions we may want to ask in the structure area are:

- Is our structure sophisticated enough to perform our work? Or should we explore more complex structure models, including matrix, business centers, process/product focused structures, and so forth?
- Have we broken our work down correctly so as to most efficiently deliver our products and services? Are cross-cutting projects and processes under control; in other words, do we have a clearly accountable project/process owner? This is particularly critical when multiple organizational stovepipes are involved.
- Have we provided for the integration of the parts of the organization to produce a seamless higher-level whole?

Finally, we must review each of our support systems and work processes. What we are looking for here is an assessment of the extent to which the systems and processes aid us in improving our performance. Too often, we assume that these systems and processes are givens and that we can do little to improve them. This assumption may sometimes be true, but before accepting that, we would want to seriously test our ability to affect them. In some organizations I have contracted with, it takes two hours to secure the contract, while in others it takes two *years!* Why the difference? The answer is that some organizations have found ways of complying with the Federal Acquisition Regulations while making the acquisition system serve their end values—they have improved performance dramatically by aligning the support systems and work processes with their vision. The systems and processes we would want to assess are our:

Support systems. These include human resources, financial management, procurement, contracting, information technology, facilities and equipment, communication, legal services, vehicle maintenance, and research and development laboratories. If these groups are not at their peak form, people in the organization will not believe that improvement is being taken seriously. We find that improvements in support systems speak louder than any other action an organization can take in making employees believe that management means what it says.

Work processes. Do we have best-practice work processes tailored to the appropriate design and features quality level delivered flawlessly? Are we continuously improving? If necessary, can we reengineer a process from the ground up?

Work management and control processes. Does every member at every level of the organization have the systems and skills to monitor and take appropriate corrective actions on our key success factors?

In the Navy's industrial facility mentioned at the beginning of this chapter, they had to work all seven Key Diagnostic Questions, but the two that drove most of the improvement were KDQ 6: How good are we? and KDQ 7: How do we treat each other and our customers? We will address the second of these below, but in the "how good are we" area, they had to reinvent how naval shipyards performed ship modernization projects. They introduced the discipline of project management and established a project-management college to prepare the workforce; installed matrix management and built an integrated top leadership team (see more in the "Tips" section below); and renegotiated an international labor contract to allow the use of cross-trained work teams to complete most of the work on the ships. The shipyard turned a $20 million "profit" on the first ship modernization completed under the improvement process, and, over a three-year period, this yard became the Navy's number one performer.

KDQs 1–6: Addressing the first six key diagnostic questions using the HPO model's visioning change lever

An organization's vision work is, perhaps, the most time consuming of all the change levers. During it, the organization has to deal with six of the seven KDQs. It is important to understand that vision work is *not* just about developing another vision statement. Let's face it: most units and organizations have enough vision statements. What they often do not have is a shared vision—that is, when members of the organization are asked where the organization is headed, they all point in the same direction and know their part in getting there.

In the HPO model, visioning moves from a more abstract, broad, and long-term focus, through a more focused set of activities, including strategic thinking, strategic planning, tactical/operational planning and execution, and monitoring and recovery. We refer to this process as the vision to performance spiral (see Figure 5.4). As Figure 5.4 indicates, the process resembles moving down a funnel or spiral from broad and general to near-term and specific. Near the point of the spiral, individuals should know what they are doing each day, with whom, and what resources they will use to move them and the organization toward the accomplishment of their vision. Each level of the

Figure 5.4 The vision to performance spiral

Key: PM = Performance measures

organization—from unit through the whole—needs a vision that is nested into the next higher level. Creating the vision does not come only from the top; it needs to come up from the units as well. A docking process then meshes these ideas into an integrated, aligned vision for the organization.

At the top of the vision spiral, units/organizations need to address KDQ 1: What is high performance for us? and KDQ 4: Why do we need to be high performing? This discussion focuses on what our *end values* are and what they should be. What is the higher moral purpose we are seeking; what is our desired future state; what outcomes/impacts are we seeking; who would miss us if we were gone? As an organization begins to settle on its desired future, we will begin the process of asking KDQ 2: How would we know? We ask this question at every level of this spiral. At the top of the vision spiral, we are future-focused, so the measures will also be future-focused. Because we cannot measure *now* whether we are *there*, the indicators are trailing or lagging indicators. Because they are trying to measure the end values we are seeking, they may also be called outcome or impact measures.

The following is an example from an Army laboratory of a vision statement being turned into a set of measurable statements. In other words, we would seek specific outcome/impact measures for each of the ten numbered parts:

[This laboratory] is (1) _recognized_ as a (2) _premier Research and Development organization_ that is (3) _sought out by customers and partners_. We (4) _develop and maintain a relevant and vibrant research program_ that includes a (5) _robust reimbursable portfolio_. We are a (6) _highly skilled, adaptable team_ with (7) _unique facilities_ that enable us to (8) _perform cutting-edge research_. We operate in an (9) _efficient and effective manner_. We (10) _provide comprehensive solutions_ to the nation's and the warfighter's toughest challenges.

As we drop down a level in the spiral, we call the next level strategic thinking, which has two parts: mission/niche thinking and theory of the business thinking. Strategic thinking is an "opening up" activity. We prefer that organizations think before they plan. We also warn organizations not to let "perfect" get in the way of "good enough." Because visioning is a cyclical process and will come around again in a year or so, we do not have to be perfect in our execution of these steps—we just need to be better this year than before. Strategic thinking includes:

Mission/niche thinking, which looks at KDQ 5. Are we doing the right "what"?—where we look at our key products and services, design and features quality, and customer value—and KDQ 3: According to whom are we high performing?

Theory of the business thinking, which looks at KDQ 6. How good are our processes at delivering our mission/niche?

We are now ready for the next level down in the spiral: strategic planning, which is a "closing" activity. The two parts of strategic planning are set direction and capacity building:

Set direction. It sounds simple. We decide where we're going and let everyone know. Yet it often becomes more complex. What if stovepiping is widespread in the organization, with many of the units going in whatever directions they want? If we want the organization to be going true north, and three-quarters of the organization is not, what must we do to redirect those units? We have found that many organizations are good at _adding_ new strategic initiatives during the strategic planning process, but rarely found an organization very good at _shutting down_ programs, units, and/or business areas when they are not going true north. In addition, the field of "change management" (sometimes defined as managing the "people-side" of change) is often overlooked when major changes are planned in an organization's direction, systems, or processes. People in organizations must be prepared for such change if it is to succeed.

Capacity building. As we exited the strategic thinking level in the spiral, we asked ourselves a series of fill-in-the-blank questions: Do we have the right ___ to achieve our vision? The missing part of the question could be key products and services, business strategy/model, partners, structure, systems and process, facilities, equipment, information technology, data, and people with the right competencies. What if the answer to any of these questions is no, and it is a serious, vision-blocking no? Now what? We have to address the issue. This is where capacity building comes in. For us, hope is not a strategy; rather, these issues must be dealt with seriously in the strategic plan, or it will not be taken seriously by employees and first-level managers.

Time for more measurement work: at the strategic planning level, we are still looking for trailing or lagging indicators, because we are dealing with strategic goals and objectives that will be measuring events three to five years or more in the future. These measures are closer-in than the outcome and impact measures at the top of the spiral, but they are still in the future.

As we reach the lower levels of the spiral and engage the tactical/operational/project planning level, the work shifts from leadership work to no-fooling, near-term, task/management implementation, grind-it-out work. At this point many organizations fail. Too often, when the strategic plan (the one with the glossy cover) shows up at the unit level, it is viewed with suspicion. Lack of participation in the strategic planning process by units at all levels often results in either direct opposition or passive-aggressive behavior at the unit level. This is precisely why we argue that units need to "run the spiral" at their level and to participate in a top down/bottom up, docking process to align the plans at each level. The two parts of tactical/operational/project planning are action planning and resource planning:

Action planning. If we are dealing with an actual project at this level, then this step creates the project plan. Usually, the plan includes a work breakdown structure and uses other techniques from the project management body of knowledge such as schedule and resource estimation, earned value, and variance analysis.[5]

Resource planning. In addition to detailing the actions/events/activities that need to occur, the unit/organization must create a matching resource plan. What if we have a brilliant causal sequence, but it will cost $1 million to execute it, and we have only a quarter of that available to pay for it? The resource plan must cover personnel, facilities, training, and other costs. Once the resource plan matches the action plan, we will be able to track the accomplishment of the scheduled activities against the estimated expenditures.

In the measurement area, we are now ready to establish some leading indicators: measures that will predict whether we will achieve our outputs and, thereby, our goals, objectives, and outcomes/impacts. The two most common are *input* measures (did we get the personnel we estimated as required for each activity in the causal sequence; did we get the required facilities, equipment, training, data, information technology?) and *throughput* measures (were the milestones accomplished when we said they would be with the resources we estimated?).

The concluding step in the vision to performance spiral is called monitoring/recovery. After the near-term, detailed, applied planning process, we turn to the actual implementation and execution. Ask the following questions: Are we on-budget and on-schedule (with the required design and features quality, execution quality, and customer value also being delivered)? If an emergency occurs or we are not on budget and on schedule, what are we going to do to recover as much of the plan as possible? What corrective actions are necessary? Did we learn anything from missing our estimates that should be factored into the planning/estimating process next time?

KDQ 7: How are we going to treat each other, our partners, our customers, and our stakeholders?

KDQ 7 is far too often overlooked in organizations. Described by some as soft or touchy-feely, it does not get the serious consideration it deserves to sustain a culture of customer satisfaction, continuous improvement, and accountability. If an organization is expected to sustain the kind of effort needed to become and remain high performing, it must, as part of that effort, consider and sustain the appropriate *means values*. These are the values that guide how we get to our desired ends values (higher moral purpose). The three types of means values we work with are:

1. Leadership philosophy is a statement of beliefs explaining the assumptions upon which management actions are based and judged. It answers the questions: What do we believe about the nature of people and their attitudes toward work? What motivates most people, once their basic needs have been met? What is the distribution of knowledge and creativity and, as a result, how will decisions be made? What is the nature of the work? Leadership philosophy imposes boundaries on the behavior of managers and team leaders with hierarchical authority over others and, as a result, will be a major determinant of work culture.

2. Individual behavioral values are a larger, overarching set of values describing how members of the community treat each other, their partners, customers, and stakeholders. They provide a standard for judging interpersonal behavior and answer the questions: "How are we going to treat each other and, by extension, our customers?" These values help define the human side of the organization's work culture.

3. Operating systems values state how we want the organization's systems and processes, such as the support systems—HR, purchasing, IT, and technical work processes—to treat the people in the organization. These values define the technical side of the organization's work culture. How organizational systems/processes *treat* employees often speaks louder than anything managers say. What if a manager says to the employee, "You're empowered, but don't forget the thirty-seven signatures to buy the pencil." Does the employee hear "We think you're responsible" or "We don't trust you"?

These means values must be translated into well-understood criteria in order for them to guide and even limit our decisions, actions, and behaviors. The work culture they create is a leading indicator of future results. What if we have a wonderful strategic plan and a perfect performance measurement system, but a really rotten work culture? Can we get to sustained high performance?

Addressing KDQ 7 using the change lever of the high performing organization model's values

In the HPO model, we take organizations through a thought process, the values to work culture spiral, designed to produce a statement of values and a plan to implement and enforce them. Although the values spiral looks only at KDQ 7—How do we treat each other, our partners, our customers, and our stakeholders?—we find that many technically oriented organizations are challenged by this work. The work contained in the values spiral is critical to a central thesis of this book: The need to build relationships and trust among the players within an organization and between the organization and the external world is critical. The values spiral is all about building trust. Like the vision spiral, the values spiral proceeds from high-level, conceptual work down the spiral, with each lower level becoming more near-term and more specific. We begin the values work by addressing the three means values that are the building blocks of our organization's work culture: leadership philosophy, individual behavioral values, and operating systems values (see Figure 5.5 on page 148).

Figure 5.5 The values to work culture spiral

Key: PM = Performance measures

Leadership philosophy is perhaps the major determinant of the trust level that will exist between the workforce and management. In the roughly left-to-right flowing causal sequence defined by the HPO diagnostic/change model in Figure 5.1, leadership philosophy is in the number one position. If an organization does not get leadership philosophy right, almost nothing downstream in the model works. We use the work of three organizational behavior research pioneers—Douglas McGregor, Rensis Likert, and Peter Block—as the theoretical base from which to view, discuss, diagnose, and finally initiate change in an organization's leadership philosophy.[6]

How organizations behave toward employees, customers, suppliers, and other stakeholders determines their leadership philosophy. At one extreme, for example, are organizations that see people as not liking to work; as not being ambitious or wanting responsibility; as not doing a good job unless directly and closely supervised or motivated by coercion, threats, and punishment; and as lacking in knowledge, talent, and creativity. Such organizations are likely to design control-oriented, multilayered hierarchies that tell workers exactly what to do at all times. Workers are not to be consulted or involved in designing work processes because they will be seen as having nothing to say. Work is reduced to discrete tasks, and workers are directed to perform the tasks exactly as directed by the supervisor or by a work rule set in a rigid, highly regulated, management-defined process. Workers are asked to check their brains at the door and are discouraged from making suggestions for improvement. "It's my way," says the boss, "or the highway." This belief set loosely corresponds to what McGregor called Theory X, Likert called Systems 1 and 2, and Block called the bureaucratic cycle.

At the other extreme are organizations that see people, generally, as wanting to do a good job because it is a core human need; as wanting to be part of something meaningful; as being motivated (once basic needs are satisfied) by challenge, responsibility, achievement, recognition, personal growth, and advancement to more challenging work; and as being knowledgeable and creative or capable of being made so by development. Such organizations view good problem-solving, continuous study and improvement of work processes, and innovation as requiring consultation with and involvement of a wide range of knowledgeable employees. Under these beliefs, work is seen as integrated processes needing knowledgeable, broadly skilled, and talented workers who collaborate to ensure that jointly held objectives are accomplished. This belief set represents the essence of Theory Y in McGregor's approach, Systems 3 and 4 in Likert's work, and Block's entrepreneurial cycle.

The following is an example of a leadership philosophy statement developed by the senior management team of a municipal government and modified by the workforce through a consultative process:

> We, the employees of [a medium-sized] City Government, want to do a good job. We will excel if we are part of something important, are consulted and involved in all aspects of our work, are provided the tools to do our jobs, and are recognized for our efforts. Knowledge, experience, creativity, and cultural diversity abound in this organization. We will use these resources to achieve [our] vision.
>
> Each of us has an important role in the "work of leadership" and the "work of management." Our work will be characterized by shared information, continuous learning, and personal responsibility. We will provide an atmosphere of competence, teamwork, trust, confidence, and respect. Our organization will succeed with clear goals and purposes. We will be mission-centered. We will make our policies and actions clear, purposeful, and consistent with our values at every level of the organization.

Addressing the individual behavioral values and operating systems values is less theory-driven and more experiential. In these areas, we normally use a brainstorming process to generate the values that the organization wants to embrace. After defining them, organizations generally synthesize these three means values—leadership philosophy, individual behavioral values, and operating systems values—into an integrated statement of their values.

Once we have described the values of our unit or organization in conceptual terms, we are ready to move to the next level of the values spiral: behaviors. To illustrate the need for becoming more specific, we often pose this question: What if we have successfully developed the best set of values known to humankind, we've posted them on the wall all over our organization, and then we watch them get violated every day? Most participants will agree that this result is worse than not having developed them in the first place, because now people can see clearly that their values are being violated instead of simply suspecting it. To stop the values work after developing the values statement, then, is to increase cynicism in the organization.

The behaviors level of the values spiral asks participants to become more specific about what behaviors they want to see from each other that support the values and what behaviors they do not want to see anymore that violate the values. A federal regulatory agency that went through this process produced the example below. It looks at one of the eight values they articulated, open communication and credibility or being believable and honest, and lists some of the behaviors that were desired and not desired:

A. Productive behaviors

- Share information up, down, and across (information should be shared with necessary individuals/teams, especially with people whose performance will be affected; inform people of the reliability of the information).
- Tell the truth. Use qualifiers, for example, "As far as I know. . ." when information is uncertain since things may change; say when you can't say; inform people if the situation changes and why.
- Actively listen (eye contact, no interrupting, undivided attention) even when you don't want to.
- Acknowledge/admit lack of information/knowledge (say when you don't know or don't understand).
- Avoid use of offensive language; important that one knows the audience/individual (no racial slurs, off-color jokes, religious/ethnic jokes, or religious profanity).
- Give and solicit frequent, polite, and constructive feedback (be specific; suggest how to improve; give positive feedback).

B. Counterproductive behaviors

- Vindictive or malicious comments.
- Being overly critical.
- Condescending tone or attitude/belittlement of employees.
- Aggressive/threatening voice tone and/or body language.
- Hidden agendas.
- Manipulation for personal or professional gain.

The final steps in the values spiral are feedback and coaching and resolution. In these steps, units need to find mechanisms for holding team members accountable for living the values. A number of organizations we've worked with have turned their behaviors-level work into 360 degree feedback instruments, which are generally used initially in a developmental way to help the person being assessed improve her performance and behavior. Eventually, these instruments feed into the appraisal process. Coaching is frequently offered as a way for individuals to see how others see them and to explore how they might improve. Resolution requires us to deal with those who choose to violate our shared values. Without this step, we don't really have values, no matter how many places they hang on the wall. We may have to ask managers to relinquish their hierarchical authority and become a nonmanager or ask that violators—whether managers or employees—"make a contribution to some other organization." This step is the ultimate test of whether we want to have a high-performance work culture or not.

Finally, just as we ask KDQ 2—How would we know?—at every level of the vision spiral, we must also ask the same question at every level of the values spiral. At the top of the spiral, for example, we might use Likert's *Profile of Organizational Characteristics* or a similar survey to assess our unit's or organization's leadership philosophy.[7] At the behaviors level, we can design customized instruments to deliver 360 degree feedback or we can develop less formal methods of feedback where individuals deliver the feedback face-to-face. Methods also are available to assess organizational/unit work culture, such as the KEYS instrument from the Center for Creative Leadership and the Organizational Assessment Survey (OAS) from the U.S. Office of Personnel Management.[8]

In our example of the Navy industrial facility, KDQ 7—How do we treat each other?—was a foundational part of the change process. The new commander of the shipyard when we began the improvement process there (he was also responsible for bringing us in to help) had been at the shipyard earlier in his career. Unfortunately, in that incarnation, he was seen as a "take-no-prisoners" kind of manager (System 1 in Likert's typology). Before we could make progress in the change effort, we needed to help him alter his leadership philosophy. Between the time he left the shipyard after his first tour of duty and his return as shipyard commander, he had participated in a number of executive development programs, including Harvard's Kennedy School, the University of Virginia's Darden School, and a program conducted by the Naval Sea Systems Command. These programs had convinced him that his leadership philosophy was not going to serve him well in the future, and, based on this insight, he engaged us to help with his personal transition. After the commander began to change his style, one of his more difficult tasks was to get the others in the yard to see him as different, rather than the person he had been.

Tips for leadership success

Although this chapter has not been a full treatment of the HPO diagnostic/change model, it has tried to lay out a good deal of the diagnostic thinking required to drive organizational improvement. As we work with organizations, several additional lessons we have learned and tips for success may be useful to keep in mind:

- **Get organized for change:** We have yet to encounter a successful organizational improvement effort that happened "accidentally." It seems that many organizations believe that sending their employees to training will, by itself, somehow result in performance improvement. Our experience is that *training does not equal change.* Instead, improvement requires a concerted effort by management to make it happen. It is necessary to build "change mechanisms" at every appropriate level of the organization in which individuals agree that a portion of their "real jobs" involves working on improving unit/microbusiness/organizational performance. The "roadmap" presented in the HPO Diagnostic/Change Model will not, by itself, cause anything to happen. We need "leadership teams" at every level of the organization who will seize the roadmap and "make it happen." It is critical that top management be involved in driving this process—a "demand function" is needed (the demand is NOT "do what I tell you," but rather is "you can't tell me you won't get organized and skilled to help improve the organization").

Further, members of such leadership teams (especially top teams) must adopt a "stewardship" mindset, in which their focus is on the success of the whole, rather than just their units. We believe stewardship can be treated as a leadership competency and can be assessed (have the individuals worked to support cross-unit projects or organization-wide process improvements; do the individuals contribute to the success and improvement of other members of the leadership team; do the individuals identify this leadership team as their "primary team," as opposed to the units that they head?). In the example that started this chapter in which a city manager inherited a group of department heads who were definitely not stewardship-minded, our first order of business in their improvement process was to begin building an integrated top leadership team. Indeed, we have rarely seen an organization achieve sustained improved performance without a successfully integrated top leadership team (remember, however, that "top" in our material is relative; top can mean a project, division, department, or organization leadership team).

- **You may need some help:** We frequently find that senior managers (especially those with technical backgrounds) need some help with the change process. Our experience is that at about the 300-person level, an organization begins needing one or more part- or full-time change professionals on staff—people with organizational development, change management, business analytic thinking, project management, and team-development skills. Experienced change agents can "staff" the senior leadership team's efforts and can deliver "just-in-time" training, change-team facilitation, and encouragement/reinforcement/coordination. These change agents also can build a network of part-time change agents dispersed throughout the organization. In addition, they can play a "sensing function," pulling information together from all the different parts of the organization that touch a microbusiness (e.g., support staff from HR, IT, finance/budget/procurement, facilities, legal, EEO, etc.). Based on this information, a picture of the microbusiness begins to emerge that can suggest (in consultation with the managers and members of the microbusiness) what specific interventions may be useful to significantly improve the unit's performance. Finally, they can integrate with any outside contract support secured to help with the change process; this will continue to increase the in-house staff's skills and may raise an alert to problems with the contractors.

- **Consider "recontracting" everyone's job to also include leadership, management, and team/networking skills and responsibilities:** Many organizations we deal with are using human resources systems from the early 1900s in which work is seen as a discrete set of tasks that an individual employee is to complete (implicitly without regard to the whole). This "task-only" focus often is called the "industrial model" of work. It does not require the workforce to focus on the whole, on "owning" unit or organizational outcomes or impacts, or on the networks that must work smoothly to yield performance. The future will require a workforce that sees work differently and possesses a wider range of skills: leadership skills, management skills, technical skills, and team skills. These individuals will need to integrate themselves into, and care about the results of, the networks of which they are a part. For organizations to de-layer, broaden spans of control, be more flexible and responsive, and reduce the cost of overhead, they will need "high-performing" employees at every level of their organizations. We've called this concept the "networked talent model."

Resources for further learning

On building high-performance organizations: James Collins, *Good to Great: Why Some Companies Make the Leap—and Others Don't* (2001). One of the best recent books on moving organizations toward high performance. His excellent monograph, *Good to Great and the Social Sectors* (2005), to accompany the book, adapts his concepts to the public and nonprofit sectors.

On project and change management: Many public sector managers, especially those with a technical background, seem to lack exposure to the concepts of project management and to the people-side of project management, often called change management. The body of knowledge surrounding project management is well established and relatively ubiquitous, and the widely acknowledged keeper of this body of knowledge is the Project Management Institute (*www.pmi.org*). In the change management area, we have been impressed with material available from Prosci (*www.change-mangement.com*). See especially Jeffery M. Hiatt's book *ADKAR: A Model for Change in Business, Government, and Our Community* (2006), which proposes a personal and organizational change management approach called ADKAR, an acronym for awareness, desire, knowledge, ability, and reinforcement.

On measurement and performance management: For public/nonprofit managers who have not been exposed to measurement theory, the following resources are useful: Mark Graham Brown, *Keeping Score: Using the Right Metrics to Drive World-Class Performance* (1996); and Robert S. Kaplan and David P. Norton, *The Balanced Scorecard: Translating Strategy into Action* (1996).

We also like the work of the Balanced Scorecard Institute at *www.balanced scorecard.com*.

Notes

1. Likert (1961); Weisbord (1976); and Peters and Waterman (1983). Note: We prefer to use the "older" seminal works in the organizational development, change management, and other literature in our HPO Diagnostic/Change Model, and then, if the client is interested, show how more modern material builds on the base laid by the giants in the fields we cover.

2. Collins (2001).

3. See Deming (1986); Juran (1988). LEAN Manufacturing is Toyota's approach to quality and process improvement, and Six Sigma is Motorola's. The Capability Maturity Model (CMM) and CMM Integrated (CMMI) were developed by the Software Engineering Institute at Carnegie Mellon University.

4. Tichy (1999).

5. For an overview of the project management body of knowledge, see the Project Management Institute Web site at *www.pmi.org*.

6. See McGregor (1960); Likert (1961); Likert (1967); and Block (1991).

7. Adapted from Appendix 11 in Likert (1967).

8. The KEYS instrument is available from the Center for Creative Leadership in Greensboro, N.C., at *www.ccl.org*; the Organizational Assessment Survey is available from the U.S. Office of Personnel Management at *www.opm.gov/employ/html/org_asse.asp*.

6 Collaborating across organizational boundaries

RUSS LINDEN, PRINCIPAL, RUSS LINDEN & ASSOCIATES

COLLABORATION—working across internal and external organizational boundaries—is one of the most critical challenges facing government in the twenty-first century. The reason is that most of the nation's major problems—immigration, global warming, pandemics, health care, terrorism—are complex by nature and cannot be solved by one unit, one function, or one technical area of expertise. Indeed, as public administration scholar Don Kettl writes, "It is virtually impossible to find any public program that matters in which a single government organization's jurisdiction can capture the features that determine success." [1]

Complex problems can be addressed effectively only when people from different disciplines and different functions work together to deal with them. And when such collaboration occurs, the results can be truly impressive. Consider the following two examples.

The U.S. Forest Service and the Bureau of Land Management (BLM) are two separate federal agencies that, to most outsiders, might well be one. They have similar missions. They often work for the same customers, members of the public who frequently want the same things—hiking trails and campgrounds. Many of their employees have similar skill sets. It would make great sense to merge them.

Despite three attempts to do so, it is unlikely that they will ever be merged, but staff of both agencies have sought ways to avoid duplication and improve customer service by working together. Their efforts are paying off through an initiative called Service First. The origins can be traced back to some bold pioneers in southern Colorado and central Oregon who began working together in the early 1990s. Their motivation was simple: Resources were becoming scarce. "Some of us started to talk about helping each other save staff time and reduce costs while improving our stewardship of the land," recalled Jim Webb, former supervisor of the San Juan-Rio Grande National Forest in Colorado.[2] The arrangement was ad hoc at first. "[One would say,] 'hey, you need a biologist, and we have one who has some slack time, and we sure could use the help of your information management people. Let's work together.' "

What began informally grew over the next fifteen years to an impressive partnership that the leaders of both agencies endorsed and Congress supported with legislation. Through Service First, local BLM and Forest Service field offices have:

- Created jointly staffed visitor services desks (customers can go to either agency and get the information they need).
- Co-located some BLM and Forest Service field offices in the same building, providing one-stop service (and saving rent and utility costs).
- Integrated certain functions such as fire management, human resources, and fleet management.
- Shared staff where appropriate.
- Given some managers "dual delegation" authority, allowing them to manage the lands, and supervise employees, of either agency.
- Developed one set of maps and permits for customers of both agencies.
- Issued one set of rules and regulations for their respective agencies, rather than two.

Both the Government Accountability Office and an independently administered series of focus groups have documented Service First successes. It is saving money, providing better customer service, and allowing the staff to manage the land in an integrated manner, which leads to better land stewardship. This kind of collaboration certainly is not easy, but many of the employees involved in Service First, and their customers, say it is exactly how government should work.

Another example of collaboration is the justice information system begun by Gov. Tom Ridge of Pennsylvania. In 1996 Ridge was in his second year as governor, and he wanted to make good on a key campaign promise to make a major reduction in crime. He believed that information sharing in the law enforcement community could make a significant difference in reducing crime, but that information was not being shared quickly or easily among the sixteen state agencies involved in law enforcement. Ridge decided it was time to act.

His administration made available $11 million to design the justice information network (soon dubbed JNET). Ridge formed a steering committee made up of leaders of the sixteen agencies. It met with a contractor and began designing the new system. The JNET Lab was soon in place, and by

1998 it had created a pilot system that was used by selected units. By 1999 the first phase of JNET was completed, and all sixteen agencies were using it.

JNET quickly proved to be a success. Using open Internet and Web technologies to link agencies using a common Web browser, JNET helps federal, state, and local officials access each other's files. Through JNET, these agencies can:

- Access offender information.
- Access digital mug shots.
- Use secure e-mail.
- Access driver's license information.
- Access searchable online reference libraries.
- Use various criminal justice Web sites not available to the public.
- Exchange photo images.

None of these functions was possible prior to JNET. Instead, it took several days to obtain hard copies of photos, suspects' criminal histories, and outstanding warrants. And sometimes the information simply was not shared at all. This information is now available to JNET members in real time. By helping law enforcement agencies share information and collaborate, JNET is making a difference in providing public safety services for Pennsylvanians.[3]

Service First and JNET are stories about successful collaboration. These short summaries make collaboration sound fairly straightforward. In fact, both projects had to overcome huge obstacles: middle managers who were threatened by a perceived loss of power, huge egos and turf concerns, and tensions between headquarters and the field, to name just a few. But the stories also reflect three common approaches to collaboration.

Three general paths to collaboration

A crisis is a terrible thing to waste.

—Paul Romer

Informal, bottom-up. Collaboration often starts informally, at the working level where employees are faced with important demands but don't have the knowledge and resources necessary to meet those demands by themselves (as happened with the BLM and Forest Service). As the collaboration proves mutually beneficial, it sometimes expands into more formalized agreements.

Formal, top-down. A more formal, top-down path also can be used. When an important need arises that one unit cannot meet on its own, the leaders sometimes form a coalition, create a governance structure and charter the effort, find a senior champion, develop a game plan, and start producing results (the JNET story).

Crisis. And sometimes a crisis spurs collaboration. The need is immediate and urgent (and often public and visible). No one party can fully meet the need; only a collaborative approach will work. That was the story at the Pentagon immediately after the 9/11 attacks. The collaboration that occurred during the weeks that followed was extraordinary. A triggering event in the JNET story was the death of a police officer. While Ridge was campaigning for governor in 1994, the officer was killed by a man who had been arrested several times using at least six aliases. Just five days before the shooting, the man was picked up on a parole violation but was then let out of jail. The lack of a comprehensive information system allowed this killing to happen, and the tragedy provided some of the urgency that led to JNET.

Each of these three approaches can produce quality services and products for the customers, and each can fail to produce such benefits. Crises don't always produce collaboration; just ask the survivors of Hurricane Katrina. But what ultimately determines if such efforts succeed?

Major collaboration drivers

Certain factors are almost always present when collaboration succeeds. I think of these factors as the basics of collaboration: necessary (but not sufficient) for it to thrive. There are five basics, and each was present in the two stories introducing this chapter:

1. *A specific, shared purpose that the parties want to meet and cannot achieve on their own.* The law enforcement agencies in Pennsylvania had a great need to exchange accurate, real-time information, but had no mechanism to do so prior to JNET. The Forest Service and BLM employees needed people and money as resources shrank; they also shared the desire to simplify services for their customers.

2. *A desire by the parties to meet now and a willingness to contribute something (people, resources) to the effort.* Collaboration rarely works unless the agencies or units at the table place a priority on the shared purpose. Governor Ridge's commitment to public safety (plus the officer's murder) made

Figure 6.1 A tool for identifying stakeholders

Influence/expertise on issue

	Low	High
High Stake in issue	Invite in	Possible champion
Low	Not usually at table	Possible champion

Source: Adapted from *The Collaborative Leadership Fieldbook* by David Chrislip (San Francisco: Jossey-Bass, an imprint of John Wiley & Sons, 2002), 75.

JNET a high priority in Pennsylvania. The difficult budget situation created a desire to meet among the natural resource agencies.

3. *Bringing the appropriate people to the table.* This task is often one of the trickiest. It is not always obvious who the appropriate people are. Collaboration scholar David Chrislip offers a useful method for identifying the necessary people on a collaborative effort. He asks who has *influence* on the particular issue, and who has a *stake* in it? I have revised his formula a bit and offer it in graphic form (see Figure 6.1).

The horizontal dimension in Figure 6.1 identifies those who have something to contribute to the initiative—influence, expertise on the issue, or both. The vertical dimension addresses those who have a stake in the issue. Starting in the upper right quadrant: those with something to contribute, and with a high stake in the issue, are clearly important players (and often champions for the effort) and must be at the table. Just as obvious, perhaps, are those in the lower left quadrant; they have little if anything to contribute, and are not affected by the initiative. They may not need to be present.

In the lower right quadrant are those with much to offer, but with little at stake. They sometimes are champions for the effort, because they often have high credibility (because they have little at stake, they can be impartial in dealing with conflicts). Those in this lower right quadrant could include people in administrative offices: finance, budget, policy shops, IT units, office of general counsel.

Finally, those with little to offer but with a big stake in the issue are in the upper left. They must be invited in because they do not have much clout. These could include customers, partner agencies, and units with few resources.

JNET was an exceptional example of bringing the appropriate people to the table. In addition to a steering group of civil servants from each of the sixteen law enforcement agencies that helped create the actual network, JNET had an executive council made up of political appointees from these agencies, which dealt with high level policy issues and provided support for the effort.

4. *An open, credible process for working together.* Once the right people are meeting, how well or poorly will they work together? Collaboration, again, is about working across boundaries. These people may have very different styles of problem solving. They may not know each other at the outset and do not have a basis of trust. It is important that they feel a primary allegiance to their home office or agency, but how to get them working well together? An open credible process is necessary to overcome these and other hurdles. Such a process includes agreed-upon ground rules, a skillful convener, transparency (agreement to make important decisions at the table), clear roles, and joint ownership of the process.

It takes considerable patience at the outset and a smart convener or facilitator to develop a credible and open process. Service First leaders have frequently held offsite meetings at which the managers from neighboring Forest Service and BLM field units develop the open communications needed to work on shared interests together.

5. *A champion or champions for the effort.* By champion, I mean someone who takes formal or informal leadership for the initiative, who has the credibility and clout to help it succeed. In large, complex collaborations, there are often two levels of champion—a senior champion (Governor Ridge for JNET) and a working-level champion (such as a manager working on the JNET steering committee). Champions are critical in helping the group overcome the myriad hurdles involved. I have seen few significant collaborative efforts succeed without the focus and energy of a committed champion.

The most effective champions are passionate about the issue being addressed, have good political and people skills, and know how to get others involved, so that the champion does not seem to be pushing her own perspective all the time. Dealing with power issues and finding senior level support are critical to most collaborative initiatives.

Going beyond the basics

> *Successful partnerships manage the relationship, not just the deal.*
>
> — Rosabeth Moss Kanter, *Harvard Business Review*

The five factors discussed above form a strong foundation for successful collaboration, but more is usually required to ensure success. Other strategies that promote successful collaboration include forming open, trusting relationships among the principals; demonstrating the stakes involved; developing a constituency for the initiative; and effective use of collaborative leadership skills.

Forming open, trusting relationships among the principals

"We had to put our money on the table, and our hands behind our backs!" That is how one senior manager described the efforts of a coalition of agencies trying to collaborate on early childhood issues. It took a lot of trust, which was not easy to form given the parties' history of competing for resources.

Trust is almost always an important factor in successful public sector collaboration. Harvard Business School professor Rosabeth Moss Kanter found the same in her research on private sector alliances around the world. After conducting more than five hundred interviews, she concluded that positive business alliances cannot be controlled by formal systems. Rather, they need a "dense web of interpersonal connections."

When trust exists, the other collaboration basics become easier to establish. People can be candid about their office's interests in the initiative, about their level of commitment to it, and about what's on the table and what's not. When trusting relationships do not exist, chances for success are low. Successful collaborative leaders understand this, and they look for opportunities to build trust among current and potential partners.

What Jay Gregorius, a Drug Enforcement Administration official, knows, what we need to remember, is that *we're all in the relationships business* (see Box 6.1). If we understand that, we'll continually scan the environment and be aware of opportunities to partner with and help others. One of the unusual aspects of Jay's story is that he found a way to form a relationship and start building trust in the middle of a crisis. People in the emergency

Box 6.1   Trust and the search for the D.C. sniper

It was October 20, 2002, and the D.C. sniper was still at large, creating fear among millions of people in Maryland, the District of Columbia, and northern and central Virginia. Fourteen people had been killed, and law enforcement agencies in dozens of jurisdictions were working overtime to find the killer or killers. Jay Gregorius, assistant special agent in charge of the Drug Enforcement Administration's (DEA) training academy, and others at the academy were looking for a way to help. Tracking down snipers is not part of the DEA mission, but Jay is a big picture guy, and he is passionate about the importance of relationships and trust in law enforcement. So he called the sheriff of Stafford County, a rural county not far from the scenes of some of the attacks.

"I didn't know the sheriff at the time," Jay recalled, "but I wanted to help. I figured he must be stretched to the limit because of the fear and media exposure given to the sniper. Besides, I live in his county. So I called him, explained that I supervise several agents, that we're trained law enforcement officers, we carry guns, and that we'd do anything at all that would help him. He wasn't used to getting this kind of call, and wasn't sure what we could do. But he told me that his deputies were spending a lot of time sitting at freeway exits off I-95, and that when the next attack came (if it was along the I-95 corridor), he'd close off every exit ramp and his deputies would have to inspect every vehicle.

"I told him that our agents could help with that task. In fact, our agents would do whatever he needed, whenever he needed them (including evenings and weekends). Further, I explained that the DEA agents would be taking orders from him and his deputies; they would be in charge, we'd be there in a support role. Well, local government officials don't usually hear that from the feds, but he really appreciated the offer; he accepted it; and the next day our agents were at the freeway exits, working with the sheriff's deputies.

"The snipers were caught a few days later, so this didn't go on too long. But my agents (who weren't excited about this initially) really liked working with the sheriff's deputies. The sheriff, of course, was delighted. Since that time, he and I have a great relationship. He'd do anything for me, and vice versa. That's how we run our office, and that's one way we build relationships." *

---

*Author's conversation with Jay Gregorius, September 2005.

management world know that whenever possible, the better time to establish relationships is *before* you have to work together.

> "You don't want to meet someone for the first time while you're standing around in the rubble," says Jarrod Bernstein, a spokesman for the NYC Office of Emergency Management. "You want to meet them during drills and exercises." New York, says Bernstein, has very tight relationships with state and federal officials in a variety of agencies. "They're involved in all our planning and all our drills. They have a seat at all the tabletop exercises we do." [4]

Bernstein's insight is important: meetings and training sessions provide better opportunities for establishing trusting relationships than when you are "in the rubble." But Gregorius's insight is also powerful. It is best captured by Stanford University economist Paul Romer's remark quoted on page 158.[5] Collaborative leaders would prefer to avoid crises, but they understand that crises create opportunities—resources become available, rigid rules and regulations are relaxed, and leaders are focused on the problem. Another opportunity is the chance to help others.

Veterans of successful collaborative efforts report some of the ways they have established trust with individuals trying to collaborate:

- Value others' input; use it whenever possible.
- Model openness; use self-disclosure and "I messages."
- Eat meals together (and make time for other informal exchanges).
- Use "careful listening" to learn underlying interests; seek common ground.
- Share accurate information, both requested and not.
- Engage in joint training (among some of the units trying to collaborate), which helps form bonds across agency boundaries.
- Set aside time to work on relationships and trust (taking a business trip together provides a good opportunity).
- Do small, work-related projects together (to build bridges and help people learn others' skills, knowledge, and interests).

Demonstrating the high stakes involved in the initiative

As noted at the start of this chapter, crises provide one of the three common paths to collaboration. It is no surprise that such conditions usually bring out excellent performance. During a crisis the priorities are clear, the goal is vivid, the consequences of getting it wrong are high, and the situation is often very visible to others.

To get some of the collaboration basics in place—in particular, having the appropriate people at the table—collaborative leaders must be clear about the high stakes involved in the initiative: the payoff to customers, the impact on the safety of the community, the need to deal with major budget cuts, and so forth. The early Service First leaders were clear with their staff about the stakes involved in working across agency lines: the workload was increasing, resources were decreasing, and there was no way to maintain quality without active collaboration.

The point is not to create false emergencies; most of us have experienced them, and they only lead to cynicism. Rather, it is about clarifying for the people at the table what the real stakes are, why the stakes are high, and why this initiative will have such a huge impact if it is done right (or wrong).

The following are examples of how to demonstrate the high stakes of an initiative:

- Bring in customers to meet with those trying to collaborate. Hearing the voice of the customer can be a strong motivator for change and action.
- Look for ways to link the initiative to the agenda of a senior leader. When leaders see how a collaborative effort can further their work (or address a problem that has been consuming their time), they sometimes become strong champions for the effort.
- Seek resources for the initiative. Many people are more concerned about what they might lose in a proposed collaboration than its benefits. When collaborative leaders line up funding for the project, it sends at least two messages: (1) the leadership is doing its homework and has gotten others to invest in the project; and (2) there may be some tangible rewards for getting involved. And that brings us to the WIIFM question: What's in it for me?
- Give the principals at the table an answer to the WIIFM question. Whether it is asked out loud or not, those invited to collaborate certainly will be asking themselves the question. Why should they spend this time and give this effort; what is the payoff for doing so? Whether this is a selfish question or not, it is a supremely human one that has to be answered candidly (see Box 6.2 on page 166).

Box 6.2   Making the WIIFM question clear

Here's how Brian Swann, an Alcohol, Tobacco, and Firearms agent, answered the WIIFM—what's in it for me?—question. He managed to demonstrate both the stakes involved and the payoff for working on the initiative. He leads a joint task force that is working to reduce violent crime in a large eastern city. Task force membership is a full-time commitment. The task force works effectively only if it includes federal, state, and local law enforcement officers, but Swann was having a hard time getting the local police chief to commit talented officers for the task force. He said:

Law enforcement folks are often competitive and territorial—they'll fight for money, for more personnel, etc. Why should the police chief give me his best people? What's in it for him to do that? So I talked with the police chief about our task force's need to have one officer from each precinct in his city's high crime areas. I promised the chief, "you give me good, young, aggressive people for two years, and I'll give you back officers ready to be detectives. I'll train them, they'll get great experience and lots of support. And when you get them back, they'll be able to handle the toughest, most complex cases." That answered the "what's in it for me?" question, and we received very good people from that PD. *

---

*Author's personal communication with Brian Swann, ATF team leader, February 2006.

Developing a constituency for the initiative

One of the many concerns that confronted the JNET leaders when they started working on their information system was that the next governor might torpedo the effort. Two previous efforts to create an information sharing network for Pennsylvania's law enforcement community had failed. Even if they got JNET up and running, what would guarantee that the next governor would support it?

The next governor (who happened to be of the other political party, which created even greater concerns) gave JNET full support. So did the state legislature. They did so for many reasons: it was fully operational, it was producing results, and all the agency heads supported it. They also backed it because JNET had developed a strong constituency at the local government level. As JNET grew, it was shared with the counties in the state. Many of the counties started sharing the system at no cost with the small towns and townships within their borders. JNET gave these county and local agencies valuable data via a system none of them could have built for themselves. The local elected officials became strong JNET supporters and told their state legislators how important it was to continue funding it. Any new governor trying to radically change JNET would have faced fierce resistance.

By constituency, I mean a group of people/organizations that are materially benefiting from the initiative and have a vested interest in its success. Constituents of a collaborative project can include customers, senior leaders, special interest groups, state and local agencies, and private sector firms. The key is to identify them, involve them, listen and use their ideas when possible, and show them how your work can help them.

The politics of collaboration can be tricky. Some agencies have stakeholders that do not like collaboration. Think about it: If you lead a special interest group that has successfully lobbied Congress to create a certain program, once that program is up and running, you want the people running it to succeed. You also want them to be accountable. And you want the funding to remain intact. If someone suggests that the program office work closely with other offices, your reactions might well be negative—where is the accountability if it is spread over several units? What happens to the program office's line item in the budget? Is collaboration just the first step toward a merger?

In addition, collaboration is not a positive word for everyone (few people become labor union leaders because they promise to collaborate with management!). Collaborative leaders therefore must develop the ability to do what the great public administration theorist Harlan Cleveland suggested years ago: *they must learn how to think politically, without becoming political.*[6] And that includes paying close attention to developing strong constituencies for the collaborative effort.

Using collaborative leadership skills

Nothing starts without men; nothing lasts without institutions.
—Jean Monnet

Jean Monnet, an early champion of the European Union, understood that most successful collaborations begin with individuals, men and women who are strongly committed to a shared goal and use their enthusiasm and persistence to gain support. Over time, these individuals seek to institutionalize their accomplishments, so that the project is not overly dependent on inspired people. But, at the start, it usually does take inspired people.

What do we know about those who effectively lead collaborative efforts? David Chrislip offers an important insight. Collaborative leaders, he writes, "lead as a peer, not as a superior." [7] That is, they typically do not have the formal authority to demand action; they are often at the same pay grade as the others at the table. Collaborative leaders rely on informal skills and tools— the arts of persuasion, negotiation, consensus building, personal appeal, and skillful listening—to help a group find common ground and move toward

---

Box 6.3   Joe Wienand and collaborative leadership

Joe Wienand was a career civil servant who rose to the Senior Executive Service level before retiring. Earlier in his career Joe managed projects as a civilian in an Army research and development lab. The work often involved meeting military officers' requirements for new equipment for troops in the field. These were high-pressure, high-stakes tasks. The timelines were strict and the projects had to hit specific milestones on schedule or risk losing funding. More important, the products were quickly tested by the soldiers in theater, and they had to work. Lives depended on it.

Wienand's project members typically came from different units and technical specialties and had not worked together. They reported to other managers, so Joe was leading the classic matrix organization, with the classic matrix dilemma: huge responsibility, but little if any authority. He was successful because he used his interpersonal and collaborative skills to get a herd acting like a team. It took careful listening, a willingness to feed big egos, reminders that troops in the field depended on them (high stakes), continual requests for input, expert negotiation skills, ample credit to the people involved, and enormous patience and persistence. As Joe puts it, "Keeping the technical people on the team happy and working together wasn't easy . . . it was by far my toughest job, dealing with those relationships. Project managers who don't have real good people skills don't succeed." [*]

---

*Linden (2002), 93.

their goal. Collaborative leadership is not the same as traditional hierarchical leadership. We will always need good hierarchical leaders, but there was no way that Joe Wienand, a civil servant, would have succeeded with his disparate group by using top-down leadership (see Box 6.3).

Beyond those skills, the position description for collaborative leaders includes the following:

- Articulate the project's purpose in a way that energizes others.
- See that the group has an effective convener.
- Help the parties identify common interests and the benefits they can realize (answering the WIIFM question).
- Create an open, candid environment, so that members can discuss their concerns as well as their hopes.
- Help the group use collaborative problem solving and decision making when issues arise.
- Assist the participants in win-win negotiations to meet three related interests: the needs of each partner, of the product they are creating, and of the relationships involved.
- Make relationship building a priority.
- Take risks as appropriate.
- Celebrate small successes, share credit widely; if any aspects of the work can be quantified, it helps to post the numbers showing the team's progress.
- Provide confidence, hope, resilience.

The last item deserves some comment. Collaboration is difficult work, and there are many reasons why collaborative efforts sometimes fall short and why members of collaborative groups lose interest or actively oppose what the group is trying to do. The benefits of collaborative work may not appear for years, while the costs are usually borne upfront. Given these challenges, collaborative leaders provide enormous value to their teams when they find ways to generate hope and confidence. One of many ways to do that is the next-to-last bulleted point: Mark small successes and share the credit.

Challenges to collaboration

At this point, a reasonable response might be "Yes, but. . . ." Indeed, the hurdles to collaboration are numerous, and many issues and challenges arise. Here are some of the more difficult ones and different ways to address them.

Lack of enthusiasm or commitment by some of the principals

The lack of commitment is a common concern. It often occurs when the initiative is led by one agency or office that has a huge stake in it and others are asked (or told) to help out. It also occurs when members of the collaborative group worry that the initiative seems to be a threat to one of their agency's interests. Such people attend the meetings primarily to play defense and to protect their home agency.

Successful collaborative leaders are not surprised by such behavior; indeed, they should expect it. Collaboration, especially in the early phases, can pose real or perceived threats to certain members' units. And those who are not threatened by the initiative still may have many unanswered questions at the start, which dampens their enthusiasm.

To deal with this problem, the initiative's leaders can try the following three suggestions:

1. Talk candidly with other principals about the WIIFM from their point of view. What would make this project valuable to them and their agencies or offices? Recognition? Access to resources available in the initiative? More control over the way the initiative is being run?

2. Talk with principals individually, outside of the group meetings, to find out what concerns they have about the effort. Do they worry that it is a threat to their turf, mission, or autonomy? Do they see it as a potential loss of control (often a huge issue)? Obtaining such information can help collaborative leaders clarify what is "on the table" and what is off, to allay people's concerns.

3. Find a senior leader who champions the project. Doing so is important for a variety of reasons; one of them is that it gives people hope and confidence that their time at the meetings will not be wasted.

A good start that stalls out

Losing momentum is a concern with a variety of projects. After several positive meetings, statements of support from leaders, and clarification of goals and roles, things slow down. Members either send their deputies to the meetings, or no one comes at all. The priority project seems to be OBE—overtaken by events.

Some collaborative leaders have avoided this dilemma when they:

• Plan the project so that it produces a series of small, visible products. JNET was designed this way. Every few months the network's planners created some new functionality that was available on the desktops of the participating members and their colleagues. Creating a network in chunks provides many benefits; one of them is that it maintains momentum. In addition, the members gain a sense of group identity (they say "we" more often, and "you" and "I" less).

• Celebrate the delivery of these products. It helps when people mark successes.

• Include customers and others who will directly benefit from the initiative. Having such people at the table helps create a sense of urgency and makes the work more meaningful.

• Shine a light on the problem. This is one way to use a strategy noted earlier: demonstrating the high stakes involved. Shining a light can be done by quantifying the cost and risk of the problem, by involving a variety of external stakeholders who want the problem addressed, by bringing in the media to discuss the problem and what is being done to address it, and by enlisting the involvement of senior leaders.

A history of distrust and conflict among the principal agencies

How do individuals work well on a collaborative team, when their offices or agencies have been feuding for decades (as has been the case with the CIA and FBI)?

The reasons for interagency feuds and turf battles are plentiful and well established. What exacerbates these tensions in collaborative efforts is that employees have stronger allegiance to their home agency (or office) than to the collaborative group they have joined. No matter how compelling the project's vision, most people keep firmly in mind that they will be going back to their own boss and worksite and that their career interests are primarily rooted there.

A strategy for dealing with preexisting distrust and conflict is to help people identify with the initiative's larger purpose. For example, create structured situations that get people from different units to work together over a period of time. These experiences often break down stereotypes and help employees trust and respect people from rival offices and agencies.

Good examples of these strategies include:

- Periodic rotations. Moving people around helps them see the larger picture. In organizations such as the Department of Defense, military personnel do not rise through the officer ranks unless they have had several rotations through joint commands (where they work with members of all four armed services).
- Co-located facilities. The Service First initiative includes more than twenty co-located units. The trend at the state level is to create fusion centers, where intelligence, law enforcement, and emergency management personnel from different agencies work together to anticipate and deal with threats to the country.
- Joint training. Such experience often helps break down agency and interpersonal barriers. Like rotations and co-location, joint training gives participants a chance to move beyond stereotypes. Relationships form that can be used when sudden challenges occur. Indeed, some of the law enforcement and emergency management managers who responded to the 9/11 attack on the Pentagon had been through many training sessions together; their relationships were critical to their extraordinary collaboration during and after the attack.[8]
- Joint task forces. In today's law enforcement and intelligence communities, joint task forces are common. When people from different agencies work together every day on high-stake issues, they tend to overcome stereotypes and forge strong bonds.

A unit-focused versus agency-focused organizational culture

One of the most common complaints in government (and in many large private firms, for that matter) is the reluctance of personnel to widen their focus. And it has some similarities to the previous issue.

Tribal loyalties can be incredibly strong. For many reasons, people at work usually find it more compelling to relate to their immediate unit than to the entire organization. The problem is that what is good for the individual units is not always what is needed for the enterprise.

I have observed two effective approaches to changing such cultures: systematic change led from the top, and the use of "multiplier mechanisms". Both require senior level commitment, and both require what quality guru W. Edwards Deming called "constancy of purpose."

Systemic change led from the top. An excellent example has occurred at the Financial Management Service (FMS) over the past decade. In December

1997, Treasury Secretary Robert Rubin asked Dick Gregg to take over the troubled FMS. The agency was in disarray, plagued by internal feuds, rigid stovepipes, divisions among senior leaders, and failure to implement an important law passed by Congress in 1996. Congressional leaders were upset, and the previous leaders were ousted. Gregg brought in Ken Papaj, his former deputy at the Bureau of Public Debt, and set about changing things at FMS.

Gregg articulated the necessary changes at the outset. At his first meeting with senior managers, Gregg recalled, "I said that we would speak with one voice, not several, that information would be shared widely, and issues would be dealt with early and directly. I emphasized that we would have a few common objectives and that we'd do business from an agency-wide perspective." [9] In his meetings with the senior managers, Gregg made clear his intention to make major changes and his expectation that the managers would support those changes. Within a month, two of the managers left; they were not forced out, but it was clear that they would not be able to function in the new environment. During the following months some other senior managers were moved to different roles, as Gregg brought in people whose leadership style fit the culture being created.

Gregg and Papaj made a number of other changes during the next year: they emphasized the values of teamwork and agencywide perspective in performance appraisals, and they saw to it that managers took them seriously. They formed matrix teams to get people working with others from different functions. Gregg and Papaj also spent countless hours meeting with small teams of employees to discuss the new direction, explain how it would affect employees, listen to the questions and concerns, and respond candidly.

The results of these and many other changes were striking. FMS developed a true culture of collaboration. The changes were done in firm but humane ways. And when Dick Gregg retired in spring 2006, it was clear to everyone at FMS that this culture was on solid ground.[10]

Multiplier mechanisms. Multiplier mechanisms describe structured management methods that make it in people's interest to work together across internal boundaries. Rotational assignments tied to promotions are a good example, as noted above.

Another example of a multiplier mechanism, the technology investment and management (TIM) council, has been used successfully at the Secret Service since 2000. TIM sets priorities on the new initiatives proposed each year (both IT and non-IT) by each Secret Service office. The TIM council has one voting member from each of the agency's offices. The agency's deputy director chairs the council, and its chief information officer is the vice chair (they are nonvoting members).

When an office director wants a new budget item that costs more than a certain amount, the office presents its business case to the TIM council. The office director spells out the need, the expected benefits, and cost. TIM council members vote on each proposal, rating it on specific criteria, such as the degree to which it supports the mission and meets the agency's strategic plan.

TIM council members use decision-support software to cast their votes and make their ratings. This tool allows members to vote anonymously, which eliminates the peer pressure to vote for each others' projects.

The TIM council puts the list of office requests into priority order. The agency director has approved these priorities every year since its inception. And TIM members say that this method also helps employees learn about the other offices, what they do, and how they might help each other. TIM is fostering collaboration as well as enterprisewide budgeting and priorities. The stovepipes are coming down in the Secret Service.

People on the collaborative team who "don't play well with others"

Many collaboration issues are organizational and structural, but some are personal. Some people simply prefer to work on their own. Some become rigid and protective in groups. And then there are those like the person that collaboration theorist Michael Shrage describes. Shrage tells of a man who was being interviewed for a senior position. After being told that the company was committed to a team concept, he was asked if he was a team player. "You bet," he answered. "Team captain!" [11]

Entire books have been written on this topic, so I will not try to give simple, six-step solutions to this challenge. One point to emphasize, however, is the importance of being clear at the outset about what is expected of the people in the collaborative group. One good approach is to ask the principals at one of the first meetings to think about similar groups they've served on in the past and describe the behaviors that were helpful and those that weren't. This technique can lead to a decision on group norms: What are the behaviors we need (and behaviors we cannot accept) to succeed? When the group members develop their own norms, these norms can be especially powerful. They still must be enforced, and it often helps to have a skillful facilitator to do that. But the first step is to discuss and agree on the acceptable behaviors and get them from the group.

The following norms can be especially helpful in dealing with difficult people:

- Candor, and no retribution for being candid.
- Mutual respect: We will be tough on the problem, not on each other.
- Park your ego and your agency (or unit) identity at the door.
- Everyone contributes; nobody dominates.
- The 70 percent rule: When making decisions, we will be satisfied if we each can get about 70 percent of what we want; holding out for 100 percent means we will never agree.

Another approach is to meet some of the ego needs of the principals early on as a way to reduce posturing at later meetings. Here is how one manager does it, especially if she knows she will be dealing with some huge egos. When she convenes a group for the first time, she goes around the room and introduces each person. She takes the time to talk about their current and past roles, some of their accomplishments, their wonderful skills, why she is so pleased that they are with "our group." She will talk about the varied contributions each can make to the team. If she does not do that, she has found that those with large egos will try to impress the group (and irritate other people in the process). By doing the introductions for them, she has found that posturing and egotistical behavior diminishes. She satisfies some of their ego needs for them, in a fair and efficient way, and the group then moves into the substance of their issue.

Good solutions that are not fully supported

The lack of support for a good solution is a difficult situation and not uncommon in collaborations. As much as we prefer win-win solutions, they are not always possible. And if the collaborative group is dedicated to finding the best solution to solve the problem or address the challenge (as it should be), that may come at the expense of one or more parties.

The first thing collaborative leaders must do is be absolutely honest about the situation. Sugarcoating it never helps. After that, consider the following options:

- Reduce the extent of the problem by anticipating it. Work on criteria that must be met for any solution to be approved (for example, it has to achieve the stated goal, achieve the agreed quality and timeliness standards, be under budget, and honor certain policy and legal requirements).

Working within these criteria can reduce the likelihood that some parties balk at a proposed solution.

- Bring in neutral outsiders who have knowledge of the issue being addressed. Ask if they can see ways to make the solution more of a win-win for all or if they can see ways to lessen the burden on some.
- See if the sacrifice can be shared. For example, if the solution costs one party some resources, can others share that burden?
- Agree to pluralistic long-term benefits. If the collaborative group will continue working together after producing this solution, agree that in the future the benefits and burdens must be rotated, so that those who lost this time can expect a different outcome next time.
- Try shuttle diplomacy. Have a neutral party go to each of the leading principals and ask what they like or dislike about the proposed solution(s). Often, someone with good mediation skills can identify shared underlying interests and develop a solution that captures most (not all) of the interests involved.

And when none of these options is effective (or seems practical), it helps to call in the project's senior champion and have that person break the tie.

Agencies or offices that refuse to join

As noted earlier, one factor for successful collaboration is to have the appropriate people at the table. But what are your options when one of the principal parties refuses to play?

A project manager at NASA had to contend with this problem a few years ago. He was the champion for a complex initiative that involved two NASA labs, the Air Force, and some aircraft companies. He started by talking informally with people at each organization to learn what they thought they might get out of the project and any concerns they had. Most seemed interested, but he was not certain about the people at one of the NASA labs. The project manager decided to take what I call an "outside-in" approach. He worked with personnel at the organizations that were most interested (even though they were not as vital to the project as the reluctant NASA lab). They developed goals, a project plan, and identified resources for the project. The project manager did not approach the NASA lab until the other partners were firmly on board. He then went back to that lab and explained what was in place. Managers there got interested in the project; they saw that it was a serious venture, were impressed by the stature of the interested organizations, and did not want to be left out.

A constitutional system that engenders distrust

The design of the U.S. government is probably the most profound challenge to collaboration in government. We are so used to our division of powers and legislative oversight that we take our fragmented system for granted, but this system is hardly a prescription for getting things done. The Framers were willing to put up with a government that was slow and clumsy because their overriding purpose was neither speed nor effectiveness; rather, it was to prevent tyranny. As Don Kettl writes, "At the very beginning, the founders decided there were two things they did not want: a single government that consolidated the states . . . and a government that consolidated governmental power in a single executive." [12]

The result: fragmented authority. We divide power between the federal and state governments, and within each level we divide power among the legislative, executive, and judicial. The Framers' goal of avoiding tyranny has been a brilliant success. But the system's way of doing so makes it very hard to move all the players in the same direction.

The U.S. constitutional system is a challenge to collaboration, but the complexity of today's problems requires that we collaborate. The major issues on the public's mind—the global economy and its impact on jobs, immigration, health care costs, global warming, the growing tribalism around the world, Iraq, and terrorism—all require extensive collaboration. No single organization can adequately address these problems. Developing the most effective options can be accomplished only by a coalition of specialists from different backgrounds and organizations, often with active public involvement.

This last issue is, in my view, the most profound problem facing government today. We are using a system of government based on eighteenth century assumptions to deal with twenty-first century challenges. These challenges do not honor traditional boundaries. And the ways we address them must reflect new ways of thinking and organizing.

The answers will not be found in the powerful new IT tools that dazzle us, even though technology will be important to our success. The answers will not be found in moving boxes around on organizational charts. Nor do I believe that merging multiple agencies will lead to serious breakthroughs. The answers are being found, however slowly, in the efforts of many informal leaders throughout government who invite others from different units to work together on complex problems. These noble collaborative leaders are experimenting, taking risks, using the methods noted here and by many others, and they are slowly creating the strategies and ways of thinking that are necessary to work across boundaries.

Some of their efforts are leading to new organizational forms such as fusion centers—places where law enforcement and intelligence agency personnel work together in one space. They share sensitive information, analyze it, and function as one unit to prevent and deal with natural and man-made threats. Other efforts are leading to more informal solutions, such as the development of human and IT networks within certain professional communities to share knowledge and develop answers to vexing problems. One of the most interesting is the new "Intellipedia," which is loosely modeled after Wikipedia, the online encyclopedia. Intellipedia is a self-governing system using content submitted by its consumers. Intelligence community analysts send postings to Intellipedia on a variety of topics. The content is subject to peer evaluation; if flawed information is submitted, others point it out quickly. (Unlike Wikipedia, Intellipedia's contributors are not anonymous, which provides accountability.) So far, Intellipedia is providing a secure and quick method for analysts at all levels and agencies to engage on important topics and emerging issues.

The collaborative pioneers who are creating these and other new forms are helping us see the world differently, and that is absolutely necessary. America's fragmented government system, for all of its blessings (and there are many), makes it very difficult to see the world holistically, find patterns, think systemically, and deal with complexity. Although it is not yet clear where these new forms will take us, what is clear is that today's major challenges will be met only through the power of collaboration.

Tips for collaborative success

In summary, those attempting to lead collaborative efforts should always keep in mind the following five "basic" conditions that form the foundation for collaborative success:

1. A specific, shared purpose that the parties want to meet and cannot achieve on their own.

2. A desire by the parties to meet now and a willingness to contribute something to the effort.

3. Appropriate people at the table.

4. An open, credible process for meeting.

5. A champion or champions for the effort.

These conditions can be difficult to achieve, so successful leaders use certain approaches to create this foundation. They can:

1. Develop open, candid relationships among the principals.
2. Demonstrate the high stakes involved in the effort.
3. Develop a constituency for the effort.
4. Use collaborative leadership skills.

Resources for further learning

To stretch your thinking about macro trends in the economy, technology, politics, and why collaboration is so central to the nation's future, two excellent books are: Thomas Friedman, *The World Is Flat* (2005), and Harlan Cleveland, *Nobody in Charge: Essays on the Future of Leadership* (2002). A report on the future of government that emphasizes the increasing role that networks will play is Donald F. Kettl, "The *Next* Government of the United States: Challenges for Performance in the 21st Century" (2005). It is published by the IBM Center for the Business of Government, which produces a variety of reports on innovations in government.

To learn how leading thinkers in public administration view collaboration and its increasing role in public management, see *Public Administration Review* 66 (Special Issue, 2006). The entire issue is devoted to the topic of collaboration.

To explore the political aspects of collaboration, how to form coalitions, how to use influence in ethical ways, see Joel DeLuca, *Political Savvy* (1999). DeLuca's excellent book describes the art of lining up support, connecting projects to others' agendas, and using relationships in positive ways.

Two fine books that describe collaboration from a private sector perspective are: Stephen Dent, *Partnering Intelligence* (2004); and James E. Austin, *The Collaboration Challenge* (2000), which offers guidance on forming alliances between nonprofits and businesses.

A fine book that focuses on the process of forming collaborative groups, and how to establish collaborative norms is E. Franklin Dukes et al., *Collaboration: A Guide for Environmental Advocates* (2001).

To learn about large federal departments and agencies trying to become "one" (gain internal alignment around common purpose), try Russ Linden, "The Quest to Become 'One': An Approach to Internal Collaboration" (2005), published by the IBM Center for the Business of Government. To learn more about the particular approach to collaboration used in this chapter, with a particular emphasis on government, try Russ Linden, *Working Across Boundaries: Making Collaboration Work in Government and Nonprofit Organizations* (2002).

Notes

1. Kettl (2006), 13.
2. Brown and Linden (2001–2002), 49.
3. The development of the JNET system is an instructive example of what it takes for collaboration to work across multiple agencies. Several other states have studied JNET and built their own systems using a similar framework. For more on JNET and how the collaboration developed, see Linden (2002), ch. 4.
4. Walters (2005), 54. For more on the importance of forming relationships prior to crises, see Moynihan (2005) on leveraging networks during emergencies, and the after-action report by Titan Systems Corporation (2001) on responses to the 9/11 attack on the Pentagon, page A-31.
5. Friedman (2005a), 306.
6. Author's personal communication with Harlan Cleveland, 2001.
7. Chrislip (2000), 23.
8. Titan Systems Corporation (2001), 12.
9. Linden (2002), 205.
10. For more on the transformation of the Financial Management Service under Dick Gregg, see ibid., ch. 12.
11. Shrage (1990).
12. Kettl (2006), 11.

7 Career-political relationships: Going beyond a government of strangers

ROBERT MARANTO, ASSOCIATE PROFESSOR OF POLITICAL SCIENCE, VILLANOVA UNIVERSITY*

Their fanatic conservatism is fine with me! It is simply misplaced in what should be a bipartisan agency. . . . My problems are not ideological. They won an election. I'll help implement policies I don' t necessarily agree with. Basically, however, most of the Reagan people couldn't operate a bingo game.

—A career executive in 1987, quoted in Robert Maranto, *Politics and Bureaucracy in the Modern Presidency,* 96.

If there truly is a move in the future to eliminate that agency or fold it back into _____, I would speak up in favor. Very little was accomplished on a day-to-day basis. When you come from a White House environment where things happen so quickly, you are always in a reaction mode and you never go to your superior and say this can' t be done—you find a way to accomplish it, and in _____ I was unable to accomplish anything in nine months and had Mr. Bush been reelected I knew I could not stay in that job, because I couldn't accomplish anything.

—A former George H. W. Bush political appointee in 2000, quoted in Robert Maranto, *Beyond a Government of Strangers,* 49.

AS THE OLD SAYING GOES, in Washington the search for the scapegoat is the easiest hunting expedition. In American politics, "political hacks" and "lazy bureaucrats" make great scapegoats. A long line of political folk wisdom, and

---

*I wish to thank Jason O'Brien, Grant Reeher, Villanova University, and the Federal Executive Institute for helping on this project, as well as the literally hundreds of government executives whose insights follow. I further wish to thank Hugh Heclo, whose classic *A Government of Strangers* (Washington, D.C.: Brookings Institution, 1977) provided both the title and many of the ideas presented here.

181

even some scholarly writing, suggests that U.S. political appointees are less expert, more politically driven, and more corrupt than career public servants.[1] Similarly, career bureaucrats are often thought to be incapable, unrepresentative, devoted to increasing their budgets, and unwilling to take direction.[2]

The reality is that political appointees and career public servants must work together. When they build relationships of mutual respect and trust, public value is more likely. In this chapter, I first outline reasons why increased distrust in government has little to do with the quality of political or career officials and why negative stereotypes about both groups of professionals are (for the most part) wrong. Second, I outline proposals (mainly from others) on how political appointees can better work with, rather than at cross-purposes with, their career bureaucrats to foster bureaucratic change and ultimately better serve the public. Finally, and most important, given the audience for this book, I suggest at some length what career officials can do to foster good relationships with the political appointees in their agencies— what a public servant can do within his or her own sphere of influence. After all, as Leo Tolstoy put it, "Everyone thinks of changing the world, but no one thinks of changing himself." [3] Or as Linda Bunker, University of Virginia education professor and sports psychologist, puts it: To succeed, executives must focus on the behaviors they can control—rather than lamenting the failures of bad karma or bad others.[4] Chiefly, political and career leaders must put themselves in each others' shoes to better serve them and ultimately the public.

Why everyone hates the bureaucracy

For decades, American politicians, media, and interest groups have railed against "the bureaucracy," by which they usually mean career civil servants. As far back as President Jackson, citizens considered the Washington bureaucracy in particular corrupt, lazy, and unrepresentative (out of touch). After all, bureaucrats live on taxes coercively collected, while most people suffer the vicissitudes of the free market.[5] Further, bureaucrats are a technocratic, at times quasi-aristocratic elite certain to draw resentment in a fundamentally populist nation. Periods of antibureaucratic sentiment have waxed and waned in the American political life cycle.[6] Since the 1950s the sentiment has been mostly antibureaucratic, with, to varying degrees, Presidents Eisenhower, Kennedy, Nixon, Carter, Reagan, and Clinton all trying to become chief executive by running against their future employees, the permanent executives. One result of these campaigns by out-parties is the inclination of the winner's political appointees to view their career officials with skepticism.[7]

Few analysts have conducted systematic treatments of public trust of the government, and those who have done so have not always asked good questions. Still, most analysts agree that public distrust in government cannot be blamed on the U.S. bureaucracy. Family breakdown, the polarization of culture war politics, and more sensationalist media coverage clearly played roles in decreasing public trust in government (and in other institutions). The inevitable comedown after phenomenal U.S. success in World War II also explains declining trust.[8]

I suspect four additional factors. First, the largest declines in public trust in government generally and the bureaucracy in particular occurred in the late 1960s and early 1970s, when homicide rates tripled, total tax bite (federal, state, and local) went up by about 25 percent, the United States lost a major war in Vietnam, and a president resigned in disgrace. In short, to some degree the level of public trust in government reflects objective conditions related to government, if not necessarily bureaucratic, failures.[9] Similarly, President George W. Bush's popularity soared after initial successes in Afghanistan and Iraq and foundered after later failures in Iraq and New Orleans.

Second, as numerous scholars have pointed out, a plethora of new ethics laws in the wake of Watergate may have made government somewhat more honest, but they have had the unintended consequence of producing more scandals. As ethics laws and regulations proliferated, politicians and bureaucrats who in the past would have been lionized today wind up in jail, disgraced, or at least under investigation by congressional committees, inspectors general, general counsels, or independent counsels. Moreover, the media and public have difficulty distinguishing minor from major transgressions. The problems of the new ethics regime are neatly captured by the titles of noted scholarly works such as *The Pursuit of Absolute Integrity* and *Innocent Until Nominated*.[10]

Third, public education has changed in ways unlikely to enhance trust in government. In the past, textbooks and curricula portrayed an overly positive and optimistic view of American history; indeed, it could be considered heritage rather than history. In contrast, public education may now portray an overly negative view of American history, emphasizing sins rather than triumphs and lacking the context of realistic foreign comparisons. Further, public education has not imparted the basic facts of American government.[11] For example, few Americans know that very little public money goes to public employees, welfare, or foreign aid, but that the budget deficit is driven by spending on middle class entitlements.[12]

Finally, during the Depression, World War II, and the early cold war, most American families included public servants, usually soldiers. Direct experience demythologized government, so citizens understood both its strengths and its limitations. Such public service generally led Americans to hold more positive views of government and to see government as "theirs" in a way that merely writing (tax) checks or cashing (entitlement) checks does not.

The truth about bureaucrats: They're (mostly) good

As Charles Goodsell, Virginia Tech public administration professor emeritus, shows at length in his classic *The Case for Bureaucracy,* contrary to popular misconceptions, American bureaucrats are reasonably representative of the public, both demographically and ideologically.[13] Further, U.S. bureaucracies generally do a good job delivering public service, with remarkably little corruption. Customer satisfaction surveys show that frequent users of agency services give high marks to the U.S. Postal Service, the Social Security Administration, and to regulatory organizations such as the Food and Drug Administration, Federal Aviation Administration, and the Environmental Protection Agency. Even the Internal Revenue Service, an organization with the truly impossible job of interpreting and applying millions of words of tax code, gets reasonably high ratings from taxpayers and very high ratings from professional tax preparers.[14] An improved environment, safer workplaces, and longer life spans all represent government (as well as private sector) success stories.[15] As I report, there is substantial evidence that the Clinton-Gore reinvention efforts have made the U.S. government more efficient and innovative than ever. The George W. Bush administration has seemingly continued reinvention, albeit with less fanfare.[16]

The good news about the U.S. bureaucracy applies particularly to the executive levels. In my three years serving in the higher civil service, I rarely encountered public servants who in dedication and smarts were not more than a match for the professors I knew during my two decades of university teaching. Public servants are not only talented, but also they recognize their roles as *public* servants, accountable not merely to their own preferences but to the political leadership of their agencies, to Congress, and ultimately to the American people. I frequently heard government executives speculate about whether one or another action furthered the public interest, something I rarely heard state university professors talk about. Regarding bureaucratic flexibility, considerable scholarship shows that for the most part, career bureaucrats do accept legitimate political direction.[17]

Despite widespread views that a declining talent pool is sapping the strength of the public service in a "quiet crisis" of ever-increasing incompetence, the intelligence and capability of the career and noncareer executives I worked with never failed to impress. In the best review of the evidence, political scientists Joel D. Aberbach and Bert A. Rockman report that "evidence on behalf of a 'quiet crisis' is itself very quiet."[18] Measures of education, class background, and job satisfaction show little evidence that the higher civil service grew any less expert from 1970 to 1992.

Moreover, for decades surveys have found political appointees giving rather high marks to their career executives. Kathryn Newcomer, public administration professor at George Washington University, surveyed sixty-nine former political appointees who also had private sector experience. She found that political appointees from the Johnson, Nixon-Ford, Carter, and Reagan administrations rated career executives as comparable to or better than private sector managers on technical skills, managerial skills, and cooperativeness, though all saw government managers as less likely to take initiative than their counterparts in the private sector.[19] (Arguably, the last point is not negative, given constitutional constraints.) My own 1987–1988 mail survey of Reagan appointees found that they rated their career executives as highly competent, and generally willing to take direction.[20] This result mirrors the Aberbach and Rockman 1991 survey, in which overwhelming majorities of political appointees report that their career executives have good management skills, try to improve government, and work hard to carry out administration goals.[21] Similarly, freelance writer and consultant Judith E. Michaels' survey of George H. W. Bush appointees found that nearly 75 percent saw career executives as competent, and nearly 66 percent saw them as responsive.[22]

Naturally, we can find exceptions. As my own work and that of American University political science professor Robert Durant[23] suggest, when political leaders impose policies in opposition to the core values or practices of agencies, career subordinates sometimes respond by failing to share information or by leaking to Congress or the press. At times, therefore, political appointees are justified in using relatively hard-nosed tactics to "tell" rather than "sell" their policies.

Political hacks as the "folk devils" of government

If the permanent bureaucracy has a (mainly) undeserved bad reputation, political appointees are even more likely to be called "hacks." As Texas A & M
University public administration professor Domonic Bearfield explains in
his brilliant essay, "The Demonization of Patronage," the reaction against politically appointed public servants often takes the form of a "moral panic," an
"exaggerated reaction of a society to events and phenomena that challenge or
upset traditional norms and values." [24] Moral panics focus on "folk devils,"
which attract public outcry and government action. Bearfield discusses the
scapegoating of two Massachusetts Port Authority executives, who had been
appointed by the governor. The press blamed them for the 9/11 terrorists' use
of Logan Airport. The two political appointees had substantial management
and law enforcement experience, had improved Logan, and did not contribute to the failures of 9/11. The press and politicians nevertheless
hounded them from office. Their political experience and connections to
governors made them immediately suspect to reporters conditioned to consider career officials as competent and political officials as hacks.

As I detail elsewhere, many public administration academics subscribe
to the dominant journalistic view of political appointees.[25] Although less biased than denizens of the ivory tower, some career public servants hold the
same views. Indeed, Georgetown University's Joseph A. Ferrara and Lynn C.
Ross see the hapless political hack as the same sort of political myth as the in-
famous "$400 hammer" or the "welfare queen." [26] In my own time in gov-
ernment, I saw many career executives "stereotype" political appointees
based on limited data, just as people stereotype those of other races.[27] One
Clinton appointee recalled, "At first my agency tried to bury me. They didn't
know what to make of me since I came in as a special assistant, so they put
me in the back with a little office and tried to ignore me." [28] Although most
career executives get along just fine with the political appointees they work
with, some still see politicos in general as incompetent, fanatical, and/or corrupt. The good ones, the folks they know, are simply exceptions to the rule.
For example, EPA careerists seemed to experience productive working relationships with most of their political appointees from the second Reagan
term and the G. H. W. Bush and Clinton administrations. Yet when asked
about EPA political appointees generally, career executives often focus on the
very controversial appointees under Reagan's first EPA administrator, Anne
Burford. Indeed, when career officials approve of the political appointees,

and when those appointees support more resources for the agency, career officials often consider them "apolitical" rather than "political." [29] I once gave a presentation on political appointees before an audience of career executives and one brave and effective Clinton political, Cynthia Brock-Smith, who had befriended many of the careerists. Several of the career executives disputed my arguments that most political appointees do a good job, often adding comments to the effect that "we don't mean you, Cynthia. . . .You're one of the good ones." [30]

Stereotypes do not explain everything. To my knowledge, only two published works, both reflecting on the Reagan presidency, have systematically examined how relations between political appointees and career executives change over the course of an administration.[31]

Defense agencies had missions that the Reagan administration prized, and largely for this reason political appointees and career executives saw career-noncareer relations as starting well and staying that way. In contrast, domestic agencies fell into two patterns. In a handful of agencies with highly controversial first term Reagan political appointees (FEMA, OPM, NHTSA, and EPA), relations started badly, as the appointees with some talent but little political acumen tried nonincremental changes in agency scope and missions. Relations improved rapidly once these agency chiefs were replaced with less polarizing and often more expert figures. In most domestic agencies, career-noncareer relations remained both stable and mixed for careerists; for political appointees, a rough first two years were followed by gradual improvement.[32] Notably, friends in government suggest that career-noncareer relations in the George W. Bush administration generally improved in the second term as polarizing leaders in the Defense Department, CIA, and elsewhere were replaced.

In part, gradual improvements usually result from personnel changes because, as a longtime political appointee, a veteran of two administrations, put it, the most ideologically zealous and least politically skilled political and career officials eventually "kill each other off." More important, however, as George Mason University political scientist James P. Pfiffner and former career government executive Paul Lorentzin have taught me, over time political appointees and career executives get to know each other and overcome the stereotypes each side holds about the other to build productive working relationships.[33] This shift comes about because most of those on each side of the divide are competent, idealistic grown-ups. Consistently, career and noncareer officials ranked public interest motives, such as "the ability to work for desired policies" and "serving my country," above pay, benefits, and other more self-serving motives.[34] Career officials view the public interest through their agency prism, while political appointees typically view the public interest through party or ideological lenses. Yet over time, through persuasion, education, negotiation, and sometimes direction by the appointees, competing views can be reconciled.[35]

In truth, new political appointees typically know far less about their agencies than career public servants who have served for years or decades. Even so, in sharp contrast to the stereotypes about appointees, very few incompetents survive an incredibly elaborate vetting process involving the White House, cabinet secretaries, the FBI, many and varied interest groups, the Washington press corps, and for high-level positions, the U.S. Senate.[36] As an Office of Presidential Personnel official in the Clinton administration put it:

> I've heard some people say that we select people for jobs by throwing darts at a dart board. Sometimes I wish that were so, but in fact it is an incredibly complex process of matching up the people to the job and going from the White House to the agencies to the secretaries to the FBI and the ethics checks back to the people. I'm against the wall. I'm working 15 hours a day five days a week; 12 to 15 hours Saturday, and two or three hours Sunday.[37]

The limited data available suggest that the vast majority of political appointees have considerable talent. As Judith Michaels found, 53 percent of G. H. W. Bush's PAS (presidential appointees, Senate confirmed) officials had an M.D., L.L.D., or Ph.D., and 78 percent had some sort of advanced degree. Sixty-five percent were over fifty, and 49 percent had prior budgetary responsibility of over $1 million. Fifty-one percent reported losing income to join government. In addition, the variety of experience political appointees bring to their new jobs helps their agencies break down traditional bureaucratic "stovepipes" and build new partnerships across sectors: 41 percent of G. H. W. Bush appointees (and far more in most administrations) had their immediately prior positions outside Washington. More than half came from the private sector or from academia.[38]

Obviously, lower level noncareer SES and Schedule C officials have fewer credentials. Still, tens of thousands want to join a new presidential administration, but only a few earn jobs. Those few typically have the competence and desire to help government. Or as a Clinton appointee told me, "Remember that every political appointee has something you don't," most typically experience in state government, business, or a congressional staff. A young Reagan-Bush appointee I interviewed started in a low level White House job, developed a good track record, and then gained advancement to higher levels in the White House and finally to an SES position in an agency, based on performance:

> [My political boss] knew I could handle people older than I was and I had experience in management. Even though I was young, they knew I would do whatever it took to learn that job and so for the first six months I lived at the White House, from eight in the morning until ten at night, until I reached a comfort level and really changed that office. . . . They knew they could use me confidentially as a sounding board [and] took a chance on me because she knew that I had what it took, which was loyalty and being willing to do whatever it took to learn the job, which I did, but that is certainly not the way a career person gets their job, and I can see how that would be frustrating to career people. I would never have survived the personnel office in an agency because I didn't have the "credentials" for the position, but in the White House it is a make or break position—you either do well or you don't.[39]

A mail survey I conducted in 1994 found that large pluralities of career executives considered appointees in their own agencies competent.[40] Similarly, Aberbach and Rockman interviewed career executives in Washington, finding that 60 percent agreed that political appointees "bring valuable experience to the job"; 52 percent agreed that appointees "have good leadership qualities"; 59 percent agreed that appointees view their jobs as vehicles to make "positive, long term improvements to government service"; and 91 percent agreed that appointees "work hard to carry out administration initiatives and priorities," but fewer than a third thought that political appointees did a good job at internal agency management.[41]

To be fair, most political appointees are not responsible for much internal management, which is left to career public servants and military officers. Instead, political appointees do *political* work: strategic planning, budgeting, regulation developing (or delaying), as well as dealing with interest groups, members of Congress and congressional staffs, the media, and state and local officials. The number of political appointees has roughly doubled since the Kennedy administration, but congressional staffers have more than tripled, and interest groups and Washington-based reporters have increased faster still. Since the 1970s Washington's *political-industrial complex* has been a growing sector of the economy, as anyone familiar with real estate prices in the Washington area knows. Political appointees have actually lagged behind the rest of the sector.[42] To reduce the number of political appointees, we would need to reeducate career public servants to play more political roles, with the attendant political risks. To my knowledge, none of those who propose reducing the numbers of political appointees have considered how to do it.

The Michael Brown fiasco suggests the dangers of having *insufficiently political* political appointees. In popular lore, FEMA Director Brown is the ultimate political hack folk devil. Yet Brown's failings lay in not being political enough. Good political appointees bring political skills to their agencies. After all, FEMA prospered under Clinton political appointee James Lee Witt, an Arkansas "crony" of the president with little formal education. Clinton relied heavily on *political appointees* Witt chose. As one FEMA appointee who served under Witt claims:

> Political directors turned out to be the best regional directors because they know how to work with the governors and mayors. . . . They could learn the program, but the political comfort level they brought there was not there with the emergency management directors there before. It made a difference with the client base, the mayors, the governors, and their chiefs of staff. They have a better understanding of the pressures on those public officials, and our success is our communicating with our state and local partners. . . . The regional directors are politically savvy because they have to be. Those political skills turned out to be very, very useful. You need experience in three areas. One is emergency management. Two is managing people; and three is political management. Over time emergency management has become less important and the other two more so.[43]

What political appointees can do

If neither political appointees nor career bureaucrats are demons, and if in fact they can come to have respect for each other, the question becomes: What can each do to hasten and improve the way they work together? If relationships and trust can be built, can they improve on the often lengthy and halting process by which that happens (or in the worst cases does not happen) now?

For their part, presidential political appointees must approach their agency bureaucrats with respect rather than seeing them as stereotypes.[44] Agencies with similar organization charts can have very distinct cultures. A wise political appointee (or indeed any newcomer) should immerse himself in the agency's culture as an amateur anthropologist. As Virginia Tech public administration professor Anne M. Khademian writes, components of culture include organization members' views of their mission, customers, commitments, and partners.[45] To this, defense analyst Andrew Krepinevich, a former Army major, adds an organization's goals and the standard operating procedures through which to achieve those goals.[46] In addition, components of culture include the agency history and how officials interpret that history. As UCLA management professor William Ouchi points out, culture includes the degree of loyalty to the organization.[47] To understand an organization's culture, one must spend time reading its history and listening to its employees, overseers, and customers. A wise political appointee will consult everyone who previously held the position not only to understand how they succeeded or failed but also to get a scouting report on the best (and worst) career employees.

Studying the agency takes time, and for better or worse most PAS officials serve for months in an unofficial capacity as consultants before formal confirmation. These months can be useful for on-site reconnaissance.[48] Without careful study of agency culture, new appointees are apt to make serious errors in communication. One hilarious example occurred when Jim Miller, President Reagan's choice to head the Federal Trade Commission, tried to explain his goals to FTC career executives. Miller, a flamboyant and highly capable former academic, introduced his agenda to a trumpet fanfare while dressed in a devil's outfit; he then tried to assure the staff that he was not going to play the devil. Unfortunately, this performance did not impress overly serious FTC attorneys.[49]

Capable appointees see part of their job as campaigning inside the agency to partner with career bureaucrats and persuade them to join the administration rather than wait it out. Appointees must listen, and, as Ferrara and Ross put it, appointees must also "communicate, communicate, communicate." [50] For example, I interviewed a Reagan appointee who found that career executives knew little about Republican ideology, so he held a sort of seminar for them:

I recommended readings that would give a full picture of Reagan policy and where it was coming from. I had a series of brownbag lunches just to kind of sit around and informally talk about policy ideas, and I found these lunches invaluable for idea exchange and clearing the air. I think every [PAS] can do this.

Skillful politicking requires the avoidance of gaffes. Like veterans, farmers, ethnic groups, and other constituencies, bureaucrats can be extremely sensitive. Career EPA staff disliked Carol Browner, Clinton's appointee as administrator, because she had made the mistake of criticizing career EPA officials during her confirmation hearings. As a Clinton EPA appointee lamented years later, "I don't know that she's ever recovered from the point of view of careerists." [51] Donald Rumsfeld, George W. Bush's first defense secretary, offered an even more extreme example in freezing out military officers. As Kansas State political scientist Dale R. Herspring writes, "Bureaucracies have a strange way of seeming to obey the person in charge even when they are being insulted, as with [Rumsfeld], but they generally have the last laugh by jettisoning most of the changes he made as soon as he is gone." [52]

In sharp contrast, numerous FEMA career and appointed officials I interviewed admired Witt's ability to persuade career executives. A Clinton FEMA appointee marveled that:

> Written mission statements, I used to think that was all bull, but the employees here needed that. There was this tension about whether we are a Cold War agency and can't talk about what we do even with each other, or we are a disaster relief agency that talks constantly with stakeholders, and is wired and interconnected, and [Director] Witt resolved that. . . . He's been real accessible, communicating his vision to the employees with lots of feedback. Of course, we're doing something most of the American public believes that government should be doing.

In addition to understanding the broader culture, capable appointees should get a feel for the change agents and laggards within their organization and how to unleash the former and encourage the latter. A good example is Steven Kelman, the Clinton appointee who led the OMB's Office of Federal Procurement Policy. Kelman spent much of his time conducting surveys and focus groups to understand how to identify those within the system who backed procurement reform, and he spent considerable time plotting with the pro-reform Procurement Executives Association. Once reformers within government showed that procurement reform could work, Kelman reinforced their efforts by publicizing successful innovators, rewarding them, and training others. Kelman also increased pressures for change by building alliances with powerful actors outside the organization, particularly in the media, Congress, and in the defense industry. Similar strategies were used successfully by FEMA's Witt, NASA's Daniel Goldin, the Veteran Health Administration's Kenneth W. Kizer, and U.S. Mint director John Martino.[53]

In general, appointees achieve the most by focusing on strategic initiatives and managing an agency's external politics. Although appointees must attempt to persuade career officials, they typically lack the time and knowledge to manage the day-to-day affairs of the agency. The exception occurs when appointees seek to reform agency core practices, which may necessitate more coercive signals. In such cases, research suggests that a single unexpected bonus, promotion, or exile to a turkey farm can send a message through an entire organization.[54]

Yet coercive means, if used too often, can prove counterproductive. Political appointees must be willing to forgive the foibles of a small minority of careerists who do more to hinder than help an uncertain transition. A few careerists may or may not fully share information, and may or may not get along with each other. One Clinton appointee in an agency not known for good management complained that two important career deputies had not been on speaking terms with each other for some time, a situation the appointee was not informed of before joining the office. The matter resolved itself when one retired. The same appointee reported that the first day on the job, one deputy greeted his new boss by saying, "You're the tenth ____ I've worked under," implying that an eleventh would be along soon enough![55] Fortunately, this leader did not allow these individuals to turn the appointee against the civil servants generally.

Finally, appointees must understand their own strengths and weaknesses, learn how to overcome their weaknesses, and use their strengths to serve the public.[56]

What career public servants can do: Managing one's own government of strangers

For better or worse, large numbers of political appointees are here to stay, and career civil servants cannot control how well those far above their pay grades manage a presidential transition. They can influence the micro-level political transition within their own organizations and how to use those transitions to build social capital within the agency. Certainly, those micro-level transitions will often be difficult. As noted above, Americans are populists: they suspect experts and hierarchies.[57] Donald Devine, a political scientist who became Reagan's OPM director, explains that such suspicion is a deep part of our collective political culture and sometimes proves useful to democracy: those in positions of expert authority are not always right.[58] Politics is a cutthroat business, making politicians doubly suspicious people. Combined, these tendencies ensure that incoming administrations distrust the bureaucrats who served their predecessors of the opposing party, especially if the incoming party has long been out or represents a fundamentally different governing philosophy, as in 1933, 1953, 1961, 1969, 1981, and 1993.[59]

Only the very centrist G. H. W. Bush administration—in some respects the first third term since Franklin Roosevelt—had the sort of kind and gentle transition in the bureaucracy that bureaucrats would want. As one career executive recalled of the 1989 transition: "It wasn't so much Bush One as Reagan Three." [60]

But such nontransitions are rare. As populists, Americans like political change, and therefore career executives must master change readiness, both psychologically and administratively. What can career executives do to hasten the eventual cycle of accommodation between the civil service and political appointees? How can career leaders help make political appointees more effective in managing the broader Washington political environment (reporters, interest groups, the White House, and congressional staffs)? After all, if the political appointee thrives, so does the agency.[61] Borrowing from others, I offer the following advice to career executives who want to do their part to smooth political transitions.

First, avoid stereotypes

Too often, career executives believe the harsh stereotype that political appointees are political hacks and that the numerous exceptions are just that, exceptions. Certainly, presidents always have a few "must-place" appointees whose clout exceeds their talent: the odd New Hampshire party official who helped win the primary or the child of a major contributor who wants to go slumming in government. But these appointments are very few in number, and, as longtime Navy career SES Harvey Wilcox points out, they typically wind up supervised by career officials who can keep them out of trouble. And a few such scions develop into effective leaders, rising in government or the private sector.[62] Career leaders can help in their ascent.

As noted above, in sharp contrast to the stereotypes, the data show that PAS officials are well-educated and have substantial experience. Lower level Schedule C political appointees are less qualified, but even so, politics is a competitive business, and successful campaigns are not run by fools. Those few who have proven themselves in a political campaign will most likely have dedication, intelligence, and commitment to public service. Even if they start out without much knowledge of the executive branch generally or the agency in particular, most are smart enough and industrious enough to learn the ropes and make a real contribution. Even the use of noncareer ambassadors, which journalists and members of Congress love to attack, may in practice prove necessary. As an Office of Presidential Personnel official told me, Congress simply does not appropriate sufficient funds to support major embassies, which makes the recruitment of wealthy (and one hopes charming) campaign contributors a practical necessity. Political ambassadors such as Nixon contributor Walter Annenberg (London), G. H. W. Bush contributor Peter Seccia (Rome), and Clinton contributor Pamela Harriman (Paris) were all successes in other fields and capably represented their presidents and their nation.

Sometimes stereotypes do come true. Presidential personnel decisions may prove perilous if the agency is not an administration priority. Just as career bureaucrats develop turkey farms to bury their own low performers, so too do presidents.[63] If one's agency serves as such a dumping ground, career leaders may have little choice but to grin and bear it and find a way to make callow political appointees as effective as possible. For solace, one can remember that unlike career turkeys, political turkeys lack tenure. If they screw up publicly, Thanksgiving dinner could come at any time.

Second, do reconnaissance

Every political appointee brings something to his or her post. It may be knowledge of the budget process or public relations skill. It may be business experience. It may be connections with the White House, OMB, Congress, or an interest group. It may simply be a fresh pair of eyes with new insights about the agency. Whatever it is, find out what talents new appointees bring, if possible even before they come on board, and think about how they can help the agency. But understand that they may already have ideas about how to make a contribution, and ultimately they must define their roles.

During the reconnaissance period, one can seek contacts in the appointee's previous workplaces to get the inside information. If the appointee has published anything, read it, which is easy to do in our online age. To find ideas about how to make a personal relationship work, see if you have anything in common. Finally, remember that like Army generals, nearly all political appointees have had patrons (mentors). Study the particular patron as best you can. For a Hill staffer, the mentor is almost invariably his or her boss, the member of Congress. I have found that appointees from the Hill whose mentors were humane and professional behave likewise; unfortunately, not all members of Congress are humane and professional.

Third, put yourself in their shoes

As one careerist put it, it is difficult to understand how lonely and unsure a new political appointee can be. If appointees are new to Washington, this may be true of their private lives as well. One Clinton appointee who moved to Washington from the West recalled that "it is very hard to make friends here. The legislative branch is very social, lots of receptions, a lot of people in their 20s, but in the executive branch people work a lot of hours and have families. You can't really socialize too much with your subordinates. It's not appropriate, so that part, leaving behind my parents and my brother and his family and my support network since high school; that was hard."

And a Clinton EPA appointee complained:

> It's completely different from a job and hiring situation anywhere else, because you don't really know what the job is, and your boss, the administrator, doesn't really know what the job is, and your boss is negotiating back and forth with the White House. In any other sector, before you are hired you would actually have discussions with the person you are working with about what their vision for this job is, to clarify the expectations of what you can achieve. I was not the only one who did not have that discussion. From my colleagues, I don't think any of us did.[64]

By exercising empathy, career public servants can better understand, respect, and serve political leaders.

Fourth, make the first move

Political appointees' biggest complaint about career executives is the same one careerists have about them: a failure to communicate. Or, as one career senior executive told me in 1993, "The trouble with the civil service during a transition is that we're just too civil. We don't say anything." As noted above, each organization has a unique culture, so new appointees may not know how to communicate with career executives. Nearly 70 percent of the Clinton appointees surveyed agreed that careerists should "initiate contacts with appointees, who may not know how to work with the bureaucracy."

During the pre-appointment process, try to see that your agency's general counsel or personnel people are keeping your appointee-designate advised as to his or her status. Offer to help with the ethics regulations. If the appointee is moving to Washington, try to arrange help. As soon as the appointee comes on board, or even before if possible, career executives should request get-acquainted meetings to explain what career officials do, to see what the appointee needs, and to find out the appointee's preferred style of interaction—in person, by telephone, or by memo. Provide a booklet with everyone's picture and basic information. Particularly for appointees who have never supervised large numbers of people, the last step can be invaluable.

Making the first move gives executives the chance to show political appointees that they know who's boss—appointees are in charge, and career public servants are there to help. In addition, career officials should ask new appointees to orient careerists as soon as they are comfortable doing so, to make sure that everyone understands the new agenda. If careerists don't know what appointees want, they can't help them get it; nor can they advise political appointees to protect them from running afoul of law or Congress. Again, see what you may have in common. One longtime career SES greeted a new cabinet secretary by pointing out that they were both from Chicago. Mentioning that made a personal connection and signaled a common way of viewing administration and a willingness to acknowledge that the new secretary might want his own person in this transferable SES position. In the end, the new secretary stuck with his incumbent career SES, a practice more typical than not.

Part of that first move should be developing an orientation plan for the new appointee, if at all possible after consulting with the appointee regarding what sort of information he wants and in what form. Some political leaders are more comfortable with paper orientations, while others prefer more personal approaches. Orientation is the first part of what may be a three- or four-year relationship, so get it right by copying from those who have done a good job orienting past appointees. Indeed, doing a good job orienting incoming officials, who often express confusion regarding the budget process in particular, may help one's own advancement. Appointees (and others!) find government budget and personnel procedures particularly obtuse, so help is usually appreciated.

As part of any orientation, career leaders should attempt to put new appointees in touch with their predecessors. New political appointees are literally "home alone," particularly if they come from outside the Beltway. Forty-five percent of Reagan political appointees reported not knowing any of their agencies' political appointees before joining government; 35 percent of Clinton appointees said the same. Fewer still knew career officials. At the same time, 81 percent of Clinton appointees reported a desire to consult their predecessors. Accordingly, the regular briefing materials for new appointees should include the names and whereabouts of all those who previously held the position, regardless of political party or administration. PAS officials, in particular, may face a stressful wait of several months from the time they are designated to the time they actually take office, so they have ample time, as well as the desire, to consult predecessors. Because most political appointees give their career bureaucrats high marks, you probably have more to gain than to lose from having the new boss consult the old one. In general, political appointees of different parties will agree about which career officials are productive and which are speed bumps.[65]

Naturally, you may not wish to share everything with new appointees, at least not during the first days of the relationship. Just as it is bad form to badmouth an ex-girlfriend to a new one, criticizing the last administration to members of the current one will have them suspect that come the next administration, you'll be saying the same things about them. Then, too, you might not want to show that picture of you getting an award from an ex-president of the other party—at least not right away.

Fifth, keep your house in order

New political appointees bring fresh eyes to the agency. Part of their job is to question agency practices in order to bring improvement or at least ensure accountability. The process may not be fun, but if your house is basically in order, the scrutiny should cause little long term discomfort. Wilcox writes:

> There's a natural tendency for appointees confronted with issues they don't yet understand and a staff they don't yet trust to call for outside help. One of the first projects most new appointees wanted to discuss with me was how to contract for a consulting firm or a renowned expert, and in their shoes I might have done the same. It's hard to argue against taking a fresh look at an old issue. Just try not to take it as a personal affront.[66]

In Wilcox's case, new Navy secretary John Lehman dispatched Yale law professor Robert Bork to grill career attorneys on contract procedures. This resulted in no changes, but did assure Lehman that the Navy's house was in order, at least regarding submarine contracts. All this recalls the old Air Force saying: The two biggest lies are when the inspector general says "we're here to help you," and you reply "we're glad you're here." Yet without such outside pressures, none of us would serve the public half so well.

As part of keeping your house in order, *practice maximum feasible transparency.* From years of interviewing hundreds of officials in dozens of organizations, I know my subjects are lying to me when they tell me that everything in the agency is "great" because they have a "great bunch of people" wonderfully effective at "interfacing with others to provide terrific public service." Often, they are also lying to themselves. In the real world, organizations do some things well, some things tolerably well, and some badly or not at all— sometimes for reasons beyond anyone's control. When a bureaucrat says his or her agency is heaven on earth, that person loses credibility. And I have to think that most political appointees are at least as smart as I am.

Sixth, forgive them their trespasses

Just as career executives often stereotype political appointees, political appointees often join government with their own negative ideas about bureaucrats, particularly if the president's party has been out of power for some time. Usually, negative views of bureaucrats soon become positive, but this may happen more quickly if you remember the biblical admonition that "a soft answer turneth away wrath." Like the rest of us, political appointees simply make mistakes. When they do, do not correct them in public.

Related to this, as Wilcox advises, *forgive every appointee at least one reorganization* as his way of marking his territory:

> Every appointee will have an impulse to reorganize. Whether that springs from a campaign promise to cut fat or whether it's to accommodate new agency duties, reorganizations are every bit as certain as death and taxes. But they're rarely as momentous.[67]

Indeed, wise career leaders should offer to lead the reorganization to make sure it goes well. Sometimes reorganizations really can bring improvement. Indeed, savvy change agents within an organization will often develop ideas in hopes of finding a new appointee with the interest and clout to make them happen.[68]

Political appointees often offend career executives by doing things demanded by their role as appointees representing the president to the agency rather than (or in addition to) the agency to the president. Appointees have an obligation to point out when the agency could better serve the public, and highly effective appointees such as James Lee Witt, Jim Miller, John Lehman, Steve Kelman, and Jim King actually began with policies that many agency insiders objected to.[69] As a Clinton EPA appointee put it, "Sometimes I have to say that OMB has a point there: maybe we are getting too much money." While perhaps true, I doubt that saying this won the appointee any friends inside EPA.

Seventh, as Colin Powell says, never step on enthusiasm

In general, political appointees join government more for patriotism (and ego) than for money.[70] Although they probably know less about the agency than career officials and may hold a different view of the public interest, they want to do a good job. As survey research shows, they are frustrated by the many constraints that frustrate all government executives.[71] Help them figure out how to overcome those constraints and buck them up when they get discouraged. At the same time, not all their ideas will be practical. When you disagree with an appointee, explain why in terms of external forces or standards. Rather than simply saying an idea is bad, say: "You have a good idea, but right now the congressional committee won't accept it. How might we develop a strategy to change that?" Sometimes, with sufficient effort and planning, political and legal obstacles really can be overcome.

Eighth, don't get in the line of fire

As scholar and occasional political appointee Richard Haass explains in *The Bureaucratic Entrepreneur,* political appointees exist in part to take risks for the agency and for the president's agenda. Their short tenure frees them to battle Congress and take on the press. The killing hours that politics requires are acceptable because appointees are running three-year sprints rather than thirty-year marathons. Finally, as politicians, political appointees are more likely to do politics better than career officials can hope to—exceptions like Michael Brown notwithstanding. Career executives are in a different position. They should support their appointees, but also understand and explain the limits of what battles they can fight, given that careerists may someday have to work for a different team. Naturally, this point might not be a subject for discussion on day one. Further, in some agencies, the organization culture does not let career officials duck political battles. In places like the Navy, which have considerable unit cohesion, and in places like the U.S. Forest Service, where even relatively low level officials must negotiate with state and local politicians, careerists are expected to fight political battles.

Ninth, disagree without being disagreeable

Survey research demonstrates that when confronted with implementing policies they disagree with, as often happens, career officials normally feel free to tell their political superiors—nine of ten report taking this course.[72] For example, in an anonymous survey one HHS career executive reported requesting different duties when detailed to develop regulations he/she strongly opposed. Political appointees respected the request and did not retaliate. "I was not detailed, and this is the way these matters usually are resolved," the respondent said. Again, negotiation over duties is more accepted in some organizations than in others. In defense organizations, such boldness might be seen as disloyalty and have serious consequences.[73]

Sometimes invoking the law to officials who genuinely may not know it can head off possible conflicts. For example, a careerist who blocked a personnel move he thought illegal recalled:

> When this individual came back to me to say the super two levels above supported him, I said there must be some misunderstanding because what he said was contrary to our legal obligations, so I

suggested a meeting with my superior and his superior, and for all the politicals to be there just to make sure we were all on the same page, and then he backed down and said he would just go with what I said. . . . There was no price for doing that.[74]

To the degree possible, career officials should try to limit disagreements until they have established trusting relationships with appointees. Dissent can use up political capital, so it should not be used too casually or too often. For good guidance on the tools of ethical dissent, political appointees and career officials would do well to read John H. Johns's Guidelines for Loyal Dissent in Government (see Box 1.7).[75]

Tenth, mobility is a possibility

Sometimes career officials disagree with a boss or a whole administration's entire agenda regarding their agency or simply cannot work with a particular political leader. In this situation, it might not make sense to wait them out. Most studies suggest appointees serve an average of about two years in their positions, but my own data from the Reagan administration suggest that in two-term administrations, political appointees serve an average of 2.6 years in their position and 3.7 years in their agencies—a long time to wait. Given that the average government executive will serve twenty-five years or so, this situation could mean spending 10 percent of one's government career in administrative purgatory—more than enough time to develop ulcers. Life is too short to suffer; rather than persevere, it might make more sense to seek a soft landing elsewhere, especially if the boss is a career executive. Most career executives are terrific, but a few seem to have studied the leadership secrets of Saddam Hussein, and there is precious little we can do about them: emigration in the face of oppression makes even more sense if a toxic boss is a careerist than a political because the career boss may be firmly entrenched.

Eleventh, careerists should show respect to lame-duck appointees

"Holdovers" from one administration to the next are rare. "Blanketing in," political appointees switching to career civil service positions, is equally rare—only twelve known cases occurred in the 1992–1993 period. Thus, sooner or later, for better or worse, any political appointee will be gone. But they may not be gone forever. Often appointees go on to Congress or to interest groups, so they continue to influence agency affairs. Many will return to government at higher levels in later administrations. Someday, in the not too distant future that GS-12 Schedule C may return as undersecretary. For entirely practical reasons, they should be treated as humanely as possible. In Washington it's nice to be smart, but it's also smart to be nice.

Unfortunately, in most cases the incoming crew will be less than respectful of the outgoing, "loser" administration, particularly at lower levels, where new politicals tend to be more passionate and less experienced. Older folks know that they too will someday be on the losing end of an election. For that reason, it may be up to the career service to buck up the outgoing (and perhaps future) politicals.

Finally, career officials must keep perspective

In our constitutional democracy, the worst ideas of political appointees seldom last long. They are blocked by other appointees, Congress, the *Washington Post,* or the mere thought of the *Washington Post.* Constitutional blocking of bad (and good) ideas is even more likely under divided party government—indeed, one career SES I interviewed longed for the days of divided government when "you could play your mother against your father or your father against your mother. Bad things could come up on the Hill and you could turn to the administration, or bad things from the administration could be stopped on the Hill." But even under united party government, such constitutional blocking occurs.

In the long run, the best ideas of political appointees, including some regarded skeptically by career bureaucrats, may live on after appointees are long gone from government. As Wilcox admits, the soft approach to military shipyards taken by political appointees in the 1970s and 1980s was not the defense policy the career executives wanted, but perhaps turned out to be what was needed to end the Cold War.[76] Policies that seem questionable in the short term may produce long-term rewards. And when all else fails, career and political officials might, as the Serenity Prayer puts it, have the strength and wisdom to change what they can and accept what they cannot because constitutional governance involves endless patience, constant struggle, and periodic change.

A final word

Rather than curse the political system in general and the political appointee system in particular, presidents, political appointees, and career leaders should seek opportunities to manage the system to produce more rather than less social capital across the career and political sectors, to get more out of the dynamic career-noncareer nexus. After all, measurements suggest that the American government is relatively innovative, efficient, representative, and open compared to foreign governments, and in part these characteristics reflect the impact of outsider political appointees keeping bureaucracies accountable.[77] In a time of challenges—terrorism, environmental degradation, and natural disasters—that cut across organizational lines, it is more vital than ever to have politically skilled outsiders able to work with career experts to find, and then politically sell feasible solutions. After all, that is what democracy should be all about.

Resources for further learning

On how to better manage presidential transitions, the best and most readable work bringing together a variety of insights is James P. Pfiffner, *The Strategic Presidency: Hitting the Ground Running* (1996).

For ideas on how to improve the "gotcha" climate of the appointment process and the appointee system generally, check out the Brookings Institution's Presidential Appointee Initiative at *www.brookings.edu/gs/pai/pai_hp.htm.*

Works advising political appointees about how to conduct themselves while in office, particularly relations with their career partners, are plentiful. Perhaps the best is John H. Trattner, *The Prune Book* (2005); the title parodies the "Plum Book" of government jobs. Trattner, who serves at the Council for Excellence in Government, does a new version for each presidential administration. Another very useful book is Richard P. Nathan, *So You Want to Be in Government?* (2000).

My own *Beyond a Government of Strangers: How Career Executives and Political Appointees Can Turn Conflict to Cooperation* (2005) offers advice to career executives dealing with political officials. Before and during a presidential transition, the Senior Executives Association, at *http://seniorexecs.org/index.php?id=117,* often issues useful pamphlets advising members on some of the finer points of political-career etiquette.

Finally, the chapters in Mark A. Abramson and Paul R. Lawrence's edited *Learning the Ropes* (2005) offer great insights for both career and political public servants.

Notes

1. See, for example, Murray and Wamsley (2007); Cohen (1998); Editors (2005). For responses, see Maranto (2005); and Maranto (1993). See also Maranto (2002); Bearfield (2007); and Bearfield (in press).

2. Niskanen (1971); Peters and Nelson (1978); Savas (1982); and Moe (1985). For responses, see Goodsell (2003).

3. "Quotes about Change" (2006).

4. Bunker (1996).

5. Van Riper (1958).

6. Hofstadter (1964).

7. Maranto (1993), 31–60.

8. See essays in Nye, Zelikow, and King (1997).

9. These failures are often state and local responsibilities. For example, I have found that on an annual basis trust in government correlates closely with the homicide rate: Americans seem to blame their national government for state and local government failures to fight crime. Notably, New York City reduced its homicide rate by more than 60 percent in the mid-1990s, with further declines since. Yet other cities have refused to copy what works in crime prevention, as former NYPD Chief William Bratton laments in *Turnaround* (New York: Random House, 1998). Despite these horrid failures, mayors still win reelection, and police chiefs keep their jobs.

10. Anechiarico and Jacobs (1996); Mackenzie (2001). See also Mackenzie (2002).

11. For two rather different, but essentially concordant views on (mis)education, see Ravitch (2003); and Zimmerman (2002).

12. Kettl and Fesler (2005), 32–33.

13. Goodsell (2003), 84–94.

14. Ibid., 27–34.

15. Ibid., 35–41.

16. Maranto (in press).

17. Wood and Waterman (1994); Meier and O'Toole (2006).

18. Aberbach and Rockman (2000), 164.

19. Newcomer (1988).

20. Maranto (1993), 85–87.

21. Aberbach and Rockman (2000), 123.

22. Michaels (2005), 13.

23. Durant (1992).

24. Bearfield (2007), 101–120; quote, page 102.

25. Maranto (2002), 175–178; Maranto (2005), 42; Maranto (1993).

26. Ferrara and Ross (2005), 42.

27. Sniderman and Piazza (1993).

28. Maranto (2005), 53.

29. Ibid., 7–8.

30. Ibid., 32. In fairness, political appointees themselves often hold negative stereotypes about career bureaucrats, a topic I have treated. See Maranto (1993).

31. Maranto (1993); Maranto (1991), 247–266.

32. Maranto (1993), 127–137; Maranto (1991).

33. Pfiffner (1996); Lorentzin (1985). Overcoming stereotypes is the main theme of Maranto (2005).

34. Brewer and Maranto (2000).

35. Maranto (2005), 20.
36. Maranto (2005); Mackenzie (2001).
37. Personal interview, March 20, 2000.
38. Michaels (1997), 198–212.
39. Maranto (2005), 31.
40. Ibid., 32.
41. Aberbach and Rockman (2000), 123.
42. Maranto (2005), 26–29, 33–36.
43. Ibid., 34.
44. Ferrara and Ross (2005), 63.
45. Khademian (2002), 108–121.
46. Krepinevich (1986).
47. Ouchi (1981).
48. Kelman (2005), 83–85; Maranto (2005), 55–58.
49. Harris and Milkis (1989), 201.
50. Ferrara and Ross (2005), 68.
51. Maranto (2005), 51.
52. Herspring (2005), 406.
53. Kelman (2005); Abramson and Lawrence (2001).
54. Maranto (1993), 103–115.
55. Maranto (2005), 54.
56. These lessons are included in a number of books, including Maranto (2005); Abramson and Lawrence (2005); Kelman (2005); Haass (1999); Nathan (2000); and Trattner (2005).
57. Hofstadter (1964).
58. Devine (1972).
59. Maranto (2005), 99–102.
60. Maranto (2002a).
61. Wilcox (2005).
62. Ibid.
63. Maranto (1993), 87–88.
64. Maranto (2005), 53.
65. Wilcox (2005). Wilcox reports that the appointee-to-appointee exchange of information regarding career public servants is particularly well developed in the Defense Department, perhaps because defense policy remains less partisan than domestic policy.
66. Ibid., 66.
67. Ibid., 68.
68. Kelman (2005).
69. Maranto (2005), 46–47.
70. Powell (1995).
71. Maranto (1993).
72. Maranto (2005), 104–107.
73. Wilcox (2005); Herspring (2005).
74. Maranto (2005), 107.
75. Maranto (2005), 133–134.
76. Wilcox (2005), 74–75.
77. Maranto (2002); see also Goodsell (2003).

7.1 Confessions of a political appointee

BILL MURRAY, ADJUNCT PROFESSOR, VIRGINIA POLYTECHNIC INSTITUTE AND STATE UNIVERSITY

WHEN—IN THE WORDS OF A FEMA CAREER ADMINISTRATOR IN THE 1990S (regularly recounted by public administration professor Gary Wamsley)—the political appointees come surfing in at the start of each administration, what is a career administrator to do? The long tradition of discussing this topic at the federal level began with Hugh Heclo starting the conversation in *Government of Strangers.*[1]

As I wrap up service for my second governor of my home state, I offer some thoughts on political appointees for the benefit of career administrators at the state level of government. I started my thinking about political appointees as a graduate student and legislative staffer who was frankly horrified at some of the behavior I witnessed by executive branch political appointees.

On the other extreme of Heclo's magisterial work, I wrote a somewhat naïve dissertation that was quite critical of political appointees at the state level.[2] I was reacting to the widespread politicization of my state's environmental regulatory agency in the mid-1990s by a former Reagan appointee who included in an interview guide for career positions the Reagan administration canard that "personnel is policy."

A short time after that, Robert Maranto wrote "The Case for Spoils" and argued for more widespread patronage.[3] Paul Light then showed that as the Clinton administration "reinvented" government, government was thickening with layers of political appointees.[4]

And then, ironically, I became a political appointee nearly six years ago. For my trouble I took a pay cut, all but dared my spouse to divorce me, and had my daughter looking for me on milk cartons. It should come as no surprise that I now have a more nuanced view of political appointees at the state level.

With this view, I'd like to offer some lessons about political appointees for career administrators in hopes of improving understanding and therefore collegiality. The upper reaches of state government are much like university faculties in that, at the end of the day, collegiality is what makes the organization either flourish or flounder.

Any such lessons always run the risk of being disproved by a contrary anecdote, and I make no claim that these thoughts are based on rigorous empirical methods, simply experience.

As I think about these lessons, I realize the Reagan people were probably onto something with the notion that personnel is policy. Personnel does matter in building an administration, but not in the way they may have thought. Rather than political zealots carrying out an ideological crusade, you want professionals who can think for themselves, make good decisions, and run government well. At least at the state level that is what works politically and managerially. Voters at the state level are notoriously uninterested in ideology as compared to political competence; that is why Hawaii and Rhode Island, two of the most heavily Democratic states in presidential elections, have Republican governors, and Wyoming and Kansas have Democratic governors.

With all the appropriate caveats, following are ten lessons on political appointees for career administrators. I learned these primarily from the two governors I have worked for; both had successful administrations due in no small part to the quality of their political appointees. (The occasional bits of trouble they had were often related to political appointees too.)

1. Not all political appointees are incompetent; some are incredibly wise. Clark Clifford was the model of the wise man, the person of affairs who acted as counselor to multiple presidents. We have people like that in state government. I served with one who had been in the cabinet of two governors. She had run statewide campaigns but was apolitical in governing. She was an unabashed partisan at one point in her career but got along very well with members of the other party. "Madam Secretary" was effective because she was wise in the best sense. She had a diverse set of life experiences at senior levels and could meld them together to make good management decisions, good policy decisions, and occasionally, when needed, good political decisions. The takeaway here is that there is nothing wrong with an overtly partisan background as long as you check the politics at the door when you start helping run government. Madam Secretary knew that campaigning and governing were fundamentally different; she just happened to be good at both.

She also proved that one of the best places for a governor to look for cabinet appointees is in the cabinet of his or her predecessors.

2. You might already be a political appointee in all but name and not even know it. The tradition of career administrators doing the work of political appointees is well established. An effective personnel strategy for governors is to figure out who is really doing the work of a politically appointed leadership position and simply formalize the arrangement by appointing that person, the loyal deputy or senior career staffer who has been running the agency for years while a parade of political appointees was installed over him or her. A great thing for governors to try (which is always greeted with the reaction of "why didn't someone think of this before?") is appointing the person who is actually capable of doing the job and in many ways has been doing it. In our state I'm thinking in particular of our budget director who had been deputy director for budget of the central budget office for approximately a decade. He had served under political appointees of varying competency but was always the one on budget day who ended up presenting the nuts and bolts of the budget. It has been very valuable to have him actually in charge of the budget agency. So, don't be too critical of political appointees; you could be closer than you think to becoming one.

3. Be wary of the campaign staff. As I mentioned above, campaigning and governing are different. A few positions crosswalk pretty well: advance, press relations, and the body person role. Some of the biggest failures in gubernatorial administrations stem from unqualified campaign staffers in over their heads in senior government positions. State governments are large, complex, and wickedly difficult to manage. Taking inexperienced campaign aides, giving them a big title and office, and printing up some business cards actually does not confer much in the way of management expertise. As a career administrator, you will sometimes need to prop up campaign staff members appointed to senior positions who don't know what they are doing. It is not fair. Neither, as John Kennedy observed, is life.

4. Some of the governor's best (and most loyal) political appointees will not even have voted for him or her. Some of them might not have voted at all. Apolitical career administrators and appointees from the other party can be valuable members of administrations. Do not assume that all of the governor's appointees are political henchmen. Americans like divided government. It is more the norm than the exception at the federal level, and it is quite common at the state level. Appointees from other political backgrounds are not only a good bridge to the other party, but also they are a

good source of ideas. It turns out that neither political party's platform, if enacted in total, would be very popular or very effective.

5. If senior appointees and senior career administrators do not know what drink to order for one another after six months, then you have a problem. The first governor I worked for was notorious for a nose to the grindstone management philosophy (reflective of his high technology entrepreneur roots). He loved Friday evening bed checks to make sure people were all still at their desks at 6:30 p.m. The one affirmative defense you could always use for his "where were you?" accusation was to tell him you had been out drinking with your colleagues (career and appointed). I still believe some of the most valuable work of this administration was done at a trendy ale house near the state capitol (and I am not even much of a drinker).

6. Even political appointees and senior career administrators have lives (and families). On the one hand, government work is mistakenly portrayed as 9 to 5. One-hundred-hour workweeks are just as common at the senior levels of government as they are in law firms and investment banks. On the other hand, it is fundamentally not sustainable to demand hours and a work schedule that prevent any type of private life. For years I told people, not very tongue-in-cheek, that if you were in a healthy relationship while serving in the governor's office, then you were not working hard enough. That was a wrongheaded view even in my state, where the governor is limited to a single, four-year term. It is absolutely wrong in a state where the governor can run for reelection. We have kidded ourselves as a society for decades about having it all. Your family life absolutely will suffer if you take a senior position in government, whether or not you are a career administrator. If you are from the corporate or trade association world, you will get to take a large pay cut to further sweeten the deal. I used to greet the resignation stories saying that someone wanted to spend more time with the family with skepticism. Absent allegations of impropriety or incompetence, I don't do this anymore. Neither should you. Senior career administrators face tremendous stress for low pay, and so do political appointees.

At the same time, viewing service at the senior level in government and having a decent family life as fundamentally incompatible is wrong. My second governor convinced me of this. I have never been very good at finding balance and would welcome an article from someone who is. I will add that this is a critical problem for senior political appointees and for senior career staff. The one refrain I hear from senior people in government when they leave is how tired they are. It is not just presidents or governors who age dramatically in government.

7. Gubernatorial administrations include people making the most they will ever make and the least they will ever make. Both can be valuable. In the administrations I served in, appointees vied for the honor of the biggest salary cut. The last administration's winner was head of corporate law at a major law firm and heir to a retail fortune. He was an outstanding cabinet secretary and part of the "Sunday morning" work club on Capitol Square; he almost never missed a Sunday. The latest winner was a top executive at a Fortune 500 health care company (and a former staff nurse). Both were stars of the cabinet. We like saying that business and government are different. That said, some people from business can be very successful in government.

8. Grow your own appointees. If you don't like the appointees you've been getting, help grow your own. Interns do grow up. By the second year, most of the kids from the campaign will have moved on to law school or other campaigns. Governors' offices have two clusters, the old people (anyone over thirty-five) and a large crop of people under age twenty-five (at least at the start; like everyone they age in place). An excellent, cheap way to combine patronage and merit selection is to run a summer internship program. You not only grow your own career staff, but also provide good candidates for the junior appointed positions.

9. It is actually pretty hard to fire a political appointee. Until recently, I used to say that it was impossible to be fired by a Democratic governor in Virginia (and the Republican governors would give you a large severance package). It is still pretty unusual. To remove a political appointee at the agency level, you need the governor's sign-off (or at least the chief of staff's, but probably both). To remove a cabinet secretary or governor's staffer, you must first endure an internal soap opera that is worthy of the *Guiding Light*. It can take six months or more from the time a governor decides someone should go until they actually leave (or as often, are found a place to land). Political appointees are supposed to have two advantages for governors: They help politically and they are easy to fire. The irony is that they often don't and aren't. So don't assume the governor will figure out as quickly as you do that an incompetent political appointee has to go. And don't assume that figuring it out is the same as making it happen. You may have to live with a bad appointee longer than is reasonable, which brings me to the last lesson.

10. Political appointees often are political liabilities. This is the corollary of lesson 4. In divided government, political appointees who lack the wisdom of Madam Secretary (lesson 1) can be trouble because legislators of the other party do not much like the extremists in the governor's party (and, truth be told, a lot of people *in* the party don't like the extremists either). Among

political operatives of different administrations, there is a spirited discussion of which party's activists are the hardest to deal with (in my experience, both Republican and Democratic operatives think their *own* activists are the hardest to deal with). Working on campaigns does not confer legislative relationships. Working actively against legislators in the other party does not always endear you to them. Campaigning is fundamentally different not only from governing; it is fundamentally different from the legislative process. After fifteen years working around our state capitol (in the legislative and executive branches and as a lobbyist), I'm still struck by how strong the legislative relationships of our career executives are and how poor the legislative relationships (and skills) of some political operatives are. Needless to say, incompetent political appointees are also a liability as are those who get involved in ethical wrongdoing or decide it is a good idea to subvert the state personnel process. This is the fundamental irony of political appointees; some of them are not very politically smart. Unfair as it may be, you may well have to help your politically appointed colleagues to become politically effective.

Notes

1. Heclo (1977).
2. Murray (1991).
3. Maranto (2001).
4. Light (1995).

8 Working with Congress: Building relationships across the constitutional divide

GRACE CUMMINGS, FOUNDER, WORKING WITH CONGRESS

ON MARCH 7, 2002, THE *WASHINGTON POST* REPORTED, "Michael Parker, the recently appointed leader of the Army Corps of Engineers, was abruptly forced to resign yesterday for failing to defend President Bush's proposed budget cuts."

The article continued: "Parker, a former House member from Mississippi who was confirmed as assistant army secretary for civil works five months ago, was the first major administration official ousted since Bush took office. He had made no secret of his disdain for the Office of Management and Budget's efforts to rein in the Corps, and recently told a sympathetic House committee that he had requested $2 billion more than the OMB proposed in the president's budget. At a Senate hearing, he questioned the administration's decision to fund no new Corps projects, adding that he did not have a 'warm and fuzzy feeling' for OMB officials." [1]

As a role model for bridging the constitutional divide between the legislative and executive branches, Mike Parker is an interesting case study. Although he was able to span the divide by establishing trust and maintaining relationships with legislators—in large part due to his tenure as a member of Congress—he ultimately failed as an effective federal manager. In bridging the chasm between these two competing branches of government, he did two things very well and one thing very wrong.

First, Parker knew that information is an important commodity up on Capitol Hill. By providing pertinent and concise information about corps activities in members' states and districts—information that was helpful to the political interests of those members—he was able to serve members' needs and establish trust while simultaneously furthering the corps' mission.

Second, Parker recognized the importance of stakeholder relationships when working with Congress. Over the years, Parker had developed strong personal and professional bonds with his congressional colleagues and continued to nurture those relationships after his departure from the Hill. More important, in his role as the civilian head of the Corps of Engineers, he identified the members who had great interest in corps projects—especially those benefiting from corps dollars spent in their states and districts. He worked closely with the committees with jurisdiction over corps programs and funding. In addition, he identified other stakeholders—business interests, local officials, military supporters—who could reach out to members of Congress and reinforce the message he wished to project for the corps.

So far, he was a model for effectively bridging the constitutional divide.

His downfall, however, came in bucking the executive branch chain of command and not appropriately representing the president's policy choices before Congress. As a federal executive within President George W. Bush's administration, Parker had the responsibility of "carrying the water" up on the Hill, even if he disagreed with the president on policy matters. In bridging the constitutional divide, federal executives must not lose sight of their role as executive branch representatives, and they must respect the separation of powers the United States has observed for more than two centuries.

The Founders envisioned a working relationship between the legislative and executive branches but knew tension between the branches helped keep them in check. More important, this balance is the foundation for trust among the American public. Former representative Lee Hamilton stresses this point by asserting, "The American people, despite their criticism of politics and politicians, have an unshakeable faith in the Constitution and in the American system and its power sharing arrangements. The performance of government may disappoint them, but they firmly support the basic structure of our government set up by the founders." [2]

Prior to being posted overseas, diplomats go through a rigorous education—on how the host country is governed, who holds power, its folkways and customs, and the locations of political landmines. To bridge the constitutional divide here at home, government executives need the same kind of education. They must first understand the overall governing structure and the place they occupy within it. And they must also understand how Congress as an institution works. This understanding in turn requires an appreciation for the specific mechanisms of congressional operations—in particular the types and roles of Capitol Hill staffers, the types and roles of committees, and the nature of the oversight process. To foster this understanding, I first offer some general advice and then describe more specific features of Congress and how these features influence congressional-executive relationships.

Challenges for federal executives when working with Congress

In bridging the divide between the legislative and executive branch, federal managers face the reality that they serve two masters within our constitutional structure. As executive branch employees, they serve under the auspices of the president in his capacity of chief executive as spelled out in Article II of the Constitution.

Article I establishes Congress as the "first branch" of government vested with the power to establish laws, appropriate funds, and maintain oversight authority to monitor how federal executives carry out their duties. The Senate has advice and consent power over presidential appointees, and senators use it to block appointees they deem not fit for the task.

Federal executives, therefore, must be responsive to the president as the chief executive and to members of Congress as those who establish, fund, and oversee what they do. As many managers can attest, although they are ultimately responsible for running efficient and effective programs, the legislators who drafted the authorizing or appropriations language for specific programs have specific ideas about the ways they want the programs administered or the money spent. By virtue of our constitutional structure, career civil servants and political appointees often find themselves caught in the crosshairs between legislative and executive branch authority.

Furthering this challenge is the highly charged relationship between the president's Office of Management and Budget and members of Congress. OMB's current mission "is to assist the President in overseeing the preparation of the federal budget and to supervise its administration in executive branch agencies. In helping to formulate the president's spending plans, OMB evaluates the effectiveness of agency programs, policies, and procedures, assesses competing funding demands among agencies, and sets funding priorities." [3] As such, OMB officials have enormous power over executive branch managers and in recent years have extended their reach beyond financial management and into performance aspects of program delivery.

The problem, however, is that members of Congress and congressional staff members often pay no attention to the hoops federal managers must jump through to satisfy their OMB examiners. Moreover, members of Congress can be openly hostile to OMB officials as witnessed in 2002 when then-OMB director Mitch Daniels went before the House Appropriations Committee. This hearing included Rep. David Obey lecturing Daniels and waving a copy of the Constitution. "This little book is not very impressive to look at, but it runs the show," he said.[4] As described in the *Washington Post,* "members were especially fond of quoting from Article 1, Section 9 which states that 'no money shall be drawn from the treasury, but in consequence of appropriations made by law.' The subtext was that unelected executive branch budget officials should butt out." [5] During the Parker hearing on the Corps of Engineers budget, Rep. Peter DeFazio referred to OMB officials as "idiots" and "thugs." [6] It is clear that federal managers are stuck between competing powers—OMB officials representing the president and members of Congress who perceive the "unelected budget officials" as trampling upon their constitutional jurisdiction.

Finally, there is the challenge of working in an environment driven by partisan politics. Although federal managers are used to working with the administration's political appointees, few are aware just how much party matters up on Capitol Hill. The atmosphere there is entirely different from the civil service environment, and navigating these rancorous waters requires political acumen.

Both the House and Senate vest the majority party with the power to chair committees, control the legislative voting schedules, and assert authority over the appropriations process. And, if the majority party chooses to do so, it can pretty much disregard the views of the minority.

Working in a nonpartisan fashion with an institution that uses partisan identification as a decision axis can be extremely challenging for federal executives. Federal executives can also become the congressional whipping boy for the presidential initiative that the majority party in Congress opposes. They must represent the administration policies, whether they agree with them or not, in a nonpartisan fashion while bombs are lobbed at them by partisan members of the House and Senate. This tension can exist even when one party holds control of both Congress and the presidency; it only increases when party control is split.

Building trust through communication

David Gergen, former White House communications director and well-known political analyst, says, "Trust is the coin of the realm," in Washington. For many federal managers, however, the concept of trust as a commodity on Capitol Hill seems to be an oxymoron. Legislative politics at its worst can be a treacherous business where veracity may be set aside with victorious ends justifying unscrupulous means. For congressional members and their staffs, however, information is highly valued and the ability to trust the individuals providing this information is essential. As Washington lawyer Donald deKieffer notes in his book, *The Citizen's Guide to Lobbying Congress,* "Accuracy and thoroughness are hallmarks of successful lobbying campaigns." [7]

Providing concise, pertinent, and reliable information to members of Congress and their staff members is the primary building block for developing trust and building relationships on the Hill. For federal managers, establishing channels of communication and developing trusted relationships with the relevant congressional offices can set the foundation for fruitful partnerships with lawmakers.

The good news for executives is they have lots of useful information for legislators (see Box 8.1). Departments and agencies can build relationships with senators and representatives by providing information that affects the economies of their states or districts and ultimately touches the lives of their constituents. Workforce plus-ups (increases), environmental superfund dollars, new soldiers transferred to military facilities, and disaster preparedness spending are all examples of opportunities for federal executives to communicate with legislative offices. Moreover, the dialogue may go beyond the economy—numbers of veterans served, new hurricane warning systems, gang eradication measures, port security enhancements are all examples of federal activities relevant to congressional offices.

Beware of misinformation. When incorrect information is discovered by legislators, it can be the death knell for any organization trying to gain support on the Hill. Legislators judge mistakes harshly, often assuming someone provided the material intentionally to mislead or gain political advantage.

Box 8.1   Sharing information

During my tenure as chief of staff for Rep. Jack Kingston, R-Ga., one of the best working relationships I developed was with John Hankinson, regional director for the EPA in Atlanta.

Our friendship hinged on periodic calls to share information. I would call John to let him know when my boss was going to criticize the EPA publicly, and John would call me when the EPA was going to do something in our district my boss was not going to like.

In most cases, one of us was not happy after the call, but we both agreed it was better than being surprised. Communicating, even under tense circumstances, was important.

Capitol Hill is a small community, and rarely is the source of bad information kept quiet. If staff members have been "burned" by bad information, they tend to share the identity of the perpetrator with their colleagues so other offices will not become victims. And a damaged reputation on the Hill is very hard to repair.

Lessons can be learned by examining the tactics of effective Washington lobbyists. Many lobbyists build trust with members of Congress by providing both the pro and con of the issue they are raising. Lobbyists know members and their staffs are smart enough to realize there are always two sides to an issue. Although lobbyists will always put the best possible spin on their side of the argument, by providing their opponents' argument, they help these offices avoid unwanted surprises. They know garnering trust within the office is essential if they are to make headway—and being upfront with all the information helps to establish that trust.

Strengthening relationships by building stakeholder support

As a representational body, the legislative branch is driven by political interests. On any given day, a member of Congress or senator may have meetings on many different issues: agriculture subsidies, high tech weaponry, wetlands protection, local transit projects, stem cell research, educational testing, and on and on and on. The number of issues Congress deals with on an annual basis is enormous, and the multiplicity of constituencies represented continues to grow.

Members, therefore, must make policy decisions based upon their own beliefs and the needs of the constituents they represent. Facts and evidence matter, but in the legislative environment, substance may not always carry the day. When approaching Congress, many federal executives make the mistake of believing that if they can make a good factual and statistical argument for a program's efficacy, Congress simply cannot reject it. This way of thinking is especially true for managers representing agencies where the scientific method rules, statistical information provides evidence, and black and white results are prized. The Hill, however, is full of gray.

Facts, evidence, and statistics all matter in the legislative process, but if executives are not cognizant of how many stakeholders are weighing in on any given issue, they are missing an important ingredient in the congressional decision-making process. To strengthen their hand, therefore, it is important that executives look beyond the substance of their programs and develop relationships with constituencies that value their work.

Box 8.2   Cultivating local stakeholders

The Federal Law Enforcement Training Center (FLETC) is located near Brunswick, Ga., an area represented in Congress by Republican Jack Kingston.

During my service in Kingston's office, I would periodically get updates from the executive staff at FLETC. More often than not, however, I would get most of my information about FLETC from our constituents. Whether it was president of the Brunswick Chamber of Commerce, the mayor of Brunswick, or the head of economic development authority for Glynn County, they all cared about the facility and made sure I knew it.

Ralph Basham, FLETC director at that time, and his executive staff did an excellent job creating local stakeholder support. Our congressional office, in turn, made certain we paid special attention to the health and well-being of the facility.

By identifying vested stakeholders, executives build political support for their work and make themselves less vulnerable to legislative intervention or funding cuts. If a member of Congress receives multiple points of input about a project or program (especially if these contacts are coming from their home district or state), it becomes much more difficult for him or her to arbitrarily cut or criticize the program (see Box 8.2). Political pressure from a wide variety of district or state interests creates an effective political buffer.

In addition, building stakeholder support for programs and projects gives executives a real reason for dialogue with legislative offices and the ability to develop working relationships that may not have existed before. By building relationships with stakeholders in districts and states, federal executives are then working with the individuals most important to members of Congress—their constituents. Congressional staff members pay particular attention to activities affecting their member's district or state and regard the federal agents who can provide such information as allies.

Stakeholder information is valuable to committee staff members because they must build political support for their bosses' policy agenda. By identifying stakeholder support for given programs or projects, executives are providing important information to the committee staff and can build valuable relationships with those who have oversight and budget authority over their programs.

Successful lobbyists know all about the importance of stakeholder support and use it to their advantage when working issues on Capitol Hill. A common misperception about lobbyists is that they cozy up to members, slide campaign contributions over, and then use their personal relationships with these members to influence legislation. Largely, that perception is a fallacy.

Lobbyists do work hard to be known by members and staff so that when an issue comes up, they are not making a "cold" sales call. Their persuasiveness with a member, however, hinges on the political stakeholders they can bring to bear in favor of their issue. Prior to approaching a member, effective lobbyists bring together a coalition of individuals who can have maximum impact on the target representative. They utilize the collective force of these individuals to champion their cause and convince the representative. Likewise, executive branch managers should be investing time building relationships and coalitions among public, private, and nonprofit entities in support of their programs or projects.

The intersection of politics, policy, and personality

Understanding the legislative environment is a little like learning how to play three-dimensional chess. In this strategic board game, players must watch each level of the playing surface and know that all three levels are interconnected. When one piece moves, it can affect any of the pieces on all three levels. Consequently, a player's strategy needs constant reevaluation with each successive move.

Working with Congress is also a multidimensional endeavor, but in this case, the three levels at play are policy, politics, and personalities. To navigate effectively in the legislative environment, executives must watch all three "P's" all the time. Moreover, as many executive branch employees can attest, personality and political factors often trump policy substance when dealing in the legislative environment.

Members of Congress are very reactive to current political situations, and executives are best able to connect with them when their substantive presentations have "real-time" relevancy. When approaching legislators, executives need to take the political temperature of the moment and judge how the current climate might influence or affect the issue at hand. Items to consider include: What are the "hot button" issues currently before Congress? Is it an election year? How high (or low) are the president's poll ratings? What is the current state of the economy? Is a particular crisis driving policy development?

An example of an agency affected by political circumstances is the attention the U.S. Agency for International Development (USAID) received on the Hill immediately after September 11, 2001. For years, USAID was an organization toiling away to build infrastructure and stability within developing nations. The agency had often been the target of anti–foreign assistance sentiment on the Hill and, for a variety of reasons, had been the focus of ire for years by Republican Jesse Helms, who chaired the Senate Foreign Relations Committee. USAID was a perpetually underfunded agency sitting on the political backburner.

After 9/11, however, its fortunes changed dramatically. With terrorism and national security on everyone's mind, USAID moved to the forefront, and members of both parties were calling for increased efforts to shore up infrastructures and economies in developing nations as a weapon to diffuse the influence of extremists and terrorists around the globe.

On Capitol Hill, policy and politics always are intertwined. All members can come up with an idea for a bill, have their legislative assistants, in conjunction with the legislative council's office, draft the proper language and then introduce it for consideration in their respective chambers. Influences that guide the formulation of this legislation might include, but are not limited to, members' ideological beliefs, their personal interests, the regional orientation of their district, or their coalitional alliances or pressures exerted by their constituents. Members, however, often introduce bills without the intention of ever having them enacted into law—in fact, in proportion to the number of bills introduced in each session of Congress, very few pass and become law. Rather, the intent of introducing the legislation may be to help the members build momentum as they run for higher office, appease a constituent group, or garner press attention during a critical political moment in time.[8]

When members wish to influence policy, drafting legislation is not the only tool in their arsenal. Congressional oversight is another path that allows members to assert policy power over executive branch organizations. Members see themselves as the principals and executive branch employees as their agents carrying out the programs and policies passed by the House and Senate. By asserting oversight pressure on an agency or department, members can have significant impact on the conduct of programs or projects.

It is also essential to understand that political timing greatly influences policy development. If the chorus "location, location, location" is true for real estate, the refrain "timing, timing, timing" is appropriate for the policy process. There are times when political pressure builds up on a given issue and Congress determines that it must act.[9]

Other times, no matter how much the president or a member of Congress wishes to move policy forward, the political timing is just not right. To illustrate, in 2005, as President Bush called for legislation to overhaul the Social Security system, Sen. Charles Grassley, chair of the Senate Finance Committee, dismissed the chances of legislative action. He said, "I don't think we can move until there is opinion coming in here [Congress] from Americans that we can't only be concerned about grandma, we have to be concerned about grandkids." [10]

Congress is an institution built on personal relationships, and the force of personalities cannot be overestimated. In an interview, the late Jack Valenti, former president of the Motion Picture Association and longtime political adviser and confidant to President Johnson, said that one of Johnson's greatest strengths, as Senate majority leader, was his understanding of human nature. According to Valenti, Johnson was extremely smart, studied issues inside and out, and devoted his full energies to his political success. His effectiveness, however, was in large part derived from knowing every member of the Senate very well and using that knowledge in leading the chamber. He not only knew all the senators' political leanings but also studied their personal likes and dislikes, their families, their political ambitions, their goals. He paid great attention to how they related to other members of the chamber. With this knowledge, he was able to influence policy decisions by playing to each member's needs, weaknesses, strengths, and political agendas. If stroking a senator's ego was in order, Johnson knew which buttons to push. If the situation called for a subtle threat, Johnson knew the personal vulnerabilities. It was through such personality-driven forces that Johnson was able to control the Senate chamber like no one before him and no one since. [11]

When working the Hill, effective lobbyists build portfolios containing personal information about each member. These portfolios include the member's legislative interests, personal interests, educational background, business and political history, family history, hobbies, and anything else they can garner. As an integral part of these profiles, the files include information on each member's political ambitions. Lobbyists then use the information to tailor their arguments to each member of Congress.

Personalities can also determine how offices function. Some offices are known to be very efficient and others frenetic and inefficient. Some offices engage in long-term planning, while others are reactive. Some offices require lengthy briefing packages, while others want nothing more than an executive brief. Most often, the member's personality dictates these peculiarities. To work effectively with an office, the lobbyist must have this information.

The bicameral body

By nature and history, the Senate and House are two very different institutions. Senators serve six-year terms with a third of the chamber up for election every two years, while the entire House goes before the voters every two years. The House debates legislation on the floor under strict rules of order, while Senate debates are freewheeling with few restrictions. House members represent a narrower constituency, while senators represent a much broader constituency. The House has a leader chosen by a vote of the whole chamber—the Speaker of the House—who has the ability to dictate activities in the chamber. The Senate has no such leader; consequently, it is harder for the majority and minority "leadership" to impose their will. In the House, coalitions matter. In the Senate, through a little-known maneuver called the legislative hold, every senator has the ability to stall legislation, so each person matters.[12]

Although the House and Senate ultimately must work in unison to produce legislation for presidential consideration, they are often at odds with each other. The consequence for executives can be devastating if they are not aware of the friction that can exist between the two chambers and the need to formulate relationships on both sides of the Hill.

When working on an issue with one side of the Hill, it is always judicious to ascertain what action is (or is not) being taken in the other chamber. Sometimes members of the House and Senate agree on an issue, but discord is common. Jurisdictional rivalries can exist between the committee chairs of the two chambers, and unsuspecting executives can become ensnarled in a bicameral conflict. During the annual budget process, the House and Senate appropriators must come up with their respective appropriation bills—and rarely are the corresponding bills the same. It is altogether possible for an agency program to receive full funding in one chamber's appropriation bill and be zeroed out in the other chamber's bill. Knowing that senators and representatives are not obligated to work together and often do not, federal executives should cultivate relationships in both bodies.

Understanding committees, hearings, and oversight

The Constitution provides federal managers with the best reason for building relationships and establishing trust with the legislative branch—in doing so, they ensure the integrity of America's system of government. The desire to limit the authority of the executive and provide direct representation for the citizenry led the Framers to make Congress the most powerful branch of government. But leery of unchecked representational government, the Framers also put into place a system of checks and balances so that the legislative branch could not act rashly or solely upon the political will of the moment. To serve as good stewards of the Constitution, legislative and executive branch employees have the responsibility to work together to ensure good governance.

Referencing James Madison and *Federalist Paper* No. 47, Walter Oleszek, a senior specialist in American national government at the Congressional Research Service, points out, "The Constitution creates a system not of separate institutions performing separate functions, but of separate institutions sharing functions (and even competing for predominant influence in exercising them). Indeed, the overlap of powers is fundamental to national decision making." [13]

On the Hill this observation plays out most directly in the work done by committees, and it is here where federal executives can develop the most important relationships. Eventually, both chambers may debate and vote on the legislation developed by committees. It is within the committee system, however, where the details of programs, projects, and funding take shape, and it is here where executive branch input is most crucial.

Committees and subcommittees do the hard work of formulating legislation. As mentioned previously, all members of Congress can come up with an idea for a bill, have it drafted into legislative language, and introduce the bill in their respective chamber. Once introduced, however, the legislation is referred to the correct committee of jurisdiction and in most cases passed on to the subcommittee that handles the issue. For a piece of legislation to come to the House or Senate floor for consideration, it must usually be discussed and "marked-up" (revised and put into final draft form) within a committee and then reported out for consideration. If at the end of a congressional session (measured in two-year increments) both chambers have not passed the bill, it dies. For further consideration, it must be reintroduced during the next session of Congress, and the process begins again.

The implication for federal executives is that contact—whether directly or through their legislative affairs office—with the committees overseeing their programs and funding is extremely important. To be at the table as initial concepts are being developed within the committee process allows federal executives to supply the statistical information pertaining to the proposed program, discuss potential pitfalls in design, and bring a "real world" workability evaluation to the discussion. Granted, federal executives cannot lobby for or against specific pieces of legislation. They do, however, have the information base that is essential material for committee staff members to evaluate as they work with their members of Congress to develop, alter, or revise current programs and funding priorities. The Founders, in establishing the balance of powers, envisioned and deemed necessary an active interchange between the executive and legislative branches for our government to function well.

Members of Congress also use the power of their committees to advance their policy objectives, and in some cases, bend the executive branch to their legislative will. Congressional hearings are an example of how legislators can use the power of their committees to bring public attention and pressure to bear on a policy they wish to advance or defeat. Although proffered as information-gathering events—witnesses are called to provide testimony—these hearings are rarely held to obtain information. Instead, hearings are called to get material on the public record—and in the media—and put a positive spin on the chair's policy objectives or a negative spin on someone else's policy objectives or programmatic performance (be it the executive branch, private sector, or nonprofit community under scrutiny).

When the Senate Committee on Science, Commerce, and Transportation questioned Jeffrey Skilling, former CEO of Enron Corporation, in February 2002, it would be hard to imagine that a single member of the committee did not already have a definite opinion about his actions or those of other Enron top executives. Clearly, the purpose of the committee hearing was to bring further public attention to the misdeeds of Enron executives. It also allowed members of Congress to publicly express their outrage on behalf of the American public and build momentum for legislation pertaining to cleaning up corporate corruption.

Likewise, when Michael Brown, former head of Federal Emergency Management Agency (FEMA), testified before the House Government Reform Committee in late 2005, new information about the Katrina disaster was not the objective. The hearing was called for members to publicly vent their outrage at what they perceived to be Brown's ineptitude, criticize the Bush administration's mismanagement of the disaster, register their criticism with the voters, and call for new policies to strengthen federal disaster assistance and reform FEMA. It was a public show to gain political capital with the American people and policy momentum for reform legislation.

Although these are high-profile and extreme examples, executive branch employees routinely deal with the same hearing dynamics on a smaller scale.

By understanding that hearings are rarely for substantive input, but are a legislative and political tool, executives can better prepare themselves for such hearings. The key to understanding the hearing process is realizing that 90 percent of what will happen in the hearing is determined before a single witness testifies.

Building relationships with committee staffers can also help protect executives from being ambushed at congressional hearings—or at least allows for some defensive preparation if the hearing is going to be hostile. Contacting a staffer prior to the hearing is an opportunity to ask some questions: What are the politics behind this particular hearing? What is the significance of calling the hearing at this particular time? What specific committee members are interested and apt to attend? Who else will be testifying at the hearing, and should we expect any surprises?

By understanding the nature of these gatherings, executives can discuss the hearings for what they are—political theater. Instead of getting angry that the committee is paying no attention to the substance, executives can work with the staff members to best position themselves in these public forums.

Legislators work in concepts, and their final output is paper. Executive branch employees are the implementers. The process works best when legislators and administrators are in dialogue about the development of legislative language and resulting programs. Without such dialogue, legislators can lose sight of the "real world" consequences of their decisions, and federal managers are stuck with administering untenable mandates.

Although law prohibits executive branch employees from lobbying on legislation, they have abundant technical, statistical, and operational material to share with their legislative counterparts. Executives and legislators may butt heads when it comes to decisions on programs and projects, but dialogue—even if it is in conflict—is far better than having committees create legislation in an information vacuum or legislation based only on information from outside forces not charged with administering these programs.

The Constitution also vests legislators with oversight responsibility to ensure federal executives do not overstep their bounds. This oversight can be a burden to executives, and in some cases administered in a heavy-handed fashion by congressional members and staff, but it is important to our system of checks and balances. For federal managers to provide critical input at all stages of the policy process, they must take the time to communicate and build relationships with their congressional counterparts. At the same time, as executive branch employees, they must respect the separation of powers and represent the president's policies and programs to the best of their ability.

Understanding and working with congressional staff

Without question, ultimate power in Congress resides with the elected members of the House and Senate. They are the only individuals who can officially introduce legislation, serve on committees, and vote on legislation brought before their respective chambers. The vast majority of the day-to-day work on Capitol Hill, however, is done not by members of Congress but by the legions of congressional staff that populate the legislative branch. The reliance of members of Congress upon their staff should not be underestimated, nor should the enormous influence these staff members can have on executive branch activities. Two distinct types of legislative staff members work on the Hill: those employed in members' personal offices and those who serve on committees.

Personal office staff

Personal office staffers serve at the pleasure of an individual representative or senator. Once elected, new members of Congress receive a budget and are able to hire a staff that serves their office needs in Washington, D.C., and in their district or state. Other than limits on the number of staff employed, members of Congress have no set standards for how they configure their offices. The General Schedule (GS) ranking system for employees does not apply on Capitol Hill; members have sole discretion over hiring and firing their teams. The rules of the House and Senate prohibit staff members from engaging in political campaign activities during their official working hours, but, unlike their executive branch counterparts, they can participate in partisan political activities after hours—and often do. Although there are no written rules, most members of Congress hire personal office staffers that share their political affiliation, and the offices are consequently very partisan in nature.

A typical Hill office employs a chief of staff and a support staff to handle all matters related to the member's legislative responsibilities. Members' offices also employ press operatives to coordinate media outreach, receptionists for front office duties, and an office manager who covers administrative duties and may serve as executive secretary/assistant to the member.

In a congressional office, federal executives will most likely deal with legislative directors and legislative assistants. These staffers are charged with briefing their members on all pending legislation, preparing members for upcoming committee hearings and mark-ups, attending meetings with constituent groups, and responding to all district or state inquiries (by phone,

Box 8.3   Building relationships

In 1998 the Navy's congressional liaison office invited me and several other congressional staff members to Kings Bay Naval Base to spend a day and a night on a nuclear submarine. For me, it was important to learn more about the base because it was one of the largest employers in our congressional district. Plus, the chance to spend a night in a submarine was just too cool to pass up.

During the trip, I learned a lot about the technology on the sub, the challenges for the crew, the mission of the base, and the base's economic impact in our district. More important, I spent thirty-six hours building relationships with the liaison officer, the base commander, and the submarine captain.

After the voyage, when one of those men called, I always answered. We had built a working relationship around mutual interests.

fax, mail or e-mail) pertaining to legislation. Federal executives will encounter this staff whenever they are dealing with programs, projects, or legislation that affect a member's district or are of special interest to that member.

Personal office staff members are extremely focused on their member's district or state; their principal concerns are the needs of their boss and the interests of his or her constituents. Although these staffers deal with national issues, the lens by which they evaluate any issue is the interest of their respective members and the interests of the district or state. These staffers tend to be legislative generalists on most issues and legislative specialists only on those matters that pertain to their member's specific policy initiatives or affect their state or district (see Box 8.3).

When a federal executive briefs staff, more information is not always better, and technical details will often elude them. An effective briefing will include material related to their member's constituent base or touch upon their member's particular policy interests; otherwise it is good information falling on deaf ears. A two-page executive brief on the most important elements of a program (wisely pointing out district or state impacts within the first two paragraphs) is far better than a 150-page report on the program. When these staff members send inquiries to government agencies, they are usually not seeking to write a thesis on the issue at hand; rather, they are responding to a constituent request—many times on an issue they know nothing about.

To build trust with personal office staff members, it is essential to remember their focus is their member and their district or state. Good material is good for them only if it relates to their boss's needs or the needs of their boss's constituents. It is an enormous relief for legislative staff members when public or private sector executives come into their office understanding that time is limited and get to the point quickly—what is the issue and why should their boss care.

Be aware that many of these staff members are in their early twenties and look even younger. It is typical for a senior federal executive to brief a twenty-three-year-old legislative assistant. Although this scenario can be disconcerting, it is, in fact, the norm on Capitol Hill. Bright young staff members populate the Hill, and their bosses rely upon them heavily. Senior executives are wise to understand this reality and endeavor to treat the "kids" with respect. Some of these staff members will be impressive, some will not. Often, however, they are the only conduit for communicating with a member of Congress and can turn into valuable allies if treated with professional courtesy.

Personal offices also include staff in members' home districts or states. The usual composition of these offices is a district or state director whose responsibility is the health and well-being of the district, a field representative responsible for outreach activities, and case workers charged with solving constituent problems. Other staffers are a receptionist for front office duties and a special projects or grant director who helps constituents seek out federal funding for local projects. Where the focus of Washington, D.C., staff is legislative, the in-state staffers are problem solvers, and their interaction with federal agencies is functional.

The district or state directors oversee the local staff, monitor current events, and most important, work for the economic well-being of the local area. They consider anything the federal government does in their district or state within their purview and are most interested in information pertaining to jobs and dollars entering or exiting their member's jurisdiction. These directors see an Army base not just as a military installation but also as a huge economic engine in the district. They see a government research laboratory not just as a scientific facility but also an employer of professionals who earn good salaries. Grants to universities, employment in regional offices, federal highway projects, crop insurance subsidies, and disaster preparedness are just a few of the areas that provide executives a reason for discourse with these directors. Federal executives cannot lobby for a given program or project, but sharing pertinent and timely information on items affecting a state or district is a terrific way to begin building trust within these offices.

District or state caseworkers are the staff members charged with working directly with constituents who have encountered problems with the federal government. Whether constituents have missed a Social Security check, need a passport expedited, have been denied service at the local veterans' hospital, or are having problems with their Medicare prescription drug plan, they can turn to caseworkers for help. Unlike the Washington staff members, who tend to be very political, the caseworkers are often less partisan and simply want to solve problems for constituents. They also tend to have long tenures, and their knowledge of how the government works and where to go to solve a problem is a valuable commodity for any member of the House and Senate. It is through these problem-solving relationships that many federal managers find their easiest and most trusted avenue into congressional offices.

Committee staff

Committee staff members, also known on the Hill as professional staff members, are a completely different type of employee with an entirely different focus. Committee staff members are broken down along partisan lines; those in the majority offices serve at the pleasure of their chairs, and those in the minority offices serve at the pleasure of their ranking minority members. These staff members are not concerned with particular districts or states; rather, their focus is the legislative jurisdiction of their committees and the policy initiatives of their respective bosses.

The core staff for most House and Senate committees and subcommittees includes majority and minority staff directors and majority and minority professional staff (also referred to as legislative analysts). Administrative staff members also work in these offices and handle functional issues such as records management, scheduling, and office administration.

Unlike their legislative counterparts in personal offices, the professional staff members are usually older, longer tenured, and much better paid. Many of them hold advanced degrees or come to the job with a legal background. More important, where the personal office staff members tend to be generalists, the professional committee staff members are experts in their field. Many are hired for their subject knowledge expertise and completely master the issues they cover for the committee. These staffers often serve for ten, fifteen, or even twenty years with a committee and consequently become the leading expert in the nation on their issues. Committee staffs deal with formulating the legislation, making detailed policy recommendations to the members, and sometimes inserting legislative language into pending legislation.

In 2004, a furor arose when a staffer inserted language into a spending bill that allowed certain congressional staff broad access to Americans' tax returns. According to the *Washington Post,* "Richard Efford, a 19-year veteran of the House Appropriations Committee, said he did not inform any elected official before inserting the provision and advised his immediate boss, Rep. Ernest Istook, only after it was too late to make changes. 'I would guess we all thought it was a housekeeping thing that would help our bosses but did not need to be elevated up to them,' said Efford, who described himself as 'dumbfounded' by the uproar." [14] Congress eventually stripped the language from the bill, but not before "irate lawmakers in both parties denounced it as a sinister encroachment on Americans' privacy." [15]

When briefing committee staff members, be aware they may feel they know more about a program than the executives who administer the program. In many cases, these staff members helped draft the original legislative language creating the programs and projects they oversee. Where a one-page executive brief is appropriate for a meeting with personal office staff members, expect to provide committee staff members with detailed technical briefings.

As a rule, committee staffers enjoy the legislative process and understand the give and take that must go on with the executive branch in order for our system of government to function. Consequently, executives have statistical, programmatic, and evaluative information to share with them and a constitutional rationale to engage on this level. These staff members seek information, and providing good, concise, pertinent input about programs and projects builds trusted relationships over time.

Conclusion

As a former member of Congress, Mike Parker knew all about how Capitol Hill worked. As an executive branch manager, Parker had been effective in communicating with his former colleagues, gaining their trust, and building stakeholder support for the Corps of Engineers. His dismissal prompted outrage on Capitol Hill, yet at the end of the day, the Bush administration had both the right and responsibility to oust Parker from his position—and members of Congress knew it. As an executive branch representative, Mike Parker was obligated to represent the president's policies and, by failing to do so, he was undermining executive branch authority.

To serve as proper stewards of the Constitution, government executives have the responsibility to play their appointed roles well. A good performance requires building relationships that bridge the constitutional divide, but it also requires a respect for the divide itself.

Building relationships and providing pertinent, accurate information to legislators is an effective way for executive branch managers to bridge the constitutional divide with the legislative branch. In bridging the divide, executives and legislators must also understand that the Founders intended tension as a means of keeping power in check and respect their wisdom. To maintain the integrity of our constitutional system, and the trust of the American people, executives and legislators must work as equals to maintain the separation of powers.

Tips for leadership success

1. Provide concise, pertinent, and correct information:
    • Make it constituent-oriented whenever possible;
    • Make it relevant to the member or committee you are addressing;
    • Provide an executive summary;
    • Double check facts and numbers and immediately correct any errors; and
    • Use the interchange to build relationships.

2. Network with stakeholders:
    • Build a support base for agency or department activities;
    • Search for political landmines;
    • Provide political cover; and
    • Share relevant information with legislative offices.

3. Be aware of the political climate:
    • Periodically check your priorities against the changing environment;
    • Keep tabs on the political circumstances of key legislators for your department or agency;
    • Avoid partisan entanglements; and
    • Build bipartisan relationships to mitigate against abrupt changes in the legislative power structure.

4. Respect the constitutional framework:
    • Represent the policies of the administration you serve;

- Seek to have substantive input with committees holding jurisdiction over your agency or department;
- Recognize legislative oversight as a necessary check on executive authority; and
- Build relationships with legislators as coequal stewards of the nation's democracy.

Resources for further learning

Books:

Donald E. deKieffer, *The Citizen's Guide to Lobbying Congress* (1997). A useful guide for accessing and influencing the congressional process.

Lee H. Hamilton, *How Congress Works and Why You Should Care* (2004). A well-known insider's insight into the process.

John Kingdon, *Agendas, Alternatives and Public Policies* (1995). A classic statement of the dynamics of policy formation, establishing the notion of "policy windows" and the importance of timing.

Thomas E. Mann and Norman J. Ornstein, *The Broken Branch: How Congress Is Failing America and How to Get it Back on Track* (2006). A powerful review and critique of Congress's recent practices, along with a prescription for change.

David Mayhew, *Congress: The Electoral Connection* (1974). A classic, succinct essay on congressional structure and behavior, viewing Congress through the lens of the pursuit of reelection.

Walter J. Oleszek, *Congressional Procedures and the Policy Process*, 7th ed. (2007). An excellent textbook providing a thorough overview of Congress.

David E. Price, *The Congressional Experience: Transforming American Politics*, 3rd ed. (2004). A first-person account of recent congressional dynamics from the perspective of a member of Congress who is a former political science professor.

Eric Redman, *The Dance of Legislation* (2001). This new edition of Redman's 1973 book includes an introduction by Richard Neustadt and an afterword by Redman. An insightful story of one piece of legislation's journey through the process; the *Gideon's Trumpet* for Congress.

Web Sites:

The following are official government Web sites related to Congress that can provide a wealth of useful information.

www.senate.gov (Official Senate Web site with links to committees and members).

www.house.gov (Official House of Representatives website with links to committees and members).

www.loc.thomas.gov (Library of Congress legislative database).

Notes

1. Grunwald and Allan (2002).
2. Hamilton (2004), 8.
3. OMB Web site: *www.whitehouse.gov/omb.*
4. Kessler (2002).
5. Ibid.
6. Grunwald (2002).
7. deKieffer (1997), 177.
8. See Mayhew (1974) for further information on legislative behavior and electoral politics.
9. See Kingdon (1995) for further information on the timing and influences around policy development in Congress.
10. "Some Wary of Social Security Plan" (2005).
11. Material based on personal interview by the author with Jack Valenti, March 18, 2005.
12. Engber (2006).
13. Oleszek (2004), 4. Also see *Federalist Paper* No. 47.
14. Morgan (2004).
15. Ibid.

8.1 Working with state legislatures

Grant Reeher, Department of Political Science,
Maxwell School of Citizenship and Public Affairs,
Syracuse University

Grace Cummings offers many useful insights in her chapter on working with Congress. Many of these insights also apply to the legislative environments federal and state government executives encounter in state capitols. They include the importance of knowing the specific political terrain and its history, the long-term damage done to relationships by "burning" a legislator with bad information, the centrality of the electoral district to the legislator's interests and attention, the key role played by professional staff, and the need to be sensitive to timing. But state legislatures differ from Congress in ways that are relevant to a government executive's ability to have successful relationships there. What I offer in this brief addendum to Cummings's chapter are some important areas of difference that executives should bear in mind when dealing with state legislatures and individual legislators.

To do this I draw on my experiences over the past seventeen years observing, interviewing, and writing about state legislators, mostly but not exclusively in the Northeast. I also draw on my experiences at FEI in facilitating honest discussions on the federal-state relationship among the executives participating in FEI's leadership programs and Virginia state executives, state legislators, and their staff. I begin with some macro-level observations about the culture and mechanics of the state legislative process and then treat more specific aspects of state legislative institutions.

The good news for government executives working with the states is that even though trust is often sorely lacking, it is not as difficult to generate in state legislatures as it is in Congress. Demonstrating a fundamental respect for the difficult and often thankless work that state legislators do, along with a helpful approach in dealing with their information needs and efforts to think through complicated policy questions, is an essential first step. Beyond that, bearing in mind the following differences between state legislatures and Congress should help.

It must be noted that state legislatures vary enormously. At one end of the spectrum are the professionalized institutions where tenures are relatively long, salaries are relatively high, the job is approached as a full-time endeavor, and staff support is relatively plentiful. At the other end are the more amateur operations where citizen-legislators earn modest salaries, cycle through the institution, and work through issues on a part-time basis with the help of a smaller cadre of shared staff. Legislatures also vary in culture. Some are quite partisan and have more clearly defined roles for individual legislators, while others are more collegial and are primarily constituted by informal networks. In addition, the culture of a single legislature can change noticeably in a relatively short period of time with a change in leadership—especially a governor or a speaker of the house—or with a change in the state's overall political climate. So before anything else, government executives should know what kind of legislature they are approaching.

In large part because of the growth in the importance of national government relative to state government during the twentieth century and the funding arrangements attending that growth, today's state legislators and their staff often feel discounted, disrespected, and overly directed by the national government. State legislators and their staff have told me countless stories of how the federal bureaucracy ignored their insights, competence, and essential local knowledge. A federal executive's sensitivity to this experience and a clearly demonstrated willingness to listen—and actually to hear—will go a long way toward establishing good relationships. For state-level executives, having information about their federal counterparts and cultivating good connections with them make them particularly valuable resources in the state legislative environment.

In a similar vein, when it comes to general policymaking and more specifically the budget process, state legislatures are not, like Congress, always open for business. They must operate within a much more compressed legislative schedule, often just several weeks. And they need to pass a balanced budget, on time. In responding to requests for information and guidance on regulations, or in negotiating proposed policy changes, federal executives need to be aware of and responsive to state legislators' particular time constraints.

In most states, the governor and the executive administration are more powerful, comparatively, than is a presidential administration—especially regarding the budget. The difference is due in part to the relative advantages in staffing and infrastructure held by many governors, as well as the compressed legislative time schedule. In turn, the gubernatorial advantage leads back to the importance of information and the civil executive's usefulness to state legislators in providing it. The information-power connection was well described to me by one state agency head who had formerly served in the legislature, including some time spent in legislative leadership:

> [W]hen I became part of the administration . . . I learned very quickly why the administration gets 90 or 95 percent of what it wants. That's something that I would never thought of, or believed, when I first went into the legislature. It has a great deal to do with knowledge and information . . . and control of information.
>
> . . . We would start at the beginning of a legislative session . . . and we would start with a legislative agenda and initiatives, budget initiatives, financially related issues, fees, taxes, and would end up, almost without exception at the end of the year—we'd have to go around the barn three or four times to get there—but we'd end up with almost 100 percent of what we asked for and started with. I was pleased by it when I was a member of the administration, but frustrated by it when I was a legislator.[*]

By the same token and for some of the same reasons, leadership *within* the state legislature, particularly in the majority party, is often stronger than in Congress. It is important for government executives to build relationships with these leaders, or someone who has their ear, even if their particular area of work does not naturally lead them to interact with these legislators. Often such leadership networks are informal and are made up of a mix of those with identifiable leadership titles, such as majority leader, assistant leader or whip, and those without a title who have demonstrated their value in moving legislation or in negotiation.

Being smaller operations than Congress, state legislatures function on a more human scale, and this extends to their physical geography. The more intimate setting provides the executive a better opportunity to establish relationships informally, through casual conversations in hallways or lobbies. In many states, most legislators eat lunch in one cafeteria in the capitol complex that is also open to the public, and there would be nothing strange about an interested member of the state or federal government joining a table of legislators. As in politics the world over, being seen in such venues, and being known for discretion, cannot but enhance one's reputation among the group.

Like in Congress, state legislative committees are central to the process of crafting legislation and exercising oversight. Some legislatures—New

York's, for example—depart from this rule and use committee meetings more as pro forma expressions of the work and negotiations that have been coordinated by party leadership and transmitted through committee chairs. But the usual pattern is that the committee staff and other professional staff, and in some states the political staff allocated to party leaders, play a larger part in the development of legislation than they do in Congress. Individual professional staffers cover more ground with fewer colleagues and necessarily have broader portfolios than their congressional counterparts. Personal staff, where it exists, tends to focus on constituency service and basic administrative support. The bottom line here is that good relationships with the professional staff are essential.

Committee meetings themselves vary in tone and style, both among and within legislatures, but compared with Congress, they tend to be more authentic working sessions, in which proposed legislation gets collectively discussed and thought through. The degree to which this is the case often depends on the personal style of the committee chair. In addition, some chairs are more closely tied to the party leadership than others—and this connection does not always correspond with the apparent, on-paper significance of the committee itself.

The same pattern holds for public hearings. Some legislators follow the congressional model and use the hearings primarily to make speeches or solicit witnesses to make their case for them, and many legislators show up with their minds already made up, but hearings can also include genuine exchanges and real learning experiences for the legislators. At one end of the axis running from scripted political theater to authentic working session are the committee hearings I observed in Vermont and in one particular case, described to me by Paul Cillo, a former majority leader in the Vermont House, who had been a leader on the reform of education financing. For public hearings, experts with a variety of viewpoints were chosen to appear before the committee. Rather than offering sequential, formal testimony, as is usually the case in a public hearing, the witnesses were asked to engage in an informal, interactive discussion among themselves while the legislators listened and interjected questions. According to Cillo, the method yielded an immensely useful—and time-efficient—learning experience for the legislators.

Like members of Congress, state legislators are concerned about reelection and the welfare of their districts, and so when dealing with individual legislators government executives should know something about their districts and the industries located there. But most state legislators are also comparatively quicker than their congressional counterparts to look at matters from a statewide perspective or to have specific policy areas that primarily drive their attention, often areas that stem from or are reflected in their committee work. Again, the reason is in part that the entire operation is on a smaller scale. Government executives therefore need not be as focused on finding specific district connections in their discussions, but neither should they ignore them.

To conclude, the tensions between national and state level government are yet another structural feature of the American political landscape making trust difficult to establish and maintain. But with a genuine commitment to honoring and respecting the state-level aspects of our governing arrangements, federal executives can advance the democratic performance of the entire system. And by being attentive to the legislative environment in their states, state-level executives can improve the operations of their own governments.

Resources for further learning

Many books have been written about—and sometimes by—state legislators and the state legislative process. The five listed here are relatively recent and in different ways shed light on legislative life in the states.

Tom Loftus, *The Art of Legislative Politics* (1994). A former Speaker of the Wisconsin House reflects on his experiences.

John McDonough, *Experiencing Politics* (2000). A former Massachusetts state representative-turned-academic applies explanatory theories popular among academics but little known outside the academy to his own experiences in the legislature.

Grant Reeher, *First Person Political* (2006). An academic author takes a more personal look at the motivations and experiences of state legislators, based on in-depth interviews and observations.

Alan Rosenthal, *The Decline of Representative Democracy* (1998). A long-time state legislative observer provides a detailed overview of the state of the state legislative process.

———— *Heavy Lifting* (2004). This work focuses in on the job of the legislator and the legislature.

Notes

* Reeher (2006), 168. The interviews are anonymous.

9 From e-government to e-governance: Harnessing technology to strengthen democracy

GRANT REEHER, DEPARTMENT OF POLITICAL SCIENCE, MAXWELL SCHOOL OF CITIZENSHIP AND PUBLIC AFFAIRS, SYRACUSE UNIVERSITY
GEORGE MITCHELL, DEPARTMENT OF POLITICAL SCIENCE, MAXWELL SCHOOL OF CITIZENSHIP AND PUBLIC AFFAIRS, SYRACUSE UNIVERSITY

Like many other states in 2004, Maine and its first-term governor, John Baldacci, faced a budget problem. To maintain a balanced budget, difficult trade-offs would be necessary. In accord with the standard process, the governor proposed a budget to the state's legislature, but accompanying it was something new: on the governor's official Web site was an interactive exercise called "The Budget Balancing Education Tool." [1]

The site invited citizens to figure out how to close the state's deficit by raising various taxes or cutting various kinds of spending. A box at the bottom of the page provided a running tally of one's progress toward a balanced budget. The exercise used Internet technology to serve at least two important democratic functions. The first was the more obvious of the two: When citizens were finished adjusting the figures, the site allowed them to register their taxing and spending preferences with the governor's office by clicking a button. But the second function was arguably more important: Participating in the exercise also allowed citizens actually to experience—and therefore better appreciate—the difficult trade-offs that the state budget process requires. The exercise was so successful that the governor decided to use it in future budget cycles.

In spring 2006 French budget minister Jean-François Cope used a similar device as his nation faced a similar problem: how to respond to an apparent national consensus to cut taxes while staying within the European Union's mandated deficit ceiling of 3 percent of GDP. His office launched a budget balancing game called "Cyberbudget," on a site that could handle up to 10,000 players at a time and included a simulation for presenting a citizen's preferred budget to parliament.

These budget-balancing tools are innovative examples of e-government—the use of recent developments in electronic technology, most notably the Internet, to improve the work of government offices and agencies. E-government can claim some notable achievements, but our central argument is that so far, the true potential for e-government–based efforts to increase the confidence and trust in government has remained largely unrealized. That potential is unlocked by increasing citizens' sense of ownership in what government does. To create this sense of ownership, government executives can learn a great deal from their counterparts in the political and commercial realms. The bottom line: To fully unleash the Internet's power, agency leaders need to think in terms of e-governance, rather than simply e-government.

Our idea of e-governance draws on more general writings about governance, which emphasize not only government institutions but the linkages between those institutions (and their personnel) and the social and political realms that surround them. Political scientist Donald Kettl has written widely on governance, and among his ten core principles for effectively building those linkages, e-governance is intimately tied to at least four: (1) the importance of networks; (2) emphasis on interpersonal processes rather than strict authority; (3) transparency; and (4) popular participation in what government does.[2] But our notion of e-governance extends beyond that literature to a more proactive and deeper involvement of the public in the central activities of government. That civic involvement can in turn generate stronger senses of investment, trust, and efficacy regarding government. Fostering greater involvement is also integral to what, in chapter 1 of this volume, Terry Newell termed values-based leadership on the public stage.

Steven Clift, the former manager of Minnesota's state government Web portal, founder of E-Democracy.org, and recent recipient of the prestigious Ashoka Fellowship for social entrepreneurship, has set his hopes on the private sector to deepen online citizenship: "With our governments and representatives ill-equipped to 'e-listen,' *civil society* needs to fill a void and create places and experiences online that allow people to learn from one another, build respect, influence agendas and over time impact decision making, and most importantly meet public challenges." [3] But we believe that government must not abandon that challenge either, and this chapter aims to provide agency executives with a framework for thinking more creatively about how to meet it.

Box 9.1   E-rulemaking

An area of e-government of particular note concerns the comment process prior to government regulatory action, often called "e-rulemaking." The use of e-rulemaking points toward some of the more genuinely interactive possibilities provided by the Internet, as well some of the pitfalls lurking in the use of the technology. Under the traditional off-line process of soliciting comments from an invited list of interested parties and through announcements via standard public notice channels, those who participate in the public comment process usually represent a narrow sliver of the nation, limited for the most part to representatives of large commercial institutions.

Using electronic technology to open up the process of submitting comments on proposed U.S. government regulations has, on the one hand, been shown to solicit a broader set of participants and a more diverse set of comments, including comments from individuals and organizations not originally appearing on the initial invitation list. It has also solicited a different kind of comment, more personal and individual in its approach, versus the more formal style of communication typical of a large organization affected by the proposed regulation. In these ways, the process has been made more democratic, and the quality of the information gathered by government through the process has been improved.[1] The government of Virginia, to take a state-level example, has also received high praise for what it has accomplished in these realms by moving most aspects of its rulemaking process online.[2] In a similar vein, the West Virginia Departments of Education and Health and Human Resources recently employed a Web portal to effectively open up the information flows related to the rulemaking process for the establishment of a universal prekindergarten program.[3]

On the other hand, large organizations and interest groups—both private and public—quickly caught up to the practice and adjusted their tactics accordingly. Now, electronic public commenting procedures often generate hundreds of thousands of duplicative, at times even "canned" comments, in much the same way that multiple political messages are e-mailed, phoned in, and sent by postcard to the White House and Congress. Such instances of

The successes, and limitations, of e-government (so far)

E-government has come a long way in a short time. Government has made use of electronic technology to make citizens' lives more convenient, in terms of obtaining useful public information, paying user fees, and filing important public action that at first appear to be spontaneous, but that in fact are orchestrated by large or wealthy organizations—"Astroturf" rather than true grassroots lobbying—can clog the system with information not especially useful to the process or genuinely reflective of public moods. And in terms of interactivity—a theme to be developed more fully in this chapter—this use of e-government is still quite limited. With e-rulemaking, the relationship between government and citizens remains essentially unchanged, as does the process, except that it has been moved online.

Stuart Shulman, a researcher at the University of Pittsburgh, has studied e-rulemaking for a number of years. Although he was originally inspired by the promise of early e-rulemaking efforts, he is now disturbed by the recent trend in the process and worries whether there is any room left for genuine deliberation. "E-mail degrades the process," he says. "Form-letter awareness campaigns educate thousands, but only in a particular viewpoint. They steer group members away from dialogue and understanding and toward a confrontation with what are, more or less, 'evil-doers,' who must be defeated in the policy process or in the court of public opinion." One way to screen out the Astroturf effect in the received comments is to craft software to pull out the unique comments and simply count up the rest. Shulman is currently working with the Fish and Wildlife Service to help them find what he terms "the needles," the useful comments, from the "haystack" of the others that he characterizes as "a global warming-sized flood of public comment." You can read his work at his research group's Web site: http://erulemaking.ucsur.pitt.edu.

---

1. For these findings and arguments, see among others Stanley and Weare (2004); Coglianese (2004a), (2004b); and Stuart Shulman's writings found on the Web site noted in the text.
2. See Holzer et al. (2004); and the Virginia portal itself at: *www.townhall.virginia.gov.*
3. Bushouse (2006).

forms. These efforts have included online tax forms, tax filing, DMV services, and information and payment of fees for national parks. It has also made available to citizens a wider and richer array of information related to what government does. As more government-generated and government-related information has become available online, greater numbers of citizens have genuine opportunities to be better informed. And by placing important political information online—for example, records of campaign donations—government can inform the public and increase the transparency of the democratic process. Running through all these advantages is the tantalizing possibility that the technology can help cut administrative costs and improve service delivery at the same time.

The general acceptance of the importance of e-government initiatives is reflected in the fact that e-government was made a centerpiece of President George W. Bush's Management Agenda in his first term of office. The main goals of e-government, the agenda stated, were to cut government spending, reduce the paperwork burden on citizens and businesses, and to improve the government's performance—primarily by easing access to information and services. The White House established an office of e-government and appointed an e-government director at the Office of Management and Budget (OMB). At the same time, states and counties were also establishing similar offices and pursuing similar initiatives.

In many respects, the initiatives seem to be working. By 2004, for example, 97 million Americans had made contact with government through the Internet for reasons other than filing tax forms. The use of the Internet to contact government grew by 50 percent between 2002 and 2003.[4] Indeed, since 1998, making use of e-government has been one of the fastest growing Internet activities. Government executives quickly found the Internet to be a handy tool. As early as 2000 they were reporting that the Internet had helped them in important ways with internal administration, public relations, and coordination with other agencies.[5] And citizens apparently agreed; based on traditional customer satisfaction measures, electronic encounters with government have rated comparably to other forms of interactions.[6] (See Box 9.1 for another way citizens and government interact via the Internet.)

There are many success stories about how government has effectively employed Internet technology to improve its operations. In collaboration with the Council for Excellence in Government, Harvard University's Ash Institute has assembled examples of these successes, which can be found on its Web site.[7] But most e-government efforts so far, especially at the national level, have left the basic relations between government and its citizens intact, and it is this relationship that must change before citizens can be fully energized by the technology. And it is this relationship that the technology invites government to change, in the same way that it has changed relationships in the political and commercial realms.

Others have noticed government's missed opportunity. In a recent overview of e-government, political scientist Darrell West, a long-time student of technology, politics, and government, offers the following conclusion about government Web sites:

> From a technical standpoint, there is no reason why government agencies have not incorporated more interactive features into their sites. The technology exists and has been well tested. Interactive technologies are common on some sites and have been used to serve customer needs. The failure to incorporate these advances is not a problem of technology as much as it represents a problem of political will and vision. . . .
>
> Public officials must recognize that government websites can do more than merely deliver information and services. They represent a powerful tool for transforming democracy and reaching out to the general public. . . . The Internet has the power to revolutionize the relationship between citizens and leaders, but realization of this hope takes more vision and political will than have thus far been established in the public sector.[8]

And, indeed, when one reads the government's published views on how it views e-government, such as OMB's reports on implementing the president's Management Agenda, it becomes clear that the emphasis has been on the government to citizen (G2C), government to government (G2G), and government to business (G2B) connections, and on internal efficiency and effectiveness (IEE).[9] Little emphasis has been placed on citizen to government (C2G) and citizen to citizen (C2C) connections, where the Internet can do the most to change the way government functions and to increase trust among citizens.

Informed by a market orientation and the "reinventing government" vein of what has come to be known as the "new public management" literature, the dominant view government has of its citizens is as customers. The resulting aim is to provide them with efficiencies in information access and service delivery, and to save them tax dollars in the process—all laudable goals. But that view does not equally emphasize citizens as active participants in a process of decision making and governance. Citizens are not seen as significant partners in what government agencies are trying to accomplish.

E-governance, as we intend it, is therefore related to the market-customer orientation—it puts customers first and listens carefully, and actively, to their concerns. Where our concept differs is in the degree to which citizens are encouraged and enabled to participate in what government produces. As we describe below, commercial and political uses of the Internet are rapidly instituting this more participatory approach.

The market view of government's online efforts is reflected in the apparent assumption that citizens will come to the sites once they are available and providing useful information. Despite greater efforts to spread the awareness of government's online features, a recent report found that most people came to government Web sites through a commercial search engine (such as Google), followed by the recommendations of friends or other nongovernment advertisements.[10] Far fewer arrived at the site because of a government publication or because a government gateway portal such as FirstGov sent them there.

The view is also reflected in a Council for Excellence in Government's survey of the benefits of e-government.[11] In the survey, citizens and government officials chose among increases in government accountability, public access to information, government efficiency, and convenience. Missing was the benefit of being more connected and involved with government. But citizens arguably expressed a desire for that benefit by selecting greater accountability most frequently, while the most favored choice of government officials was information access.

We need to broaden our consideration of the values and purposes of e-government, and doing so will yield constructive engagement of the problem of trust. Research on trust in government has suggested that trust may not have a close connection with government performance, as indicated by objective measures, nor with the ideological fit between specific government policies and the beliefs of respondents.[12] Instead, e-government may be best able to engender trust by inviting citizens to become more active in the work of government agencies and, through that process, instill a sense of ownership in government.

And though it is not our focus here, it is worth noting that similar approaches might be employed within a government agency and between government agencies or offices to improve levels of involvement, investment, and trust among employees. Toward that end, after reading this chapter the reader would be well-served to review chapter 6, Russ Linden's discussion of collaborative leadership, and consider the possible linkages.

The Internet versus democracy

Two worries are frequently expressed about the Internet's effects on politics, which extend to how an increased emphasis on e-government might adversely affect the public. The first concerns the digital divide—the worry that if access to the Internet is skewed by income, race, and even gender, and in particular if access to the Internet remains elusive for the poor, the Internet's ultimate effects will be antidemocratic.[13] Power to communicate, persuade, and organize will further accrue to the educated and affluent, strengthen a class-based governing system, and reinforce traditional social hierarchies. That concern is real, but the digital divide has significantly closed since these concerns were first raised in the late 1990s. In May 2006, for example, Nielsen//NetRatings estimated the number of people with access to the Internet through a home or nonshared workplace personal computer to be 205 million, a figure that includes the majority of all adults.[14] Active users were estimated at 143 million. Recent studies by Pew and others indicate that in terms of race, the gap in Internet access is steadily closing.[15]

A new laptop computer developed by the nonprofit organization One Laptop Per Child, and currently being sold to governments in developing countries to distribute to school children, suggests what might be possible here in the United States, with the appropriate public sector commitment.[16] Costing approximately $150—and providing wireless network capability, a sturdy structure, a rechargeable power source, a video camera lens, programs for Web browsing, word processing, and other learning purposes, and an energy-efficient screen easily viewable in direct sunlight—the computer is being bought on a mass scale by the governments of Argentina, Brazil, Libya, Nigeria, and Thailand, to help their children learn. The governments will employ various techniques to provide wireless access to users. It is worth noting that the cost of the computer is a sliver of the average amount spent per child per year in the Medicaid program.

Another kind of divide in the United States has surfaced regarding the quality of Internet access and the skills and knowledge to make the most effective use of digital technology. But even here, the signs are hopeful. According to Nielsen//NetRatings, in May 2006, 76 percent of active home Internet users in the United States had a broadband connection, up 15 percent from the year before.[17] In addition, the user-friendliness and affordability of a variety of communication tools available on the Internet has dramatically increased, as blogging and sites such as MySpace.com and YouTube.com have grown in popularity and as the mastery of an increasing array of mobile phone functions has had spillover effects in the computing realm.

A second commonly expressed concern is that the Internet will degrade the political process by introducing more divisiveness, harshness, misinformation, social isolation, and even passivity. These criticisms are taken up at length in *Click on Democracy: The Internet's Power to Change Political Apathy into Political Action.*[18] Many of the concerns are speculative and theoretical or based on impressions of Internet use and behavior that in "Internet years" are decades old. We note here that this question is ultimately an empirical one, and the recent empirical evidence that we are aware of points in a different overall direction. In addition, one must ask "as compared to what" in response to these worries. Given the recent trends in *off*-line American politics, noted briefly in the introduction, the Internet is unlikely to make things worse.

Possible models of interactivity: Political and commercial spheres

If e-government's greatest potential to invigorate agency-citizen relations and generate trust remains largely untapped, clues to unlocking that potential might be found in electoral politics and political advocacy as well as business. These two realms have shown much innovation, which has mirrored the rapidly changing landscape of the technology itself. Because we are political scientists who study the political uses of the Internet, we focus our attention on politics, but comment on commerce along the way.

Here is the clear lesson from observing six years' worth of innovations: the central need to generate authentic two-way interactions between citizens and the organizations working with and for them (C2G), and to facilitate more horizontal, multiway communications among citizens, which are centered on the mission of the organization (C2C).[19] In pondering how to get the most out of e-government, federal executives should recognize that in politics and commerce, a learning curve had to be traveled before the lesson was internalized. An initial impulse to approach the Internet as another vehicle to deliver the same services and messages yielded only limited successes; it was only as the Internet began to be viewed in distinctive terms, with the potential to help change the very nature of the approach taken toward citizens and customers, that it demonstrated greater success.

Granted, there are limits on the kinds of techniques from politics and commerce that a government agency can adopt wholesale—limits generated by legal-liability concerns, the need to maintain control over the integrity of both the content and the presentation of the agency's central mission, as well as the more general need for greater top-down control over what an agency does. While we are sensitive to these limitations, we nevertheless believe the basic insight can be imported to good use. And we believe that more can be done to invite the participation of citizens.

What has the Internet realized so far? The following sketch of its use is primarily modeled on the election cycles of 2000, 2004, and 2006. While Internet-based and Internet-facilitated political participation obviously exists between elections and extends beyond them—indeed, one of the Internet's principal values is its ability to *sustain* civic activity and create alternative forms of political engagement—elections mobilize and concentrate a great deal of political activity. For that reason, we have chosen to anchor our discussion in the people and events surrounding those years. Our discussion of election 2000 relies in particular on *Click on Democracy*.[20]

First steps: The Internet in election 2000

We begin our account in 2000, when the Internet's impact was first readily seen.[21] Just two years earlier, Jesse Ventura had ridden the Internet to victory in the Minnesota governor's race. The Internet was credited with helping Ventura raise money, organize volunteers, and respond to the opposition. In the following year, Steve Forbes announced his presidential candidacy online, and Bill Bradley became the first candidate to raise $1 million online. More and more people were going online, and applications of the technology for political uses were expanding rapidly. Consequently, expectations that the Internet would have a dramatic impact on the 2000 election reached a high point going into the cycle's final year.

And from one perspective, election 2000 did indeed look like a watershed moment. Sen. John McCain gathered more than $2 million online in one week; Arizona conducted a binding online primary; and presidential candidate George W. Bush posted his campaign contributors online. Interest groups such as Moveon.org, which started in 1998 to oppose the impeachment of President Clinton and then morphed into a broad-based liberal organization, were getting real political traction through the Internet. More political information with greater depth and variety was available online, and many citizens were making good use of it.

But in the end, particularly when we look at how large political institutions and the media used the Internet, the reality fell so far short of the hype that a chapter of *Click on Democracy* was titled "Election.dud." [22] Perhaps the best metaphor for the Internet's trajectory in the election was the contrast between the Republican and Democratic conventions, held just two weeks apart in the summer. The Republicans went first, staking their claim to the presidency in Philadelphia. Soon after the start-up dot com Pseudopolitics arrived on the scene, it became the media darling of the festivities. Its skybox was the trendiest place for politicos to be seen. Fifty-five other Internet outlets were there, too, housed in a media pavilion dubbed "Internet Alley." On-line chats, instant polls, Web-cams mounted to roving reporters' heads, and interviews that included questions fed to anchors through chat rooms were some of the innovative and at times irreverent features they added to the traditional mix of excerpted speeches and media commentary.

But the initial buzz created by the Web's presence at the convention did not translate into anything more significant among citizens or advertisers, and the politics-cum-business ventures failed to generate expected revenues. Two weeks later, when the Democrats convened in Los Angeles, the Internet-based coverage had been dramatically scaled back. Pseudopolitics dropped its live, interactive features, and its skybox appeared placid. The buzz evaporated, and many of the people involved in the different Internet operations there used the convention to network for new jobs.

That was not the whole story, however. A deeper look beyond the traditional campaign events and institutions revealed something quite hopeful: Groups of individuals, some loosely organized and others more formally organized, were using the Internet in more genuinely interactive ways to form political communities and pursue collective action. These groups included one called 80-20, a national-level group of Asian Americans trying to raise their political clout; the People's Campaign, a local group trying to contest elections in New Brunswick, New Jersey; and loosely linked sets of groups trying to protest the Republican convention. After surveying the entire political field during the election cycle, we discovered the central conclusion of the book: the importance of interactivity and horizontal connections, which in turn helped to create and foster political communities.

Like their present-day e-government counterparts, the political and media institutions had approached the Internet largely as a new version of the older, one-to-many TV, radio, and print media, and they were in fact able to achieve some notable innovations in political communication and collective action. But they failed to change political life in the dramatic ways many Internet and political observers had hoped to see. Neither the media nor the candidates used the Internet effectively for interacting with voters, essentially short-circuiting any chance they had of truly connecting with the online electorate. Their notions of the Internet's political role were limited for the most part to a few narrowly defined, traditional uses.[23] In their mind's eye, a campaign's Web site or a political news story sat at the hub of the political wheel, and individual citizens logged on as spokes, received the broadcast information, and sent back financial contributions through cyberspace.

All the while, the Internet's most profound and positive political impact was the way informal groups and individuals used it to create and enhance political communities. The Internet made its most effective contribution to politics—and held its greatest future promise—as a facilitator of political community building and multiple-way communication, rather than as a one-to-many broadcast device employed to capture viewers, money, and votes. Furthermore, the Internet was more useful in achieving even those more mercenary purposes if it was used in ways that challenged the command-and-control model and encouraged people to connect with each other under the aegis of the organization's ultimate aims.

Commercial enterprises certainly understood, as a *BusinessWeek* article called it, "The Power of Us." [24] "User-generated content," "peer-production," "co-production," and "architectures of participation" were some of the buzzwords hinting at the new approach. Consider, for example, the way Amazon and Travelocity employ (with minimal cost) their customers to review its products, or the way Google uses the accumulated decision making of Web page designers to organize its search output. Despite being vulnerable to sabotage by political partisans, the citizen-crafted Wikipedia is remarkably useful and accurate. (Wikipedia is nonprofit, but it illustrates the point.) Mostly free Craigslist has captured a lot of the classified advertising business in large cities, from help-wanted to personal ads, and made the information deeper, the process more interactive, and the experience better. It has also fostered spin-off communities of shared interest and action, both online and off-line.

Writers, pundits, and activists who understood the importance of the difference in approach encouraged the candidates and the political institutions to appreciate the value of a more inclusive and participatory framework, pointing out the few interactive glimmers of hope supplied during the 2000 election. They also encouraged the candidates and institutions to open up back channels and relax top-down control. And indeed, many of them made these changes in the 2004 election cycle, which is one reason that 2004 looked more like a genuine breakout year for the Internet.

But most of them also struggled, and continue to struggle to this day, with the tension between facilitating the co-creation of the political efforts on the part of their would-be supporters—which requires giving up some control and authority—and the desire to control the messages coming out of the organization and manage the activities occurring under its umbrella.[25] That tension is something that government executives attempting to employ the Internet more creatively will feel with a vengeance, a topic we return to below.

It walks and talks: The Internet in election 2004

By all measures, the political force of the Internet could not be ignored in 2004. The largest, most established political institutions turned to interactive, horizontally focused grassroots models with great success. To list just a few of the Internet's biggest steps: It supplied the organizational glue and logistical resources for Howard Dean's volunteers; facilitated much of Dean's financing, allowing him to smash Bill Clinton's record for Democratic fundraising in the twelve months before an election year and propel himself from dark horse to frontrunner; gave John Kerry a similar fundraising boost and in particular helped him to make up ground on President Bush's huge early-money lead in the critical later months of the campaign; underwrote the grassroots movement to draft Wesley Clark into the race; supplied the primary organizing and fundraising device for myriad 527 organizations, such as Moveon, America Coming Together (ACT), Democracy for America (formerly Dean for America), and Swift Boat Veterans for Truth; got millions of people to talk politics and organize local political efforts through Meetups and other similar venues; and enhanced Bush-Cheney '04's massive ground-level volunteer effort, a critical component in an election that turned on approximately 120,000 voters in Ohio.[26]

Larger numbers of informal groups and individuals turned to the Internet for political information, communication, and organization, including heretofore nonpolitical individuals making their first real foray into political activity, people organizing carpools and chartering buses to register voters in swing states, and those starting their own interest and activist groups.

At the same time, blogging became an Internet phenomenon of its own. Millions of blogs emerged, and a few, such as DailyKos, Talking Points Memo, Power Line, InstaPundit, and Little Green Footballs, worked their way into political discussions at elite levels. Perhaps their greatest influence was that many reporters and editors in the traditional media canvassed the blogs, which then became, according to Internet observer Michael Cornfield, "the agenda setters for the agenda setters." [27] But the blogs were also drawing many ordinary people into active discussions, and the cross-posting and cross-linking among the blogs generated a sense of community among large subsets of them. Smaller, locally oriented blogs helped to stimulate meaningful political dialogues. Individual blogs, even those read by just a handful of friends and family, unleashed the personal political expression of countless citizens.[28]

A few aggregate-level statistics suggest the positive effect of the Internet on political life. In 2004, 37 percent of all adults, 75 million people, used the Internet to get political news and information, discuss candidates, donate money, or otherwise volunteer their political services. A Pew Research Center survey of those making election-related uses of the Internet in 2004 found that half believed that the Internet had supplied them with important information that made a difference in their vote, and a quarter of them said that what they found on the Internet made *the* difference in their vote.[29] A quarter of the respondents also reported that their use of the Internet encouraged them to vote. More than half thought that the quality of the political debate was raised by the information available on the Internet, and that the Internet supplied them with information they could not get through the print media or television. Additional evidence from a separate Pew survey suggested that the people using the Internet to get political information were not just seeking out items with which they agreed; in fact, they were exposed to a greater diversity of views than off-line citizens.[30]

Arguably more important, the available evidence also suggested that the Internet was instrumental in bringing new people into the political system. A study by the Institute for Politics, Democracy, and the Internet (IPDI) of on-line political activity during the primary season found that almost half of those who were the most active politically through online means had not been previously involved in politics.[31] Additional research on presidential campaign Meetups during the early months of 2004 suggested that the Internet-organized get-togethers brought new people into the system.[32] Another study found that the Meetups were important in fundraising efforts.[33] It is also worth noting that in the major conferences on Internet politics held since the election, the political professionals—left, right, and center—have agreed that the Internet contributed significantly and independently to the rise in political interest and participation. As we write, the Internet is proving vital in the highest profile early campaign efforts of the 2008 presidential election cycle.

Perhaps the most telling aggregate-level evidence concerns campaign finance. Between 2000 and 2004 the number of people who contributed to campaigns online doubled.[34] An IPDI study of small donors and online donors to the presidential campaigns contained a number of intriguing and hopeful findings about how this change affected the pool of donors.[35] First, the percentage of large donations accounted for by the extremely wealthy appeared to drop. Second, although all groups of donors were still wealthier than nondonors, smaller donors were relatively much closer in income to the average citizen. Third, the numbers of small and large donors both increased between 2000 and 2004, but the increase in the number of small donors was approximately four-fold, and much of that increase came from online donations—high percentages of first-time donors gave online. Most important, however, was the finding that small, online donors were just as politically active as large donors—they were more likely than other small donors to solicit others to give and to attend political events. Based on those findings, the study's authors argued that:

> The Internet is leveling the playing field. Small donors lack the resources and social networks that large donors have, but the Internet in 2004 helped connect them in ways that made up for fewer resources. Online small donors are just as likely as large donors to try to convince someone to support their candidate, and soliciting others to donate seems particularly spurred by being online.[36]

And, after reviewing all the evidence they had gathered about the demographic changes in donors and the Internet's role in the influx of new and small donations, the authors concluded their study with the hope "that [the Internet] can help bring to campaign fundraising a richer social and political diversity that marks the American political system at its best." [37]

Further maturing: Election 2006

The election cycle in 2006, for all its rancor—especially in the form of the televised attack ads run by the national party committees in the final months of the campaign—nevertheless demonstrated additional hopeful signs about how the Internet was being used for political purposes, large and small.[38] Activist and writer Nancy Scola, who also served as an aide to former Virginia governor Mark Warner and a Capitol Hill staffer, contended that by 2006 familiarity with the new communication technologies had spread to the point where "some degree of fluency is almost part of the shared American experience. . . . There are just more of us now who are comfortable expressing [online] who we are and want our leaders to be." [39]

The Republican Party followed the lead it established for itself in 2004 by using its "Action Center" Web site feature to channel potential volunteers into well-defined but horizontally interactive online and off-line activities designed to garner votes, and the party provided them with the online information and tools to accomplish those aims. These activities included walking one's neighborhood and talking to potential voters, networking with activists in one's area, hosting parties for networking and fundraising, recruiting other volunteers, and building personal Web sites. The Democratic Party followed suit, but took a more open-ended approach that emphasized social networking and information sharing through its "Partybuilder" feature. Individual candidates attempted to shed their brittle shells and mass media images. They tried in particular to connect with young voters, by placing themselves on social networking sites such as MySpace and Facebook and by sending their own video and commercials to YouTube. Public interest groups also turned to the social networking sites to help with their campaigns.[40] Individuals who had donated to campaigns online in 2004 now turned to the Internet to start or be part of coordinated fundraising efforts on behalf of candidates and causes, and these efforts were often fostered by political groups, such as ActBlue. Many similar efforts have sprouted in the 2008 presidential election cycle.

Syracuse University's Maxwell Poll on Civic Engagement and Inequality (discussed in the introduction to this volume) also reveals some hopeful indications about the Internet's broader impact on political engagement.[41] When respondents were asked in early autumn 2006 about the Internet's effect on the ability of average citizens to influence political decisions, 17 percent responded that it had "greatly increased it," and 48 percent responded that it had "somewhat increased it." Only 18 percent responded that the Internet had not changed their influence, and a mere 1 percent responded that it had somehow lowered it. More telling perhaps, when asked how the Internet had affected their own levels of political activity, 34 percent responded that it had either greatly or somewhat increased their activity—a sizable percentage to report that kind of change.

Applying the insights in a government agency context

Government agencies have different kinds of missions and therefore different needs for control over what they make available to citizens. Executives at the CIA necessarily work within a set of constraints different from those at the National Park Service, but even the CIA has recently jazzed up its Web site with an interactive personality quiz designed to invite applicants (also see Russ Linden's discussion of the CIA's "Intellipedia" in chapter 6). Not all the possibilities suggested here will be viable in all agencies; nevertheless, we believe that some core principles are widely applicable. Government agencies have one advantage over the other areas we are citing as examples: the citizens' needs for government services and information.

How to realize these ideas on the ground? Web page design is obviously important—the sites must be inviting, easy to navigate, and supply smooth paths leading to greater activity. But that is just the beginning. The agency must be committed to interaction and horizontal activity and be ready both to respond and instigate.

To start, it is essential to *reach out to citizens where they already are*—and then encourage them to join the agency in going further. This principle operates at three levels. The first level is quite literal. Agencies must be proactive in reaching out to potentially interested citizens in the places they already visit online. Although many agencies have captive audiences for their online efforts, they cannot rely solely on them. There is no reason why agency employees could not frequent Internet crossroads related to the agency's mission, and alert the people congregating there to the agency, its work, and the possibilities for their involvement.[42]

These efforts could be as simple as posting agency-approved video archives to YouTube.com or having employees contribute relevant entries on Wikipedia (see below) that invite a visit to an agency's Web site. On a governmentwide scale, a good illustration is Prime Minister Tony Blair's invitation to his fellow citizens to post online petitions—an already popular form of electronic political participation—to his Web site.[43] He probably got more than he bargained for, as the call quickly resulted in an avalanche of petitions protesting the war in Iraq, as well as asking for the absurd—3,700 British citizens signed their names to a request that Blair do a headstand and then juggle ice cream. On the other hand, they did appear to spur greater public response from Downing Street.

The second level is the way citizens are engaged once they arrive. To illustrate this point, in a Federal Executive Institute seminar held last year, Reeher asked his government executive participants to adopt a fictional identity, with accompanying interests or concerns, and then spend an evening accessing the federal government's online presence as if they had those identities.[44] Many of the executives reported back the next day that they were appalled at how technical and uninviting the available information seemed to their fictional characters—ordinary citizens with specific concerns. It is imperative that citizens find easily understandable language in the government's Internet space. Speaking clearly is necessary for all governments in all mediums; in the United States, Washington State has been leading the way with its "plain talk" principles.[45] But such plain talk is especially critical in creating an Internet environment that citizens will want to join.

The third level is what efforts citizens are asked to join. The citizens' prior interests and concerns must overlap with the projects for which the agency is soliciting their help. As a first step, the Internet can be employed to discover what those interests and concerns are. The agency must then offer citizens activities and information that provide multiple connections between agency and citizen, facilitate horizontal connections among citizens, and encourage them to undertake related but new activities. Accomplishing that transition leads us to our second set of core principles.

In the Federal Executive Institute seminar exercise mentioned above, Reeher also asked the executives to pay particular attention to what they were invited to do, and what tools they were given to become more active in their fictional character's areas of interest or concern. The answer that quickly emerged from the following day's reports back to the group was: precious little.

Agencies must *keep the back channel genuinely open*. Again, this principle has several dimensions. Citizens must have ways to communicate their views back to government, and the government must establish ways to acknowledge, respond to, and use this feedback, beyond an automated response. Citizens must also have the option of making their views known to others; it is important to them that other citizens can know what they think and respond if they wish. As we have stressed before, citizens need to be encouraged and provided with the means to establish horizontal connections and communication networks around shared interests or concerns. And for all these methods to work, another core principle must be followed: *The experiences created must be authentic* for the individual citizen.

Many kinds of material can be put online that invite response or participation. Podcasts, videos, and blogs related to the work of the agency can be posted for viewing and comment. Some of these items can be informal and personal, communicating the sense of agency mission that brought public servants to their work in the first place. Elected officials, including President Bush, have enjoyed great success posting informal and human-interest focused communications on their Web sites.[46] Such material can both inform

Box 9.2   Tapping e-governance with DanmarksDebatten

Many of the examples we discuss in the text conjure up networks with subsets of citizens interested in particular aspects of an agency's work. But the insights apply on a mass public scale as well. Steven Clift's "E-Democracy" online forums, for example, are used by communities in the United States and the United Kingdom to discuss public issues.[1] Participants are required to use their real names, can only post twice in any 24-hour period, and are gently guided by online facilitators. Also consider the following story from Denmark, which illustrates a stirring progression from enhancing service delivery to realizing an active vision of e-democracy.

How will your next e-government initiative enhance democracy? This was the question on the minds of the developers of "DanmarksDebatten" (The Denmark Debate), an interactive forum first introduced by Denmark's IT and Telecoms Agency in 2004, through which citizens and public officials can actively debate local and national issues.[2]

According to a case study published by the agency, the program in Denmark is designed to "rehumanize" electronic citizen-government interaction through what they term "situational engagement." [3] Instead of visiting a government Web site simply to retrieve information or submit an electronic form, citizens are also invited to participate in public debates on relevant issues. The moderated forums give citizens the opportunity to actively participate in public policymaking and provide public officials with a wealth of authentic citizen-centered ideas and commentary. DanmarksDebatten transcends the traditional service delivery paradigm by emphasizing interactivity and activating the potential of Internet technology to promote public dialogue and enhance democracy.

Citizens log in to the portal with unique user IDs and can then engage in both local and national debates. During the program's initial pilot phase, citizens and public officials debated diverse issues such as how to solve the inner-city traffic problem in Aarhus, whether to introduce a new payments system for an adult education center in Funen, and what to do with the outdated military airbase in Vaerlose.[4]

Rather than being defensive about having that level of openness lead to more criticism of government, the Danish approach appears to invite it. Here is how the government sees the way this might work: "DanmarksDebatten is

and help to generate empathy for the agency and its employees, as citizens are invited to virtually walk in someone else's shoes.

And in most agencies there is plenty of additional room for digital public discussions coordinated by agency representatives, from lightly moderated to create the framework for debates where citizens want them. For instance, if a family can see from the municipality's website that the waiting time for [day care service] is six months, the municipal authorities may on the same page invite the family to discuss the municipality's future childcare policy. There may be links to similar debates at local, regional or national level, where the family may find inspiration or voice its opinion. From a discussion of municipal childcare policy the family may thus rapidly proceed to . . . a debate on government family policy." [5]

What's next for e-democracy in Denmark? DanmarksDebatten II is a combined e-debate and e-voting initiative scheduled to be launched in 2007, in conjunction with Denmark's new citizen e-government portal, "borger.dk." Following on the heels of DanmarksDebatten I, the new initiative will enable citizens to provide advisory and referendum-style votes online on issues at all levels of government. Using digital signature and pin-code technology, the e-voting software will give public officials the flexibility to delimit their appropriate voter bases. Eligible voters can be defined by adding restrictions on demographic characteristics such as age and location, for example.[6]

But why stop there? Why not let citizens produce their own policy alternatives from the ground up? This is what the Telecom Agency officials in Denmark call their new "debating data" initiative, which is currently under development. Debating data would give citizens and public officials access to the data used in actual government decision making, helping to improve both transparency and the quality of public debate, and increasing citizens' capacities for enlightened participation in the democratic process.

---

1. See the Web site at *www.e-democracy.org*.
2. See Thuestad (2004); Rasmussen (2006); Lukensmeyer and Torres (2006).
3. Thuestad (2004).
4. Ibid.
5. See the English language version of the Web site located at *www.dan marksdebatten.dk/sitemod/design/layouts/default/index.asp?pid=5020& ContentArea=1*. See also OECD (2005), 138.
6. Rasmussen (2006).

---

informal discussions to actively led forums in a more formal Q & A format, if that is more appropriate for the topic.[47] These spaces can be divided up into areas of specific interest, which correspond to different divisions of the agency or the branch. Other possibilities include simulations similar to the

Maine budget exercise described at the beginning of this chapter and kindred "TurboTax" approaches, in which a software package or simulation available on the agency's Web site demonstrates to individual citizens or businesses how a particular set of rules, regulations, or benefit eligibilities would affect them in terms of an outcome, rather than just describing through text how the provisions work.[48] Citizens could also sign up with an agency for automatic updates and alerts to any changes or proposed changes that might affect their interests. Virginia already uses a version of this with its e-rulemaking process. Abroad, Seoul, South Korea, provides reports to the online forums it sponsors regarding actions the government takes that are related to the discussions generated there.[49]

With genuine feedback, critical thoughts about what an agency is doing will get voiced, and not all of them will be benign or even fair. That is the cost of complete transparency. But if the experience so far in other realms on the Internet is any indication, an agency having both the courage and confidence to let these views stand and be seen by others visiting the site will earn more respect than enmity (see Box 9.2).

For government executives the greatest power of the Internet lies in drawing citizens into the work of agencies as coproducers of value, which can be done by further opening up the space created for agency-oriented discussions, providing tools for individuals to do things, and then actually using what they do. The core principle to unlock this last stage is: *Remember that citizens already want to help.*

By allowing others to respond to and evaluate comments posted on their sites, and then employing metrics to accumulate these reactions, agencies can enlist citizens in highlighting the most useful comments, and to place ideas on the agency's agenda for further consideration. Consider, for example, how Travelocity employs its own customers to rate the accommodations it lists, or how Amazon asks customers not only to review its books, but also to rate the usefulness of the posted customer reviews.

An agency might also provide a space for citizens and groups to post information about nonagency events that are related to the agency's mission, in much the same way as politically related event-sharing sites currently do. The agency could go a step further and invite those who signed up for an event through the site to evaluate that event after the fact, and then post on the site a cumulative rating for that event or an entire organization's events. Working Assets does something similar on its "Volunteer for Change" site. As activist and writer Greg Bloom points out, asking for feedback causes the sponsoring organization to take greater care with the quality of the events it is posting to the site.[50]

But such approaches can be taken even further and ask individual citizens to help with the central aspects of an agency's mission. An off-beat (but spot-on) example of this potential can be found in Australia, created by the government's "National Continence Management Strategy," part of the Department of Health and Ageing. The program offers an interactive online map of all public restrooms in the nation.[51] Citizens planning a trip can generate a customized toilet map for their travel route. It is an extremely handy device when one pauses to consider it—very practical, very British.

But now imagine adding to that map a system for individual travelers to report on the quality and cleanliness of the facilities, and feed their reports back into an Amazon-type automatically updating rating system, which was in turn integrated into the map. Note that when Reeher posed this possibility to the executives in his Federal Executive Institute seminar, they looked at him like he was in the loo. The prototype of such a system exists, but it is found in the private sector, in the form of a site called "The Bathroom Diaries," which rates more than 8,000 public bathrooms in more than 100 countries around the world.[52]

Another imaginative potential use emerged in Texas in summer 2006, when Gov. Rick Perry proposed making available online live video streams from cameras installed along remote stretches of private land bordering Mexico.[53] The specific placement of individual cameras would not be made public. Citizens viewing the videos could report suspicious activity, presumably by a camera identification number, by dialing a toll-free telephone number. The governor presented the idea as a way to respond to cuts in federal homeland security funding and increases in border violence; he characterized it as a broader, virtual equivalent of a neighborhood watch program. What would have made the idea even more intriguing from an Internet networking standpoint would have been to provide a way for the citizens watching the site at any given time to communicate with each other, should they choose to do so. That way, they could alert each other to activity that they saw and get second and third opinions on whether the activity was indeed suspicious.

To be sure, the politics surrounding the proposal and its possible effects made it controversial—it was dubbed the "virtual posse," and denounced as crazy, half-baked, race-baiting, even illegal. In addition to legitimate concerns about the political message that such a system of monitoring might convey and how some individuals and organizations might use it, what also appears to be embedded in the critiques is an assumption that the general public cannot be trusted to help the state do its job. And this leads to another core principle: At some meaningful level, agencies must *trust the people.* Trust, after all, is not unidirectional; it is a mutual relationship, and that aspect of it must be taken seriously.

Agencies can choose less-controversial actions. Individuals expressing kindred views or sharing kindred problems or concerns could be encouraged to join together, and agencies could supply them with the networking tools to sustain those initial connections. Agencies could also, after obtaining the permission of the individuals, share information about them with others who might want to join them, and in that way actively facilitate the creation of networks. Citizens coming together through these means could share their experiences with each other and, for example, discuss practices they have learned for coping with whatever problem or concern brought them to interact with government in the first place. These practices are already primary features of the most effective online party-based and campaign-oriented organizing efforts.

Agencies can also provide tools for individuals to create and carry out activities on their own. The Dean presidential campaign did this with its legions of online volunteers in 2003 and 2004, when it latched on to the gatherings in support of Dean—and against the Iraq war—that were already happening through Meetup.com. Bush-Cheney '04 took a more coordinated and planned approach to the same strategy by supplying willing e-volunteers whom it had been cultivating since before 2000 with walk lists of registered Republicans in their own neighborhoods, contact information for other volunteers in their area to join in, and contact information for other potential supporters across the country with shared occupations or interests.

Agencies could take such efforts even further, into the realm of "wikis," for example. A wiki allows individual participants to change the product that is being created collectively, either by adding or editing. Probably the best-known example is the online encyclopedia, Wikipedia, which is remarkably accurate and useful on the whole.[54] But here is a more suggestive example of how an agency might use the wiki approach: In the aftermath of Hurricane Katrina, John Scalzi, a writer and blogger, posted on his Web site a poetic essay, "Being Poor," intended to counter criticisms of those who did not evacuate New Orleans.[55] Others began to add to his essay, wiki-style. The result was a moving and insightful tapestry of reflections on poverty and the tragedy in the Gulf Coast.

For all the important civic reasons discussed throughout this chapter, government agencies should be among the leaders in supplying interactive outlets for our citizens. And agencies are uniquely situated to act as effective instruments for civic bridging. But there is another reason for them to do this, and that reason is our final core principle and the conclusion of our argument.

Agencies need to move forward on e-governance because they have to. Citizens who use electronic technology as a primary way of communicating expect and demand this kind of interactivity. As the worlds of politics and commerce have illustrated, interactivity is an essential part of the new digital culture. Government agencies—and the executives who manage them—simply cannot afford to be left behind.

Resources for further learning

For a thorough overview of the state of e-government, see Darrell West, *Digital Government: Technology and Public Sector Performance* (2005), but note that works such as this, despite anyone's best efforts, become somewhat dated fairly rapidly.

Books that might help stimulate some big-think ideas about innovations include Steve Davis, Larry Elin, and Grant Reeher, *Click on Democracy* (2002); Allison Fine, *Momentum* (2006); Malcolm Gladwell, *The Tipping Point* (2002); Howard Rheingold, *The Virtual Community* (2000), and Rheingold, *Smart Mobs* (2003). But what is probably better is to wade into the deep and see what is actually being done by others. Try some of the many Web sites referenced in the text and in the endnotes for this chapter.

For case studies of innovative e-governance initiatives, see Steven Clift's Democracies Online Web site, *www.dowire.org*. Also see his organization's Web site facilitating online public discussion forums, *www.e-democracy.org*. In addition, Carolyn Lukensmeyer and Lars Hasselblad Torres, "Public Deliberation: A Manager's Guide to Citizen Engagement," is a report on public deliberation from a government agency perspective. It includes a rich discussion of online deliberation, with several useful examples, and is available at *www.businessofgovernment.org/pdfs/LukensmeyerReport.pdf*.

For ongoing updates, feature essays, and informed discussions of how the Internet is affecting the conduct of electoral politics and political advocacy, check out the Personal Democracy Forum, at *www.personaldemocracy.com*.

The nonprofit Sunlight Foundation is pushing the boundaries of transparency when it comes to elected representatives, particularly Congress. Its Web site is worth exploring and could generate specific ideas. See *www.sunlightfoundation.com*.

For more "traditional" forms of innovation in government administration, including e-government efforts, see the Ash Institute at Harvard University, at *www.innovations.harvard.edu*.

Regarding blogs, to get a sense of their culture and framework, the best thing to do is to read some of them. We could list thousands, but our recommendation is to follow your own political inclinations and interests and pay attention to what draws you in and prompts you to share your own comments, and then think of that in terms of your own agency's work.

Online organizer and activist Alan Rosenblatt has assembled his favorite blogs that deal with politics and the Internet. Rosenblatt's own blog is at *www.drdigipol.com*. Here is his list, minus repeats from above, and without annotation:

www.epolitics.com

www.Frogloop.com

www.mobileactive.org

http://nten.typepad.com/newsletter

www.politicsonline.com/blog

www.ipdi.org/Blog

www.zackexley.com

www.idealware.org/blog

www.bivingsreport.com

Notes

1. The current year's simulation can be found at *www.maine.gov/governor/baldacci/policy/budget*.
2. See Kettl (2002).
3. Clift (2006), emphasis added.
4. See Horrigan (2004) for these and other figures on Internet use.
5. Council for Excellence in Government (2001).
6. See Horrigan (2004); Stowers (2004).
7. See the Web site at *www.innovations.harvard.edu*.
8. West (2005), 113.

9. See, for example, Willemssen (2003).

10. Horrigan (2004).

11. Council for Excellence in Government (2001), 25.

12. See the discussion of trust appearing in the introduction to this volume; and Tolbert and Mossberger (2006).

13. See, for example, Norris (2001); Mossberger, Tolbert, and Stansbury (2003).

14. Nielsen//NetRatings (2006a). According to the U.S. Census Bureau, in 2005 there were 230 million people over the age of sixteen in the United States.

15. See Marriott (2006).

16. See Markoff (2006); and the "One Laptop" Web site at *http://wiki.laptop.org/go/One_Laptop_per_Child.*

17. Nielsen//NetRatings (2006b).

18. Davis, Elin, and Reeher (2002).

19. See, for example, Davis, Elin, and Reeher (2002); Reeher and Davis (2004); Reeher, Davis, and Elin (forthcoming); Armstrong and Moulitsas Zuniga (2006); Fine (2006); Trippi (2004).

20. Davis, Elin, and Reeher (2002). Material similar to some of what follows can be found in that work, and in Reeher, Davis, and Elin (forthcoming).

21. In selecting many of these signposts, we were guided by "The First Digital Decade" (2004). More generally on the Internet in 2000, and for more detail on some of the stories that follow, see Davis, Elin, and Reeher (2002).

22. Much of this and what follows is taken from Davis, Elin, and Reeher (2002); and Reeher and Davis (2004).

23. The observation extends to the way scholars have tended to study Internet politics. Their principal focus has been on the Internet as an effective, efficient, flexible, and low-cost substitute for traditional one-to-many activities. This assumption has restricted the consideration of the role of the Internet in many different aspects of political life. In electoral politics, the Internet has been viewed primarily as another vehicle for broadcasting information, raising money, and publicizing a highly focused message. In public administration, the attention has centered on analogous efforts by government, such as communicating agency information and regulations or enrolling clients online. Typical academic studies of the Internet's political use have followed from these assumptions and have tended to focus on content analyses of candidate and government agency Web sites, studies of user-friendliness and participation rates for candidate sites and for online government forms and applications, or qualitative evaluations of online services. While useful to other researchers and some political practitioners, these works have been rather dry affairs, which fail to capture much of the Internet's true political value and are unlikely to inspire readers to greater civic engagement. Beginning in 2004, and in particular with studies of the Dean campaign, this began to change, but the weight of scholarship is still centered in these kinds of efforts.

24. Hof (2005).

25. Greg Bloom (2006) reports on his experiences attending the New Organizing Institute's three-day training seminar and nicely reveals these tensions.

26. To get a sense of Meetup, see its Web site at *www.meetup.com.*

27. Brooks (2006).

28. The seemingly endless discussions at conferences and in the media about whether blogs are an alternative form of "legitimate" journalism, while an important topic, largely miss their political and social significance. Millions are writing them, billions are reading them, and billions are talking about them. On June 27, 2006, for example, Technorati.com, the well-known tracker of blogs, was keeping tabs on 46.1 million blog sites and 2.6 billion links on those sites. On the same day, a Google search of the word *blog* recorded 2,100,000,000 sites containing that word. Now Podcasts and uploaded video are adding to the richness of blogs and other sites. The blogs provide interactive hubs for participation, in

the form of political expression in a variety of forms. More important than the people running the blogs and the content of the main pieces they write on them are the many others who contribute and post to them.

29. Rainie, Cornfield, and Horrigan (2005). Subsequent data reported in this paragraph are also taken from this report, unless otherwise noted.

30. Horrigan, Garrett, and Resnick (2004).

31. Graf and Darr (2004).

32. Williams, Weinberg, and Gordon (2004).

33. Graf et al. (2006).

34. Rainie, Cornfield, and Horrigan (2005).

35. Graf et al. (2006). The study places the line between "small donors" and "large donors" at $200.

36. Ibid., 32.

37. Ibid., 44.

38. The following is based on the authors' own research as well as the reports of others who either observed or actively participated in the election. In particular, see Sifry (2006); Bloom (2006); Levy (2006); and Defeo et al. (2006).

39. See her comments in Defeo et al. (2006).

40. Not all expert observers and participants agreed that the networking sites, at least as they were used, added much of value to political efforts, either for the candidates and group campaigns or the citizens who normally visit the sites. In a similar vein, the use of mobile phone technology did not appear to realize the expectations that many pundits placed on it for the 2006 cycle.

41. The poll can be found at *www.maxwell.syr.edu/Campbell.*

42. See similar advice for political organizers in Levy (2006).

43. Stringer (2007).

44. The identities ranged from "the mother of a 5-year-old child diagnosed with autism, wanting to find out what kinds of federal programs apply to them, and what kinds of support are available," to "a 70-year-old widow with a Medigap insurance plan who is concerned about the new Medicare drug benefit plan—how the benefit plan will affect her insurance, and what its advantages are." Other identities were persons interested in space travel, the environment and national parks, and policies in Africa, among others.

45. La Corte (2006).

46. Among the most frequently viewed and downloaded sets of materials from the White House site are the "Barney" videos which, although at first viewing appear to be lighthearted treatments of the West Wing as seen through the eyes of the family dog, are, upon closer analysis, savvy, effective communications of some of the central political themes of its occupants. See *www.whitehouse.gov/barney.*

47. For an intriguing model of an EPA discussion, along with some best practices for leading these discussions, see Holzer et al. (2004). See also a broader discussion of electronic public deliberation, including deliberations sponsored by government, in Lukensmeyer and Torres (2006).

48. See, among others, Coglianese (2004a), (2004b).

49. Clift (2006).

50. Bloom (2006). The Web site is: *http://volunteerforchange.org.*

51. For the map, see *www.toiletmap.gov.au/default.aspx.*

52. See *www.thebathroomdiaries.com.*

53. Caldwell (2006).

54. Wikipedia can be found at *www.wikipedia.org.*

55. The essay, with comments, links, and additions, can be found at *www.scalzi.com/whatever/003704.html.*

10 Engineering experiences that build trust in government

LOU CARBONE, FOUNDER AND CEO, EXPERIENCE ENGINEERING, INC.

IN 1994 THE U.S. MINT WAS 202 YEARS OLD and acted like it. Although it produced 20 billion circulating coins a year for the Federal Reserve system, it was an old-line manufacturing outfit with terrible labor relations and, for its commemorative coins, equally poor customer service. If you called the Mint, it took on average two minutes before anyone answered, and if you sent a letter, you could wait forty-two days for an answer. If you actually ordered something, you could wait eight weeks or more to get it. Needless to say, the Mint engendered little loyalty or trust from its customers.[1]

After becoming director of the Mint, Philip Diehl changed all that. By 1999 the buyers of its numismatic and commemorative coins gave the Mint a higher score than any other government agency measured by the American Customer Satisfaction Index. Calls were answered on average in 17.5 seconds, letters in three days, and orders were filled in less than two weeks. More important, the Mint rediscovered the magic in its product, turning its customers on to the fact that buying its new fifty state quarters was a way to emotionally connect parents and grandparents with children through the nation's history. The Mint discovered the Web, exciting and enabling the public to participate actively in designing the Sacagawea dollar and inviting children to play games on its H.I.P. (History in Your Pocket) Pocket Change site. These changes became possible because Diehl listened to customers. The customer experience improved dramatically, and along with that came financial success. Diehl found new support in Congress as well. In short, by changing the customer's experience, one of the oldest manufacturing companies in the United States rebuilt trust, strengthened loyalty, and emerged as a government success story.

As Phil Diehl recognized, the way we as citizens experience government services and leadership today has changed dramatically since the Founders established our democratic form of government. The changes are due in great part to instantaneous communications and the complex global, political, and economic frameworks that have evolved. As we discuss throughout this chapter, managing how citizens experience government in this environment presents a major opportunity to build trust and value in government and its leaders.

How people feel about the experiences they have with government services and leadership greatly influences their value assessment. A systematic and holistic framework for managing experiences that build trust and commitment should be foundational to every government leader's vision and the keystone of the execution of their duties.

Experience and trust

In both the private and public sectors it is clear that consumer and citizen trust is earned or revoked based on our experiences.[2] The private sector, for its part, has become increasingly aware that trust built by a good customer experience correlates positively with business success.

- Dr. Leonard Berry of Texas A&M University states that the basic components of trust are rooted in behaviors that foster feelings of reliability, competence, and fairness.[3]
- A 2004 Yankelovich State of Consumer Trust report states that a large majority of consumers will shop at companies that have earned their trust even if they charge more.[4] If trust is violated, however, 96 percent spend less, 76 percent tell family and friends, and 49 percent increase business with competitors.
- A Harvard Mind of the Market case study ("Companies that have Consumer's Best Interest at Heart, a ZMet(r) Study") directly linked trust to honesty, dependability, and continued patronage.[5] It concluded that to build trust, companies must consistently send cues that the consumer can interpret as "caring," which leads to trust, which leads to loyalty.

Customers behave like detectives in the way they unconsciously organize "clues" embedded in their experiences into a set of feelings. They recall these feelings when deciding whether to use, not use, recommend, or reuse a product or service. Where those feelings are positive, trust is developed. The more important, complex, and personal the service, the more deeply rooted the feelings. The more deeply rooted the feelings, the more important the experience clues are, and the more the bond of trust can be built.

The same process correlates to citizens' experiences with government. For example, dealing with the IRS could leave someone with a feeling of vulnerability, injustice, and insensitivity or with a sense of fairness, openness, and empathy. The signals or clues that exist in the experience with the agency range all the way from language used in correspondence to the demeanor of a telephone representative. An experience with the Veterans Administration, the Social Security Administration, or an agency of the Department of Homeland Security has the potential to emit a set of "favorable" feelings or "negative" feelings that profoundly impact perception. Considering how to manage the customer experiences of government services may seem over-whelming, but we can bring it into focus by first understanding what feelings customers want an experience to evoke.

In some of his earliest work involving how customers think and process the experiences they have, Gerald Zaltman, professor emeritus at Harvard Business School, stated that "the tangible attributes of a product or service have far less influence on consumers than the unconscious sensory and emotional elements derived from the total experience." [6] After standing in two different lines for nearly an hour and a half at the Department of Motor Vehicles, your driver's license may have been renewed, but chances are the experience will have left you irritated and angry as well as bored and tired. Your memory of this government office and more generally your trust in government will have been negatively affected. In other words, loyalty and trust are more a result of how customers feel in the overall experience they have, rather than the rational functional service they receive. Feelings shape how customers think about and behave with regard to an organization's products or services, and this point is equally true in government and the private sector. An experience with the IRS might be efficient yet not engender any positive feelings that would cause a tax-payer to feel the agency is trustworthy or reflects any value the citizens derive.

This gulf between the government's service and the customer's feelings about it underscores the need for a monumental shift in the focus of think-ing in many government agencies, where the focus has traditionally been on efficiency (doing more with less). Leaders in government, for the most part, have not seen themselves in the customer experience business, but as Table 10.1 on the following page suggests, all government agencies are serving cus-tomers for whom the emotional part of the experience matters.

Whether serving citizens directly on a fee-for-service basis (a common occurrence as government struggles to earn the revenue it needs), in a fran-chise operation that sells services to other government agencies, in a regula-tory or law enforcement mode, or even in just the effort to recruit and retain employees in a competitive labor market, government agencies can reap

Table 10.1 Government services and their customers

Type of service	Agency examples	Customers
Direct service	Social Security (SSA) IRS Transportation Security (TSA)	Pensioners Taxpayers Travelers
Fee-for-service	U.S. Postal Service National Park Service Agricultural Marketing Service	Postal patrons Vacationers Produce shippers/receivers
Interagency franchising	Financial Management Service (Treasury)	Agency financial managers
Technical assistance	General Services Administration	Users of the federal supply service
Law enforcement	Inspectors general (IG) Bureau of Prisons FBI	Agency managers Incarcerated felons State/local law enforcement, citizens, and suspects
Regulatory	Federal Aviation Administration	Commercial airlines and pilots
Employee recruitment	All agencies	Potential hires
Employee retention	All agencies	Existing employees

significant benefits if they pay attention to what customers feel in their encounters with them.

This point may not always be obvious. Consider services where cooperation is essential, such as law enforcement, judicial proceedings, corrections, and immigration. Positive feelings among those served make such agencies function more smoothly. For example, jurists who experience inadequacy and inefficiencies in the legal system consequently view this duty of citizenship as an inconvenience or waste of time rather than an honor and obligation to others in a democratic society. Leaders in correctional facilities can attest to the dramatic difference that the cooperation (as opposed to the resistance) of incarcerated felons can make in achieving the objectives of their organizations at reasonable cost, not to mention the impact on the experience (and therefore morale and retention) of their employees.

Government agencies have the opportunity to create value for their constituents, leaders, and the organizations themselves by understanding, designing, and managing their agencies' value propositions around the total experience they deliver rather than simply the efficiency of the service or function they perform. Many leaders may find themselves solely focusing on achieving the fundamental goal of the efficient delivery of government services, when greater attention to experience management on both an emotional and rational level can increase effectiveness, help maintain funding, improve customer satisfaction, and decrease oversight.

Perceptions of government agencies

How well do government agencies currently address the emotional needs of their customers? This is not an easy question to answer. The data most often collected about government services focus on broad measures of trust, satisfaction, or how efficiently government agencies serve the public, not on how well the emotional needs of citizens are met. Indeed, many government agencies have long followed the way of most private sector businesses and focus on efficiencies rather than the experiential emotional equity being built (or diminished) for customers.

If an organization focuses on efficiency to the exclusion of effectiveness (on behalf of customer needs), it will always fall short in building long-term advocacy, value, and loyalty. How leaders in government manage experiences will impact how leadership and government services are valued. Experiences can be purposefully managed to create emotional connections that build powerful relationships and trust. How people feel in an experience is unconsciously the basis for how they feel about an agency, and by extension, the leadership of the agency and of government.

At present, the American Customer Satisfaction Index (ACSI) is the best tool we have to gauge the emotional perceptions of customers to the services they receive from government. The ACSI is a sophisticated customer survey conducted quarterly by the University of Michigan for private and public sector agencies that pay to be included. The ACSI measure of customer satisfaction, on a scale of 0 to 100 (100 is the highest possible score), includes measures of the perceived quality of government services (including customization and reliability), the extent to which customer expectations are met, a comparison of services provided to the customer's ideal for those services, the extent of customer complaints, and the customer's perception of the service outcomes.

Table 10.2 on page 272 provides a sample of 2006 data for selected federal agencies. The overall average for all government agencies included in the ACSI is 72.3 (by comparison, the private sector average is 74.4).

Table 10.2 ACSI data for selected federal agencies, 2006

Service Area/agency	Recipients	ACSI Score
Individual benefits		
Social Security Administration	Retirement benefits recipients	80
Centers for Medicare and Medicaid Services/HHS	Medicare and Medicaid recipients	73
Information providers/technical assistance/supply		
General Services Administration	Users of the Federal Citizen Information Center	82
Treasury Franchise Fund	Recipients of Federal Consulting Group, Consulting, and Performance Measurement Services	81
Specialty retail–collectibles		
U.S. Mint, Treasury	Buyers of numismatic and commemorative coins	87
Financial services		
Federal Student Aid, Education	Borrowers with federal student loans in repayment status	79
Small Business Administration	Applicants for a Disaster Recovery Administration low-interest loan	57
Tax collection		
Internal Revenue Service–Treasury	All individual tax filers	65
	Individual electronic tax filers	76
	Individual paper tax filers	51

Source: American Customer Satisfaction Index, *www.theacsi.org/index.php?option=com_content&task=view&id=164&Itemid=160.*

As the data demonstrate, the customer experience with government differs dramatically across agencies. Not surprisingly, the two services shown in the table that have the lowest scores are also associated with some of the most emotionally frustrating experiences citizens currently have with government—applying for a loan to help recover from a natural disaster and filling out and seeking personal help with the maze of paper tax forms. In the latter case, as the 25-point spread between the experience of paper and electronic filers demonstrates, it is not surprising that the IRS is encouraging more people to file their taxes electronically.

Despite these striking results, the ACSI does not give us a full picture of the emotional reaction of citizens to government. Indeed, customer satisfaction is a proxy and incomplete measure. Current studies and writings in the private sector by business consultants such as Fred Reichheld, author of the *Loyalty Effect* and the *Ultimate Question,* counter the idea that customer satisfaction measures are viable in accurately determining an organization's customer advocacy or ability to create loyalty and growth. In the private sector at least, many customers who respond on surveys that they are "satisfied" or "very satisfied" defect to other providers. "Satisfaction" does not ensure loyalty. In the public sector, there may not be another organization to which one can turn to meet a need, but citizens who want to express their displeasure do have other places to turn—535 other places on Capitol Hill to be exact.

> *Satisfaction surveys are a far less accurate test of satisfaction than behavior. In business after business, our research has shown that 60 to 80 percent of customers who defected had said on a survey just prior to defecting that they were satisfied or very satisfied.*
>
> —Fred Reichheld, *The Loyalty Effect,* 237.

So there is an apparent opportunity, just as the private sector discovered, to enhance the value that constituents sense they receive from government. Government agencies need to focus on the experiences they deliver, and to succeed at this they must understand how customers think about and process the experiences they have.

Customers filter experience clues

Basic to managing experiences is the premise that customers consciously and unconsciously filter experience clues when they interact with an organization. They organize the clues into a set of impressions, some rational and calculative, and others more emotional.

Passengers going through a Transportation Security Administration (TSA) airport screening will encounter a barrage of clues, including the orderliness or confusion of the surroundings, the way their privacy is respected, and the speed and quality of the screening itself. They will have an emotional as well as a cognitive reaction to the screening experience and draw conclusions that, collectively, have a profound affect on TSA.

What exactly is an experience clue? It is anything present in the experience that the customer can see, hear, taste, touch, or smell. Each clue carries a message, and added together the clues help create the customer's total experience. Clues tell a story in the most powerful of ways. It is far more beneficial to weave a consistent, cohesive, and compelling story than an inconsistent, disjointed one that does not engage individuals. Even the absence of clues is part of an experience. Private sector organizations such as Starbucks, the Mayo Clinic, Federal Express, and Target have long realized the value of developing their stories and creating supporting evidence through purposeful, systematic clue management. Some federal agencies have also mastered clue management. One outstanding example is the Department of Veterans Affairs National Cemeteries Association, which conducts the emotionally compelling and flawlessly managed burials at, among other places, Arlington National Cemetery.

Customers unconsciously work out the "clue math." They add up the clues and unconsciously compute intricate calculations that will affect their decisions, opinions, and preferences as a result of their assessment of a service. They decide whether clues are emotionally positive (differentiate the service in a memorable way), negative (are destructive of loyalty and trust), or neutral (fail to differentiate the service provided in any helpful way) (see Figure 10.1). Although an organization may or may not understand that this process is happening, the reality is that experience delivery can range from very purposeful to haphazard. Thinking about experiences in this way helps an organization take a more systemic and focused approach to the management of clues in the experience.

Figure 10.1 Experience preference model™

A tool to visualize how clues in an experience add up
to a positive, negative, or neutral feeling

rejection	acceptance	preference
Negative differentiation	No differentiation	Positive differentiation
—	commodity zone	**+**

Source: Experience Engineering Inc.

Building a new competency

As never before, today's environment requires government leaders to recalibrate their perspectives on how they create value for the people they serve. A systematic focus on experience can provide the framework to influence the creation of feelings of trust and value. To fully leverage experience, organizations must manage the emotional components with the same rigor they bring to the management of product and service functionality and efficiency.

How do you design, create, and manage the appropriate clues in a customer experience to make it more valuable and sustainable? How do you structure efforts to optimize the value their experiences can create for customers? Leaders and managers must develop new perspectives and skills, with associated tools that are rooted in the following fundamental experience management principles:

Understand customers on a deeper level. Critical to optimizing experiences is to first understand the emotional needs and desires that drive your customers' preferences and advocacy. Invest in learning what customers want to feel in the experience, what will engage them cognitively and emotionally in a manner that creates strong preference and loyalty. Success requires a commitment to research.

Be clue conscious. Cultivate a sensibility about the experiences you deliver. Understand what customers see and hear, touch, smell, and taste. Most important, develop a sensitivity for what they are feeling throughout the experience. By understanding what customers sense in an experience, you will understand the story that stringing clues together creates. By comparing what customers feel in an experience to what they want to feel, you will begin to identify how to modify current clues and add new ones to deliver the desired experience in a predictable, powerful way.

Understanding customers at a deeper emotional level—the experience motif

The results of identifying customers' deeper needs, along with consideration of an organization's overall market strategy, form the basis for the creation of an "experience motif." The experience motif is ideally a three-word expression of the customers' desired feelings in an experience. The reason for choosing three words rather than a longer phrase or a sentence is to keep the expression simple and focused so that it can be an effective tool for the assessment, design, development, and management of experience clues. Otherwise, the motif may resemble a conventional mission statement and make the interpretation considerably less focused and more diffuse.

Consider the case of Doylestown Hospital's Health and Wellness Center in Warrington, Pennsylvania, which developed an experience motif of "understood, strengthened, and renewed." This motif clearly articulates what patients want to feel, and it offers a concise directive to staff for the design, development, and management of each subexperience to get people to feel understood, strengthened, and renewed. Compared to a mission statement such as "The Center will provide a world-class healthcare experience that provides for the health and well-being of the community," Doylestown's motif is far more actionable and focused.

Clue management

The experience motif becomes the North Star—the foundation for integrating and reconciling all elements of the experience. It is the unifying element for every clue in an experience. It becomes the filter that facilitates alignment of what would otherwise be a collection of random clues into a well thought-out, purposefully designed set of clues orchestrated to create certain feelings and tell a certain story.

Clues generally fall into three main categories:

1. *Functional* clues concern the technical quality of the offering. Functional clues are the "what" of the experience and reveal reliability and competence. Anything that indicates or suggests the technical quality—its presence or absence—is a functional clue. Does the key issued at the front desk open the hotel room door? Does the television set work? Was the wake-up call made as promised? Is the room service order correct? In a government agency, is the application for assistance clear and easy to understand? Is all the needed information—and only the needed information—collected on one form? Does the agency Web site enable you to drill down to get needed information quickly and easily?

2. *Mechanic* clues come from the sensory presentation of the service. Whereas functional clues concern reliability, mechanic clues concern the sights, smells, sounds, tastes, and textures of the surroundings. The wide aisles, signature red color scheme, and numerous check-out counters serve as mechanic clues in Target stores. Consider the sign shown below, which appeared on the door of a state government's highway welcome center. In this

case, the mechanic clue counteracts the very purpose of a welcome center, which is to encourage people to visit and spend their dollars in the state.

3. *Humanic* clues come from the behavior and appearance of service providers—choice of words, tone of voice, level of enthusiasm, body language, neatness, and appropriate dress. Southwest Airlines' flight attendants' typically friendly manner as they interact with passengers on a

```
NO SMOKING

NO FOOD OR DRINKS
ALLOWED INSIDE

SHOES AND SHIRTS
REQUIRED

NO PETS
```

Welcome center sign

flight and their distinctive polo shirt and khaki slacks uniform illustrate humanic clues. The way you are greeted on entering a National Park or the tone of voice you hear on an 800-helpline are humanic clues in government settings, and they contribute to citizen loyalty or disaffection. Humanic and mechanic clues, the "how" of the service experience, reveal much about an organization's commitment to understanding and satisfying customers' needs and wants.

The distinction among functional, mechanic, and humanic clues can be subtle. For example, a retail salesperson who answers a customer's question about when an out-of-stock item will be available is producing both functional and humanic clues. The accuracy of the information is a functional clue. The salesperson's choice of words and body language are humanic clues. One salesperson may answer the question disinterestedly—"Sorry, we're out of that"—and another may answer enthusiastically—"We expect a shipment next week. Would you like me to hold the item for you?" A customer's emotional response to these humanic clues is likely to be quite different even if the information is accurate in both cases.

The power of different humanic clues to produce different customer feelings among competent professional service providers showed up dramatically in a study of patients who filed and did not file malpractice claims against fifty-nine primary care physicians in Oregon and Colorado. When audiotapes of routine office visits were analyzed, the no-claims physicians (compared with those with two or more lifetime malpractice claims) used more statements of orientation (educating patients about what to expect and the flow of the visit), laughed and used humor more often, and used more behaviors that invited patients' opinions, checked for understanding, and encouraged patients to talk. No-claims physicians also spent longer in routine visits. Although the difference in time was small (18.3 minutes versus 15.0 minutes), it represented greater communication with patients and made a real difference in the patient experience.[7]

Subtleties aside, managers who wish to improve their customers' service experience must effectively manage the clues that make up the experience. The different clues play different roles and can vary in importance. It is a rare organization, however, that can deliver truly excellent service and be deficient in any of the clue categories: functional, mechanic, and humanic.

Conducting an experience audit

Organizations and leaders embracing experience management typically make a commitment to research by conducting a customer experience audit. This process is a thorough analysis of the current customer experience that can reveal customers' emotional needs as well as an understanding of their response to specific experience clues.

Videotape and digital photography may be used to document actual customer experiences. Managers might accompany and observe customers as they go through an experience. In-depth interviews may be held with customers and employees to learn their feelings about different aspects of an experience.

Doylestown Hospital conducted an extensive experience audit and came to understand that their customers unconsciously evaluate the experience they create based on how understood, strengthened, and renewed they feel, and the hospital made these values into its experience motif. The audit allows the organization to set an emotional compass upon which it can evaluate existing clues in the experience or create new clues that engender those feelings and emotions.

The Federal Executive Institute (FEI) in Charlottesville, Virginia, is a residential executive education campus for senior career leaders in government. FEI's staff sought to understand the current experience from the customer's vantage point, especially during the first (and critical) twenty-four hours an executive lives on campus. FEI's experience audit included interviews with executives; "clue scanning," in which staff used digital photography and guided observation techniques to see the experience as the executives might see it; and a thorough analysis of all printed and online material executives received prior to the start of the program. At the same time, a contractor

Figure 10.2 Federal Executive Institute: Experience
audit – partial results

FEI experience motif:
At FEI, we want executives to feel valued, strengthened, and inspired.

Registration experience clues
and their emotional impact

rejection	acceptance	preference
Negative differentiation	No differentiation	Positive differentiation
–	commodity zone	**+**

- Lack of signs to find FEI/parking spaces
- Dim lighting in entry
- "Poverty" look:
  - stains on flooring
  - worn furniture
- Lack of readiness
  - empty water cooler
  - bathrooms being cleaned
  - empty brochure rack

- Welcome signage
- Organized

- Warm smiles and greetings
- Smells of cider and cookies
- Registration process — smooth, easy, straight-forward
- Walking tour orientation

Source: Experience Engineering Inc.

conducted a metaphor analysis with potential customers to see what they expected to feel during the FEI experience. The combination of these techniques yielded an experience motif and the kind of audit data illustrated in Figure 10.2.

When the actual clues in the audit (organized by whether each clue was positive, neutral, or negative in the feelings produced) were held up against the desired feelings in the motif, the gaps became evident. As Figure 10.2 shows, the positive feelings produced by a warm greeting and registration process had to struggle to overcome the anxiety and confusion created for executives who had trouble locating the facility and finding a parking space, and then noticing facility maintenance problems that should have been corrected before they arrived.

This combined picture has enabled the institute to redesign many of the experience clues and create new clues more likely to produce arriving participants who feel valued, strengthened, and inspired.

Designing experiences

The audit process leads to designing experiences from the customer's perspective ("customer-back" or "citizen-back") versus the agency's perspective ("agency-out") and involves paying closer attention to what customers are sensing and feeling—much of which will be at an unconscious level. If you are not thinking of the experience from inside the customer's mind, you can easily miss not just minor nuances but also important pieces of the experience that shape customer perception.

Avis Car Rental learned that the way they store and handle infant car seats at the rental facility has a greater impact on customers' perceptions of the cleanliness of the rental car than anything they could do to clean the inside or outside of the vehicle. By looking at the experience customer-back through an experience audit, they discovered that the Avis locations that put infant seats in poly bags and placed them neatly on shelves within customer view (previously they had been piled on an oil-stained floor) found themselves being rated higher for the cleanliness of their cars.[8] This nuance would never have been revealed without the benefit of a customer experience audit.

The FEI audit indicated that many executives felt their arrival was like checking into a hotel, whereas the staff wanted them to feel they were being welcomed to a home. This information led to changes in everything from how visitors find the institute from the highway, to how they are guided to parking spaces, welcomed into the building, and escorted to their rooms.

A commitment to experience management affects all levels of an organization. It is important to understand the roles and responsibilities in carrying out experience initiatives, and even more important for leadership to foster and manage those roles and responsibilities. As summarized in Table 10.3, all levels of the organization play vital roles in extracting the most value from managing experience clues.[9] Senior leadership must set the tone and focus attention on the importance of experience management. Middle managers must be clue conscious: They must incorporate clue language into daily discussion, become personally involved in improving the company's clue presentation, support direct reports who are invited to serve on cross-functional clue management project teams, and, in general, empower, encourage, and facilitate systematic clue management. Middle managers must also select, orient, teach, encourage, assess, and reward employees who perform the service and provide the clues that play such a dominant role for many services.

Table 10.3   Clue management in the organization

Organizational level	Role	Action
Senior leadership	Create and support imperative for clue management	Demonstrate a strong commitment to understanding the role of managing clues and its importance to customers' preference and loyalty. Establish and stay focused on a mandate for systematic experience clue management.
Middle management	Understand and empower clue management	Demonstrate understanding of the role of managing clues and establish it as a high priority. Support the development of clue management proficiency within the organization.
Frontline workers	Sense and respond to clue management	Become sensitive to the presence and absence of clues with a bias for action in the management of clues. Be aware of customers' emotional and functional needs in an experience and respond to customers accordingly.

Frontline employees are powerful generators of experience clues and need to be clue conscious as well. It is critical for leaders to share with these employees relevant market research that distills what customers value in the service experience—their emotional needs, not just their functional needs. To provide the humanic clues that support the organization's strategy, service providers need to know their customers, and they need to be armed with a customer experience "emotional compass" that clearly and concisely articulates customers' desired feelings. In addition, employees need ongoing training, education, and reinforcement to effectively present the right clues.

Benefits to leaders in democracy

The ultimate measure of success is how people feel in the experiences they have and how they associate those feelings with the experience. If people feel insignificant or undervalued in a government experience, they are more likely to develop negative perceptions—and share them with others—that shape the reality of the reputation of an agency. Whether leaders put this all together—or not—customers and constituents do. They work out the "clue math" in every interaction they have. They add up the clues that shape their assessment of government agencies and services. Experience management presents the opportunity to positively imprint with constituents on a deeper and more lasting level and create greater advocacy and loyalty.

As government leaders continue to face higher costs, increased oversight, and the need for new ways to maintain funding, they will benefit by focusing with greater rigor on the experience created for all their constituents. They can accomplish this by assessing what systems they have in place to learn how customers feel in the current experience and understand how customers want to feel on a deep, unconscious level, and then design and consistently manage clues that could close any gap between the two.

Leaders embracing experience management as a competency in their organization are far more likely to connect with their constituents, foster emotional engagement, and create a deeper sense of value and commitment from them. They will also reap the benefits of greater trust and loyalty that so many leading companies in the private sector are beginning to realize through experience management initiatives.

Leaders in government may think experience management applies solely to enhancing the experience of outside customers and constituents, so we end with the story of Michael Abrashoff, former commanding officer of USS *Benfold*, a $1 billion advanced Navy warship with a crew of more than 300 that in the late 1990s was assigned to duty near Iraq. The ship won the Spokane Trophy for having the best combat readiness in the fleet—the first time in at least ten years that a ship of its class had received that honor.[10] The *Benfold* became known not only for its operational and financial success (in fiscal year 1998 it returned $600,000 of its $2.4 million maintenance budget and $800,000 of its $3 million repair budget to the government), but also for its innovative practices that created a culture of excellence.

From finding pumpkins for a pumpkin-carving contest while deployed in the Middle East to ditching traditional and costly Navy food for tastier commercially available menu items (the savings sent five of the ship's cooks to culinary school), the *Benfold* was able to create a crew experience unparalleled in the fleet. Listen to its creative commander talk about how he fashioned an unparalleled experience for all newly arriving crew members and for those new recruits whose first on-ship experience he was charged with creating:

Within two days of when new crew members arrive, I sit down with them face-to-face. I try to learn something about each of them: Why did they join the navy? What's their family situation like? What are their goals while they're in the navy—and beyond? How can I help them chart a course through life? Ultimately, I consider it my job to improve my little 300-person piece of society. And that's as much a part of the bottom line as operational readiness is.

  …I looked at what usually happens when new 18- or 19-year-old recruits check in: They fly in from boot camp on a Friday night. They feel intimidated and friendless. They stow their gear in their berths and immediately get lost in San Diego. To change all of that, we've created a welcoming plan: Now, when new recruits come on board, their bunks are assigned, their linen and blankets are there, and we match them with a hand-picked sponsor who shows them the ropes. They can even call home—on my nickel—to tell Mom and Dad that they've made it.[11]

Michael Abrashoff may not have talked about enhancing the employee experience, but it was in his work and in his heart, and it produced a ship of loyal sailors that cut the time needed for redeployment training from twenty-two days to five days in port and from thirty days to fourteen days at sea. The experience of employees is vital to earning their trust and loyalty, just as the experience of customers is important for achieving the same gains. When employee trust and loyalty are matched with customer trust and loyalty through the power of exceptional experiences, government works.

Tips for leadership success

How citizens experience government presents a major opportunity to build trust and value. Leaders may find the following framework valuable for embarking on an experience management strategy.

- Assess the experience: identify and prioritize the various potential experience audiences in your agency or department.
- Audit the experience: understand customer needs and desires. Research the experiences you are currently delivering through customer interviews and mystery shopping. From these insights generate an experience motif that guides clue creation.

- Design the experience: identify and create preferential clues in your environment, processes, and behaviors that reflect the experience motif.
- Implement the experience design: plan and execute implementation of specific experience clues into business operation; set metrics.
- Steward the experience: monitor the experience design through feedback and metrics; adjust clues as needed.

Resources for further learning

Leonard L. Berry, *Discovering the Soul of Service* (1999). Berry offers a systematic way to think about great customer service. His nine core drivers of exceptional service are illustrated with examples from the real world. The drivers include: leading with values, strategic focus, executional excellence, control of destiny, trust-based relationships, investment in employee success, acting small, brand cultivation, and generosity.

Leonard L. Berry, Eileen Wall, and Lewis P. Carbone, "Service Clues and Customer Assessment of the Service Experience" (2006).

Lewis P. Carbone, "What Makes Customers Tick" (2003).

——— *Clued In: How to Keep Customers Coming Back Again and Again* (2004). Carbone focuses on why the customer experience matters so much in the modern economy and how to craft experiences that build customer loyalty. Meeting the deeper emotional needs of the customer takes center stage along with the management of sensory clues (sights, sounds, smells, taste, texture) delivered by the functional aspects of the product or service, the setting in which it is offered, and the people who provide it. This book also offers an approach to customer experience management over time and descriptions of tools for use at various stages of the experience management process.

Gerald Zaltman, *How Customers Think* (2004). Zaltman runs a market research lab at Harvard that accepts the notion that 95 percent of what customers think is below the level of their own conscious recall. The implication is that you cannot get into the mind of the customer by simply asking. Using traditional means such as surveys and focus groups is not adequate. Instead, you need to penetrate the subconscious through techniques such as using metaphors to probe for the customer's deeper feelings by bypassing rational thought processes. The Zaltman Metaphor technique plays a major role in helping organizations identify what matters most when they decide to focus on the customer experience.

Notes

1. Muoio (1999).

2. The terms *citizen, constituent,* and *the customer* are used interchangeably in this chapter. We believe that experience management applies at all levels of government, in all branches of government, and in all interactions of government workers with their colleagues, other agencies, citizens, and elected and appointed officials they serve.

3. Berry (1999).

4. Wood (2004).

5. Braun and Zaltman (undated).

6. Zaltman (2003).

7. Levinson et al. (1997).

8. Carbone (2004).

9. Berry, Wall, and Carbone (2006).

10. LaBarre (1999).

11. Ibid.

11 Global leadership: Strengthening a skeptical world's trust in America

PETER RONAYNE, DEAN OF FACULTY, FEDERAL EXECUTIVE INSTITUTE*

There is nothing we need to build here except relationships.
—Col. Thomas Wilhelm, U.S. defense attaché, Mongolia,
quoted in Robert Kaplan, *Imperial Grunts,* 129.

IN A NONDESCRIPT WHITE TRAILER at the Marine Corps Training and Education Command in Quantico, Virginia, innovation in global leadership is under way. Marines have reflected on their experience in Iraq and elsewhere and have acted to significantly enhance the cultural capabilities of their forces. At the new Center for Advanced Operational Culture Learning (CAOCL), training is focused on getting marines to view cultural understanding as a tool that can help them in conflict, in nation building, in whatever high stress, high threat international environments they face. Whether dealing with Islamic allies in Iraq, training indigenous military forces in Africa, or collaborating with local leaders in Mongolia, the twenty-first century marine will be able to use cultural knowledge "to establish rapport and build relationships, a key aspect of successful counterinsurgency operation," and a major component of trust. As Barak A. Salmoni, the center's deputy director, explains, "Three plus years ago the moniker was 'cultural sensitivity.' But being sensitive is not the same as being aware, and being aware is not the same thing as being capable—being able to apply your knowledge so as to have any effect on the people with or against whom you're operating." [1]

Indeed, this is not sensitivity for sensitivity's sake. As the CAOCL's goal statement lays out, it "does not teach culture for its own sake, or for a non-directed appreciation of or sensitivity towards foreign peoples. CAOCL executes operationally focused training and education in individual training, PME [professional military education], and pre-deployment phases, reflecting current and likely contingencies and functions, to ensure Marines and

---

* The views expressed here are the author's and do not necessarily reflect those of the Federal Executive Institute or the U.S. Office of Personnel Management.

leaders deploy a grasp of culture and indigenous dynamics for use as a force multiplier." [2] The effort is now under way to build this "operational cultural learning" into all levels of the vast Marine Corps professional education system and embed it as one of their "bread and butter skills." [3] This is the new frontier of global leadership in the public sector—and the time is now for such perspectives and programs to permeate every corner of American government.

As its practitioners know, there is no more demanding context for leadership than in the public sector. A dizzying array of issues, actors, and interests challenge even the most savvy leader in ways not likely imagined or envisioned even half a century ago. As best-selling business and leadership writer Jim Collins observes in his monograph, *Good to Great and the Social Sectors,* "Social sector leaders are not less decisive than business leaders as a general rule; they only appear that way to those who fail to grasp the complex governance and diffuse power structures common to social sectors." [4] An era of succession planning, knowledge management, emotional intelligence, and network government is rendered exponentially more complex and perilous (and interesting) by the ever-accelerating pace of globalization and our deepening awareness of its impact.

The concept of trust in government, the core idea behind this book, also resides at the center of the global leadership issue. At this macro level—the world stage—in which the United States seeks to promote its interests and create a broader international milieu of security and prosperity, trust is absolutely imperative. Global military reach and an economic preponderance of power are indispensable tools in the promotion of U.S. national security abroad. Yet, without a strong measure of trust, an important part of what we might call America's "soft power," the elements of hard power will have limited impact and fall short of their vast potential. Indeed, mistrust of American intentions, goals, and purposes on the world stage is like a viral insurgency, slowly but surely eroding the nation's ability to lead collective action against security threats such as terrorism, nuclear proliferation, and transnational diseases.

The equation is, in fact, a simple one: today's most pressing national security priorities are global issues; global issues demand global leadership; and successful global leadership requires global trust. At present, the worldwide reservoir of trust in the United States is at an alarmingly low rate for a number of reasons. A government tuned into these issues and capable of deploying a cadre of public servants with a heightened level of global perspective and savvy can set about reversing this trend and reviving trust. With enhanced trust and improved global relationships, the United States and its partners can play a stronger hand and maximize the opportunities for significant progress on the pressing issues of the day.

> *The United States, working with the governments of the other major powers, can still shape the course of the twenty-first century and bring about a world that is to a striking degree characterized by peace, prosperity, and freedom for most of the globe's countries and peoples. Opportunity, though, is just that. It represents possibility, not inevitability.*
>
> —Richard Haass, *The Opportunity*

This opportunity cannot be emphasized enough. Perhaps never before in the history of the world has a nation enjoyed such a dominant combination of military, economic, cultural, and political power. Shorn of trust, however, the United States is hobbled in some areas, impotent in others.

Like fish in water, Americans can be remarkably oblivious to the nation's power. A quick survey of the scale and scope of American power provides an important element of the self-awareness and global perspective that today's leaders must possess. The United States has:

- More than 750 military installations in 130 countries;
- A military budget equal to the combined military budgets of the next fifteen nations;
- Nearly 10,000 nuclear weapons (half of them operational and active);
- Close to one-third of the world's economic output;
- The world's third largest population (but less than 5 percent of the total global population);
- Nearly half of the world's top 500 global businesses;
- More than 60 of the world's top 100 brands; and
- The world lead in exporting film and television.

How should we label this power? Empire? Hegemony? Sole superpower? Semantics aside, the simple fact remains that the United States is a world power on a scale not seen since the days of Rome's ascendancy. But, paradoxically, as Kennedy School of Government professor Joseph Nye and others point out, the United States on its own cannot solve the most pressing and challenging national security issues facing it.[5]

Yet what word but "empire" describes the awesome thing that America is becoming? It is the only nation that polices the world through five global military commands; maintains more than a million men and women at arms on four continents; deploys carrier battle groups on watch in every ocean; guarantees the survival of countries from Israel to South Korea; drives the wheels of global trade and commerce; and fills the hearts and minds of an entire planet with its dreams and desires.

—Michael Ignatieff, *New York Times,* January 10, 2003

America in the mirror

We have it in our power to begin the world over again.

—Thomas Paine

Americans have a nearly unwavering trust in America on the world stage. While seemingly obvious to the point of silliness, probing that statement and understanding its origins and enduring nature are critical to the trust enterprise in America's global leadership. Furthermore, meaningful attempts by presidents, policymakers, and public servants to enhance trust in the United States on the world stage require an understanding of the nature and size of the gap between America's sense of self and international perceptions. If we are oblivious to the extent of the nation's power, we are equally oblivious as to how other countries feel about us. As Terry Newell argues in compelling fashion in chapter 1, effective leadership requires an understanding of and connection to one's own core moral values. His point applies equally to a nation acting and attempting to lead on the world stage. And as Beverly Fletcher and Alfred Cooke describe in chapter 2, "know thyself" is the first step on the path to leading others.

As noted in chapter 1, a foundational piece of that understanding for America at home and abroad comes from John Winthrop and his 1630 "A Model of Christian Charity" sermon delivered to his Puritan congregation. Known widely as the "City on a Hill" speech and based on the New Testament's Sermon on the Mount, the oration urged the fledging Massachusetts Bay Colony to see their colonial enterprise within the broader trajectory of history. Argued Winthrop:

For we must consider that we shall be as a city upon a hill. The eyes of all people are upon us. So that if we shall deal falsely with our God in this work we have undertaken . . . we shall be made a story and a by-word throughout the world. We shall open the mouths of enemies to speak evil of the ways of God. . . . We shall shame the faces of many of God's worthy servants, and cause their prayers to be turned into curses upon us til we be consumed out of the good land whither we are going.

From that stridently religious and teleological origin has come a more secularized and powerfully enduring concept: American exceptionalism.[6] The vision of the City on Hill/American exceptionalism has resonated through the ages, from the founding period and "Manifest Destiny" through to present-day America, and emerging with particular prominence in the political rhetoric of Presidents Kennedy and Reagan. Colin Powell referenced the concept at the 2000 Republican National Convention. The Clinton administration coined their own synonym, referring to the United States as "the indispensable nation."

Thus, from Puritan origins came a powerful and resonant core belief in, first, the American experiment as unique, as world-historical, as qualitatively different from other attempts at government, and, finally, as having great power. Coupled with exceptionalism comes a prosletyzing element in which the United States believes that the basket of democratic values (or "constitutional values" as *Newsweek*'s international affairs editor Fareed Zakaria would emphasize[7]) it holds dear—freedom, equality, self-determination, rule of law—are not only American or Western values but instead have universal applicability and desirability.[8]

> *These are American principles, American policies. We could stand for no other. And they are also the principles and policies of forward-looking men and women everywhere, of every modern nation, of every enlightened community. They are the principles of mankind and must prevail.*
>
> —Woodrow Wilson

This merging of the American and the universal and the accompanying champion's role strikes some as proud, enlightened commitment to principles larger than one's parochial interest; others see it as prideful, narrow, a symptom of hubris, or blatant self-interest clothed in hypocritical self-righteousness.

How to put into practice this American exceptionalism or this peculiar "American mission" has caused much debate since the nation's founding. Early incarnations argued that the City on a Hill concept best promoted its values and vision by serving as a model, as an example for the world to observe and emulate. This "exemplarist" school of thought has a distinguished pedigree and enjoyed decades of ascendancy following President George Washington's Farewell Address.[9] In that precedent-setting speech, Washington put pragmatic borders around the City on a Hill: "The great rule of conduct for us in regard to foreign nations is, in extending our commercial relations to have with them as little *political* connection as possible. . . . It is our true policy to steer clear of permanent alliances with any portion of the foreign world." Thought leaders and political actors such as Jefferson and John Quincy Adams followed suit, anchoring American exceptionalism solidly at home. Indeed, one recent observer of the philosophy of American foreign policy labeled this exemplarist tendency the Jeffersonian School.[10]

Rising globalism

Modern American global leadership has, however, been shaped and characterized by the other vision, the opposing pole, the competing model for the United States in the world: internationalism. This more active, some would say aggressive, approach blends the language of duty, responsibility, and leadership. The exemplarist's fraternal twin is active rather than passive, external instead of internal, bold where the other is retiring. Because of its conviction, the internationalist variant of exceptionalism, together with the emergence of America's quasi-imperial power, poses a significant challenge to building and maintaining trust on the world stage. Here we see the most striking clash of perceptions between self (America) and others (much of the rest of the world).

America's precipitous and nearly unbroken rise to globalism began after the Spanish-American War in 1898 and led to a concomitant rise in internationalist outlook, bedazzled in the language of duty, responsibility, and mission. Sen. Albert Beveridge's speech on American responsibility in the Philippines in 1900 captured perfectly that ascendant sentiment (complete with period ethnocentrism). Urged Beveridge, "God has not been preparing the English-speaking and Teutonic peoples for a thousand years for nothing but vain and idle self-contemplation and self-admiration. He has given us the spirit of progress to overwhelm the forces of reaction throughout the earth. . . . We are the trustees of the world's progress, guardians of its right-eous peace."

What Walter Russell Mead of the Council on Foreign Relations calls the Wilsonian school of thought inched toward newfound primacy first with the onset of cold war in 1947 and today finds expression in the so-called "neo-conservative" and "liberal internationalist" movements. Echoing Winthrop's mantra but in a secularized and sanitized version, this variant of exception-alism urges the United States to embrace activist, impassioned global leader-ship. Proponents call for an enlightened, almost benevolent empire to pursue its interests, which by their nature simultaneously champion the cause of democracy, open markets, and rule of law everywhere.

Today's Americans might not be powerfully interventionist (particularly when chastened by the Iraq War). They nevertheless maintain a reservoir of internationalism coupled with pride and the conviction that American ideas and beliefs are good for the rest of the world. Contemporary research by the Pew Research Center clearly illustrates this:

- Sixty percent of Americans agree with the statement "Our people are not perfect, but our culture is superior to others."
- Seventy-nine percent of Americans believe it is a good thing that U.S. ideas and customs are spreading around the world.
- Seventy percent of Americans think it is a good idea to promote "Amer-ican style" democracy in the world.[11]

Data from the Pew Global Attitudes Survey and similar outlets also con-firm that despite such attitudes, the American public is not imperial or ex-pansionist in their mindset or goals and prefers multilateral action and shared leadership when possible. Still, empire is in the eye of the beholder. External attitudes about America's efforts at global leadership strongly sug-gest that trust in the United States has eroded significantly.

Trust: Contemporary global context

America defines itself as the leader of the free world, and there is much truth in that idea. But leadership requires having fol-lowers who are prepared to move in the same general direction. And walking a path without followers, allies or partners can quickly become self-isolation—even for the sole superpower.

—Paul Saunders, National Interest Online, March 1, 2007

Effective leadership at any level requires understanding the context in which you are trying to lead. That context includes the way the leader is perceived, viewed by those around him or her. In the end, one might disagree with or have relevant variables that explain or illuminate some of the more negative perceptions. Still, perceptions matter; image isn't everything but it is something of importance. And understanding how (and perhaps why) others view you is a major element in designing a leadership style and strategy that allows for the steady accumulation of trust.

One cannot fully understand the issue of trust and global leadership without briefly surveying the landscape of global perceptions and attitudes—namely, how sizable portions of the rest of the world view the United States and its claim to leadership. The point here is not partisan or unnecessarily provocative. Widespread in the field of leadership development today is the well-researched and supported concept that feedback is critical to leadership success. Individual leaders in organizations can benefit tremendously from receiving candid, honest feedback from those around them—360 degree feedback, as it is described in the field of leadership development. So, too, 360°-feedback is required reading for American leaders, including the dedicated public servants implementing the myriad U.S. policies that extend to and influence every corner of the globe. This element of national self-knowledge is even more critical because the story of the United States and trust on the world stage is experiencing a troubling chapter.

The view from abroad

Anti-Americanism (for lack of a better phrase) is nothing new and at a certain level should not generate surprise. With great power comes not only great responsibility, but also a potent mix of jealousy, admiration, fear, and emulation. As survey data show, much of America's self-image and sense of its historic role on the world stage clashes with or contradicts how others see the so-called last remaining superpower. It is also important to note that some of the world's misgivings spring both from specific U.S. policies—particularly in the Middle East—and more deeply from America's sense of self and perceived missionary zeal.

Recent findings from the Pew Global Attitudes Project provide remarkable and compelling insight into how the world views—and distrusts—the United States. In Europe, ambivalence about America, its perceived inexperienced arrogance, and its rise to power has festered for decades. Today, it runs much stronger. From 2000 to 2005, U.S. favorability dropped by as many as ten, even twenty, percentage points in Britain, France, and Germany, traditional allies and NATO colleagues since the end of World War II. Non-Western attitudes toward the United States also have turned sour. As Pew director Andy Kohut highlights in his book *America Against the World,* "In Brazil, for example, where 52 percent of the public expressed a favorable opinion of the United States in 2002, the pro-American portion of the population had dropped to 34 percent. In Russia, there was a 25-percentage-point decline in the U.S. favorability rating, from 61 percent to 36 percent, in the course of less than a year." [12]

Of equal or even greater concern are the levels of fear and distrust evidenced by recent global survey data. As Pew uncovered:

- After the Iraq invasion, majorities in seven of eight predominantly Muslim nations feared that the United States might target them, including 71 percent of people in NATO member Turkey.
- Europeans, too, distrust the United States. Greece, Spain, Finland, and Sweden view the United States as a greater threat to world stability than Iran or North Korea.
- According to the Eurobarometer in the UK, 55 percent of the people regard the United States as a dangerous nation. [13]

In any organization, it is difficult to trust a boss, a manager, a leader who one believes does not take into consideration the interests, concerns, and perspectives of others. The United States suffers in world esteem in this regard as well, with clear majorities viewing American leadership as increasingly unilateral, even imperial, with little regard for the rest of the world community, even its allies. Sizable majorities in Britain, Germany, Spain, and Russia, and eight in ten French respondents, believe that American leaders do not take their interests into account when making policy decisions. This perception diminishes trust. Simultaneously, two-thirds of Americans believe that the U.S. government, at least to a fair amount, does concern itself with the interests of other nations before acting. [14] Add to the ledger that the world exhibits marginal trust for the United States to lead in international efforts against genocide and holds rock bottom levels of trust for U.S. leadership on environmental issues. [15]

No one would expect Finland, Australia and Botswana to have identical foreign policies simply because each enjoys a

representative form of government. And even when democra-
cies share both values and interests, they often have different
priorities. Without understanding these realities and develop-
ing strategies to manage them, the United States cannot main-
tain a position of real leadership, even within the "free world."

— Paul Saunders, National Interest Online, March 2007

Furthering the mistrust and concern about American power is that, for many around the globe, the phenomenon known as "globalization" has come to mean "Americanization" or to be seen as predominantly associated with American values and American economic reach.[16] In short, the most recent wave of globalization involves highly interdependent economic activity around the world; revolutions in information technology and communication, making the world more of a global village than ever before; and a sharp spike in transnational issues, communities, and interests.[17]

Globalization is not Americanization, even though the core assumptions behind the economic side of the phenomenon do represent core U.S. interests and values. The fact remains that in many corners of the world, the exponential growth of cross-border economic integration and tremendous technological advances that facilitate the transmission of Western (often American) culture, lead to heightened levels of anxiety about weakness, the decline of one's own nation-state, and the Borg-like march of American-led globalization.[18]

Americans do not appear to waltz along, oblivious to their nation's public relations challenge. Exceptionalism and world-historic mission aside, a strong majority, 66 percent, of Americans believe that the declining image of the United States on the world stage is a major problem for the country.[19] Repairing that damage will require multitiered and multiyear action. And part of the solution rests in developing globally aware, savvy public servants to represent the United States in its myriad international dealings.

The transnational agenda

It's nice to say we can do it unilaterally, except you can't.

Secretary of State Colin Powell[20]

Synonymous with Americanization or not, globalization has a major impact on even its most ardent proponent and symbol. The United States and therefore the public sector find themselves in an unprecedented maelstrom of globalization. Name an issue, really any issue, and it likely has a relevant global component. Trade policy. Drug interdiction. The AIDS pandemic. Labor practices and protections. Biological diversity. Clean air standards. Food and drug safety. Transportation security. Nation building. Disaster relief. At least eight of twelve critical issues the GAO's report on challenges facing the federal government have significant global content, as do a preponderance of forces shaping the world. Whether it's columnist Thomas Friedman's "flatism" or the new map drawn up for the Pentagon by analyst Thomas Barnett, the combined and accelerating forces of economic integration, networking across national borders, an exponential communications revolution, massive proliferation of NGOs and international organizations, and the rise of transnational issues are dramatically reshaping the contours of world politics and the issues facing governments everywhere.[21]

The work and responsibilities of the federal sector are clearly a sprawling microcosm of these trends, even in traditionally domestic agencies and organizations (the Social Security Administration, after all, manages more than thirty bilateral agreements). With each passing day the traditional division between the domestic and the foreign is more of a fiction, a concept that helps us mentally map and order our world but describes it less and less accurately. The long-standing, knee-jerk presumption that "global leadership" and related issues are limited to the foreign affairs and defense agencies alone is invalid and dangerous. Indeed, the new face of "national security" reflects truly transnational issues and challenges. Energy, environment, economic growth, population, science and technology, AIDS and other pandemics, and terror networks are all national security priorities, and none of them can or will be solved solely through the application of American power, however dominant.

For all its merits, globalization comes with significant demerits, too. Moises Naim, editor of *Foreign Policy* magazine, chronicles this downside of our global society in his succinctly titled book *Illicit*. What emerges is a compelling, if troubling, vision of the future of American foreign policy and the challenges facing America's public servants as global leaders. To the list above, Naim highlights:

- Human trafficking—4 million people smuggled or sold (500,000 into the United States) a year for a value of $7 to $10 billion;
- Money laundering—estimated between $800 billion and $2 trillion annually;

- Violating intellectual property rights, which cost the United States almost $10 billion in 2001;
- Arms trafficking—more than $1 billion a year in small arms with potentially devastating consequences in stolen weapons of mass destruction technology; and
- Drug trafficking—more than $400 billion a year (larger than the Spanish economy).

For too long, the domestic and foreign policy arenas have been viewed as mostly separate and distinct spheres of action. Government leaders who worked in domestic agencies felt they needed to know little about world affairs or other countries and had little, if any, international interaction. But the combined and accelerating forces of globalization and technology have forged an interconnected world in which change—and the need to anticipate and respond to it—are both faster and more complex, the international and the domestic are inextricably linked, and trust is in short supply.

The imperative of global leaders(hip)

The leadership development agenda for today's public servants must now include the international, intercultural, and strategic perspectives essential for success in this rapidly changing, globalized world. Patricia McGinnis, president and CEO of the Council for Excellence in Government underscores this point: "The Council believes that career federal executives must be able to lead for results in all aspects of their work. Today, an increasing number of career public servants outside the federal government's traditional foreign affairs community have responsibilities with an international dimension. Improving their ability as leaders in a global context has therefore become a very important goal." [22] Similarly, in a report on the future of human capital in the federal workforce, the GAO states, "Government organizations must undergo a cultural transformation allowing them to work better with other governmental organizations, non-governmental organizations, and the private sector, both domestically and internationally, to achieve results." [23]

Despite awareness of the need for change, most federal civil servants—particularly in "domestic" agencies—have received little preparation for their global roles and have minimal understanding of critical global trends shaping the world. America faces unique leadership demands and possibilities, which in turn require that we invest time and resources to ensure that every federal public servant is the best and brightest global leader possible, whether one of more than 90,000 civilian government employees stationed overseas or one of the legions stateside working on issues with vast and expanding international implications.

The global leadership gap

So far the United States has not placed anything close to a premium on overcoming its parochial tendencies and developing globally savvy leaders. According to a 2003 RAND report on developing global leaders, "The nation is producing too few future leaders who combine substantive depth with international experience and outlook. So, too, managers with a broad strategic vision in a rapidly changing world are in short supply." [24] In research by the Federal Executive Institute (FEI), more than two-thirds of federal leaders surveyed rated their own proficiency for international work below the midpoint of a five-point scale. According to the U.S. Advisory Commission on Public Diplomacy, training is an essential yet underutilized pillar of public diplomacy, as the United States tries to make itself and its policies understood and works to project a positive and respectful image in the world. In its September 2004 report, the commission faulted the current state of training to foster U.S. international goals in several areas, including media skills and cross-cultural communication skills.[25]

America's well-known language limitations have deep, early roots and may prove insurmountable given the country's relative geographic isolation and the emergence of English as the modern world's *lingua franca*. For now, only one-third of the nation's seventh through twelfth graders study a foreign language; that drops to fewer than one-in-ten students at the college level—with the vast majority studying Spanish. Interest in Arabic is growing but still accounts for just .8 percent of foreign language enrollments in postsecondary institutions. Study abroad numbers are on the rise, with greater percentages of students going to India and China than ever before—but a mere 1 percent of undergraduates study abroad.[26] The National Security Language Initiative launched in early 2006 to increase the number of Americans with advanced proficiency in critical languages is an important step forward. And building language skills is important not just for intelligence and national security. It signals engagement with and respect for other nations, and fluency adds immeasurably to one's ability to interact with, understand, and ultimately influence international counterparts. As a former dean of the School of Language Studies at the State Department's Foreign Service Institute put it: "Part of the reason for our difficulty is that we simply don't have enough competent speakers of Arabic with credible policy context and an ability to connect with the intended audience so they will at least listen to what we are trying to say and give us a hearing." [27]

But fluency in a foreign language is only one of the necessary global leadership skills. In the past decade, a significant body of literature has examined, defined, and refined the competencies leaders need for success in international activities. In a 2001 study, "Accelerating International Growth," Philip Rosensweig and his colleagues outline five global leadership capabilities worth noting:

1. Strategic capability: Develop and implement strategy in a global context, not just national or regional.

2. Partnership capability: Work effectively with cross-border partners dealing with similar issues. Partners include global alliances; bilateral, multilateral, and international organizations, where cultural sensitivity and perspectives are important.

3. Staffing capability: Develop global teams where employees and contractors from different countries and cultures can work together without one dominating the other.

4. Learning capability: Hardwire international learning as part of development, so as not to be blindfolded by or exclusively wedded to one's national perspective and biases or force international experiences into one's national lens.

5. Organizational capability: Arrange organizations in a way that facilitates and capitalizes on leadership, not through host country dominance but through a true global network of executives.[28]

All five of these capabilities translate well in a public sector context.

In FEI research, government executives cited the following five elements as critical in developing their global perspective:

1. Content learning on topics such as the global economy, national security issues, protection of intellectual property, export control, and global environmental issues;

2. Cultural awareness and regional/country-specific overviews along with information on government structures, the economy, and the regulatory framework in which a host country operates;

3. Protocol and suggested success strategies for dealing with and doing business with foreign governments and corporations;

4. Overviews of the ever-growing international governance networks—international agreements between the United States and other nations; international institutions—and their impact on U.S. global policies and efforts; and

5. Skill building in areas such as negotiation and strategies and communication to international audiences (public diplomacy).[29]

Armed with leadership enhanced by these capabilities and competencies, our local, state, and national public servants can be better agents of what Nye refers to as "soft power." As Nye perceptively explains, "A country may obtain the outcomes it wants in world politics because other countries want to follow it, admiring its values, emulating its example, aspiring to its level of prosperity and openness. In this sense, it is just as important to set the agenda in world politics and attract others as it is to force them to change through the threat of military or economic weapons. This aspect of power—getting others to do want what you want—I call *soft power.*"[30]

Developing global leaders

The private sector is at least a decade into its global leadership epiphany. A 1998 survey by the Conference Board of senior managers and executives pointed to the importance of developing global leaders for business success.[31] Research a year later involving 108 Fortune 500 companies also highlighted competent global managers as "the factor most critical to achieving international success."[32] Signaling this evolving mindset, the August 2003 *Harvard Business Review* focused entirely on global perspectives and leadership for a changed world. For the public sector, the massive and multiplying effect of globalization, the 9/11 attacks, and America's waning image abroad, and the Iraq conflict should combine to create a Sputnik moment for global leadership development. Thomas Friedman sounds the clarion call when he says that meeting the challenges of globalization "requires as comprehensive, energetic, and focused a response as meeting the challenge of Communism."[33]

Within the federal sector, outposts of global perspective have slowly emerged. At NASA, the agency's leadership and management development program includes an international competency (see Figure 11.1). FEI's flagship Leadership for a Democratic Society program now includes global

Figure 11.1 NASA leadership development model

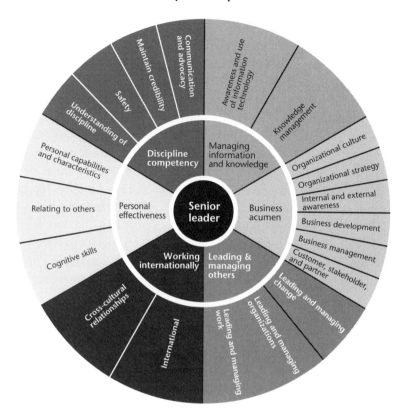

perspectives as a core curriculum theme for its interagency audience, and the institute in September 2001 convened public, private, and nongovernmental thought leaders to explore the issue of developing global leaders. One downstream impact of that gathering is the recently formed Global Leadership Consortium, founded by FEI, the National Academy of Public Administration, and the Graduate School, USDA.

The military's firm commitment to growing leaders often pushes it to the forefront in certain areas of professional development. The defense community has shown some forward thinking on international skills. According to the Defense Language Transformation Roadmap, "Language skill and regional expertise have not been regarded as war-fighting skills, and are not sufficiently incorporated into operational or contingency planning. Language skill and regional expertise are not valued as Defense core competencies, yet they are as important as critical weapon systems."[34] Now, efforts to overcome past deficits in language skills are under way across the Department of Defense.

Commenting on his early experiences in Iraq with the 101st Airborne Division, Gen. David Petraeus, commander of Multinational Force Iraq, revealed, "We had terrific situational awareness; what we lacked was cultural awareness." To improve that situation, the U.S. Army has used a small cadre of specialists known as foreign-area officers. Equipped with language skills and cultural knowledge, they support the combat troops in various missions. Although debate continues in the Pentagon over the long-term role of the foreign-area officers, many believe it represents the future of development for all officers.[35] At Fort Leavenworth American and allied soldiers engage in true post–cold war programs developed to learn lessons from experiences in places such as Bosnia and Iraq. The programs emphasize the complex cultural conditions surrounding policing and nation-building efforts.[36] As mentioned at the beginning of the chapter, the Marine Corp's Center for Advanced Operational Culture Learning is another fine example—perhaps even a best practice—of such efforts.

The private sector, too, offers innovative and replicable models. To help its emerging leaders develop a broader international view and earn valuable global experience, PricewaterhouseCoopers founded the Ulysses program in 2001. Young partners participate on cross-cultural teams drawn from PWC firms spread around 139 countries. The action learning teams travel abroad for up to three months to help tackle challenges faced by various developing nations, including Belize, Moldova, Namibia, and Zambia. Ralf Schneider, PWC's head of global talent development, says that learning in the Ulysses program takes place at the individual, team, and organizational levels, and includes a new appreciation for collaboration and for cultural differences as a spark to innovation.[37]

Similarly, the Boeing company is energizing its efforts to create a truly global cadre of leaders. Based on the philosophy that with increased global activity must also come a new human resources approach, Boeing launched the Global Leadership Program, a twenty-seven-day course that sends managers to Europe, Asia, or South America to learn about Boeing suppliers, customers, and competitors in their own surroundings. While learning the business side of Boeing, executives are also steeped in the history, politics, culture, and traditions of a specific region. To widen the global knowledge circle within the company, the senior vice president for international relations, Thomas Pickering (former U.S. ambassador to the United Nations), and his staff pick up their pens. The team "regularly writes articles and analysis pieces about the world's political and economic situation. These are forwarded to members of Boeing's Executive Council, providing timely information on world business prospects and political changes that could affect business units and Boeing markets." [38]

The way forward

The fact remains that despite some innovation and true strategic thinking, few public sector leaders receive any globally oriented leadership development or formal preparation for international assignments. The public sector has not yet developed a comprehensive approach or system to prepare leaders for success in their critical global work. Until there is such a system, global leadership competence remains a promise not a program, and public servants will not be a significant factor in overcoming the nation's trust deficit. In the meantime, individual leaders and federal organizations must take responsibility for incorporating the "global" into their vision, values, and vital strategies. Without it, they will continue to cling to the comfortable yet fictional notion of a line delineating the foreign and the domestic, the national and the international. And in an ongoing embrace of that fiction, they will limit now and in the future their ability to successfully implement their agency's efforts to advance the interests of the American people. Indeed, U.S. relationships, enhanced trust, and effective leadership in the world demand public sector leaders prepared for the dynamic global context in which they operate. We can imagine no greater leadership development priority.

Tips for global leadership success

The following ideas and principles are worth considering by individuals and organizations seeking to become truly "world class" by developing global leadership skills:

- Use cultural awareness inventories to gauge needs and design professional development opportunities.
- Structure all management and leadership development programs to include global content and awareness building.
- If possible, require even short-term global assignments, exchanges, and action learning for high potential leaders. Similarly, invite international

peers to join leadership development programs and for short-term work assignments in your organization.
• Subscribe to an international newspaper or journal such as *The Economist* or even the *International Herald Tribune* as a relatively easy and inexpensive way to grow global perspective.

Resources for further learning

Maxine Dalton et al., *Success for the New Global Manager* (2002). A useful and basic "global leadership handbook" by a team from the Center for Creative Leadership. Dalton and her colleagues combine qualitative and quantitative research to craft a practitioner-oriented book with several tools and recommendations for emerging global leaders and those working to develop them.

Francis Fukuyama, "Nation-Building 101" (January/February 2004). In his article for the *Atlantic Monthly,* Fukuyama builds on the Earthlights/Liotta/Miskel thesis (see below) and stresses that the future of America's global leadership will in fact involve helping other nations find stability and then sustainable political and economic institutions. To do so, Fukuyama argues, will require involvement from a wide range of the federal sector.

P. H. Liotta and James F. Miskel, "Redrawing the Map of the Future" (2004). In this *World Policy Journal* article, Liotta and Miskel—both faculty at the U.S. Naval War College—provide compelling insight into the future of American foreign policy. They argue that the NASA "earthlights" map (a composite of images of the world's city lights) provides striking visual evidence of the growing divide between light and dark, developed and underdeveloped, north and south—and it is in these dark regions and zones where failed states and feral cities take shape and threaten stability and ultimately U.S. interests. "Earthlights" can be seen at *www.cojoweb.com/earthlights.html.*

Harvard Business Review, "Leadership in a Changed World," Special Issue. Released in August 2003, this edition of HBR focuses almost exclusively on global leadership, global economy, and global competencies from the perspective of business. Also valuable because it includes three "Best of HBR" global articles reprinted from years past.

Joseph Nye, *Soft Power* (2004). A book-length exposition on the term he coined. Nye explores in a coherent and convincing way the necessity of multilateral and multinational cooperation by the United States as it grapples with increasingly difficult and complex transnational security threats.

Notes

1. Peters (2007), 14.
2. United States Marine Corps (2007).
3. Peters (2007), 15.
4. Collins (2005).
5. Nye (2003).
6. Most analysts credit Alexis de Tocqueville with first coining the term in his classic *Democracy in America.*
7. Zakaria (2003). In both this book and in a 1997 article for *Foreign Affairs,* Zakaria stresses the importance of "constitutional liberalism" versus "democracy."
8. It is interesting to note that Winthrop was powerfully anti-democratic. His vision of the City on a Hill did not include such values. Winthrop stated, for example, "If we should change from a mixed aristocracy to mere democracy, first we should have no warrant in scripture for it: for there was no such government in Israel. . . . A democracy is, amongst civil nations, accounted the meanest and worst of all forms of government. To allow it would be a manifest breach of the 5th Commandment."
9. Brands (1998). Brands suggests that the term *exemplar* is more appropriate to American foreign policy than *isolationist* and explores the tension between this approach and what he calls the "vindicator" tradition in American foreign policy.
10. Mead (2002).
11. Kohut and Stokes (2006), 44, 46, 71; Pew (2002–2005).
12. Kohut and Stokes (2006), 25–26.
13. Ibid., 26.
14. Ibid., 169.
15. Pew (2002–2005).
16. For some elaboration on globalization and the mental/political/identity divisions it might be fostering, see Barber (2003) and Friedman (2000), the writer's first book-length foray into the topic.
17. Countless descriptions and definitions of globalization exist, but all tend to revolve around the main issues listed here and drawn from Huddleston (2000).
18. The Borg are a cyborg race featured in the *Star Trek: The Next Generation* television series. Characterized by cold and constant pursuit of other cultures for assimilation and an ability to surmount almost any defense, they have become a pop culture synonym for any homogenizing juggernaut against which "resistance is futile"—their robotic catchphrase.
19. Pew (2004).
20. Secretary of State Powell speaking to President George W. Bush, August 5, 2002, as reported by Woodward (2002), 333.
21. Friedman (2006); and Barnett (2004).
22. Brower et al. (2002).
23. Walker (2002).
24. Bikson et al. (2003).
25. U.S. Department of State (2004).
26. Committee for Economic Development (2006).
27. Lemmon (2004).
28. Lorange (2003).
29. Weiser (2003).
30. Nye (2003).
31. Conner (2000), 156.
32. Morrison et al. (1999), 45.
33. Friedman (2005), 37.

34. U.S. Department of Defense (2005).
35. Jaffe (2005).
36. Fichtner (2006).
37. Hempel (2004).
38. Beck (2002).

C onclusion

What, then, is the job of the government leader?

DAN FENN JR., ADJUNCT LECTURER IN EXECUTIVE PROGRAMS, KENNEDY SCHOOL OF GOVERNMENT, HARVARD UNIVERSITY

AS THE READER KNOWS BY NOW, this book opens a dialogue on a critical topic for government officials and, for that matter, for citizens generally: Trust is important for public officials whatever the form of government. Even in authoritarian systems, leaders have to stay somewhere in range of public opinion, although, given repressive tools and a culture of compliance, that range may be extremely broad.[1] Shakespeare's Richard III paid close attention to the public's acceptance and cultivated it as he pursued the crown; Nicaragua's Somoza, until his ultimate downfall, was adept at managing the electoral process and keeping his constituency, in the words of the onetime Yale football coach referring to his alumni, "sullen, but not mutinous."

Thomas Jefferson told us in the Declaration of Independence that governments derive "their just powers from the consent of the governed." The Founders, who disagreed so deeply and often bitterly, even personally, on so much that was so important, came together in their commitment to creating a new kind of government, rooted solidly in the American ethos, based not on the divine right of the rulers to rule but on public accountability and participation. They sought new ways to effectuate the "consent of the governed." It was explicitly to implement that commitment to popular sovereignty that James Madison fashioned the U.S. Constitution.

But, as we have learned from living the great American experiment, if Jefferson's revolutionary idea is to work in practice, mutual trust is indispensible—and the more trust, the better it will work. Trust, of course, is not blind acceptance; rather, it is a basic, often unexpressed, assumption that not just me, but others are acting to an acceptable degree with the public interest in mind.[2]

307

All well and good. But, as with so much in the real world, the challenging dilemmas arise when the tires and the macadam meet. Viewed from the perspective of the public executive, the nagging question is "how?" Faced with a culturally and congenitally suspicious and skeptical public—another historical characteristic of Americans—what specifically can public executives do to create a level of understanding, acceptance, and trust so the tasks assigned and assumed can be carried out with a maximum of effectiveness and efficiency? To help respond to that question is the task of this book.

Every leader in every sector of the society—private, nonprofit, and public—knows full well that there is a degree of confidence that must be developed between herself (throughout this chapter, I use gender terms interchangeably) and her colleagues and especially her subordinates. "After all," as one Navy captain said to me, "They do the work!" A great deal has been written on this topic, some of it even useful.

We are concerned here with the peculiar set of relationships in a free society between the governing and the governed, between the citizen and public officials. We focus on this subject and, staying within the parameters of the book, we concern ourselves with the career executives—federal, state, and local—rather than elected or appointed officials, who are subject to the ultimate term limits: elections!

Unfortunately, it is not enough just to turn in a solid professional performance; we have consciously to work on building trust—which is hard to earn and easy to lose. That charge needs to be built into our job descriptions.

Participation and trust

One of the pillars of a structure of trust is participation in those decisions, which I believe impact on my life and well-being. When Maine's Department of Mental Retardation (DMR) tried to establish a halfway house for six of their clients in a suburb of Bangor, the officials went about it exactly the wrong way. Working through a nonprofit, the DMR bought the dwelling and then began to talk to the neighbors about the plan. The uproar was almost instantaneous, and the opponents seized every tool at hand to block the project, including the local zoning ordinances. We often airily dismiss this all-too-familiar community reaction to NIMBY (not in my backyard) or BANANA (build absolutely nothing anywhere near anybody), but in fact it is far more profound than that. When we disregard or disrespect the deeply held sense of the right of participation, we tap into a powerful American assumption about what we as government officials are supposed to be doing and how we are supposed to do it.

In some quarters, the feeling is that we should adopt the "moonless night" strategy: don't ask, don't tell, buy the house through a proxy, wait for dark, move the patients in, and then tell the community what you've done. Saves a lot of time and money to skip all that public relations stuff, right? But, in addition to the normative issues around the matter of how a government should behave in a free society ("consent of the governed"), there are the pragmatic ones. What is likely to happen? All of us who have been involved in or a witness to adverse community reactions to government action can testify that keeping citizens out of a decision is likely to stir up even more resentment than the substance of the decision itself. I often think that the action of the British redcoats who began to tear up the planks on the Old North Bridge in Concord on April 19, 1775, must have done as much as anything to arouse the colonials: "Who do you think you are, tearing up our bridge?"

I submit that as a society, we are more demanding today than ever before that we have a voice and a hand in government decisions. I remember a friend and constituent of mine who once asked me—perhaps in the late 1950s—why the water pressure in his house was so low. I went to the town engineer to check and found that the pipes were too small for all the development that had taken place in his community and that they were plugged up with accumulated rust and calcium. When I reported to him, my friend simply said: "Oh. Thanks." He had asked a question, and I had answered it. Today he would form a group, write chants, circulate petitions, and march on Town Hall complete with candles and battle cries. "I'm sick and tired of this and I'm not going to take it anymore," cried the character in the movie *Network*. Rosa Parks really started something.

Jefferson, who thought the New England town meeting, invented in the "plantation" in Dorchester, Massachusetts, by the first Puritans to establish themselves on these shores (1630), was the best form of government designed by mankind, would applaud our insistence on being players. Cicero told us, "Freedom is participation in power," so he would have liked it too. The decisions made at that first town meeting exist: If you don't keep up your fences, and your cattle drift into your neighbor's yard, they belong to him. Pretty clear what had happened. The elders, frustrated by the inaction of one of the company, came up with the idea of getting together and setting some rules for the community. Jefferson wanted to have what we came later to call "maximum feasible participation," with all male taxpayers getting together at the precinct level to decide the issues that concerned them. He wanted, in short, to establish the mechanisms for participation right from the start.

Alexander Hamilton's thinking was quite different. He could not see how national issues could be resolved on a precinct-by-precinct basis, nor did he see Jefferson's ideas as a viable prescription for building a nation. To make sure that the public interest, which, he said, "to my mind is sacred," could be accomplished, he believed it necessary to find those few men (in his time, it would be men) who had a sense of interests and concerns larger than their own and put them in charge. This kind of meritocracy was based on breadth of vision, not the accident of birth or the acquisition of wealth.

But President Truman's Administrative Procedures Act and the Freedom of Information amendment thereto; President Nixon's National Environmental Protection Act with its built-in public participation; all those local, state, and federal requirements and provisions for public hearings and publication of proposed regulations, and so many other laws reflect the Jeffersonian insistence of Americans to have a say in government.

I submit, however, that the formal requirements, useful as they are, have not proven to be sufficient. One of the frequent complaints from citizens is that government people are not open enough and do not seek out the opinions of the people.

The fact is, however, that in this country the sense of trust among the citizenry rises and falls with their sense of participation. Creating new mechanisms, experimenting (some ideas will work, some won't), opening and clearing channels, and using the new technologies—all of these activities, as we have seen in the preceding chapters, are part of our job descriptions, whether or not they are written down (they ought to be). The specifics of the techniques will vary with the issue, the constituency, the timing, the personalities of the players. The point is that we need to use our energy and imagination to find ways not just to communicate but to build structures of participation. In this regard, Jefferson was wiser than Hamilton. And we need to exchange views with one another on what works and what does not. Municipal associations, professional groups, as well as state and federal training programs need to focus on initiating such exchanges of experience. It is the way this society is supposed to function, and it helps us do our jobs by developing more trust in those we serve.

Since the 1980s, the Kettering Foundation has been paying attention to social capital, citizen action, and public opinion. The "Right Question Project" in Cambridge, Massachusetts, trains citizens in effective ways to approach public officials. Similarly, other organizations have helped groups of citizens mobilize and deal with problems. The War on Poverty put considerable emphasis on empowering and enabling people. Erwin Canham, the late editor of the *Christian Science Monitor*, wrote about what he called "The Authentic Revolution" in the 1940s, talking about the tradition of joint volunteer activity in America going back to the old New England barn-raisings; John Gardner, founder of Common Cause, also turned our attention to citizen action. I often wonder why those of us in government fail to devote attention to stimulating and helping and working with citizen organizations instead of either coping with them or dismissing them or even wondering what they are doing on our turf. Wouldn't positive behavior on our part serve to build trust?

Moreover, listening offers other obvious benefits. First, believe it or not, we can pick up some information that we may have missed before. And, second, if we listen—really listen—to what people are saying, we may well find ourselves reordering our priorities and thinking more deeply about what we are doing and why.

Helping the public understand how government works

Useful as all those approaches and the many more presented in this book may be, a massive obstacle looms up as we seek to cultivate a population that trusts us—or at least distrusts us less! Sargent Shriver, that great public servant who fashioned the Peace Corps and the War on Poverty, said to me at the time of Richard Nixon's resignation: "You know, the Russian people understand what it was that Stalin did but our country does not understand what precisely Nixon did that was so bad. They knew he was doing things they didn't like, but they couldn't articulate just what they were and why they were wrong." What he was saying, I think, is that the American people, at a fundamental level, do not understand how their own government works or is supposed to work.

I am told that the civics courses that many of us had in school simply do not exist any more. That may be—but remember those textbooks that instructed us that we have (in most places) bicameral legislatures and that money bills start in the House and that most of the work is done in committees and that the president or the governor or the mayor is head of the executive branch and that there are two others known as the legislative and the judicial and that they are separate and that is called checks and balances and, like, who cares and how dull can you get? I am not convinced that phasing them out, if indeed it has happened, is such a great loss. I never learned what really happened in government, what those people did, and how and why; all that attention to the architecture, to the posts and beams of the structure, gave me no sense of the drama, of the *Sturm und Drang,* of the reality, of the people, of the actual play that was taking place within that structure. How can we expect people to trust us if they do not understand what we are doing and why we are doing it?

Superficially, the government of New York State looks like IBM. There is a CEO, the governor, and he has people working for him separated into different departments that are headed by bosses and local divisions that are subject to what headquarters wants. The whole thing is shaped like a pyramid with a place for everyone and everyone in his place and orders going down from the top and reports going up from the bottom. There are rules and regulations and policies and processes and budgets and tasks and inspections and evaluations, and products are supposed to be coming out of all this. No wonder they tell us government should be run like a business—why not?

But as anyone who has ever worked in a business knows, this picture is far more myth than reality. Businesses are run by people acting like people. There is pulling and hauling and conflict and cooperation and confusion and mistakes and success and near misses and good luck. It's called human behavior in organizations, and it provides us with a concept, caricature though it be, of a company.

We have no such image of government, so we naturally adopt the prevailing one we have of another big organization, namely a corporation. But the American government, hammered out during that summer in Philadelphia, was never designed to look like IBM—quite the contrary—nor was it conceived to function like IBM. Nor was it to serve the same purposes as a company.

The function of a business is primarily (though not exclusively) to generate profits for the shareholders, management, and employees. It accomplishes this end by producing goods and services that appeal to customers and potential customers. To maximize the income, it maximizes efficiency, producing as much output as possible with as little input as possible. The continuing search for ways to become more efficient, more cost effective, and more appealing to buyers is a demanding and intellectually stimulating endeavor. It calls for imagination, perception, clarity, creativity, and devotion to the bottom line. Business is critical to our well-being as a nation, as a society, and to our comfort as individuals.

But government, as Woodrow Wilson observed, is "not business. It is organic social life." And the ends of business are not those of government. The task of the public servant is to deliver service and to do that in a fair, equitable, accountable fashion. It is to seek out and implement the common good and to do so in a way that attracts and holds the support of the public. Part of the job of the government official, therefore, is to encourage public participation in her affairs so that "consent of the governed" can be ascertained and maintained. Government's role is to serve the common good and to deliver public value.

The fifty-five delegates—with shifting attendance, as we know—who gathered in Philadelphia that critical summer did not think they were starting up a new business, a new bank, canal company, or sawmill. They were well aware that they were drafting a formal document describing the way their new nation was to be governed. The Declaration of Independence had set forth the aspirations, the values, purposes of their new nation, won in what Washington called "The Glorious Cause." Their job was to raise the beams, the walls, the roof of this new government, indeed, a new *kind* of government. They set about replacing the Articles of Confederation with something more workable and serviceable and at the same time making operational the idea of popular sovereignty. Madison's two scholarly papers, one on the history of confederations and the other on the weaknesses of the existing American version, set the stage for their work.

However much they disagreed, however many different ways they interpreted the same words and phrases, however profound the conflicts between the small and the large states, they stood together in agreement on their conviction that the nation should be something new and different, above all that it should not be a monarchy.

But how, without a monarch, could all the ongoing differences be reconciled? They knew there was no such thing as "the public interest"; instead, as Madison was well aware, there were countless "factions," groups of citizens with roughly common views of just where the public interest lay—and they knew those views often directly contradicted each other. Similarly, there was no such phenomenon as "public opinion," but many different opinions about matters of great importance—economic, religious, political—and all were represented at Philadelphia. So when modern pundits talk glibly about the "intent of the Founders," I always wonder precisely which "Founders" they mean—Hamilton? Jefferson? Madison? Adams? Washington? Randolph? And at what stages of their careers, for their views changed with the changing times.

At any rate, Madison, "little Jemmy," seized the initiative in thinking specifically about what this Constitution should look like. Able to read Latin and Greek, backed by his library and the "cargo of books" Jefferson sent him from Paris, he sawed and hammered away at Montpelier, his estate in Virginia, and came up with a model. As shrewd a politician as he was profound as a thinker, he brought the Virginia delegation together at the same boardinghouse in Philadelphia two weeks before the first gavel sounded; they worked over his ideas and, ultimately, his formulation went before the convention as the Virginia Plan. The advantage still goes to the person who has something on paper at the start of the meeting to which the others will react!

And what was at the heart of Madison's grand plan? Not "separation of powers," to which they were all committed, given the British experience, rather it was "countervailing powers" (*Federalist* 10 and 51). Fearful that one or another of the "factions" could take over one or more of the branches, he mixed and matched, giving each some of the traditional powers of the others. In this way he set "ambition to counter ambition," meaning, I think, policy ambitions as well as personal ambitions.

Was this a recipe for business-like efficiency in an organization? Not hardly. It was a recipe for a cumbersome decision-making process. It was a recipe for "maximum feasible participation" of many players inside and outside the formal structure. It was a recipe for almost limitless accessibility to the decision makers and to the decision-making process from the governed. It is as though Bill Gates, Paul Allen, and Paul Balmer when they started Microsoft got together and said: "How can we make it as hard as possible to get decisions made? How can we bring as many people as possible into the decision-making process? How can we make our decisions as transparent as possible so as many folk as possible will know what we are doing?"

We all know this. We took civics or American history in school, and we all heard about checks and balances until we were sick of it. But we were not made aware of how these basic concepts have evolved and how they play out in the America of today.

But Bill Kelly, director of Job Corps under President Johnson and Sargent Shriver, head of the Office of Economic Opportunity (the so-called Poverty Program)—he knew all right.

Of all the OEO programs, the Job Corps was in the most trouble. Its appropriation and authorization legislation were both coming up in June, and harsh criticism was heard everywhere, threatening its survival. The communities where the camps were located did not like it, wondered what all these

Figure C.1 The power center wheel of Bill Kelly

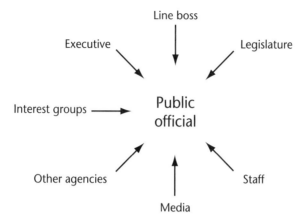

Source: Dan Fenn, "Making the Madisonian System Work: Case Studies in Contemporary American Government, Notes on Classroom Use," John F. Kennedy School of Government, 2004, 5.

African American kids were suddenly doing in their towns; Congress thought it was wasteful; the Office of Management and Budget was circulating memos against it throughout the government; the press was filled with stories about riots and high costs; the staff was demoralized, plagued by all this criticism and frequent turnover of leadership.

But Kelly, unfazed by all this as he sought to save the program, well understood the situation in which Madison's plan had placed him. He was in the middle of a wheel of power centers, each one of which could impact his program—perhaps terminally. His situation looked like Figure C.1.

In reality, things were not that simple because, with the exception of Kelly and his staff, all the other players had different sets of concerns and orders of priorities. It looked more like Figure C.2 on page 316.

But even that was not the whole story: there were all kinds combinations and networks and lash-ups among and between the players. So his world really looked like Figure C.3 on page 317.

Systematically, Bill Kelly went around the wheel, building relationships of trust in all the power centers. He met constantly with members of Congress and their staffs, stayed in close touch with his boss, worked with his staff to make sure they understood what was going on and what he was doing,

Figure C.2 The power center wheel of Bill Kelly —
because others have their own concerns

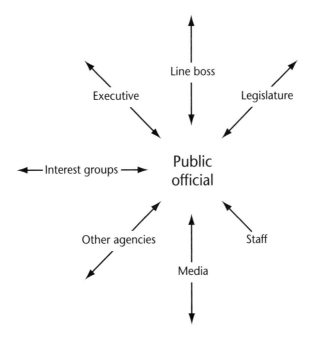

Source: Dan Fenn, "Making the Madisonian System Work: Case Studies in Contemporary American Government, Notes on Classroom Use," John F. Kennedy School of Government, 2004, 6.

courted the media and kept them informed, worked with the local communities on local projects and local purchases, was responsive to complaints, took action to improve the program. In short, he added to Speaker Tip O'Neill's famous dictum "all politics is local" his own: "all politics is personal."

The upshot of his work was that the Job Corps not only survived but also received an increase in its budget. And, despite many attempts over the years to do away with it, it exists today, larger and better funded than it was when Kelly left it.

I find it interesting that a program director in another agency recently described to me just how he had managed not only to protect his project against the pressures of a hostile administration but also increased its scope and funding. Literally, I could almost have substituted his name for Bill Kelly's, so closely had he followed Bill's script—without ever having been aware of the Job Corps story.

Figure C.3 **The power center wheel of Bill Kelly —
with combinations and networks considered**

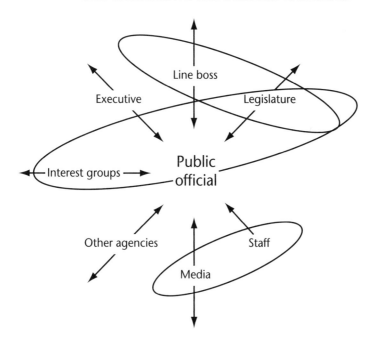

Source: Dan Fenn, "Making the Madisonian System Work: Case Studies in
Contemporary American Government, Notes on Classroom Use," John F. Kennedy
School of Government, 2004, 6.

Ah well, I can hear some say: That kind of interplay, the checks and balances system through which Kelly had to work himself, goes on way above
me in the food chain.

So thought a supervisor in an agency when he was trying to deal with an
employee with a great résumé but a poor record of performance. His story is
a familiar one. Try as he would to help Neil Cooper become a productive
member of his staff, Bob Morgenstern (not their real names) simply could
not make it work out. Finally, he started the termination process. To his
shock and distress, he learned that Neil had just gone to the FBI complaining
that he (Morgenstern) was covering up wrongdoing. Suddenly, what looked
like, and was, a standard personnel supervisory matter had exploded into the
whole Madisonian system. Or take the time the Nixon administration
wanted to move the VA administrator in Boston to Minneapolis because
Nixon's people thought he was too political, too close to the Kennedy family.

His bags were packed—when suddenly a line appeared in the VA appropriation bill saying that no part of these funds shall be used to move the regional administrator in Boston to Minneapolis.

In short, no one and no action of a public official is immune from the workings of Mr. Madison's system, because it provides so much leverage for so many people, inside and outside the government itself.

One public executive once told me: "In this country, to varying degrees, everyone wants to do their own thing, make things come out the way they want. Business is designed to channel that drive; government to empower it!"

Vice President Al Gore allegedly tells a story on himself. When he was first elected to the Senate, he held a dinner party for some of his closest friends. As they were having drinks in one corner of the room, he noticed a waiter putting down a pat of butter at each place. "Two pats," Gore commanded. The waiter kept putting down one pat. Gore said again, more forcefully: "Two pats." The waiter kept on as before. Gore, by this time quite irritated, said: "Do you know who I am?" "Yes," the waiter replied calmly. "And I know who I am. I'm the man in charge of the butter."

The American system of government was not put together with efficiency in mind, but with accountability and participation foremost. It was fashioned more than two centuries ago to protect the people against tyranny, arbitrary government people carrying out arbitrary policies. For there is no such thing as "the government"; that term is merely a convenient shorthand we commonly employ. Rather, there are thousands of men and women drawing a check from the U.S. Treasury or state or municipality taking certain actions. (It is strange how we have trapped ourselves by our own shorthand. If someone asks me whether I mind that "the government" may be reviewing my overseas calls, I would answer, "no, not particularly," because I have a more benign view of government in the abstract than most Americans. But if I am asked how I feel about some GS 9 working for some agency somewhere listening in on my calls, I can get very upset because I don't know this person, his abilities, his degree of discretion, his level of wisdom or his motives.)

Does all this mean that government officials aren't supposed to be concerned about being efficient, accomplishing their tasks in a timely and cost-effective manner? Of course not. The people have lent us their authority and provided us with their resources. It is incumbent on us to use them responsibly. It is thoroughly appropriate that we should be scrutinized to make sure that we are doing so.

It is only to say that for government people, efficiency is not the major goal and purpose. Responsiveness is.

Why has the U.S. Constitution stood fundamentally unchanged for all these decades? Because it was rooted in a set of values that are still dear to us: the values of John Locke, the Enlightenment, the social contract, self-reliance, freedom, liberty, and doing our own thing. And having a hand and a voice in matters that concern us. The traditions of congregational polity, expressed in that very first town meeting when the landholders came together to enact the rules for their new "plantation" and invented a new form of self-government, are alive and well.

As a matter of fact, as I said above, I would postulate that our generation is even more insistent on being a player than were our forebears. Woodrow Wilson in 1887 complained that the American public was all too involved in government and was often like a "clumsy rustic tinkering with delicate machinery." He should see us now! We are all children of Rosa Parks.

Attempts to change the fundamentals of decentralization and participation have taken place over the years, either formally or informally. Many of the so-called "management reforms" are basically attempts to shift power upward and remake our Madisonian system into a more pyramidal shape. During the Nixon years the President's Advisory Council on Executive Organization made recommendations to that end, but they foundered on Watergate. Calls for a "robust" executive today are part of that same effort. And the dilemma is indeed a taxing one—getting product out is hard in our government organization. It was meant to be. Hamilton is said to have complained to Madison: "You have created an organization to impede action, not to facilitate it." Madison is said to have smiled benignly and said something like "Yup."

Happily for the public servant, the American people understand all this, appreciate the fact that the jobs we do and the way we do them are directly traceable to Philadelphia in 1787, and so realize just how difficult it is for us to get things done.

Sure they do. "What's the matter with you government guys?" they ask. "In private industry we get things done while you screw around and screw around. Government should be run like a business."

And there goes the trust.

But if we adopt the Hamiltonian style, occupy ourselves with the task at hand, and do not stop to listen to their comments, complaints, chants, petitions, and songs, they say, "What's the matter with you, you pointy-headed bureaucrat? You work for me, remember?"

And there goes trust.

We are then, caught. If I am getting the job done, in response to their request, I am not being responsive. If I am listening to the public, I'm not getting the job done. So these two completely legitimate demands are irreconcilable, and either way I lose trust. That is the nature of the organization in which we find ourselves.

President Kennedy liked a stanza translated from the Spanish by Robert Graves:

> Bullfight critics, ranked in rows
>
> Crowd the vast arena full.
>
> But only one is there who knows.
>
> And that's the one who fights the bull.

What are those of us who fight the bull to do when the organization with which and through which we work, the very Constitution which we have sworn to uphold and defend, deprives us of the public trust because it often prevents us from acting with crispness and dispatch?

We need to see as part of our jobs the never-ending search for new and effective ways to build public participation into our decision-making processes. Naturally, we run some risk here. That little dog Toto really messed up the Wizard's operation when he pulled aside the curtain and we all saw the little man pulling the levers and manipulating the big awesome machine.

But I am convinced that the gains outweigh the hazards and the difficulties inherent in exposure because, as the curtain is pulled away, people will see how the system really works, not in junior high textbooks but in real life. They will see us struggling with many players, many interests, many viewpoints—as in fact the Constitution meant us to do. And, at some level, as they want us to do. We can, in short, transform an interface with a citizen or another player into a learning experience.

Suppose I am one of five people on an elected school board. Someone comes up to me at a party, as they often did in my hometown, and says: "I really think we should have four years of Latin in our high school curriculum." I recognize her all right—a friend. What do I say?

Recalling my own behavior, probably I would say something like "Interesting idea!" Going through my mind, however, would be: "Oh lord, I hope she doesn't pursue this. I have enough on my plate already, and I am not even sure it is a good idea, never mind a doable one."

Then suppose a week later she calls me and says: "You know, I have been talking with friends of mine and there is a group of ten of us parents who really think four years of Latin is important for these high school kids. What do you think?" What I think is that I wish she'd forgotten it; what I think is, "How do I handle this?" But what I say is: "Okay, I'll look into it for you. Latin certainly is important, isn't it?"

I make the calculation that she isn't going away. I call the superintendent, who tells me we're short of classrooms and have no teachers capable of doing the job. Dutifully, I pass that along to my friend, hoping that will end it. But no. "Well, I'm sure there are logistical issues," she says. "But we think this is so important!"

Recalling my own public career, I would figure out some bob or weave—unfortunately. Probably ask her to put it all on paper so it could be considered carefully and blah blah blah.

What I could do is to sit down with her and say: "Let me walk through this process with you. First, as you know, I am only one of five members. There have to be three to move ahead with this. But then there is the superintendent. He actually runs the schools and, though formally he works for us, we wouldn't push something like this without his cooperation. Whatever the legal lines may be, the actual power to get things done is divided here between us and the professional staff. They implement, and furthermore, in virtually every situation, we confer and discuss and reach agreement with the superintendent and other school staff. And then he has the principal and the teachers' views to take into account. Beyond all that, we would have to displace another language to make room for the fourth year of Latin. Other parents may think Chinese is more important than Latin, or French, or Spanish. And there are teachers who feel that way, too. And they would fight this proposal very hard." And so on and so forth, trying to lay out the realities of the system for her. I could then guide her through the process.

I could have done that sort of thing in my career—but I didn't. I could have searched for chances to explain the realities to people. But I didn't.

What happens when we pull the curtain away like that? All of a sudden we don't look so all powerful. All of a sudden we are forced to admit that their priorities—a heart, a brain, courage—aren't necessarily our priorities. All of a sudden, instead of the big shot who gets things done, I am merely the AAA or MapQuest supplying them with the roadmap. Furthermore, that process is time-consuming and diverts me from all those other demands facing me.

But would it build understanding? Would it build trust? Would it mean that in future interactions with other public servants, my friend would be both more effective and more realistic? Would it be a better way to bring people to a recognition of just how our system works than all the talks to all the service club luncheons? I think so, and I wish I had done it.

In short, the problem for us public officials is that the community expects us to behave as they believe (fantasize?) IBM executives behave. But we cannot and we should not. So we are trapped. Consciously seizing opportunities to show our publics why and how, in fact, we *do* function can, gradually, incrementally, build a richer, deeper understanding and, with it, increased trust.

No one said this would be easy

"Building trust" in our relations with the public, our colleagues, other parts of the government, our staffs, and the press; adjusting to change; being change agents; doing the technical parts of our work well and effectively; working with a variety of bosses of varying abilities; finding new methods of public participation; being sensitive to our responsibility to the system itself, to its meaning and purpose as well as to its letter; and making sure that we, as the current stewards of the gift that Madison and his colleagues gave the nation, turn over to our successors a government even sturdier than it was when it was entrusted to us—that's the job description. And nobody promised us a walk in the park when we signed on.

We have, then, myriad responsibilities—many more even than I have listed above. That, in itself, is one reason our jobs are so tough—the most difficult managerial jobs that society has to offer, in fact.

Of course, all executive positions are hard. The facts, the scientific evidence, run in conflicting directions; judgment calls are often close ones; we never know all we need to know; and then there are all those pesky personnel matters—"time vampires" someone has dubbed them—which pervade all human organizations.

But our jobs in the public sector are especially taxing—and for several reasons. First, we are going where no one has gone before. How do you educate a widely diverse group of young people for a rapidly changing world? How do you provide decent health care at a reasonable cost? How do you clean the planet and halt global warming and not go broke in the process? How do you battle and defeat a shadowy and omnipresent enemy?

Second, there are so many players and potential players out there. Thank you, Mr. Madison, for making it possible for them to get into our business so much and so often!

Third, when you think of it, we are so often at the nexus of issues that deeply divide us as a nation, issues that may shift with changing circumstances. For example, the appropriate, acceptable, and working balance between our privacy, a freedom we cherish, and the security of the community as a whole needs constant rethinking and adjustment. I recall a customs chief at a busy airport who must give performance ratings to his people. One of his officers, remembering that he is supposed to knock and get a response before exercising a search warrant, dutifully does so; a second officer stations an agent at the back of the house who yells "come in" at the first knock, enabling his colleagues to come crashing into the building and preventing the inhabitants getting rid of dangerous or incriminating material. For this public official, the proper balance between individual and community rights is no mere topic for school debates or bull sessions; it is an ever-present reality.

It is unfortunate that those whom we serve, on whose trust we depend, not only fail to understand why we do what we do and how we do it, they do not think what we do is very important. I remember hearing of one woman, in a class of business and public executives, saying proudly that she had spent her life making lemon-scented furniture polish. Nothing intrinsically wrong with that—but where did the American people ever get the idea that figuring how many blue chips to put into laundry powder so it could be called "NEW Swish" and increasing point-of-sale purchases is more important than keeping the nation and our homes safe and mapping the oceans and managing the infrastructure of a free society and providing food and housing and caring for the most vulnerable among us—all the tasks to which public servants devote their minds and hearts?

The fact is that we work in a country whose citizens are basically opposed to government and, consequently, to government workers. Certainly one reason for this attitude is that, with the exception of most African Americans, our ancestors came over here precisely to get away from arbitrary government officials and government actions. So it is bred in our bones.

Finally, and perhaps most important, our jobs were explicitly designed to be tough. That is what those men in their powdered wigs and funny knickers, with their quill pens and parchments, set out to do. Checks and balances and countervailing power indeed! Who, exactly, were they checking and balancing? Us, that's who. Whose powers were they trying to limit? Ours, naturally.

What other executive in the society works in an organization specifically fashioned to make it hard for him to do his job?

How often do I wake up in the middle of the night, faced with three boxes: "IN," "OUT," and "TOO HARD," and wonder why I'm not engaged in doing something sensible like selling shoes? Why did I choose this work? Because I figure that, one day, the lobby of my office building will feature my portrait or maybe a life size statue outside the door? Not likely. Or because the public will know and appreciate what I did and how hard it was? Equally unlikely. My spouse may have some ideas, but wonder why I was so preoccupied with the job that I never remembered to pick up the milk; my kids only know I couldn't often help them with homework; my father will know I did something but won't be quite clear what; and my mother always knew I would accomplish wonderful things, so I get no points there. And eventually—too soon—what I accomplished will be generally accepted as having always been there, my struggle to achieve it lost in the mists of history.

Discouraging? Maybe. But I recall a woman named Ramona Barth who, in the 1930s and 1940s, battled for the outrageous idea that women could be something other than housewives, teachers, and nurses, that they could be doctors and lawyers and Speakers of the U.S. House and business leaders. She was thought crazy and obnoxious in her time. In the last paragraph of her autobiography, she wrote: "What greater reward can a good worker desire than that the next generation should forget her, regarding as an obsolete truism work which her own generation called a visionary fanaticism?"

And then it could be the very fact that our work is so difficult and so important that gives it a special appeal to us. It is our full engagement—heart and mind—in matters that are at once extraordinarily difficult and vitally important to our generation and to our posterity that gives our lives purpose and meaning.

Over my desk I have a cartoon of two newly minted angels rising through the clouds with their wings and halos. One is saying wistfully to the other: "I spent my life making a difference—but in an area that didn't matter."

Notes

1. Given new technologies, which make control of information to a populace so much more difficult to accomplish and communication between them so much easier, that range may be narrowing.

2. In modern America, people will cut their leaders a good bit of slack—but as the elections of 1994 and 2006 showed dramatically, their patience is not without limits.

References

Aberbach, Joel D., and Bert A. Rockman. 2000. *In the Web of Politics.* Washington, D.C.: Brookings Institution.

Abramson, Mark A., and Paul R. Lawrence. 2001. *Transforming Organizations.* Lanham, Md.: Rowman and Littlefield.

———eds. 2005. *Learning the Ropes: Insights for Political Appointees.* Lanham, Md.: Rowman and Littlefield.

Anechiarico, Frank, and James B. Jacobs. 1996. *The Pursuit of Absolute Integrity.* Chicago: University of Chicago Press.

Arendt, Hannah. 1963. *Eichmann in Jerusalem.* New York: Viking Press.

Armstrong, Jerome, and Markos Moulitsas Zuniga. 2006. *Crashing the Gate: Netroots, Grassroots, and the Rise of People-Powered Politics.* White River Junction, Vt.: Chelsea Green.

Barber, Benjamin. 2003. *Jihad vs. McWorld.* New York: Ballantine.

Barnes, Cheryl, and Derek Gill. 2000. "Declining Government Performance? Why Citizens Don't Trust Government." Working Paper No. 9, State Service Commission, New Zealand (February).

Barnett, Thomas. 2004. *The Pentagon's New Map: War and Peace in the Twenty-First Century.* New York: G. P. Putnam's Sons.

Bearfield, Domonic A. 2007. "The Demonization of Patronage: Folk Devils and the Boston Globe's Coverage of the 9/11 Terrorist Attacks." In *American Public Service: Radical Reform and the Merit System.* J. S. Bowman and J. P. West, eds. Boca Raton: Taylor and Francis Group, 101–120.

———. In press. "Patronage: A Critical Reexamination."

Beck, Katherine. 2002. "Going Global: How Boeing Is Changing the Way It Works Around the World." *Boeing Frontiers Online,* June 1. www.boeing.com/news/frontiers/archive/2002/june/cover.html.

Bennis, Warren. 1989. *On Becoming a Leader.* Cambridge, Mass.: Perseus Books.

Berry, Leonard. 1999. *Discovering the Soul of Service: The Nine Drivers of Sustainable Business Success.* New York: Free Press.

———, Eileen Wall, and Lewis P. Carbone. 2006. "Service Clues and Customer Assessment of the Service Experience." *Academy of Management Executive* (May).

Bikson, Tora, Gregory F. Treverton, Joy Moini, and Gustav Lindstrom. 2003. "New Challenges for International Leadership: Lessons from Organizations with Global Missions." Santa Monica: RAND Monograph Report.

Block, Peter. 1991. *The Empowered Manager: Positive Political Skills at Work.* San Francisco: Jossey-Bass.

Bloom, Greg. 2006. "Meet the New Organizing—Same as the Old Organizing?" Personal Democracy Forum, September 8. www.personaldemocracy.com/node/1002.

Bok, Derek. 1997. "Measuring the Performance of Government." In *Why People Don't Trust Government.* J. Nye, P. D. Selikow, and D. C. King, eds. Cambridge: Harvard University Press.

Bok, Sissela. 1978. *Lying: Moral Choice in Public and Private Life.* New York: Vintage Books.

Bolino, Mark, William Turnley, and James Bloodgood. 2002. "Citizenship Behavior and the Creation of Social Capital in Organizations." *Academy of Management Review* 27 (4): 505–522.

Bossidy, Larry, and Ram Charan. 2002. *Execution—The Discipline of Getting Things Done.* New York: Crown Business Press.

Brands, H. W. 1998. *What America Owes the World: The Struggle for the Soul of Foreign Policy.* New York: Cambridge University Press.

Bratton, William. 1998. *Turnaround.* New York: Random House.

Braun, Kathyrn A., and Gerald Zaltman. Undated. "Companies that Have Consumers' Best Interest at Heart, a zMet Study." Mind of the Market Lab case study for classroom use. Boston: Harvard Business School. www.hbs.edu/mml/hide/MMLCBI/.

Brewer, Gene A., and Robert Maranto. 2000. "Comparing the Roles of Political Appointees and Career Executives in the U.S. Federal Executive Branch." *American Review of Public Administration* 30 (March): 69–86.

Bridges, William. 2004. *Managing Transitions: Making the Most of Change,* 2nd ed. Reading, Mass.: Perseus Books.

Brooks, Jennifer. 2006. "Power of Blogs on Rise in Politics." *Detroit Free Press,* June 6.

Brower, Dana, Terry Newell, and Peter Ronayne. 2002. "The Imperative of Developing Global Leaders." *The Business of Government.* (Winter).

Brown, Hutch, and Russ Linden. 2001–2002. "Daring to Be Citizen Centered." *The Public Manager.* Washington, D.C.: 49–52.

Brown, Mark Graham. Annual. *Baldrige Award Winning Quality.* Milwaukee: ASQ Quality Press.

———. 1996. *Keeping Score: Using the Right Metrics to Drive World-Class Performance.* New York: Quality Resources; distributed by AMACOM.

Bunker, Linda. 1996. *Winning Strategies for the Executive Playing Field.* Charlottesville, Va.: Federal Executive Institute.

———. 2001. *The Johari Window [What Is It? Why Use It?]* A monograph written for use at the Federal Executive Institute, Charlottesville, Va.

Burns, James McGregor. 1978. *Leadership.* New York: HarperCollins.

Bushouse, Brenda. 2006. "West Virginia Collaboration for Creating Universal Prekindergarten." *Public Administration Review* 66 (Special Issue): 154–155.

Caldwell, Alicia A. 2006. "Texas May Stream Border Video on Web." *Syracuse Post-Standard,* June 9.

Canfield, Jack. 1989. *Self-Esteem and Peak Performance.* An audiocassette seminar. Boulder: CareerTrack Publications.

Carbone, Lewis P. 2003. "What Makes Customers Tick." *Marketing Management* (July/August).

———. 2004. *Clued In: How to Keep Customers Coming Back Again and Again.* Upper Saddle River, N.J.: Financial Times Prentice Hall.

Chapman, Alan. 2003. *The Johari Window.* Online presentation at: http://unpan1.un.org/intradoc/groups/public/documents/UNSSC/UNPAN022136.pdf.

Chrislip, David. 2000. "The New Civic Leadership." In *Cutting Edge: Leadership 2000.* B. Kellerman and Larraine R. Matusak, eds. James McGregor Burns Academy of Leadership, University of Maryland, College Park, 18–24.

Clift, Steven. 2006. "Citizens 2.0 and Governance 2.0." Personal Democracy Forum, November 14. www.personaldemocracy.com/node/1096.

Coglianese, Cary. 2004a. "Information Technology and Regulatory Policy: New Directions for Digital Government Research." *Social Science Computer Review* 22 (1): 85–91.

————. 2004b. "E-Rulemaking: Information Technology and the Regulatory Process." *Administration Law Review* 56 (2): 353–402.

Cohen, D. M. 1998. "Amateur Government." *Journal of Public Administration Research and Theory* 8 (4): 450–497.

Collins, James. 2001. *Good to Great: Why Some Companies Make the Leap and Others Don't.* New York: HarperCollins.

————. 2005. *Good to Great and the Social Sectors: A Monograph to Accompany Good to Great.* Self-published.

————, and Jerry Porras. 1994. *Built to Last: Successful Habits of Visionary Companies.* New York: HarperCollins.

Columbia Accident Investigation Board Final Report. 2003. Vol. 1, chap. 8, 201. For the full report, go to the board's Web site at http://caib.nasa.gov/.

Committee for Economic Development. 2006. *Education for Global Leadership.* Washington, D.C.: Committee for Economic Development.

Conner, Jill. 2000. "Developing the Global Leaders of Tomorrow." *Human Resource Management* 39, nos. 2, 3 (August): 147–157.

Cooke, Alfred L. 1995. *The Individual and the Organization.* Unpublished monograph.

————et al. 1999. *Reading Book on Human Relations Training,* 8th ed. Alexandria, Va.: NTL Institute.

Cooper, Terry. 1998. *The Responsible Administrator: An Approach to Ethics for the Administrative Role,* 4th ed. San Francisco: Jossey-Bass.

Cooperrider, David L., and Diana Whitney. 2005. *Appreciative Inquiry: A Positive Revolution in Change.* San Francisco: Berrett-Koehler.

Council for Excellence in Government. 2001. *E-Government: The Next American Revolution.* Washington, D.C.: Council for Excellence in Government.

Covey, Stephen R. 1989. *The 7 Habits of Highly Effective People: Restoring the Character Ethic.* New York: Simon and Schuster.

————. 1997. Foreword to the twenty-fifth anniversary edition of Greenleaf's *Servant Leadership.* Mahwah, N.J.: Paulist Press, 2.

Defeo, Chuck, et al. 2006. "Technology's Role in 2006 and Beyond." Personal Democracy Forum, November 14. www.personaldemocracy.com/node/1095.

deKieffer, Donald E. 1997. *The Citizen's Guide to Lobbying Congress.* Chicago: Chicago Review Press.

Delmhorst, Frederic P. 2006. "Self-awareness and Leadership Development." Ph.D. diss., Columbia University.

Deming, W. Edwards. 1986. *Out of the Crisis.* Cambridge, Mass.: MIT Center for Advanced Engineering Study.

Denhardt, Janet, and Robert Denhardt. 2003. *The New Public Service: Serving, Not Steering.* New York: M. E. Sharpe.

DePree, Max. 1992. *Leadership Jazz.* New York: Dell Publishing.

Devine, Donald J. 1972. *The Political Culture of the United States.* Boston: Little, Brown.

Diamond, Jared. 1997. *Guns, Germs, and Steel.* New York: W. W. Norton.

Durant, Robert. 1992. *The Administrative Presidency Revisited.* Albany: State University of New York Press.

Editors. 2005. "Welcome to the Hackocracy." *New Republic,* October 17, 21–25.

Engber, Daniel. 2006. "The Senate's Darkest Secret: The Cloak-and-Dagger History of Legislative Holds." *Slate Magazine,* September 1.

Federal Executive Institute and Federal Consulting Group. 2002. *Guidelines for Federal Agencies Considering Executive Coaching.* Jointly developed document.

Ferrara, Joseph A., and Lynn C. Ross. 2005. "Getting to Know You: Rules of Engagement for Political Appointees and Career Executives." In *Learning the Ropes: Insights for Political Appointees.* Mark A. Abramson and Paul. R. Lawrence, eds. Lanham, Md.: Rowman and Littlefield, 37–80.

Fesler, James W., and Donald F. Kettl. 2005. *The Politics of the Administrative Process,* 3rd ed. Washington, D.C.: CQ Press.

Fichtner, Ullrich. 2006. "Civilized Warriors: The US Army Learns from Its Mistakes in Iraq." *Spiegel Online,* December 18. www.spiegel.de/international/spiegel/0,1518,455165,00.html.

Fine, Allison. 2006. *Momentum: Igniting Social Change in the Connected Age.* San Francisco: Jossey-Bass.

"First Digital Decade, The." 2004. Washington, D.C.: Institute for Politics, Democracy, and the Internet, George Washington University; and Rightclick Strategies.

Friedman, Thomas L. 2000. *The Lexus and the Olive Tree.* New York: Anchor Books.

———. 2005a. *The World Is Flat.* New York: Farrar, Straus and Giroux.

———. 2005b. "It's a Flat World After All." *New York Times magazine,* April 3.

Fukuyama, Francis. 1995. *Trust: The Social Virtues and the Creation of Prosperity.* New York: Free Press.

Gardner, Howard. 1983. *Frames of Mind: The Theory of Multiple Intelligences.* Cambridge, Mass.: Perseus Books.

———. 1999. *The Disciplined Mind: Beyond Facts and Standardized Tests.* New York: Simon and Schuster.

Garrett, Thomas A., and Russell M. Rhine. 2006. "On the Size and Growth of Government." *Federal Reserve Bank of St. Louis Review* (January/February).

Gawthrop, Louis C. 1998. *Public Service and Democracy: Ethical Imperatives for the 21st Century.* New York: Chatham House Publishers.

Gilligan, Carol. 1982. *In a Different Voice.* Cambridge: Harvard University Press.

Goldfinger, Charles. 1994. *The Useful and the Futile: The Immaterial Economy.* Paris: Odile Jacob.

Goleman, Daniel. 1995. *Emotional Intelligence: Why It Can Matter More Than IQ.* New York: Bantam Books.

———. 2000a. *Working with Emotional Intelligence.* New York: Bantam Books.

———. 2000b. "Leadership That Gets Results." *Harvard Business Review* (March-April).

———, Richard Boyatzis, and Annie McKee. 2002. *Primal Leadership: Realizing the Power of Emotional Intelligence.* Cambridge: Harvard Business School Press.

Goodsell, Charles. 2003. *The Case for Bureaucracy: A Public Administration Polemic,* 4th ed. Washington, D.C.: CQ Press.

Graf, Joseph, and Carol Darr. 2004. *Political Influentials Online in the 2004 Presidential Campaign.* Washington, D.C.: Institute for Politics, Democracy, and the Internet, George Washington University.

Graf, Joseph, Grant Reeher, Michael J. Malbin, and Costas Panagopoulos. 2006. *Small Donors and Online Giving: A Study of Donors to the 2004 Presidential Campaigns.* Washington, D.C.: Institute for Politics, Democracy and the Internet, George Washington University.

Greenleaf, Robert. 1977. *Servant Leadership: A Journey into the Nature of Legitimate Power and Greatness.* Mahway, N.J.: Paulist Press.

Grunwald, Michael. 2002. "Army Corps Chief's Ouster Prompts Outrage on Capitol Hill." *Washington Post,* Web edition, March 7.

———, and Mike Allan. 2002. "Corps of Engineers Civilian Chief Ousted," *Washington Post,* March 7, A1.

Haass, Richard N. 1999. *The Bureaucratic Entrepreneur.* Washington, D.C.: Brookings Institution.

Halverson, Stefanie K., et al. 2002. *Self-Other Agreement on a 360-Degree Leadership Evaluation.* Paper presented at the seventeenth annual conference of the Society for Industrial and Organizational Psychology, Toronto, Canada. April.

Hamel, Gary. 1994. *Competing for the Future.* Boston: Harvard Business School Press.

Hamilton, Lee H. 2004. *How Congress Works and Why You Should Care.* Bloomington: Indiana University Press.

Harris, Richard A., and Sidney M. Milkis. 1989. *The Politics of Regulatory Change.* New York: Oxford University Press.

Hart Research Associates. 2006. "Partisanship Up, Confidence Down: Americans Want Compromise and Competition." Based on a survey in behalf of the Council for Excellence in Government, Washington, D.C.

Heclo, Hugh. 1977. *A Government of Strangers.* Washington, D.C.: Brookings Institution.

Heifetz, Ron. 1994. *Leadership Without Easy Answers.* Cambridge: Harvard University Press.

Heim, Pat. 1995. *The Power Dead-Even Rule (and Other Gender Differences in the Workplace.* Video. Libertyville, Ill.: CorVision Media.

Hempel, Jesse. 2004. "It Takes A Village—And a Consultant." *Business Week Online,* September 6. www.businessweek.com/magazine/content/04_36/b3898097_mz056.htm.

Herspring, Dale R. 2005. *The Pentagon and the Presidency.* Lawrence: University Press of Kansas.

Hiatt, Jeffrey. 2006. *ADKAR: A Model for Change in Business, Government, and Our Community.* Loveland, Colo.: Prosci Learning Center Publications.

Hill-Stoks, Hattie, et al. 1990. *Women, Power, and Self-Esteem: Take Charge of Your Own Well-Being.* Audiocassette seminar. Boulder: CareerTrack Publications.

Hirsh, Elizabeth, Katherine W. Hirsh, and Sandra Krebs Hirsh. 2003. *Introduction to Type and Teams,* 2nd ed. Palo Alto, Calif.: Consulting Psychologists' Press, 2003.

Hoagland, Jim. 2006. "A Change in Tone—and a Stumble on Iraq." *Washington Post,* September 3.

Hof, Robert D. 2005. "The Power of Us." *Business Week,* June 20.

Hofstadter, Richard. 1964. *Anti-Intellectualism in American Life.* New York: Vintage.

Holzer, Marc, James Melitski, Seung-Yong Rho, and Richard Schwester. 2004. "Restoring Trust in Government: The Potential of Digital Citizen Participation." Washington, D.C.: IBM Center for the Business of Government.

Horrigan, John. 2004. *How Americans Get in Touch with Government.* Washington, D.C.: Pew Internet and American Life Project, May 24.

———, Kelly Garrett, and Paul Resnick. 2004. *The Internet and Democratic Debate.* Washington, D.C.: Pew Internet and American Life Project, October 27.

Huddleston, Mark W. 2000. "Onto the Darkling Plain: Globalization and the American Public Service in the Twenty-First Century." *Journal of Public Administration Research and Theory* 10 (4): 665–684.

Jackson, Phil. 1995. *Sacred Hoops.* New York: Hyperion Press.

Jaffe, Greg. 2005. "In Iraq, One Officer Uses Cultural Skills to Fight Insurgents." *Wall Street Journal,* November 15.

Janis, Irving. 1989. *Crucial Decisions: Leadership in Policymaking and Crisis Management.* New York: Free Press.

Jefferson, Thomas. 1801. *First Inaugural Address.* March 4. A copy of the address can be found on the State Department's Web site: http://usinfo.state.gov/usa/infousa/facts/democrac/11.htm.

Jehn, Karen, et al. 2001. "The Dynamic Nature of Conflict: A Longitudinal Study of Intragroup Conflict and Group Performance." *Academy of Management Journal* 44: 238.

Johnson, Spencer. 1999. *Who Moved My Cheese?* New York: G. P. Putnam and Sons.

Jones, Gareth, and Jennifer George. 1998. "The Experience and Evolution of Trust: Implications for Cooperation and Teamwork." *Academy of Management Review* 23: 531–547.

Juran, Joseph. 1988. *Quality Improvement: Service.* Wilton, Conn: Juran Institute.

Kanter, Rosabeth Moss. 1994. "Collaborative Advantage: The Art of Alliances." *Harvard Business Review* (July-August): 96–108.

Kaplan, Robert. 2005. *Imperial Grunts.* New York: Vintage Books.

———, and David P. Norton. 1996. *The Balanced Scorecard: Translating Strategy into Action.* Boston: Harvard Business School Press.

Katzenbach, Jon R., and Douglas K. Smith. 2003. *The Wisdom of Team.* New York: Harper Collins.

Kelman, Steven. 2005. *Unleashing Change.* Washington, D.C.: Brookings Institution.

Kessler, Glen. 2002. "Budget Director Lectured by House Appropriators." *Washington Post,* March 15, A21.

Kettl, Donald F. 2002. *The Transformation of Governance: Public Administration for the Twenty-First Century.* Baltimore: Johns Hopkins University Press.

———. 2006. "Managing Boundaries in American Administration: The Collaboration Imperative." *Public Administration Review* 66:6 (Supplement): 10–19.

———, and James W. Fesler. 2005. *The Politics of the Administrative Process,* 3rd ed. Washington, D.C.: CQ Press.

Khademian, Anne M. 2002. *Working with Culture.* Washington, D.C.: CQ Press.

Kidder, Rushworth. 1995. *How Good People Make Tough Choices: Resolving the Dilemmas of Ethical Living.* New York: Fireside Books.

———. 2005a. *Moral Courage.* New York: William Morrow.

———. 2005b. "Auschwitz at 60: The Lesson of Moral Perimeters." Camden, Maine: Institute for Global Ethics. www.globalethics.org/newsline/members/issue.tmpl?articleid=01310517581288.

King, David C., Joseph S. Nye, and Philip D. Zelikow, eds. 1997. *Why People Don't Trust Government.* Cambridge: Harvard University Press.

Kingdon, John W. 1995. *Agendas, Alternatives, and Public Policy.* New York: Harper-Collins.

Kohut, Andrew, and Bruce Stokes. 2006. *America Against the World: How We Are Different and Why We Are Disliked.* New York: Times Books.

Kotter, John P. 1996. *Leading Change.* Boston: Harvard Business School Press.

Kouzes, Jim, and Barry Posner. 2002. *The Leadership Challenge,* 3rd ed. San Francisco: Jossey-Bass.

Krepinevich, Andrew F. 1986. *The Army and Vietnam.* Baltimore: Johns Hopkins University Press.

LaBarre, Polly. 1999. "The Agenda: Grass Roots Leadership." *Fast Company,* March.

La Corte, Rachel. 2006. "Washington State Personalizes Interfaces with Constituents." *Syracuse Post-Standard,* December 10.

Lash, Rick. 2002. "Top Leadership; taking the inner journey; developing self-awareness is the first step in becoming a leader. . . ." *Ivy Business Journal* (May).

Laszlo, Ervin. 2006. *The Chaos Point: The World at the Crossroads.* Charlottesville, Va.: Hampton Roads.

Lemmon, Michael. 2004. "Meeting the Need for World Languages." States Institute on International Education in the Schools. http://internationaled.org/statesinstitute2004/MichaelLemmon.pdf.

Lencioni, Patrick. 2002. *The Five Dysfunctions of a Team: A Leadership Fable.* San Francisco: Jossey-Bass.

Levinson, W., et al. 1997. "Physician-Patient Communication: The Relationship with Malpractice Claims Among Primary Care Physicians and Surgeons." *Journal of the American Medical Association* 27 (7): 553–559.

Levy, Joshua. 2006. "Rules for Using MySpace in Politics." Personal Democracy Forum, December 4. www.personaldemocracy.com/node/1116.

Lewis, Carol. 1991. *The Ethics Challenge in Public Service: A Problem-Solving Guide.* San Francisco: Jossey-Bass.

Light, Paul C. 1995. *Thickening Government: Federal Hierarchy and the Diffusion of Responsibility.* Washington, D.C.: Brookings Institution.

———. 2002. *Government's Greatest Achievements: From Civil Rights to Homeland Security.* Washington, D.C.: Brookings Institution.

———. 2006. "The Tides of Reform Revisited: Patterns in Making Government Work, 1945–2002." *Public Administration Review* (January/February): 6–19.

Likert, Rensis. 1961. *New Patterns of Management.* New York: McGraw-Hill.

———. 1967. *The Human Organization: Its Management and Values.* New York: McGraw-Hill.

Linden, Russell. 2002. *Working Across Boundaries: Making Collaboration Work in Government and Nonprofit Organizations.* San Francisco: Jossey-Bass.

Lipnack, Jessica, and Jeffrey Stamps. 1997. *Virtual Teams: Reaching Across Space, Time, and Organizations with Technology.* New York: John Wiley and Sons.

Lorange, Peter. 2003. "Developing Global Leaders." *BizEd.* (September/October). www.aacsb.edu/publications/Archives/SepOct03/p24-27.pdf.

Lorentzin, Paul. 1985. "Stress in Political-Career Executive Relations." *Public Administration Review* 45 (3): 211–214.

Luft, Joseph. 1969. *Of Human Interaction.* Palo Alto, Calif.: National Press. 1, 41.

———, and Harry Ingham. 1955. *The Johari Window: A Graphic Model for Interpersonal Relations.* University of California, Los Angeles, Western Training Lab. http://sol.brunel.ac.uk/-jarvisibola/communications/Johari.html.

Lukensmeyer, Carolyn J., and Lars Hasselblad Torres. 2006. "Public Deliberation: A Manager's Guide to Citizen Engagement." Washington, D.C.: IBM Center for the Business of Government.

Luks, S. 2001. "Information and Complexity in Trust in Government." Princeton Conference on Trust in Government. November 30–December 1.

Mackenzie, G. Calvin, ed. 2001. *Innocent Until Nominated.* Washington, D.C.: Brookings Institution.

———, with Michael Hafken. 2002. *Scandal Proof.* Washington, D.C.: Brookings Institution.

Maranto, Robert. 1991. "Does Familiarity Breed Acceptance? Trends in Career-Non career Relations in the Reagan Administration." *Administration and Society* 23 (2): 247–266.

———. 1993. *Politics and Bureaucracy in the Modern Presidency: Appointees and Careerists in the Reagan Administration.* Westport, Conn.: Greenwood Press.

———. 2001. "The Case for Spoils," in *Radical Reform of the Civil Service.* Steven E. Condrey and Robert Maranto, eds. Lexington, Mass.: Lexington Books.

———. 2002a. " 'Government Service Is a Noble Calling': President Bush and the U.S. Civil Service." In *Honor and Loyalty: Inside the Politics of the George H. W. Bush Presidency.* Leslie D. Feldman and Rosanna Perotti, eds. Westport, Conn.: Greenwood Press, 97–108.

———. 2002b. "Praising Civil Service but Not Bureaucracy: A Brief Against Tenure in the U.S. Civil Service." *Review of Public Personnel Administration* 22 (Fall): 175–192.

———. 2005. *Beyond a Government of Strangers: How Career Executives and Political Appointees Can Turn Conflict to Cooperation.* Lanham, Md.: Lexington Books.

Markoff, John. 2006. "For $150, Third-World Laptop Stirs a Big Debate." *New York Times,* November 30.

Marriott, Michel. 2006. "Digital Divide Closing as Blacks Turn to Internet." *New York Times,* March 31.

Mayhew, David M. 1974. *Congress: The Electoral Connection.* New Haven: Yale University Press.

McGregor, Douglas. 1960. *The Human Side of Enterprise.* New York: McGraw-Hill.

McKay, Matthew, and Patrick Fanning. 2000. *Self-Esteem: A Proven Program of Cognitive Techniques for Assessing, Improving, and Maintaining Your Self-Esteem,* 8th ed. Oakland, Calif.: New Harbinger Publications.

Mead, Walter Russell. 2002. *Special Providence: American Foreign Policy and How It Changed the World.* New York: Routledge.

Meier, Kenneth J., and Laurence J. O'Toole Jr. 2006. *Bureaucracy in a Democratic State.* Baltimore: Johns Hopkins University Press.

Michaels, Judith. E. 1997. *The President's Call.* Pittsburgh: University of Pittsburgh Press.

———. 2005. "Becoming an Effective Political Executive: 7 lessons from experienced appointees." In *Learning the Ropes: Insights for Political Appointees.* Mark A. Abramson and Paul. R. Lawrence, eds. Lanham, Md.: Rowman and Littlefield, 11–36.

Moe, Terry M. 1985. "The Politicized Presidency." In *The New Direction in American Politics.* John Chubb and Paul Peterson, eds. Washington, D.C.: Brookings Institution, 235–271.

Morgan, Dan. 2004. "Aide Takes Blame for Tax Return Provision," *Washington Post,* December 3, A1.

Mossberger, Karen, Caroline J. Tolbert, and Mary Stansbury. 2003. *Virtual Inequality: Beyond the Digital Divide.* Washington, D.C.: Georgetown University Press.

Moynihan, Donald. 2005. "Leveraging Collaborative Networks in Infrequent Emergency Situations." Washington, D.C.: IBM Center for the Business of Government.

Muoio, Anna. 1999. "Mint Condition." *Fast Company* (December).

Murray, William L. 1991. *Effects of Politicization on the Agency, Subsystem, and Policy Level: A Case Study of the Commonwealth of Virginia.* Ph.D. diss., Virginia Polytechnic University.

———, and Gary L. Wamsley. 2007. "A Modest Proposal Regarding Political Appointees." In *Strategic Public Personnel Administration.* Ali Farazmand, ed. Westport, Conn.: Praeger, 199–226.

Nahapiet, Janine, and Sumantra Ghoshal. 1998. "Social Capital, Intellectual Capital, and the Organizational Advantage." *Academy of Management Review* 23 (2): 242–267.

Nathan, Richard P. 2000. *So You Want to Be in Government?* Albany, N.Y.: Rockefeller Institute Press.

Neill, Margaret James. 1999. "The Learning Journal." In *Reading Book for Human Relations Training,* Alfred Cooke et al., eds. Alexandria, Va.: NTL Institute, 209.

Nelson, Michael, and Charles Peters, eds. 1978. *The Culture of Bureaucracy.* New York: Holt, Rinehart, and Winston.

Newcomer, Kathryn. 1988. "Public Versus Private Executives: A Competence Gap?" Paper presented at the annual conference of the Senior Executives Association, Washington, D.C. (July).

Newell, Terry. 2004. *The Ladder of Inference [What Is It? How to Use It].* A monograph written for use at the Federal Executive Institute, Charlottesville, Va.

Nielsen//NetRatings. 2006a. "United States Monthly Web Usage Data." www.nielsen-netratings.com/news.jsp?section=dat_to&country=us.

———. 2006b. "U.S. Broadband Composition Reaches 72 Percent at Home, a 15-Point Year-Over-Year Increase, according to Nielsen//NetRatings." www.nielsen-netratings.com/pr/pr_060621.pdf.

Niskanen, William A. 1971. *Bureaucracy and Representative Government.* Chicago: Aldine-Alherton.

Norris, Pippa. 2001. *Digital Divide: Civic Engagement, Information Poverty, and the Internet Worldwide.* New York: Cambridge University Press.

Nye, Joseph, Jr. 2002. *The Paradox of American Power: Why the World's Only Superpower Can't Go It Alone.* New York: Oxford University Press.

———. 2004. *Soft Power: The Means to Success in World Politics.* New York: Public Affairs.

———, Phillip Zelikow, and David King. 1997. *Why People Don't Trust Government.* Cambridge, Mass.: Harvard University Press.

O'Leary, Rose. 2005. *The Ethics of Dissent: Managing Guerrilla Government.* Washington, D.C.: CQ Press.

Oleszek, Walter J. 2007. *Congressional Procedures and the Policy Process,* 7th ed. Washington, D.C.: CQ Press.

Organisation for Economic Co-operation and Development. 2005. "Peer Review of E-Government in Denmark." (September).

Ouchi, William G. 1981. *Theory Z.* New York: Avon.

Patterson, Thomas. 2000. "Doing Well and Doing Good: How Soft News and Critical Journalism Are Shrinking the News Audience and Weakening Democracy—and What News Outlets Can Do About It." Typescript. Cambridge: Harvard University.

Peters, Charles, and Michael Nelson, eds. (1978). *The Culture of Bureaucracy.* New York: Holt, Rinehart, and Winston.

Peters, Katherine McIntire. 2007. "Culture Club: The Marine Corps Aims to Add Cultural Knowledge to Its Arsenal." *Government Executive,* April 1.

Peters, Thomas, and Robert Waterman Jr. 1983. *In Search of Excellence.* New York: Harper and Row.

Pew Global Attitudes Survey, 2002–2005. www.pewglobal.org.

Pew Research Center for the People and the Press. 2004. "Foreign Policy Attitudes Now Driven by 9/11 and Iraq." http://people-press.org/reports/display.php3?ReportID=222. August 18.

Pfiffner, James P. 1996. *The Strategic Presidency: Hitting the Ground Running,* 2nd ed., rev. Lawrence: University Press of Kansas.

Phillips, Donald T., and James M. Loy. 2003. *Character in Action: The U.S. Coast Guard on Leadership.* Annapolis, Md.: Naval Institute Press.

Porter, Lawrence. 1999. "The Learning Journal: Some Mechanics." In *Reading Book for Human Relations Training.* Alfred Cooke et al., eds. Alexandria, Va.: NTL Institute. Page 217.

Porter, Margaret. 2000. *Definition of Mentoring.* Developed for the Federal Executive Institute's Coaching Program, Charlottesville, Va.

Powell, Colin L., with Joseph C. Persico. 1995. *My American Journey.* New York: Random House.

"Quotes About Change." http://quotations.about.com/cs/inspirationquotes/a/Change7.htm?terms=matter+of+chance. Accessed November 10, 2006.

Rainie, Lee, Michael Cornfield, and John Horrigan. 2005. *The Internet and Campaign 2004.* Washington, D.C.: Pew Internet and American Life Project, March 6.

Rasmussen, Eva Born. 2006. "E-debate and E-voting in Denmark." Presentation for the European Union Good Practices Workshop, November 23.

Ravitch, Diane. 2003. *The Language Police.* New York: Knopf.

Reeher, Grant. 2006. *First Person Political: Legislative Life and the Meaning of Public Service.* New York: New York University Press.

———, and Steve Davis. 2004. "The Political Life of the Internet." *The Responsive Community* 14 (2/3): 26–31.

Reeher, Grant, Steve Davis, and Larry Elin. 2002. *Click on Democracy: The Internet's Power to Change Political Apathy into Political Action.* Boulder: Westview Press.

———. Forthcoming. *The Political Life of the Internet.* New York: New York University Press.

Reichheld, Frederick F., with Thomas Teal. 2001. *The Loyalty Effect: The Hidden Force Behind Growth, Profits, and Lasting Value.* Boston : Harvard Business School Press.

Roet, Brian. 2001. *The Confidence to Be Yourself.* London: Piatkus.

Rohr, John. 1998. *Public Service, Ethics, and Constitutional Practice.* Lawrence: University Press of Kansas.

Savas, E. X. 1982. *Privatizing the Public Sector.* London: Chatham House.

Schwartz, Shalom. 1994. "Are There Universal Aspects in the Structure and Contents of Human Values?" *Journal of Social Issues* 50 (4): 19–45.

Seligman, Martin. 1998. *Learned Optimism: How to Change Your Mind and Your Life.* New York: Pocket Books.

Senge, Peter M. 1990. *The Fifth Discipline.* New York: Doubleday.

————, et. al. 1994. *The Fifth Discipline Fieldbook.* New York: Doubleday.

Shackleton, Ernest. 1998. *South.* New York: Carroll and Graf.

Shrage, Michael. 1990. *Shared Minds: The New Technologies of Collaboration.* New York: Random House.

Sifry, Micah L. 2006. "RNC vs. DNC Online: Precinct-Walking or Social-Networking?" Personal Democracy Forum, October 9. Available at www.personaldemocracy.com/node/1036.

Sniderman, Paul P., and Thomas Piazza. 1993. *The Scar of Race.* Cambridge, Mass.: Belknap Press.

"Some Wary of Social Security Plan." 2005. *Baltimore Sun,* February 10, 3A.

Sosik, John J., and Lara E. Megerian. 1999. "Understanding Leader Emotional Intelligence and Performance." *Group & Organization Management* 24 (3): 367–390.

Stanley, J. Woody, and Christopher Weare. 2004. "The Effects of Internet Use on Political Participation: Evidence from an Online Discussion Forum." *Administration & Society* 36 (5): 503–527.

Stowers, Genie N. L. 2004. "Measuring the Performance of E-Government." Washington, D.C.: IBM Center for the Business of Government.

Stringer, David. 2007. "Britons Protest, Request in E-petitions for Blair." *Syracuse Post-Standard,* February 22.

Sunstein, Cass. 2003. *Why Societies Need Dissent.* Cambridge, Mass.: Harvard University Press.

Surowiecki, James. 2004. *The Wisdom of Crowds.* New York: Doubleday.

Tannenbaum, Robert. 1999. "Self-Awareness: An Essential Element Underlying Leadership Effectiveness." In *Reading Book for Human Relations Training.* Alfred Cooke et al., eds. Alexandria, Va.: NTL Institute, 221.

Thuestad, Arvid Bro. 2004. "Creating Dialogue in an Effective Democracy: The Danish Case." National IT and Telecom Agency, Denmark.

Tichy, Noel. 1999. "The Teachable Point of View: A Primer." *Harvard Business Review* 77 (2): 82–83.

————, with Eli Cohen. 1997. *The Leadership Engine: How Winning Companies Build Leaders at Every Level.* New York: HarperBusiness.

Titan Systems Corporation. 2001. "After Action Report on the Response to the September 11 Terrorist Attack on the Pentagon." Arlington County, Virginia.

Toffler, Alvin. 1980. *The Third Wave.* New York: William Morrow.

Tolbert, Caroline J., and Karen Mossberger. 2006. "The Effects of E-Government on Trust and Confidence in Government." *Public Administration Review* (May/June): 354–369.

Tolle, Eckhart. 1999. *The Power of Now.* Novato, Calif.: New World Library.

Trattner, John H., with Patricia McGinnis. 2005. *The Prune Book: Top Management Challenges for Political Appointees.* Washington, D.C.: Brookings Institution.

Trippi, Joe. 2004. *The Revolution Will Not Be Televised: Democracy, the Internet, and the Overthrow of Everything.* New York: HarperCollins.

Ulrich, David. 1998. "A New Mandate for Human Resources." *Harvard Business Review* (January-February).

United States Marine Corps Center for Advanced Operational Culture Learning. 2007. www.tecom.usmc.mil/caocl.

U.S. Department of Defense. 2005. *Defense Language Training Roadmap.* Washington, D.C.: U.S. Government Printing Office.

U.S. Department of State. 2004. *2004 Report of the United States Advisory Commission on Public Diplomacy.* Washington, D.C.: U.S. Government Printing Office.

Vaill, Peter. 1989. *Managing as a Performing Art.* San Francisco: Jossey-Bass.

Van de Walle, Steven, and Geert Bouckaert. 2003. "Public Service Performance and Trust in Government: The Problem of Causality." *International Journal of Public Administration* 26 (8/9): 891–913.

Van de Walle, Steven, Jaal Kampden, Geert Bouckaert, and Bart Maddens. 2002. "Service Delivery Satisfaction and Trust in Government: The Micro-Performance Hypothesis." Paper presented at the 63rd national conference of the American Society for Public Administration, Phoenix, March 23–26.

Van Riper, Paul P. 1958. *History of the U.S. Civil Service.* Evanston, Ill.: Row, Peterson.

Waldo, Dwight. 1988. *The Enterprise of Public Administration.* Novata, Calif.: Chandler and Sharp.

Walker, David M. 2002. "Maximizing Human Capital in the Government Workforce." Washington, D.C.: Government Accountability Office.

Walters, Jonathan. 2005. "Contention Over Catastrophes." *Government Executive* (December): 51–57.

Waterman, Richard W., and B. Dan Wood, 1994. *Bureaucratic Dynamics.* Boulder: Westview Press.

Weisbord, Marvin. 1976. "Six Places to Look for Trouble With or Without a Theory." *Group & Organization Studies* 1 (4): 430–477.

———. 1978. *Organizational Diagnosis: A Workbook of Theory and Practice.* Reading, Mass.: Perseus Books.

———. 1988. *Productive Workplaces.* San Francisco: Jossey-Bass.

Weiser, Carl. 2003. "Report Lists Public Diplomacy Failures." *USA Today,* September 16.

Weisinger, Hendrie. 1998. *Emotional Intelligence at Work.* San Francisco: Jossey-Bass.

Werhane, Patricia. 1999. *Moral Imagination and Management Decision Making.* New York: Oxford University Press.

West, Darrell M. 2005. *Digital Government: Technology and Public Sector Performance.* Princeton: Princeton University Press.

Wilcox, Harvey. 2005. "A Careerist's Perspective: Keeping Bad Ideas from Becoming Presidential Policy," in Robert Maranto, *Beyond a Government of Strangers.* Lanham, Md.: Lexington Books, 63–79.

Willemssen, Joel C. 2003. "Electronic Government: Success of the Office of Management and Budget's 25 Initiatives Depends on Effective Management and Oversight." Testimony before the Subcommittee on Technology, Information Policy, Intergovernmental Relations, Census, Committee on Government Reform, House of Representatives. Washington, D.C.: Government Accounting Office, GAO-03-495T.

Williams, Christine B., Bruce D. Weinberg, and Jesse A. Gordon. 2004. "When Online and Offline Politics 'Meet Up': An Examination of the Phenomenon, Presidential Campaign and Its Citizen Activists." Paper presented at the annual meeting of the American Political Science Association, Chicago, Ill.

Winthrop, John. 1630. "A Modell of Christian Charity." http://history.hanover.edu/texts/winthmod.html.

Wood, B. Dan, and Richard W. Waterman. 1994. *Bureaucratic Dynamics.* Boulder: Westview Press.

Wood, Craig. 2004. "State of Consumer Trust: A Crisis of Confidence—Rebuilding the Bonds of Trust." Presented to the 10th annual Fred. Newell Customer Relationship Management Conference, June 2–4, 2004, Chicago, Ill.

Wooden, John R., and Steve Jamison. 1997. *A Lifetime of Observations and Reflections On and Off the Court.* Lincolnwood, Ill.: Contemporary Books.

Woodward, Bob. 2002. *Bush At War.* New York: Simon and Schuster.

Zakaria, Fareed. 2003. *The Future of Freedom: Illiberal Democracy at Home and Abroad.* New York: W. W. Norton.

Zaltman, Gerald. 2003. *How Customers Think: Essential Insights into the Mind of the Market.* Boston: Harvard Business School Press.

Zander, Benjamin, and Rosamund Stone Zander. 2000. *The Art of Possibility.* Boston: Harvard Business School Press.

Zimmerman, Jonathan. 2002. *Whose America? Culture Wars in the Public Schools.* Cambridge: Harvard University Press.

Index

Efford, Richard, 231
E-governance, defined, 240–241
E-government, 240–266. *See also* Internet
  civic involvement and, 241
  DanmarksDebatten (The Denmark Debate),
    258–259*b*
  e-rulemaking, 242–243*b*
  goals of, 244
  resources for further learning, 263–264
  success and limitations, 242–246
80-20 group, 250
Election 2000 and Internet use, 249–252
Election 2004 and Internet use, 252–254
Election 2006 and Internet use, 254–255
Electronic technology and government. *See*
    E-government
Emerson, Ralph Wado, 49
Emotional intelligence, 12, 13*b*
Empathy
  career public servants for political
    appointees, 196
  coaching and, 78, 82–83
  listening and, 29
Enron hearings, 225
Enthusiasm, 200
  lack of, and commitment, 170
Entrepreneurial cycle, 149
Environmental Protection Agency, 186, 192
  Office of Inspector General (IG), 139
Environment and teams, 102–104, 106*t*, 109
E-rulemaking, 242–243*b*
Ethical culture, 38–39, 39*f*
Ethics
  Code of Ethics for Government Service, 24
  laws and regulations enacted post-
    Watergate, 183
  of public servants, 34–35, 34*b*, 40
  European view of U.S., 293–294
Execution and organizational success, 12
Execution quality, 133–134, 133*f*
Executive branch, relationship with Congress,
    213–216
Executive coaching, 67–70
  defined, 68–69
Exemplarist school of thought, 291
Experience
  benefits to government leaders, 281–283
  customer, 267
  emotional reactions, 268–273, 270*t*
  engineering, 267–285
  resources for further learning, 284
  tips for leadership success, 283–284
Experience audit, 278–279, 279*f*
Experience clues, 273–274, 275

functional clues, 276
humanic clues, 277, 281
management of, 274, 276–278, 280–281, 281*t*
mechanic clues, 276–277
Experience design, 257, 280–281
Experience motif, 275–276
Experience Preference Model, 274*f*

F
Federal agencies. *See* Government; *specific*
    agency by name
Federal Aviation Administration, 184
Federal Emergency Management Agency
    (FEMA), 190, 192, 193, 225
Federal Executive Institute (FEI)
  experience audit, 278–279, 279*f*, 280
  Global Leadership Consortium, 301
  Leadership for a Democratic Society pro-
    gram, 300–301
  MBTI used at, 101
  midcourse correction at, 117
  oath of office administered to graduates of,
    39
  online sites of government, review of use of,
    256–257, 261
  research on international proficiency of
    federal leaders, 298
  teambuilding, 100, 111, 114
  training models used by, 98
  virtual teams at, 119, 120
Federalist Paper No. 10, 314
Federalist Paper No. 47, 224
Federalist Paper No. 51, 314
Federal Law Enforcement Training Center
    (FLETC), 219*b*
Federal-state relationship, 236
Federal Trade Commission (FTC), 191
Feedback, 63–67, 65*f*
  coaching and, 63–67
  high performance and, 151
  multirater (360), 66–67
FEI. *See* Federal Executive Institute
Ferrara, Joseph A., 186, 191
Financial Management Service, 172–173
Financial performance, 134–135
527 organizations, 252
Fletcher, Beverly, 289
Folk devils, of government, 186–190
Food and Drug Administration, 87
Forbes, Steve, 249
Force field analysis, 117
Foreign language skills, 298–299, 301–302
Foreign policy, 293–295
Framers. *See* Constitutional framers

Schneider, Ralf, 302
Scola, Nancy, 254
Secret Service, and collaboration, 173
Seinfeld, Jerry, 76
Self-affirmation, 51, 53
Self-awareness, 12, 13*b*, 49–73, 100
   autobiography, method of, 56–58
   defined, 52
   feedback and, 63–67, 63*f*, 65*f*
   finding time for, 70–71
   journal method, 58–60, 59*b*
   ladder of inference, 60–63, 61*f*
   mentoring and coaching for, 67–70
   in model of leadership success, 50–52, 51*f*,
      101
   resources for further learning, 71–72
   self-exploration to achieve, 52–54
   tips for leadership success, 71
   tools for building, 54–70
   values exploration, 54–56, 55*b*
Self-discovery, 66
Self-efficacy, 51, 53
Self-management, 12, 13*b*
Self-pride, 138
Self-reflection, 40, 62
Senate, U.S. *See* Congress
September 11, 2001
   communication failure and, 96
   government response to, 97
Servant Leadership (Greenleaf), 20
Service, customer. *See* Customer satisfaction
   with agency services; Experience
Service, public, 36–37
Service First, 156–157, 159, 161, 165, 172
Set direction, 143*f*, 144
Seven S model, 128
Shackleton, Ernest, 102
Shakespeare, 67
Shared purpose, 159
Shrage, Michael, 174
Shriver, Sargent, 311
Shulman, Stuart, 243*b*
Six-box model, 106*t*, 107, 128
Skilling, Jeffrey, 225
Skills, leadership, 27–31, 167–169
Social awareness, 12, 13*b*
Social capital, 12–13, 204
Social Security Administration, 3
Soft power, 21, 287, 300
Sports coaching, 75, 82, 83
Stakeholders, 129, 160–161, 160*f*, 218–220,
   219*b*
Stamps, Jeffrey, 119

State government
   legislatures, 235–239
   political appointees and, 207–212
State of the World Forum, 26
Stereotypes, 194–195
   of career civil servants, 191, 199–200
   of political appointees, 187, 188
Stovepipes, organizational, 127
Strategic thinking, 144
Strategy, 139–140
Structure, organizational, 140–141
Support systems, 141
Swann, Brian, 166*b*
Syracuse University's Maxwell School Poll on
   Civic Engagement and Inequality, 5, 255
Systemic change, 172–173
Systems 1 and 2, 149
Systems 3 and 4, 149
Systems support, 132, 141
Szasz, Thomas, 70

T
Talmadge, Herman, 32
Tannenbaum, Robert, 50
Task forces, joint, 172
Task interdependence, 104
Tax returns, congressional access to, 231
"Teachable point of view," 137
Team identity, 116
Teams
   acceptable behaviors on, 174–175
   assessment of, 117
   communication in, 119
   decision making and, 118
   elements of, 110, 111*t*
   environment and, 102–104, 106*t*, 109
   gender differences and, 110
   helpful mechanisms for, 108
   leadership of, 103, 109
   macro environment and, 106–109
   member contributions to, 118
   membership issues, 112
   micro environment and, 111–118
   midcourse corrections of, 117
   names of, 107
   organizational culture and, 109–110
   orientation of, 115–116
   processes of, 115–118
   purpose of, 103–104, 105–106, 107
   relationships in, 105, 107–108
   resources for further learning, 122–123
   rewards, 108
   roles, 110–111

Virtual teams, 119–121
Vision
  and high performance, 143
  and organizations, 142
Vision statements, 143–144
Vision to performance spiral, 142–146, 143*f*

W
Waldo, Dwight, 34
War on Poverty, 311
Washington, George, 22, 43–44, 291
Webb, Jim, 156
Websites. *See also* E-government; Internet
  design, 255–256, 260–261
  government, 245–246, 255–263
Weisbord, Marvin, 106, 107, 128
Welch, Jack, 86–87
West, Darrell, 245
West Virginia Departments of Education and
    Health and Human Resources, 242*b*
Whistle-blowing, 41*b*
Wienand, Joe, 168*b*
"WIIFM question," 165, 166*b*
Wiki approach, 262
Wikipedia, 178, 251, 256, 262
Wilcox, Harvey, 194, 199, 200, 203
Wilson, Woodrow, 290, 313, 319
Wilsonian school of thought, 292
Winthrop, John, 19, 289
Witt, James Lee, 190, 192, 193, 200
Women and teams, 110
Woodcock, Janet, 87
Wooden, John, 82
Working Assets, 260
Working of government, helping public to
    understand, 311–322
Work processes, 141

Y
Yankelovich State of Consumer Trust, 268

Z
Zakaria, Fareed, 290
Zaltman, Gerald, 269